MARKETING
THEORY AND PRACTICE

MACMILLAN STUDIES IN MARKETING MANAGEMENT

General Editor: Professor Michael J. Baker
University of Strathclyde

This series is designed to fill the need for a compact treatment of major aspects of marketing management and practice based essentially upon European institutions and experience. This is not to suggest that experience and practice in other advanced economies will be ignored, but rather that the treatment will reflect European custom and attitudes as opposed to American, which have tended to dominate so much of the marketing literature.

Each volume is the work of an acknowledged authority on that subject and combines distillation of the best and most up-to-date research findings with a clear statement of their relevance to improved managerial practice. A concise style is followed throughout, and extensive use is made of summaries, checklists and references to related work. Thus each work may be viewed as both an introduction to and a reference work on its particular subject. Further, while each book is self-contained, the series as a whole comprises a handbook of marketing management.

The series is designed for both students and practitioners of marketing. Lecturers will find the treatment adequate as the foundation for in-depth study of each topic by more advanced students who have already pursued an introductory and broadly based course in marketing. Similarly, managers will find each book to be both a useful *aide-mémoire* and a reference source.

The titles so far published in the series are:

Michael J. Baker (ed.), *Marketing: Theory and Practice*
Michael J. Baker and Ronald McTavish, *Product Policy and Management*
J. R. Bureau, *Brand Management*
Gordon R. Foxall, *Consumer Choice*
Roy W. Hill and T. J. Hillier, *Organisational Buying Behaviour*
Frank Jefkins, *Public Relations for Marketing Management*
Geoffrey A. Lancaster and Robert A. Lomas, *Forecasting for Sales and Materials Management*
Joanna Kinsey, *Marketing in Developing Countries*
James M. Livingstone, *International Marketing Management*
Arthur Meidan, *Bank Marketing Management*

MARKETING
THEORY AND PRACTICE

Second Edition

Michael J. Baker
A. J. Brown
Douglas Brownlie
Keith Crosier
Jennifer L. Drayton
Anita Kennedy
Joanna Kinsey
Stephen T. Parkinson

MACMILLAN
EDUCATION

First edition 1976
Reprinted 1979 (twice), 1981
Second edition 1983
Reprinted 1987, 1988

Published by
MACMILLAN EDUCATION LTD
Houndmills, Basingstoke, Hampshire RG21 2XS
and London
Companies and representatives
throughout the world

Printed in Hong Kong

ISBN 0-333-35392-7 (hardcover)
ISBN 0-333-35399-4 (paperback)

Contents

Acknowledgements

The author and publishers wish to thank the following who have kindly given permission for the use of copyright material:

The Advertising Association for a table from *Advertising Quarterly*.

AMACON, a division of American Management Associations, New York, for extracts from *Putting it all Together* by William Rothschild © 1976 by AMACON.

Louis P. Bucklin for a diagram from *Vertical Market Systems*.

Business Horizons, Indiana University, for two figures from 'Where Long-Range Planning Pays Off' by Thune and House, August 1970.

Cambridge University Press for a table from *Retail Distribution in Great Britain 1850–1950* by J.B. Jeffreys.

The Controller of Her Majesty's Stationery Office for a table from *British Business*.

The Economist Intelligence Unit Ltd for a table from *Retail Business*.

Euromonitor Publications Ltd for data and figures.

Harvard Business Review for tables from 'Strategies for Diversification' by Igor H. Ansoff (*HBR*, September–October 1957).

Institute of Grocery Distribution for data from *Retail Grocery Trade Review*.

Institute of Marketing for a table from an article by Peter Doyle in the *Quarterly Review of Marketing*.

Journal of Consumer Research, University of California, for two figures from *Psychological Theories of Consumer Choice* by Hansen.

McGraw-Hill Book Company for figure from *Corporate Strategy* by Ansoff.

Prentice-Hall Inc. for a table from *Strategic Market Planning: Problems and Analytical Approaches* by Derek F. Abell and John S. Hammond. © 1979.

West Publishing Company for figures from *Strategy Formulation: Analytical Concepts* by Charles W. Hofer and Dan Schendel. Copyright © 1978 by West Publishing Company.

Every effort has been made to trace all the copyright holders, but if any have been inadvertently overlooked the publishers will be pleased to make the necessary arrangement at the first opportunity.

Preface to the first edition

The enigma of marketing is that it is one of man's oldest activities and yet it is widely regarded as the most recent of the business disciplines. In this book we examine some of the reasons which seem to us to account for this apparent contradiction as well as indicating why the theory and practice of marketing must be integrated if the profession of marketing is to achieve the status and credibility of professions such as the law or medicine.

In fact many interesting parallels may be drawn between the evolution and growth of these latter professions, especially medicine and marketing. Like medicine, marketing has been practised for thousands of years and has built up an enormous wealth of descriptive information concerning the 'art'. Familiarity with this descriptive base has now become an essential prerequisite, for it contains both the language or 'jargon' which is a feature of any specialised activity as well as the 'case-law' which enables past experience to be applied to present and future problems. However, as we note in Chapter 2, the foundation of the modern profession of medicine is generally agreed to have been laid with the transition from description to analysis which accompanied Harvey's discovery of the circulation of the blood. Since this discovery medicine has borrowed extensively from other sciences in developing its own theory and body of knowledge, but at the same time it has recognised that the practice demands the establishment of a relationship with the patient which mitigates direct translation of theory into practice.

It is our view that if marketing is to progress it must achieve a similar transition from art to applied science as has been attained by medicine and that to do this it must establish a sound theoretical foundation in its own right. Further, we would argue that, in time, knowledge of this theoretical basis should become an essential qualification for practice and that those without it will become the 'quacks' of their profession. Much of this book constitutes an elaboration of this view.

In Part I, 'The Foundations of Marketing', we trace the evolution of

vii

the marketing concept from its origins in barter to its modern statement as a managerial philosophy of business. Based on this historical review we next consider the need for theory in marketing as a preliminary to a survey of possible sources for such a theory. In Part II, 'Evolution of Marketing Thought', we examine the theoretical foundations of four areas of central importance to the practice of marketing – consumer behaviour, communications, distribution and innovation. Of necessity such a review must be eclectic, but it is hoped that it will suffice to substantiate our claim as to the practical value of developing theory in marketing and will encourage the reader to extend his studies of the sources cited. Finally, in Part III, 'New Directions in Marketing', we summarise current thinking on the application of marketing concepts and techniques beyond consumer-goods markets, with which it is traditionally associated, before concluding with a brief look at some of the sources of criticism of marketing.

Given the scope which we are attempting within such a small volume it will readily be appreciated that our efforts must represent a compromise between the breadth of coverage necessary to sustain our basic purpose of establishing the nature and relevance of marketing and the inextricable relationship between theory and practice, and the depth essential to raise the discussion above the trivial. To help reconcile these conflicting aims five authors have co-operated in developing material and their contributions are as follows:

Chapters 1, 7, 8 and 9	Michael J. Baker
Chapters 2 and 3	Michael J. Baker and D. E. N. Dickson
Chapter 4	Jennifer L. Drayton
Chapter 5	Stephen T. Parkinson
Chapter 6	A. J. Brown

While each of these authors is responsible for his or her own contribution and any merit which the book possesses in whole or in part is to his or her personal credit, any deficiencies are the sole responsibility of the principal author.

Strathclyde University   Michael J. Baker
August 1975

Preface to the second edition

It is always gratifying to be invited to prepare a second edition of a book, for it is a clear indication that the first has enjoyed more than a modicum of success. However, it also presents a dilemma that is familiar to every marketer with a successful product: namely, what changes (if any) should be made to sustain this success?

From the feedback that we have received it would seem that the first edition met the need we had experienced ourselves for a review of the role of theory in marketing supported by a detailed analysis of a number of specific topics and rounded off with a look at emerging trends. Seven years later this need is still apparent and so we have decided not to change the original formula. That said, it is clear that the second edition is almost twice the length of its predecessor – which suggests some fairly radical changes. In the main these changes are largely represented by the inclusion of several new chapters and a radical rewrite of the core of the book concerned with the evolution of marketing thought.

Since the writing of the first edition there has been a rapid increase in the faculty of the Department of Marketing at Strathclyde University to the point where it is now believed to be the largest concentration of marketing teachers and researchers in Europe. Given such a wealth of expertise it was inevitable that subject specialists should be invited to contribute a chapter summarising the 'state of the art' with the result that each of several chapters could almost stand alone as a mini-textbook in its own right. Indeed, within the Department of Marketing these chapters are being used as core teaching materials and the book itself is to be used as one of three required texts for the open learning MBA to be launched in 1983.

Eight authors have contributed to this volume and their contributions are as follows:

Chapters 2, 3	Michael J. Baker and Joanna Kinsey
Chapter 6	Keith Crosier

Chapters 9, 10	A. J. Brown
Chapter 11	Douglas Brownlie
Chapter 6	Keith Crosier
Chapter 4	Jennifer L. Drayton
Chapter 5	Anita Kennedy
Chapter 7	Stephen T. Parkinson

Readers familiar with the first edition will find modest changes in the chapters that deal with the general issues (for which I am principally responsible) but the remainder is almost entirely new. We hope that the changes meet with your approval.

Strathclyde University   MICHAEL J. BAKER
July 1983

List of tables

List of figures

PART I

THE FOUNDATIONS
OF MARKETING

CHAPTER 1

Evolution of the marketing concept

Contents

Introduction

In this chapter we seek to provide some answers to the frequently posed question 'What is marketing?' We will argue that, essentially, marketing is concerned with exchange relationships between producers and users, suppliers and customers, and will suggest that uncertainty, confusion or misunderstanding as to the scope and nature of this exchange relationship would seem to stem from the fact that all of us have participated in such interchange and have formulated our own interpretation of its nature.

However, despite the multiplicity of definitions that are bound to arise from such a process, we propose that consensus is possible by distinguishing between marketing as a philosophy of exchange between persons and/or organisations and marketing as it has emerged as a business function. To establish this proposition we describe briefly the evolution of exchange from its early beginning in the form of barter to the sophisticated operation of a modern market economy. Against this background we identify the three managerial orientations which have characterised the development of the modern business organisation–production, sales and marketing–and argue that the recent development of a marketing orientation reflects a return to the original basis of exchange 'consumer sovereignty'.

Finally, some reference will be made to the relevance of a marketing orientation in the changing economic and social conditions which seem likely to obtain during the final years of the present century (a full discussion of this issue is undertaken in Part III, 'New Directions in Marketing').

Marketing=exchange

It is universally accepted that the lowest (and simplest) form of economic organisation is the subsistence economy in which each individual family unit is wholly dependent upon its own productive resources to satisfy its consumption needs. For our purposes it is unimportant to inquire into the precise social organisation of subsistence economies, for while this is of fundamental interest to the anthropologist, the distinction between gathering, hunting and/or pastoral nomadism is irrelevant in the absence of exchange, for, as Kotler has noted, 'it is a stage (of economic development) devoid of a concept of marketing'.[1]

Exchange first comes about where a producer creates a surplus in excess of the immediate needs of himself and his family, a surplus which he is willing to trade for some other good. Clearly, the potential for exchange is limited by the availability of other producers of different goods (or services) with surplus units which are intrinsically more attractive to the first producer than increased consumption of his own output (in the language of the economist they have a greater 'marginal utility'). In turn, the owners of these surpluses must seek supplies of the first producer's surplus. Assuming, therefore, that two producers of different products are brought into contact, each of whom has a desire for units of the other's surplus, it is logical to assume that any exchange effected by them is to their mutual satisfaction. In my opinion this is the essence of marketing–a mutually satisfying exchange relationship.

However, if we were to suggest this as our definition of marketing, that is 'Marketing is a process of exchange between individuals and/or organisations which is concluded to the mutual benefit and satisfaction of the parties', then clearly this proposition would go far beyond what most people consider to be the scope of the subject. In no small measure such rejection would arise from the modern interpretation of marketing as a business function which has evolved in its most extreme form in the sale of mass-consumption, packaged convenience products. As such it is appropriate to stress the point in the preceding paragraph that the essence of an exchange relationship is freedom to decide how much of one's own surplus of any good or service, or title to any good or service, one is prepared to commute into supplies of some other good or service. Whether in fact this constitutes 'marketing' in the modern idiom can only be established by tracing the development of exchange relationships from their first beginnings in barter.

As a result of chance, application or natural aptitude most persons develop a particular skill in some aspect of life. If such skill yields an output of goods or services in demand by other persons, then the benefits of specialisation are immediately apparent. Increased productivity arising out of task specialisation results in a concomitant growth in the potential for exchange and this stage of economic development is generally associated with the genesis of the marketplace. The need for an agreed meeting place where exchanges might be effected is obvious, for otherwise much productive time will be lost in seeking out potential customers for one's output who also possess supplies of desired goods or services. Similarly, as the degree of specialisation increases so does the assortment of goods, which further complicates the problem of bringing together two parties with a mutual interest in exchange.

To facilitate barter, at least two interrelated problems must be resolved—the problem of timing and the problem of value. Value is an essentially subjective concept and, like beauty, lies in the eye of the beholder. However, for an exchange to meet our criterion that it be 'mutually satisfying' it is clear that the parties to the exchange must agree on the basis for a subjective opinion as to 'value'. In formulating this value judgement the parties are bound to be guided by the more generalised value system evolved by the social grouping of which they are members. However, it would seem that there are certain concepts fundamental to most value systems among which may be numbered scarcity, utility and skill.

While scarcity may result from a natural deficiency, as is the case with precious metals, or from the time and effort required to create a unit of supply, physical scarcity in and of itself is insufficient to invest an object with value. Only if it is perceived as possessing utility in the widest sense of the word will people prize its ownership. Thus utility is inextricably linked with concepts of value, as it is with concepts of skill, that is the scarcity value of a skill is also proportionate to its perceived utility.

Given that one has developed generalised criteria for judging value, it is obvious that agreement on a unit of measurement will greatly facilitate comparative judgements on the exchange value of widely differing goods and services. Such a unit of measurement may take any form so long as it is universally recognised and accepted within the community which wishes to use it, and has been expressed in terms of cattle, shells, beads, and so forth, as well as its modern equivalent, money.

Evolution of a standard unit of exchange goes a long way to solving the problems of barter, for it provides a common denominator for estimating the value of goods and services as well as mitigating problems of timing. These latter are bound to arise as a result of disequilibrium between supply and demand, and, in the case of barter, are exacerbated by differences in the value and divisibility of different outputs. Universally acceptable units of exchange act as a store of value and so alleviate these timing problems.

Clearly the evolution of a money economy greatly encouraged increased specialisation and led to the development of sophisticated institutions for facilitating exchange both nationally and internationally. However, while increased specialisation led to enormous improvements in productivity in the manufacture of products, primary and tertiary activities—mining and farming—distribution and personal services were less amenable to improvement through specialisation and the division of labour.

Eventually the benefits of the division of labour were subject to diminishing returns in manufacturing industry too and the next step forward had to await the application of technology to the productive process. With the development of steam power an industrial revolution was set in train which enabled man's productive capacity to break through the plateau which it had reached when limited by natural power sources—wind and water—and the slow increase in population.

The history of the Industrial Revolution is familiar to us all and does not bear repetition here. Suffice it to say that increased productivity enabled a rapid increase in population which provided both the need for more sophisticated marketing institutions as well as the means of supplying them. However, it is important to recognise that while we speak of an industrial 'revolution' the actual process was more evolutionary and extended over a much longer period of time than is consistent with the connotations of revolution. Certainly there was no immediate solution to the grinding poverty which the working classes had endured since time immemorial, and the critical problem remained that of increasing the supply of the basic necessities of life. It was this emphasis which has led to the era being characterised as production orientated.

From production to marketing orientation

Nowadays it is fashionable to distinguish different managerial approaches to the conduct of business and to suggest that there are fundamental differences between a production, a sales and a marketing operation.[2] The validity of such a proposition must of course depend upon how one defines a production, a sales and a marketing orientation, and it is necessary to put forward and examine such definitions before passing judgement.

As indicated in the preceding section, the endemic problem of mankind was (and still is in many developing countries) a basic disequilibrium between supply and demand. In the face of such disequilibrium the concept of homeostasis predicates the action of natural forces to restore balance in the system. Clearly, the restoration of balance may arise or be brought about by either increasing supply, through increased productivity, or by reducing demand. In the nature of things man is a wanting animal and so seeks to increase supply, although in the case of warfare this is pursued in a negative manner more akin to demand reduction. Generally, however, demand reduction results from natural causes beyond man's immediate control, such as famine and disease, and history clearly demonstrates that population growth has been checked or declined when demand has caught up with or has overtaken available supply.

Because of the unpredictable incidence of the natural population controls of famine and disease, and recognising the need to increase the labour supply to maintain or improve production, most human societies have encouraged fertility. Indeed many religions contain a positive invocation to 'go forth and multiply' which has not been challenged seriously until very recent times. Thus, although Malthus warned in his *Essay on Population* that if the population continued to expand geometrically while production expanded in an arithmetic progression there would develop a major disequilibrium between supply and demand which could only be resolved by the natural controls, his warning fell into disrepute due to its failure to come into early effect. With the benefit of hindsight we can now see that supply did not expand arithmetically in the nineteenth century–it grew exponentially and more rapidly in the industrialised economies than did population, thus giving rise to a very significant improvement in the standards of living enjoyed by the members of those economies.

Today, however, there has been a Malthusian revival which has received perhaps its greatest support from the work of Jay Forrester[3] at the Massachusetts Institute of Technology (MIT) and from the project sponsored by the Club of Rome which developed from this, preliminary reports of which are contained in *The Limits to Growth*.[4] The thesis underlying neo-Malthusianism is essentially that the world is a finite resource which will be rapidly exhausted if present consumption trends are allowed to continue, being reinforced by the multiplier effect of a rapidly expanding population.

In the medium term of three or four generations it is not too difficult to reject the pessimism of the Meadows model which predicts catastrophe long before this, by pointing out that Meadows, like Malthus, has fallen into the trap of extrapolating population and consumption geometrically and technological innovation and pro- duction arithmetically. However, for the longer term, even if one assumes that the means of sustaining life are available, it is clear that this planet can only physically accommodate a certain level of population. In recognition of this fact, as well as the validity of many of the arguments of the neo-Malthusians, the case for stabilising demand by population control is considered a much more viable and realistic solution to the human predicament than are attempts to increase supply. If, therefore, a production orientation is considered synonymous with efforts to increase supply, we can readily under- stand why it should have occupied a central place in the thinking of entrepreneurs from time immemorial. Further, given that the capac- ity to create over-supply only exists in a limited number of the world's economies it is not difficult to see why it should remain the focus of immediate effort in those countries with a supply deficiency *vis-à-vis* their present population.

King summarises the period of production orientation as 'an era of managerial concern with problems of capacity creation, work methods, and volume production'.[5] However, as he continues to point out, 'Although it is not suggested that corporate management gave no consideration during this period to the markets for which they produced, it appears that, generally, problems related to manu- facturing assumed greater significance than did those related to identification and development of markets.'

While King is confining his discussion to the twentieth century, it is quite obvious, for the reasons discussed above, that his comments are equally applicable to preceding centuries. It seems to me, therefore, that we render entrepreneurs a grave disservice if we use 'production orientated' in a pejorative sense and with overtones which imply that such an orientation ignores consumer needs. Rather, it seems to me that the production-orientated manager got his priori- ties right, in that demand for basic goods and services was clearly identifiable and that an emphasis upon volume rather than dif- ferentiation or choice was eminently sensible in that it went a long way towards maximising total satisfaction. Certainly, by achieving the economies of mass production, Henry Ford made his model-T available to vast segments of the population who otherwise would never have had the opportunity to own the basic product–a car– which they sought, the colour of which was essentially irrelevant. Yet today we cite 'You can have any colour of car as long as it's black' as the antithesis of marketing–a view that it is difficult if not impossible to sustain if one adopts the definition proposed earlier that marketing is concerned with mutually satisfying exchange relationships. As more than 60 per cent of American car sales in 1920 were Fords, we must accept that two-thirds of American car buyers felt this to be a more satisfying situation than buying (or not being able to afford to buy) the products of the myriad producers who collectively accounted for the remaining third of the market.

The situation that was to bring the production orientation into disrepute was what I have referred to elsewhere as 'the creation of "excess" supply'.[6] Excess supply is of course a comparative state and applies only to certain categories of products under very limited conditions, foremost among which is a presumption of available discretionary consumer purchasing power that is only satisfied, and then only partially, in the most affluent societies. However, from the firm's point of view, a state of excess supply begins to become apparent when the market ceases to absorb all of its output and exhibits price inelasticity of demand within the range which would be acceptable to the firm, that is to stimulate increased consumption, it would be necessary to sell at an unacceptably low price.

Faced with price inelasticity of demand for its output, and a situation in which the joint potential supply of the firm and its immediate competitors exceeds effective demand, managements' immediate reaction tends to be to maintain volume through non-price competition and especially by means of product differentiation, promotion and selling effort.

In the short term it is easiest to increase the sales effort, and for this reason there was a transitional period which King identifies as the sales-management orientation between the production-management orientation and the present emphasis upon marketing. Simplistically, the sales-management orientation, which prevailed between 1930 and 1950 in the United States, may be characterised as 'selling what we can make' in contradistinction to 'making what we can sell' which is considered a central feature of the marketing concept. However, these catch phrases do scant justice to the philosophical difference between a sales-management and marketing approach.

From the sales manager's standpoint, products and services are given and potential customers must be persuaded to see them as the solution to a generalised consumption need. From the marketer's standpoint customers are given and potential products must be developed or modified to match specific consumption needs. Thus, where the production- or sales-orientated manager would tend to ask himself 'What do customers want?', the marketer would ask the customers themselves and then proceed to organise a supply of the desired objects.

One of the first firms to embrace a marketing approach was the American General Electric Company, and King cites two quotations which help spell out this fundamental difference between selling and marketing:

> Under the traditional 'sales' concept, engineering designed a product, manufacturing produced it–and then the sales people were expected to sell it. Under the modern 'marketing' concept, the whole business process starts with marketing research and sales forecasting to provide a sound, factual customer-oriented basis for planning all business operations, and the business function which has sales responsibility now participates in all the stages of the business planning process.[7]

> [the marketing concept] introduces the marketing man at the beginning rather than the end of the production cycle and would integrate marketing into each phase of the business. Thus marketing, through its studies and research, will establish for the engineer, the designer and the manufacturing man what the customer wants in a given product, what price he is willing to pay, and where and when it will be wanted. Marketing would have authority in product planning, production scheduling and inventory control, as well as in the sales, distribution and servicing of the product.[8]

Similarly, Robert J. Keith's description of the role of marketing in the Pillsbury Company serves to reinforce this point:

> Marketing is viewed in our company today as the function which plans and executes the sale–all the way from the inception of the idea, through its development and execution, to the sale to the customer. Marketing begins and ends with the consumer. The idea for a new product is conceived after careful study of her wants and needs, her likes and dislikes. With the idea in hand, the marketing department functions as a universal joint in the corporation, marshalling all the forces of the corporation to translate the idea into product and the product into sales.[9]

Full circle

In describing the evolution of the marketing concept it appears that we have been guilty of considerable arrogance in presuming it to be of recent origin. In reality it seems to me that if our early definition of marketing as 'a process of exchange between individuals and/or organisations which is concluded to the mutual benefit and satisfaction of the parties' is acceptable, then marketing is as old as exchange relationships themselves. However, as society has developed, and has harnessed the power of science and technology to assist it in meeting the apparently insatiable demand for goods and services, so it has been necessary to evolve new institutions and new mechanisms to cope with the complexity which has accompanied this development.

It follows that if the criterion to be used to judge or measure the effectiveness of a single exchange relationship is the mutual satisfaction derived from it, then, in the aggregate, marketing (exchange?) will be at its most efficient when it maximises aggregate satisfaction. If this is so, then, as we have already argued, the much despised production orientation with its emphasis upon manufacturing and volume of output may be the most appropriate to conditions of chronic under-supply. Under such conditions the nature of demand is likely to be as self-evident to the entrepreneur responsible for setting up and controlling a factory with an output measured in millions of identical units as it was and is to the supplier who engaged in a direct one-to-one relationship with his customer.

Thus it would seem more accurate to speak not of the emergence of the marketing concept in the 1950s but rather to talk about the need to reappraise the precise nature of consumer demand due to the changes brought about by the physical separation of producer and customer (accompanied by the potential to create excess supply in some sectors of production) in order to ensure that we maximise aggregate satisfaction. Asking customers what they want can hardly be as revolutionary a step as some writers would have us believe! More likely it reflects the basic and continuing nature of exchange, that is consumer sovereignty.

Marketing–philosophy or function?

Unfortunately, while the philosophy of marketing is firmly rooted in the principle of consumer sovereignty, even if only out of enlightened self-interest, there is a growing body of criticism which believes and argues to the contrary. It would be naive to deny that this criticism has foundation for there are sufficient well-established examples[10] to warrant a case against modern marketing practices. However, to establish that some members of a community are criminals is not to prove that all are. Similarly, to identify some misleading advertisements or malpractices such as pyramid selling (albeit that the latter only thrives on the greed of the victims who want something for nothing) is not to substantiate a case that marketing as a whole is against the consumer interest.

Further, it seems to me that most criticism is directed at the practice, or perhaps it would be nearer the truth to say the malpractice, of marketing and not against the philosophy or principles as we have outlined them above. Indeed, given our definition of marketing it is difficult to see how anyone could ever take exception to it. On the other hand, it is not difficult to understand how ordinary consumers can become dubious about marketing when they have no clear definition of what the marketing concept is supposed to be, save possibly a cliché such as 'the customer is always right', and so can only judge from their own direct experience at the hands of marketers.

However, while one is forced to acknowledge defects in the function of marketing arising from certain marketing practices, it would be unwise to accept all of the criticism directed against it by consumerists. Because consumerists are intelligent, articulate and often highly vocal one should not automatically assume that they have a monopoly of the truth nor that one must accept their point of view. Accordingly, while most advertisers, and certainly all responsible ones, would agree with the desirability of truth in advertising, this is not to concede that all advertising should be purely factual and devoid of any subjective associations or connotations.

Where the consumerists go wrong in their condemnation of marketing is in their insistence upon a concept of objective rationality the origin of which would seem to be a simplifying assumption necessary to make early price theory work. As economics has become more sophisticated it has become possible to relax such rigid assumptions as homogeneity of demand and supply and to admit, as Lawrence Abbott[11] has pointed out, that 'What people really desire are not products but satisfying experiences.' Thus, as Abbott comments,

> what is considered satisfying is a matter for individual decision: it varies according to one's tastes, standards, beliefs and objectives–and these vary greatly, depending on individual personality and cultural environment. Here is a foundation for a theory of choice broad enough to embrace Asiatic as well as Eastern cultures, nonconformists as well as slaves to convention, Epicureans, stoics, cynics, roisterers, religious fanatics, dullards, and intellectual giants alike.

In fact, a theory of choice founded on consumer sovereignty.

To criticize 'Admass' (mass advertising) for treating all consumers as the same, and mindless automatons to boot, would seem contradictory to say the least when reinforced by an all-embracing demand that we all buy on the basis of price and product specification while ignoring all aesthetic and/or subjective associations.

But merely to deny the consumerists' case against marketing is insufficient. Rather it is necessary to show that marketing too possesses a theoretical foundation which, without claiming it to be a better theory than any other theory of how people behave, at least deserves equal consideration. Only if marketers can raise the argument above the trivial of the rights and wrongs of specific marketing actions does it seem to me that we may be able to persuade our critics that marketing is a subject worthy of serious study, and an honourable profession as well. Further, I believe that it is essential to establish that marketing is not merely another transitional phase, like the sales-management orientation of the 1930s and 1940s, to be characterised as one of 'demand stimulation' and 'conspicuous consumption' and wholly inappropriate to the growing awareness of the need to conserve our limited resources, but a social philosophy of increasing relevance.

To this end, in the next two chapters we examine the need for a theory of marketing, and its likely nature and sources before considering how theory may improve our understanding of specific areas such as marketing communications and distribution. Finally, we broaden our review once again to discuss the role marketing has to play in the changing social and economic conditions likely to obtain in the final years of the century.

CHAPTER 2

The need for theory in marketing

Contents

Introduction

The purpose of this chapter is to establish why it is considered essential that the study and practice of marketing should be founded upon a sound theoretical base.

To do this one must first specify what one means by 'theory' and then identify its role. Equipped with a definition of theory we may then enquire into its nature, which in turn will allow us to focus attention upon its function. This consideration suggests that theory is essential to the development of an integrated body of knowledge and raises the question as to how theory evolves or is developed.

14

A basic distinction is frequently drawn between 'art' and 'science' and we review what appears to us to be the difference between the two prior to a fuller consideration of the nature of science and the scientific method in the context of its possible relevance to marketing.

The definition of theory

The word 'theory' is normally associated in people's minds with the development of ideas or conjectures about the manner or ways in which part of the world works. From the Oxford dictionary we find that one derivation of theory is from the Greek *oewpia* which was used in the sense of 'pertaining to or connected with public spectacles, religious functions and solemn embassies', which we presume were looked at by spectators as an attempt on the part of actors or participants to interpret one way of looking at part of the real world. With the passage of time the meaning of theory became more generalised and the Latin root *theoria* was used to mean 'a looking at or a speculation or a contemplation'. Today, however, we have endowed the word 'theory' with a more specific meaning and for our purposes will adopt the working definition suggested in the Oxford dictionary which defines a theory as being 'a scheme or system of ideas or statements held as an explanation of a group of facts or phenomena'.

The nature of theory

A review of human progress would seem to suggest that the main catalyst is a change in emphasis in the orientation of critical thought from a 'descriptive' basis to a basis which may be defined as primarily 'analytical'. For example, in the field of medicine early developments were confined to general descriptions of the human body and the naming of its various parts. In turn this descriptive base permitted the transference of ideas concerning the nature and causes of disease from one case to another. However, with Harvey's discovery of the circulation of the blood the orientation of medicine changed from being one of description to one of analysis based upon a theory which satisfies the definition advanced earlier.

Just as Harvey's discovery provided the foundation for the modern profession of medicine so too have similar breakthroughs provided the basis for the development and extension of other fields of human endeavour. At the same time it must be recognised that many breakthroughs in thought and practice have occurred without the application of developed theory. Thus most early innovations were developed by inventors whose approach could be defined as pragmatic, as was the case when James Watt designed the first rudimentary steam-engine based upon his observations of the pressure exerted upon the lid of a kettle as a result of the build up of steam which took place when it boiled upon an open fire. The thermo-dynamic theory of heat transfer had not been developed yet steam-engines were constructed and worked successfully for over a century before this theory was evolved. But, with the development of a theory of thermo-dynamics the design of the steam-engine underwent a revolutionary change, and from that time onwards they were designed largely according to theoretical principles rather than by studying and applying empirical data concerning the past design and operation of steam-engines. As a result of this application of theory the efficiency of the steam-engine increased geometrically by contrast with the arithmetic rate of progress which had characterised it prior to a statement of theory concerning its operation.

This same process of development from applied art to analytical or theoretical knowledge has held good in many fields of human activity. When these activities first developed they were essentially based upon the application of skill or technique and characterised as 'arts'. However, with the formulation and statement of a sound theoretical base a whole new insight into the activity began to emerge and the transition took place from art to science.

However, before going on to consider the nature of the differences between art and science it will be helpful if we delineate three basic requirements which any theorist must satisfy.

A basic requirement of any theory are definitions which state clearly the meaning of the various terms which will be used in that theory. The need for clear and precise definitions is obvious, for without them we will be uncertain as to what constitutes a relevant observation and how to interpret it in order to test the theory. In addition to defining the terms that are to be used, an area of science frequently termed 'semantics', the statement of an adequate theory also requires that we define the conditions or assumptions under which the theory will hold. The third requirement of a theory is that it should be built upon hypotheses about the way in which things actually behave or about relationships between things in the real world. In essence hypotheses are working guesses to which we attach a high antecedent probability that they will be validated by the collection and analysis of evidence or data. Thus a hypothesis differs from a theory in that it has not been demonstrated to yield predictions with an accuracy greater than that which could be achieved if predictions were made by some random device. However, once a hypothesis has been shown to be able to yield predictions with greater accuracy than would arise from such a random process, then we will term it a 'theory'. In turn, if a theory can be demonstrated to yield perfectly accurate predictions every time it is used, then that theory will take on the status of a 'law'.

The usefulness and quality of marketing theory will depend upon the way in which definitions, assumptions and hypotheses are combined together. The theory or model which is produced may be regarded as a simplification of a part of reality which usually fits the observed facts approximately rather than exactly. Thus the role of a researcher in any field is to try and impose order upon the observations he makes of that part of the real world which is his area of interest, for otherwise these observations will be little more than a confused jumble of facts and ideas. The statement of a theory demands that these facts and ideas should be brought together in a related and meaningful way. Thus in many respects a valid theory is very similar to a road map. A valid theory, like a valid road map, requires to be based on facts if it is to be realistic and useful. If it is too detailed and incorporates every hedge and post upon the road it will be confusing and of little use to the driver using it as a means of getting from one place to another. On the other hand, if it is insufficiently detailed, it will be inadequate as a guide to real-life situations.

To be useful, then, a theory, like a road map, must satisfy certain functions, functions which to some degree are dependent upon the structure of the theory itself. Until now, researchers in the field of marketing have tended to limit the functions of theory to those of description and prescription, that is the ability to give direction. These two functions are basic to all theory but in addition there are others which should be performed by any theory with pretensions to adequacy, namely the functions of delimitation, generation and integration.

Delimitation function

While the basic function of any theory is to describe part of reality such description must operate selectively. This selection is the delimiting function and means in effect that the theory cannot include everything in the world of reality. Thus a theory which does not delimit in this fashion would break under its own excess of explanation. The process of deciding what to include and exclude from a theory through this process of delimitation depends very much upon the purpose for which the theory is being constructed.

The generative function

The generative function may be defined as the capacity to create testable hypotheses and encompasses the processes which we otherwise describe as theoretical speculation, creativity, or even 'hunch'. Thus as well as being founded upon tested hypotheses a theory must also generate new hypotheses which will permit us to extend our understanding and knowledge.

When a theory is used to stimulate empirical investigation it is spoken of as using the theory 'heuristically'. The heuristic use of theory is often made by analogy, for example Freud used the physical concepts of hydraulic fluid to express mental states.

The integrative function

This function of theory refers to the ability to bring together the various constructs and propositions which have been elucidated by the researcher into a more or less consistent and useful whole. Thus the objective of theorists working in an area such as marketing must be to endeavour to integrate and pull together their ideas into a coherent and interdependent unit which warrants identification as a formal theory.

However, such a process of formalisation can have side-effects such as confusion and inconsistency. For example, in the field of marketing a number of independent researchers have attempted to construct complex theories of consumer behaviour in order to explain the buying process. As Jennifer L. Drayton points out in her discussion of these theories in Chapter 4, these theories contradict as much as confirm one another.

The integrative function is of prime importance in the development of theory. In many ways marketing like psychology has been going through a period in which the emphasis has been upon a number of micro or miniature theories which constitute an adequate explanation of some part or parts of the subject (the 'piecemeal' approach). Thus some observers such as MacInnes are of the opinion that the first priority in developing theory in marketing must be the integration of these various pieces of emerging theory into a consistent whole (a 'holistic' approach).

The need for a theory in marketing

As we indicated in Chapter 1, the practice of marketing has existed since the first exchange relationship. However, in tracing the evolution of marketing from the early days of barter through to the statement of the modern marketing concept in the early 1950s, it became apparent that the need for a formal restatement of the basis upon which such relationships exist arose out of the separation which had occurred between buyer and seller. In turn the degree and extent of this separation reflects the development of a very complex and sophisticated system for matching highly specific wants with supplies of goods and services capable of satisfying these wants.

In recent years it has been fashionable to decry the operation of the marketing system and to give great attention to its deficiencies rather than to its achievements. In large degree it is felt that many of the deficiencies which exist in the marketing system arise out of a lack of understanding as to its actual operation. It is recognition and acceptance of the need to improve our understanding of the manner in which the system works which underlies the need to develop a workable theory of exchange. It must be stressed that the key word in the preceding sentence is 'workable' for clearly there are well-developed theories of exchange in economics and in the behavioural sciences. However, from our point of view these are inadequate for they are an oversimplified and stylised representation of real-world behaviour. Further, it is our opinion that a theory of marketing demands a synthesising of concepts from both the economic and the behavioural sciences if it is to constitute an adequate explanation of the true nature of exchange.

In many senses the practice of marketing today is in a very similar situation to that which obtained prior to the statement of the law of thermo-dynamics in terms of the development of the steam-engine. Thus, as Halbert has pointed out,[1] marketing needs to develop a theory both to improve operational performance as well as to satisfy an intellectual desire to evolve an explanation of a confused world. With the formulation and statement of a theory of marketing we could look forward to the more effective solution of immediate operating problems and so could concentrate our attention on the more important and basic problems which underlie them. Further, increased operational efficiency would also free practitioners from 'fire-fighting' activities and so leave them with more time in which to solve these problems. Thus the increasing complexity of business makes the need for theory even more pressing than hitherto in order to speed up and improve our decision-making capability. At the same time it appears that developments in other sciences have created the intellectual and analytical tools necessary to the statement of a theory of marketing.

Marketing and the scientific method

At a number of places in the preceding pages we have referred to science and scientific method and it is appropriate that we should now consider the relevance that these may have for the formulation of a theory of marketing.

As hinted earlier, the factor that tends to differentiate science from art or applied skill is that science goes beyond mere description and seeks to provide an explanation of why things are what they are. Thus one of the main objectives of science has been that of spelling out the interrelationship between the parts of the structure in order to derive laws or principles which may serve as a basis for prediction, decision and action. Prediction in any field of study is possible only to the extent that uniformity exists in the phenomena under study. Indeed it is probably because the conditions and events of a physical nature are found to have a relatively higher degree of uniformity that predictions regarding them can be thought of as comparatively reliable with the result that the methods by which such phenomena have been studied have become the standards for scientific research and the basis of what has been termed 'the scientific method'.

In an article entitled 'Is Marketing a Science?' Robert D. Buzzell[2] suggests that a science is 'a classified and systemized body of knowledge...organized around one or more central theories and a number of general principles...usually expressed in quantitative terms...knowledge which permits the prediction and, under some circumstances the control of future events'. Invariably science that conforms to this definition is the outcome of a process known as 'the scientific method' which is usually recognised as possessing a number of clearly defined steps: (i). observation and measurement, (ii). experimentation, (iii). classification, and (iv). accurate generalisation.

Is marketing a science?

The question posed by Buzzell has long been debated by marketing academics being originally sparked off by Converse[3] in 1945 and raged in the 1950s and 1960s fuelled by such authors as Alderson and Cox (1948),[4] Vaile (1949),[5] Bartels (1951),[6] Hutchinson (1965),[7] Jueck (1953),[8] Baumol (1957),[9] Buzzell (1963),[10] Halbert (1965)[11] and Taylor (1965).[12] Three definite schools of thought can be identified:

1. Those who say marketing is not and never will be a science.
2. Those who believe marketing is a science.
3. Those who presuppose the attainment of science is possible and who either do not concern themselves with justifying their position or suggest that as marketing matures it will become worthy of the title 'science'. Others who may be included in this school are those who point out marketing's use of scientific method as justification of its evolving status.

Vaile[13] was one of the earliest critics of the 'marketing is a science' school. In answer to Alderson and Cox's[14] attempt at a single theory in 1948, he said 'When all is said and done, marketing will remain an art in which innovation and extravaganza will continue to play an important, albeit unpredictable part'.[15] Hutchinson[16] similarly eloquently dismisses marketing as a science. He too believes that marketing should be considered as an art or practice, more closely resembling engineering, medicine and architecture and that marketers should follow the medical profession whose members are called practitioners and whose work it is, 'as it is of any practitioner, to apply the findings of many sciences to the solution of problems'.[17] Levitt suggests science is only used as a limited background to help marketers make decisions and reduce risks, but their objective must always be the practical application and thus 'The highest form of achievement is always art, never science'.[18] He further believes that marketing will probably never be a science because little day-to-day guidance is possible. Taylor is also of the opinion that 'the act of marketing is an art'. He does, however, admit that in the course of the marketing practitioner's work 'he may publish observations and conduct experiments. To the extent that he does so and contributes to the field of conceptual schemes that are fruitful and that extend the range of theory in marketing, he functions as a scientist'.[19] Weiss[20] is perhaps the most scathing, suggesting that the Marketing Science Institute in the United States should drop 'science' from its title for all social sciences are merely disciplines and 'undisciplined disciplines at that'. Since behaviour can never be 'average', to develop diagnostic tools to analyse it, he insists, is irrelevant.

The 'marketing is a science' school is less polemic. Bartels[21] suggests one commonly held view is that 'Marketing thought is...seen beginning as simple inquiry and findings, progressing to the status of a discipline and emerging as science'.[22] Most marketers, however, are more cautious and fall into the third category, believing marketing will be worthy of the title of science eventually, provided marketers do not concentrate on borrowing theories from other disciplines without validating them, but stick instead to building up theory from observation and the measurement of raw data.

Whether marketing is classified as a science or art is largely dependent upon the author's perspective and approach. If he is a practitioner, or favours the view that marketing should be approached in a managerial or institutional way, he is likely to insist that marketing is an art. The academic and researcher are more likely to believe that marketing is, or has the potential of being, a science. Numerous definitions of science have consequently been quoted to prove or disprove that marketing is a science. For example, Buzzell says that since science is 'a classified and systematic body of knowledge...organised around one or more central theories and a number of general principles' and since marketing lacks the requisite central tendencies, it cannot be termed a science. In addition, he suggests its ability to predict (another of science's criteria) is limited. However, even the critics have to admit that marketing uses science and scientific techniques. Hutchinson[23] seeks to resolve the problem by drawing a distinction between the scientist pushing back the frontiers of knowledge and the practitioner applying that knowledge. Ramond[24] suggests the linkage is much closer, 'using science is an art'. He goes on to show how scientific knowledge and methods can help practitioners operate most effectively. 'Marketing, like medicine and engineering, requires the practice of many arts, important among which is the use of science.'

The supporters of marketing being a science frequently quote Homans,[25] 'What makes a science are its aims, not its results', while others have taken dictionary definitions of science, for example, 'any distinct branch or department of systematized knowledge considered as a distinct field of investigation or object of study, it is concerned with observation and the classification of facts and with the establishment of general laws, chiefly by induction and hypotheses'[26] and matched the function of marketing accordingly. They point out that science is built up through the scientific method–the selection, registration and rearranging of facts into some workable form from which conclusions can be derived–and since marketing already uses this process it must be at least a potential science, but may not yet be science because it is still a young discipline. They refer to the fact that physics achieved the status of science before psychology, and psychology before sociology. Since marketing has not progressed very far along the evolutionary spectrum, it is only a matter of time before it arrives.

The battle tends to focus on one or two controversial areas. One is whether marketing meets the objectives of science. Most accept that science's objectives are to derive laws and principles from studying underlying uniformities to serve as the basis for prediction. The 'marketing is an art' school argue that marketing phenomena are different from those in the physical sciences and do not therefore have a sufficient degree of uniformity to serve as the basis for prediction. The 'marketing is a science' school argue that there is sufficient uniformity and stability for making valid and reliable predictions, and measurement can be used in marketing equally well as it is used in physics or chemistry–the only difference being that 'precision is a relative matter'.[27] Also, while it is true that marketing is a complex discipline with numerous variables interacting within a wider dynamic framework, complexity is also common in physical sciences, but here it is often assumed away.

Another point of disagreement is whether the scientific approach is inductive or deductive. The 'marketing is an art' school say that true science is made up of laws that are empirically derived (and therefore more objective) while the social sciences have tended to rely on theoretical laws (i.e. rules of inference). Supporters of the 'marketing is a science' school are prepared to accept either or both types, for even subjective factors, they say, can be reduced to scientific statement in law.[28]

Perhaps Bartels sums up the definition of science debate the best by showing how marketing can be described to fit the definition of an art, a discipline or a science. The only reason for one's choice is one's approach. To define marketing as an art puts the emphasis on doing. To define marketing as a discipline stresses the academic side. To define marketing as a science is to see it as a body of knowledge with concepts, theories, principles and laws.

It would seem that to consider marketing solely as an art is myopically to deny the utility and function of science and restrict marketing's development in the future. Despite the fact that most marketers will always be concerned with the discipline's practical application, all effective practice is dependent upon evolving theory. Without better theory practice cannot become more effective and to regard theory as the opposite end of the continuum from practice is to exemplify the misunderstanding portrayed by many of the 'marketing is an art' school. The purpose of science as a problem-solving tool for society should be sufficient reason to regard marketing as a science, and theory, an integral part of science, therefore has an essential role.

Science and marketing

While we have suggested that the basic distinction between art and science rests on the fact that the latter goes beyond description to explanation, none the less it is clear that the first step in the scientific method must be the collection and description of facts. Based upon observation the first distinction which a person is likely to make is qualitative, for example A is bigger than B and A is bigger than C. It is immediately apparent that such qualitative statements severely limit our ability to make inferences about the relationship between B and C. For this reason science lays great emphasis upon precise measurement and quantification and so enables us to make much more accurate and elaborate statements about the relationship between objects.

If we assume that the first step in the evolution of scientific methods is the chance or random observation of objects and events, then it is clear that our knowledge and understanding will be greatly improved if these observations are undertaken in a systematic manner. Even greater progress becomes possible when such systematic observation is complemented by experimentation. Experiments may be conceived of and undertaken for a variety of reasons but all rest upon the principle that every natural event is a consequence of preceding and ascertainable conditions of its physical environment. It follows, therefore, that if one changes the conditions in the physical environment then one will produce corresponding changes in the event. Amongst the various types of experiment may be distinguished exploratory investigations in which one varies inputs in a controlled manner in order to determine the effect upon the outputs; experiments to test accepted principles, for example Gallileo's experiments with weights whereby he disproved the Aristotelian law that material bodies fall with velocities proportional to their weights; experiments to check on chance observations; and experiments to test hypotheses.

Clearly, experimentation results in a great improvement in both the quantity and quality of data available to scientists. However, to be meaningful this data must now be classified as a basis for analysis and a statement of accurate generalisations. This process whereby one develops generalisations from particular instances and events is known as 'induction' and, irrespective of the name given to them, all models, principles, laws and theories possess the common property that they are generalisations about an area of reality arrived at by the process of abstracting from reality.

Good representations of phenomena abstracted from reality can also be used to explain occurrences or even to make predictions. This method is known as 'deduction'–a process of reasoning from general assumptions or statements to particular conclusions. It is clear that deductive methods permit the verification of conclusions arrived at by inductive reasoning, and thus the cycle of induction, deduction and verification constitutes the framework of the scientific method.

The need for a scientific approach to the solution of marketing problems was well exemplified in a paper delivered by Colin McDonald at the Market Research Society's Seminar on Strategic Advertising Decisions in November 1974.[29] Given the magnitude of advertising expenditures (£874 million in 1973 in the United Kingdom at the time at which McDonald was writing and now (1982) estimated at £3,126 million) it is not surprising that marketers have long sought for some measure of the return on this outlay but, so far, with a singular lack of success. In McDonald's view this lack of success is due to speculative theorising which fails to observe the rules of the scientific method, and especially its failure first to observe and describe the phenomenon. Thus he comments:

> I find myself very much in agreement with David Berdy[30] when he categorises most of the approaches to advertising as ideological, or fundamentalist, and for that reason sterile, and complains of its failure to adopt a true scientific approach in spite of trying: Outside the pure sciences…there is an inverse relationship between preoccupation with theoretical structures and the understanding of practical techniques or processes. You cannot observe a theory without observing facts; such short cuts are a negation of the scientific method.

In deciding just what one should observe, McDonald cites three basic questions posed by advertisers:

1. How should we decide the size of the advertising appropriation?
2. How should we decide the media mix?
3. How should we decide whether to have continuous or burst advertising?

He goes on to say that 'The second and third of these questions are subsidiary to the first one. The first question involves *what* advertising is trying to do (objectives) and how we measure that it is doing it; the other two questions are about how to achieve what is determined by the first.'

But, after reviewing the advertisers' viewpoint, McDonald is forced to conclude that an approach based upon measuring advertising's success (or lack of it) in achieving predetermined objectives is doomed to failure. As he trenchantly points out, 'The trouble is that, *because* there is ignorance of advertising effect, people have no basis on which to *set* objectives in the first place. Thus the objectives they do set (when indeed they propose any) tend to be circular; they reflect their existing preconceptions'. Accordingly, it follows that one must first observe, record and measure what actually happens as a result of advertising in terms of perception, awareness, attitude and behavioural change. In turn, as we are concerned with people, we must study them as individuals and over time, which militates against the type of aggregate and cross-sectional studies which have predominated in the past.

Once we have built up a sound base of observations, McDonald feels that we should not be so constrained by the true scientific method as to become heavily involved in experimentation. This opinion is predicated on the belief that the high level of interdependence between many marketing variables (for example distribution and promotion) makes it very difficult to separate out their effects and that attempts to do so may be sterile and self-defeating (as they often have been in the past). Thus experimentation should be used where feasible and appropriate but should not be regarded as a *sine qua non* of progression to the stages of classification and generalisation.

Throughout his paper McDonald returns again and again to the need for a sound empirical basis to theory founded upon observation and testing of these observations, for otherwise there is a considerable danger of falling into the trap of circular reasoning. As an example of this he cites the DAGMAR model which is postulated on a premise that this is how advertising 'should' work and validated by data or evidence which proves the point–in other words a self-fulfilling prophecy.

The development of marketing theory

Much of what McDonald has to say about the measurement of advertising effectiveness would seem to be equally true of many other areas of marketing. Perhaps marketers lack sufficient humility to get back to first principles and collect raw data as the basis for developing their own theory, or perhaps we place too much reliance upon the theories which we have borrowed from other disciplines without validating them. Whatever the reason we are inclined to subscribe to the general view that while marketing is not yet worthy of the title 'science', there is no reason why it should not become so. However, to achieve scientific status we must accept the rigour implicit in the scientific method and begin at the beginning with observation and measurement and not jump into experimentation, classification and generalisation without this essential foundation.

Assuming then that we accept the desirability of committing effort and resources to the development of marketing theory, and are prepared to adopt a scientific approach, what criteria should we seek to satisfy? On this issue we can do no better than reproduce Leslie Rodger's statement of the requirements of good theory.[31]

(a) it must provide the means of classifying, organising, and integrating information relevant to the factual world of business;
(b) it must provide a technique of thinking about marketing problems, and a perspective for practical action;
(c) it must make available an analytical tool-kit to be drawn on as appropriate in the solution of marketing problems;
(d) it should provide a basis for the explanation, prediction, and perhaps even the control of marketing processes and events;
(e) it should, in time, permit the derivation of a number of principles, possibly even laws, of marketing behaviour.

If we adopt these criteria then it is apparent that there are at least some ideas and concepts which enjoy currency among both academics and practitioners that go a long way towards satisfying them. Thus, while this chapter has been concerned primarily with establishing the need for theory and the benefits of a scientific approach to its formulation, in the process of which we have been critical of non-scientific methods, this is not to say that marketing lacks any theoretical foundations at all.

To date, however, theory is poorly developed in marketing. It can be evaluated in terms of (i) integration or cohesion, (ii) consistency of approach, (iii) practical applicability, (iv) sophistication, and (v) origin. While its role and function have varied through time–from a means of identifying problems to facilitating solutions and today helping to organise a much wider social system to explain the exchange relationship–theory on both the overall and the specific levels remains relatively unintegrated and its practical utility is limited in scope, lacking in sophistication, and its foundations lie largely within other disciplines. In terms of its inconsistency of approach, nowhere is this more clearly seen than in early attempts to develop a marketing 'theory'.

Early approaches to marketing theory on the overall level

By considering the historical evolution of marketing theory on the broad level, it is obvious how disparate, eclectic and inconsistent in approach attempts at such a theory were. Marketing was conceived, or discovered, according to Bartels, between 1900 and 1910. Previously it had been incorporated into macroeconomic theory but at the beginning of the century the scientific study of management practice was developing. Attention thus turned from the public to private economic problems. Economic theory was seen to be inadequate and marketing began to borrow theory from other disciplines. Overall, however, marketing theory received little interest before 1941. Between 1940 and 1950, and closely associated with the 'is marketing a science?' debate, it was felt that there was an insufficient theoretical basis in marketing. The most significant contributions to emerge were those developed by Alderson and Cox[32] and Bartels.[33]

Cox and Alderson suggest that two factors promoted the call for a new theoretical perspective–first, dissatisfaction with the numbers and kinds of generalisations thus far achieved through sedulous accumulation of innumerable facts; and secondly, and perhaps more importantly, dissatisfaction with the adequacy of individual theories already incorporated within marketing, notably economic theory. Nevertheless, they believe that marketing is not doomed to a 'fragmentary, superficial and inaccurate' future, but that 'the accumulating elements for at least a rudimentary theory of marketing are scattered throughout the literature of the social sciences'. Thus, while they dismiss the idea that a definitive theory of marketing can be developed immediately, they suggest certain insights and borrowings from such fields as group behaviourism and ecological studies, could, using a creative approach, help to develop some basic overall theory.

Wroe Alderson attempts his own creative approach through functionalism. Functionalism, first introduced into marketing by Shaw[34] in 1912, is defined as an approach to science which first identifies some system of action and then tries to determine how and why it works as it does. Alderson's normative theory of marketing systems examines the way organised groups function in continuous adjustment to an operating environment. The normative aspect of his discussion specifies how decision-makers (problem-solvers) ought to behave if they want to achieve their goal–which is seen as survival. The economic, social and ecological environments offer various choices on both the supply and demand sides. Problem-solving is seen as an attempt to reduce the uncertainty. Thus the theory resolves problem-solving by decision-makers in different operating environments. It suffers several limitations. For example, Alderson assumes marginal utility theory in consumer behaviour, suggesting that two-thirds of all American consumers are rational problem-solvers, but to justify its claim to being a first step in marketing theory, it should not have to mirror reality in all its complexity. Such an approach, says Alderson, can be applied to all types of commodities and firms on the individual level, and will help explain how an entire marketing system continues to evolve through the activities of its components on the macro-marketing level. Thus Alderson provides a perspective for future model-building directed at either the general interpretation of marketing or the solution of individual problems.

Alderson is not the only writer who has attempted to use functionalism. McGary[35] in 1953, identifying six marketing functions (contractual, propaganda, merchandising, physical distribution, pricing and termination), attempted to develop a theory of marketing. It is a deductive, speculative approach that envisages marketing as a social mechanism that develops with the growth of an economy and aids the adjustment of man to his environment. McGary, unlike Alderson, believes the consumer is imperfectly rational. While such controversies are inherent in a subject-matter with so many unknown variables, both McGary and Alderson provide the beginnings of an overall theory which simplifies, explains, may eventually predict, and which would seem to be of great potential value today.

Bartels, the other major contributor to general marketing theory, is concerned about the cohesiveness of marketing. He believes a holistic theory is necessary to bind together the proliferation of facts and the various viewpoints, concepts and approaches, which are constantly changing as marketing becomes more people-oriented and more subject to public and environmental constraints.

Bartels's perspective of marketing is summarised by his statement 'Marketing is the process whereby society, to supply its consumption needs, evolves distribution systems composed of participants, who, interacting under constraints—technical (economic) and ethical (social)—creates the transactions or flows which resolve market separations and result in exchange and consumption'.[36] He then attempts to expand this into a general theory summarised in Figure 2.1.

Whether such a diagram can be regarded as an overall theory is open to debate. Certainly it serves to epitomise the lack of sophistication associated with theory at this level. Bartels is the only author to call his work 'a general theory'. Others readily admit that their suggestions are merely perspectives that might form the beginnings of general theory.

Figure 2.1   Bartels's summary of marketing theory

Source: R. Bartels, 'The General Theory of Marketing', *Journal of Marketing*, vol. 32 (Jan. 1968) p. 32.

Problems involved in the use and development of theory

Many of the major problems involved in using and developing theory are interrelated with the acceptability of marketing as a science. The youth of the discipline and the nature of marketing phenomena are obvious initial handicaps. If it is assumed that any science starts with curiosity and that it is first necessary to understand and explain in order to predict and eventually control the future, marketing's progression along this path has been hindered from the early stages. Curiosity and inspection of marketing phenomena calls for definition, since it is difficult to predict without some precision of language. Unfortunately the essential step of formulating a language is still underway. The problem of definition revolves around three areas of controversy: (i) what kinds of phenomena and issues are perceived to be in the scope of marketing, (ii) what kinds of phenomena and issues should be included in the scope of marketing, and (iii) how can marketing be defined so as to encompass systematically all the phenomena and issues that should be included, while at the same time systematically excluding all other phenomena and issues.[37] Since the scope of marketing is very broad, and the phenomena are complex, interacting and dynamic, responding to a much wider system, it is not surprising that the definition of marketing's boundaries and functions has varied according to individuals' perspectives.

Major perspectives adopted can be identified by using three dichotomies–micro/macro, descriptive/decision-oriented, profit/non-profit. By examining the various approaches and allocating authors to these categories, it is easy to understand why marketing is considered a science by some and not by others, and why theoretical development and agreement is more difficult. The practitioners like Levitt, Buzzell, Vaile and Taylor would suggest that marketing should be restricted to the profit/micro/normative definition, which can be traced to the 1920s, but received greatest emphasis in the early 1960s when the managerial approach to marketing was in fashion. Since marketing is purely evaluative and prescriptive if this approach is adopted, not unnaturally the authors regarding it in this light see marketing as an art. However, it is unnecessary, unrealistic and undesirable to restrict the definition of marketing to this extent. Marketing also includes positive dimensions which can be understood, explained and predicted, and therefore involves science. Furthermore, because marketing deals with the real world which is constantly changing, corresponding changes in foci and priorities are essential. The growth of the public sector, social and societal issues and other new values and priorities are now forcing the traditional definitions of marketing like 'the performance of business activities that directs the flow of goods and services from producer to consumer or user in order to satisfy customers and accomplish company objectives'[38] to be broadened. Thus profit/macro/normative and non-profit macro/ and micro/normative approaches to marketing are the most fashionable today.

In the past the problems of definition and the widening scope and changing foci of marketing have been exacerbated by the lack of interaction between academic marketers and marketing practitioners. The practitioner has tended to dismiss marketing theory as irrelevant, or an impossible dream, since (i) the various assumptions made by the theorist can always be disputed, (ii) marketing models are often seen as reductionistic and therefore useless, concentrating on the individual as opposed to aggregate factors like market demand, and (iii) static equilibrium models are worthless in the dynamic real world.

Yet, even the practitioner has 'rules of thumb' which could be seen as models to help him predict. Furthermore, his function of setting goals, analysing, planning, implementing and control corresponds to normative prescriptions given by the theoretician. Therefore, while the idea that theory and practice are separate is clearly wrong, at the same time, because the academic has in the past been of little help with his theories, which seek to explain the variables originating from other disciplines or which incorporate *ceteris paribus* assumptions, the gap between theorist and practitioner has been maintained. In an increasingly dynamic, unpredictable and complex world, new models, even if simple, are essential to allow the decision-maker to identify correctly the basic structure of the environment in which his organisation operates and allow him to predict relationships, for example, that between advertising outlays and company demand.

Certainly some cohesion within the discipline is necessary and some framework which will be accepted by marketers must be developed. The answer would seem to lie in using criteria sufficiently broad to enable both schools of thought to regard marketing as a science. Since marketing has (i) a distinct subject-matter, being centred on the transaction, (ii) can be described and classified (as well exemplified by the marketing literature), (iii) has underlying uniformities and regularities on both *a priori* and empirical grounds, and (iv) can be studied by using the methodology of science, it should be regarded as a science. Such criteria overcome the criticism like lack of central theories, while the focus of the transaction provides some solution to the problems of definition. Through reconciling the two schools of thought in this manner, the way ahead to develop better theory specifically suited to marketing's needs rather than reliance on theories borrowed from other disciplines is open. The purpose of theory in broad terms is to increase understanding through systematised structure but the practitioner's co-operation will ensure that theory is developed in the right direction to maximum utility. It may be that some business practitioners are already coming round to this way of thinking if Newman[39] is to be believed. He suggests that dating from the 1960s there has been a shift from the 'seat of the pants' type of decision-making to a new era of professional management based on regularly sought, expertly interpreted information. The practitioners' acceptance of marketing as a science can also be witnessed by the establishment of associations like the United States's Marketing Science Institute which has the specific aim of contributing to the emergence of science in marketing, stimulating increased applications of scientific techniques.

The case for accepting marketing as a science is clearly a good one. It diverts energy spent on arguing over the criteria of what is science to more fruitful application elsewhere and ensures a more integrated approach towards marketing from both the academics and the practitioners.

CHAPTER 3

The sources of marketing theory

Contents

Introduction

In the preceding chapter we were concerned primarily with defining the nature and function of theory in order to justify our view that a theoretical foundation is essential to the development of any body of knowledge. Further, we endeavoured to show that improvement in practice is dependent upon the development of such a body of knowledge which, in turn, would seem to proceed most effectively when based upon a scientific approach. In this chapter we turn our attention to an examination of the progress made towards the evolution of theory in marketing.

Our examination of the present state of marketing theory commences with a review of the proposition that we must draw upon concepts and hypotheses developed in other disciplines, notably the social sciences, as the basis for such theory. Accordingly we consider 'borrowing' on three levels–content, techniques and concepts. This survey leads naturally to a discussion of the way in which different facts or other evidence may be combined into a distinctive or coherent body of knowledge and to a brief synopsis of the development of marketing thought along the lines proposed by Bartels. Finally, we examine specific sources of marketing theory, such as economics and the behavioural sciences, as a preliminary to the detailed analysis of the particular marketing topics which comprise Part II of this book.

Basic sources

In his seminal contribution *The Meaning and Sources of Marketing Theory*, Michael Halbert makes the point early on that 'marketing, however, has no recognised central theoretical basis such as exists for any other disciplines, notably the physical sciences and, in some cases, the behavioural sciences'.[1] At first glance the absence of such a recognised theoretical core seems somewhat surprising, particularly if one accepts that theory usually develops out of practice and that marketing has been practised ever since the first exchange relationship was entered into. However, as we noted in the previous chapter, the development of a theory usually results from a coalescing of two parallel forces, a practical desire to improve operational performance and an intellectual desire to evolve an explanation of a confused world. But, as a review of the evolution of the modern marketing management concept out of the production- and sales-management orientations which preceded it makes clear, in conditions of chronic under-supply improvement of operational performance demands that, before anything else, we must satisfy first-order needs which in turn places a premium upon increased productivity and output. Similarly, the intellectual desire to evolve an explanation of a confused world would tend to reflect this reality, which is why the problem of maximising the satisfaction to be derived from the consumption of scarce resources is central to economic theory.

If one believes in the 'needs hierarchy' such as that proposed by Maslow, that is (i) physiological needs, (ii) safety needs, (iii) love needs, (iv) esteem needs, and (v) the need for self-actualisation, in which each higher order of need only emerges when all needs on the preceding and lower levels have been satisfied, one can readily understand why the social sciences are of relatively recent origin. In a situation where virtually all needs are concentrated at the lowest physiological level we may anticipate that patterns of behaviour will be relatively simple and focused upon the acquisition of basic food, shelter and clothing. Only when these basic needs are satisfied and we move up the hierarchy does the intrinsic complexity of human behaviour become sufficiently marked to warrant investigation and explanation. Thus we can speculate that the development of conditions in which supply caught up with and sometimes exceeded demand, conditions that were to give rise to the function of marketing as we know it today, also created the conditions which favoured the development of the behavioural sciences.

It is our belief that any theory of marketing must be synthetic, in the sense that it must combine major concepts and ideas from both economics and the behavioural sciences. Although there is now a trend for each of these disciplines to consider the findings and theories of the other and to attempt to incorporate them in their own theories, the earlier development of both these disciplines has shown a marked neglect of the other. Thus, as we argue later, the theory of buyer behaviour based solely upon concepts of economic rationality, or alternatively one based upon behavioural concepts which ignore economic constraints upon behaviour, is unlikely to prove a satisfactory explanation of the way in which people behave in the real world. It is possible, therefore, that the need for a theory of marketing arises from recognition of the enormous complexity associated with exchange relationships and recognises that neither economics nor the behavioural sciences fully satisfies this need. If this is the case then it is not difficult to understand why progress towards a theory of marketing must of necessity be both painful and slow.

'Borrowing' as a basis for marketing theory

Halbert suggests that if we are seeking a basis for marketing theory then we should be prepared to borrow from other fields. This we may do at three different levels of generality–content, techniques and concepts. When we are dealing with content we are concerned with the question of 'what' to study, that is with facts or data; when we are concerned with techniques we will be studying 'how' to apply certain methods to the generation of the content material; and when we are concerned with concepts, we will be referring, or endeavouring to refer, to 'why' the phenomena take place.

Content refers to the most specific class of material since it is concerned with observations, measurements and descriptions of the phenomena which are to be studied; thus content concerns facts or data from which a theory may be abstracted.

In Halbert's words, techniques are 'ways of generalising the content material' and so include techniques of research investigation and analysis. It is in this area that the most active and effective borrowing has taken place, and applied to marketing. Techniques include the processes of both measurement and analysis. From mathematics we borrow techniques like 'multiple regression' while from psychology we are liable to borrow the 'intelligence test' and the 'questionnaire', and from statistics analytical techniques which allow us to estimate percentages of a population likely to possess, or not possess, given characteristics based upon samples of that population.

In his search for appropriate techniques which may be applied to marketing, Halbert looks to the behavioural sciences, the business disciplines and the methodological sciences. He suggests that while few of the techniques developed and in common use are already well integrated into marketing many are beginning to exert considerable interest at the fringe of research.

However, borrowed and adapted techniques, no matter how powerful and useful they may be in their own area, offer no easy solution to marketing problems. Some of the most enthusiastic advocates of the management sciences have suggested that some of their techniques such as, for example, linear programming and operations research provide the means whereby many marketing problems could be solved more realistically. At best, however, these techniques probably offer us an additional analytical device the value of which depends very much upon the skill of the marketing analyst and upon the clarity with which problems can be stated and analysed when first identified.

While the borrowing of content and techniques often goes a long way towards the objective of improving operational performance, it

Table 3.1   Contributions of various sciences and disciplines to a science of marketing

Science or discipline	Type of contribution		
	Content	Technique	Concept
Marketing	Major	Minor	
Business disciplines	Major	Minor	
Behavioural sciences	Minor	Major	Minor
Methodological sciences		Minor	Major

Source: M. Halbert, *The Meaning and Sources of Marketing Theory* (New York: McGraw-Hill, 1965).

is to concepts that we must look to provide the intellectual and explanatory aspects of theory. For, as Halbert notes, it is *'concepts, theories,* and *generalised ideas* that form the abstract but essential element that distinguishes a science from an art of practice'. As can be seen from Table 3.1, reproduced from Halbert, marketing has been least successful in borrowing concepts, and, according to Halbert, has developed no concepts of its own.

Contributions to a theory of marketing

The increase in knowledge of most marketing specialists has come about as a result of utilising descriptive material, techniques and concepts from different fields of knowledge. As can be seen from Table 3.1, marketing has drawn from many different source areas, and these borrowings have often been so numerous and extensive that one can be forgiven for wondering whether they can be ever welded together into a coherent whole warranting recognition as a general theory of marketing.

This doubt is well founded, for most marketers have come into the subject from other disciplines and their view of it is imbued with concepts and ideas appropriate to this original discipline. Thus economists regard marketing as being primarily an area of applied economics and think about the subject in a very different way from behaviourists and management scientists.

In an article entitled 'The General Theory of Marketing'[2] Robert Bartels suggests that, just as in other areas of scientific and behavioural knowledge the subject area has moved through the process of development of practical ability to theoretical knowledge, so in marketing we may be already witnessing a similar move towards the development of a cohesive theory. In fact he argues that the very proliferation of facts may be forcing an integration of knowledge on a higher plane of unification and abstraction.

Bartels continues to argue that growth of theory in the marketing area may be thought of as analogous to the growth of a pile of sand or sand-castle which one builds on the beach when on holiday; the higher the sand-castle has to be, then the broader must be its base; the broader its base, the higher it must be built before a sharp peak or focus is obtained. The process of abstraction applied to the field of marketing may indeed be similar to this in its nature. If we are to give any credence to this point of view then a given base of fact supports its own structure of generalisation and abstraction as indicated in Figure 3.1(a). Further study may reinforce the theory

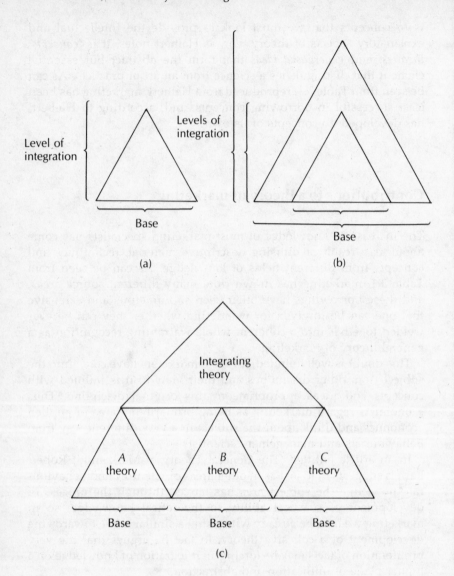

Figure 3.1   Levels of integration

Source: R. Bartels, 'The General Theory of Marketing', *Journal of Marketing*, vol. 32 (Jan. 1968) pp. 32 ff.

which has already been devised through broadening the basis of enquiry. This has two effects upon the structure of thought. It may either, as a result of more and more empirical observations, raise the level of generalisation which can be based upon the myriad of facts, as for example is shown in Figure 3.1(b), or it may provide certain theories with relevant concepts and techniques which may or may not be capable of being unified into a more general theory, as is indicated in Figure 3.1(c). If there is any possibility of the development of what could be called 'a general theory of marketing' then it will probably grow out of the approach suggested by Figures 3.1(b) or 3.1(c).

However, most observers are agreed that in its current state of development marketing still consists of a number of separate theories or piecemeal approaches which by and large fall into the pattern suggested by Figure 3.1(c). These separate theoretical areas may in time build up through a process of integration with the result that we may be able to apply theory to much larger areas of empirical fact, many of which would not be currently classed within the area of knowledge covered by the discipline of marketing.

Marketing and other disciplines

Marketing men traditionally regarded themselves as economic men. However, as non-economic motivations have become recognised, and different patterns of behaviour have been observed, so new areas of study have been opened to marketing. New views were not easily integrated with the assumptions and observations which represented the viewpoint of the economic man, but as we have suggested earlier the behaviourist theories have now been applied increasingly to the field of marketing. Alderson, for example, considered participants in the marketing process as being the same people whom sociologists studied within the context of the firm itself, and therefore he advanced a view that sociological theories had an important role to play in helping to understand marketing and to extend the basis provided by economic theory. Marketing has also drawn upon a number of other areas including the management sciences, social and behavioural sciences and the methodological sciences but, as noted above, so far each of these areas of thought has tended to develop separately in a piecemeal way and very little attempt has been made to integrate these separate areas and move towards a more general theory of marketing. However, before examining the contributions from these different areas it will be useful to trace the developmental stages through which marketing thought has progressed.

The development of marketing thought

Probably the best-known chronicler of the history of marketing thought is Robert Bartels.[3] According to Bartels we may distinguish six different periods in the history of marketing thought since its 'discovery' between 1900 and 1910. In Bartels's view, prior to 1900 market behaviour and trade practice were explained mainly from the macro viewpoint in economic theory. However, while the emphasis upon scientific management, exemplified *inter alia* by the studies of Frederick Taylor, diverted attention from the public to private economic problems virtually no attention was given to the distribution activity. As a result, as Bartels points out, there developed

> a gap in theoretical explanation as social and economic conditions departed increasingly from the assumptions concerning the market on which existing trade theory was built. Competition no longer characterised some markets: demanders and suppliers were farther removed from each other; customary relations of demand and supply were becoming reversed; and new patterns of living were evolving. New interpretations of economic activity were needed, as were new applications of management science to distributive business. These needs nurtured the discovery of marketing.

Thus Bartels's period of *discovery* may be summarised as a period in which the early teachers of the subject sought facts about the distributive trades. In the process of this search, theory was borrowed mainly from economics, particularly in the fields of distribution, world trade and commodity markets, and the term 'marketing' was selected to describe this particular activity.

The years between 1910 and 1920 are characterised by Bartels as a period of *conceptualisation*, and in this era 'basic concepts on which the structure of marketing thought was built for the next forty or fifty years emerged and were crystallised'. It was during this period that many marketing concepts were initially developed and classified and terms defined. It was also during this time that three lines of approach to the analysis of marketing were identified–the institutional, the functional and the commodity approaches. Significant among early contributions to the functional approach are the writings of Shaw, Weld and Cherington.[4]

Weld also contributed to the institutional approach, as did Paul H. Nystrom whose *Retail Selling and Store Management* and *The Economics of Retailing* did much to elucidate the operation and structural elements associated with retail distribution.[5] Many other notable contributions were made during this period relating to advertising, the provision of credit, selling and sales management, and so on, and the reader seeking a description of these is recommended to refer to Bartels for a detailed review.

Following on the many and diverse contributions made during the decade 1910–20 the next decade is characterised as a *period of integration*. As Bartels comments, 'the years between 1920 and 1930 mark the coming of age of the discipline of marketing. During that decade not only did all the branches of the subject attain a general or integrated statement, but two additional areas of specialisation appeared–wholesaling and marketing research'. At this stage of its development the marketing concept was defined as comprising 'all of those activities involved in the distribution of goods from producers to consumers and in the transfer of title thereto'. It is not surprising therefore that the emphasis was again placed upon the physical activities such as wholesaling, retailing and their relationship to one another in the concept of a marketing channel. However, during the 1930s changes in social and economic conditions had a marked effect moulding the direction of thinking and practice in marketing with the result that Bartels describes the 1930s and 1940s as a *period of development*. Synoptically this phase is characterised as one during which 'specialised areas of marketing continued to be developed, hypothetical assumptions were verified and quantified, and some new approaches to the explanation of marketing were undertaken'. In turn, the developments of the 1930s laid the basis for the next decade–typified as a *period of reappraisal*. It was probably during this period that academics and other thinkers concerned with the development of marketing began to ask themselves whether the body of knowledge had achieved, or could aspire to, the status of a science. With the benefit of hindsight it would seem fair to say that by 1950 marketing thinking encompassed an impressive array of content and techniques that was short of concepts and certainly lacked any general theory or theories of marketing. It was with these latter issues that we have been concerned in the second half of the twentieth century commencing with Bartels's *period of conceptualisation* (1950–60) which he summarises as being the period during which 'traditional approaches to the study of marketing were supplemented by increasing emphasis upon managerial decision making, the societal aspects of marketing, and quantitative marketing analysis. Many new concepts, some borrowed from the field of management, some from the other social sciences, were introduced into marketing.'

In Halbert's opinion the evolution of marketing thought described by Bartels has been accompanied by a shift in both approach and method *vis-à-vis* marketing theory. Thus there has been a shift from:

1. Subjective approaches to objective ones.
2. Less formalised approaches to more theoretical ones (models, mathematics, statistics, marketing research).

3. The qualitative to the quantitative, even in unlikely areas of attitudes, opinions, and motivations (scaling, and projective techniques).
4. Rigorous classifications to gradations and refinements.
5. Classification to causation.
6. Static to dynamic theories (classical statistical approaches, to Markov processes simulation).
7. Disjointed facts and descriptions to a search for generalisations, principles, theories, and laws.
8. Surface analysis to depth investigations.
9. Sheer speculation (which is necessary) to realism and more directly applicable concepts and theories.[6]

Throughout this process the budding marketing theorist has drawn heavily upon other disciplines, especially economics, the behavioural sciences and, more recently, the management sciences. We conclude this chapter by considering the relationship between marketing and these source disciplines in slightly greater depth as a basis for the detailed review of the selected marketing areas discussed in Part II.

Marketing and economics

As indicated earlier, the study of marketing developed as a branch of applied economics concerned with the study of channels of distribution. Thus the macroeconomic model of resource allocation recognises four principal activities:

1. extractive and agrarian
2. manufacturing, assembling and fabricating
3. distribution
4. consumption

The model locates marketing in the third category. Within such a scheme, marketing is viewed as part of the theory of economic allocation and its contribution is considered to be the creation of value through time, place and possession utilities.

However, while the study of distribution in economics was concerned with flows at the macro level, marketing is concerned primarily with micro flows of goods and services between organisations and persons. Accordingly, borrowing from economics has tended to be concentrated more upon price and output theory and has drawn heavily upon such concepts as 'price elasticity', 'market equilibrium', 'diminishing marginal utility', 'economies of scale', and so on.

Marketing has also made frequent use of the concept of 'economic man' which holds that purchasing decisions are largely the result of rational and economic calculations on the part of the buyer. However, as Halbert comments, 'Economic man is assumed to have full and complete information about the decision under consideration. In classical economics when the problem of price is being considered, it is assumed that all customers and all suppliers know the location of all products, and that the information about price, quality, quantity, and availability is instantly available and completely correct.'[7] Such simplifying assumptions are essential to the development of a theory which has proved of enormous value, as both a general statement of how the price mechanism operates under changing conditions of supply and demand, as well as specifying which variables need to be monitored in the real world if the model is to have practical application.

However, the economist's emphasis upon a single equilibrium point ignores several facets of behaviour which are of central importance to the marketer. The economist has not concerned himself with the manner in which preferences are formed, nor how they are rank-ordered, both of which constitute a major preoccupation of marketing practitioners. Similarly, economists are not concerned with the manner in which preferences may be psychologically modified or altered by new stimuli, yet this area is a major preoccupation of advertising and sales-promotional efforts. In the same manner, economics pays scant attention to the interaction between buyer and seller in the negotiation of a sale—yet another vital area for the marketing man.

In essence, therefore, economics provides a rich source of theory, concepts and ideas but is an inadequate explanation of the real world. Indeed, if it were an adequate explanation of the real world it is very doubtful that there would have been a need for the new composite discipline of marketing. Fundamentally the inadequacy of economic theory rests on the concept of 'rationality', the definition of which is tautologous, as is apparent in this quotation from Halbert:

> The concept of rationality, so central to economic theory on examination, appears to be a very difficult concept indeed. If we define rationality as behaviour designed to maximise utility and then define utility as that which behaviour tends to maximise, we are not very far ahead.

Clearly, the marketer is in need of a better explanation of behaviour than this and it is for this reason that he has also borrowed extensively from the behavioural sciences.

Marketing and the behavioural sciences

In Halbert's view the major contribution of the behavioural sciences–among which may be numbered anthropology, demography, political science, psychology and sociology–lies not so much in specific techniques or ideas but in the fact that they require 'that marketing science take explicit account of the human and social aspects of individuals and groups engaged in marketing behaviour'.[8]

While this is not to say that marketing cannot borrow specific concepts, such as stimulus-response models or Freudian psychodynamic personality theory, it underlines the fact that the behavioural sciences have tried to grapple with the complexity and uncertainty implicit in the real world rather than assume much of it away as the economists have done. Thus it is from the behavioural scientist's *approach* that marketing theorists and researchers probably have most to learn. At the same time it should also be recognised that marketing has made many notable contributions of its own in the methodology of social surveys since it first adopted these techniques, and it is not overstating the situation to claim that nowadays marketing researchers are leaders in the development of new techniques. However, the warning sounded in the previous chapter must also be recognised–namely that preoccupation with techniques, especially in a pseudo-experimental setting of the marketing laboratory, may tempt us to ignore the real world outside.

Another major contribution of the behavioural sciences is its treatment of values and their effect upon human behaviour, especially in the context of decision-taking. Thus, while decision theory provides a logically compelling framework for analysis, its utility is constrained to the extent that we can identify and measure values. In this context the behavioural sciences have made a signal contribution by pointing out that while people tend to obey the pleasure/pain principle by maximising the former and avoiding the latter, none the less people tend to like what they do–not only do what they like. In other words, a person's values may be as much conditioned by his behaviour as the other way around. Certainly, values change over time and marketing has made its own contribution to the sociologists' and anthropologists' studies of maturation and changing value systems with its concept of 'life-style' and consumption behaviour.

In fact, marketing has drawn extensively upon the behavioural sciences in developing its own specialism of consumer behaviour, which is the subject of Chapter 4, as well as the field of marketing communications (Chapter 6) and diffusion of innovations (Chapter 8). Accordingly, further discussion is deferred at this juncture.

Marketing and the management sciences

A study of the development of 'management science' is felt to have particular relevance to the marketing theorist and, at the very least, he should read Chapter 9 of Halbert's book. This view is predicated by the observation that in many ways management scientists have achieved that which marketing scientists are seeking–acceptance and recognition in their own right–within the past twenty to thirty years. Further, they appear to have done this by the same processes of borrowing, synthesising and integration which reflect the efforts of marketing scientists. Thus Halbert notes that:

> their [management scientists and operation researchers] activities have been characterised by emphasis on the mathematical modeling of systems and the development of decision rules for making 'optimal' choices among alternative courses of action. Their techniques have been drawn from a wide variety of disciplines, including applied mathematics, economics, statistics, and psychology.[9]

One might comment that of these disciplines psychology is probably least in evidence and that the early acceptance of management science owes much to its concentration on 'soluble' problems in which the key variables could be both specified and quantified. More recently, management science has turned to less tractable problems incorporating judgement and uncertainty, and thus more characteristic of marketing situations. In these areas their success and credibility is of a much lower order. This is not to argue that the techniques and methods of the econometrician, operation researcher and management scientist are without value–it merely underlines the normal human propensity to solve the easy problems first and defer consideration of the more difficult issues.

It is our view that the emergence of a discipline of marketing represents a conscious attempt to grapple with and explain the real world and that we should not be discouraged if progress is both painful and slow. That progress has been made is readily apparent in the contributions to Part II of this book and we should take heart from this rather than be overly impressed with the initial acceptance accorded management science and so attempt to emulate it. Certainly, this danger is apparent in the emphasis upon experimentation outlined in Chapter 2 which has contributed little to a real understanding of the problem of how advertising works.

Theory–the current status

In many areas of marketing the amount of theory is not commensurate with the research done in the field. International marketing is a good example. Despite remarkable growth in world trade and new forms of international marketing resulting from the growth of multinational corporations, the most common theoretical approach is still traditional trade theory (that is, comparative advantage dating to Ricardo, 1817). As with most economic theory, it suffers limitations owing to its assumptions of perfect competition, factor immobility among nations, and its perspective from one national economy, though the theory still has relevance in helping to identify opportunities, especially in developing nations. The few alternative models that have been produced include Root's enterprise theory–focusing on the market behaviour of an international enterprise and Linder's per capita income theory which proposes that there will be large trade flows between rich countries and small flows between rich and poor countries. Once again it can be seen how the author's perspective is important in determining the scale and spatial dimensions included in the theory used, and once again lack of a unified approach is apparent.

Indeed, there are few universal theories which have relevance in various marketing areas and the practical utility of most theories on the specific level remains limited. Diffusion theory is one exception, being used in the product-life-cycle concept and the adoption process by consumers. Generally, even within specific marketing areas, there are few widely accepted theories. For example, as already noted, there is still no one widely accepted model to explain purchasing. Instead there is controversy as to what and how much of other disciplines should be borrowed. 'If the economists have done marketing a disservice by overemphasising the rational and economic motives for human behaviour, the social scientists, and in particular, the psychologists, have attempted to swing the pendulum to the opposite extreme by emphasising irrational and psychodynamic motivations.'[10]

Clearly, some borrowing is necessary 'for the enrichment of its perspective and for the advancement of marketing as an empirical science'.[11] But while there is much common ground between disciplines, the difference lies in the point of view with which they see the same subject. It is therefore rare that the theoretical approach of one discipline is directly relevant to another, and marketing must, consequently, rely less on other disciplines and develop its own body of theory.

The way in which, and the extent to which, these numerous extensive borrowings can be welded into a coherent whole warranting recognition as a general theory of marketing is a controversial area. At the general overall level, marketing can still be seen as a conglomerate of many disciplines. As shown above, the numerous micro theories provide explanation in some parts of the subject but 'scholarly efforts to integrate the fragments into a coherent general theory have yielded little that is conclusive'.[12]

The need for overall theory, however, is even more urgent today as environmental problems (e.g. explosive population growth, world-wide inflation, environmental destruction, etc.) shake the conceptual foundations of marketing and call for new definitive frameworks. Marketing has always evolved in response to wider economic, social and environmental change. Between 1900 and 1930 when demand was greater than supply, firms were production-orientated, the desire being to increase output with little marketing effort being necessary. In the next twenty years mass production and an era of abundance necessitated a sales orientation. But as some customer needs became satiated and technical and social factors shifted buyer preferences, it was necessary to develop a consumer-orientation. Hence the marketing concept was born around 1950. For almost twenty years it was seen to have relevance in the Western world in an era of rapid economic growth, growing affluence and important inventions, for example xerography. Today this concept is seen as inadequate (and even the cause of present problems, according to some critics), since by focusing on demand–directing the producers to increased satisfaction of consumer wants–it puts us on a collision course with Malthusian arithmetic. Certainly, it ignores the non-profit sector and wider social responsibility issues. In addition, social objectives have changed–quality of life overtaking quantity of goods as a major concern. As a result, Kotler has suggested a societal marketing concept–a management orientation arrived at generating customer satisfaction and long-run consumer and public welfare as the key to satisfying organisational goals and responsibilities. To take care of the non-profit sector, Kotler and Zaltman[13] suggest social marketing–the design, implementation and control of social ideas involving considerations of product planning, price, communications, distribution and market research. Such extensions of the boundaries of marketing, and marketing's changing role within a changing wider system, is summed up in Kotler's generic view, which shows how marketing has developed from a branch of applied economics devoted to the study of distribution channels, through a management discipline concerned with increasing sales, through an applied behavioural science directed at understanding consumer behaviour, to 'the disciplined task of creating and offering values to others for the purpose of achieving a desired response'.

However, while the generic view may help put individual theories embodied in specific areas of marketing into context and may even continue the 'Is marketing a science?' debate under another guise–the more recent 'nature of marketing' debate–it does not in itself provide a theory, nor will it provide a springboard for a vigorous new marketing theory. It is merely a reaction to dissatisfaction with marketing theory on both the overall and specific levels and the growing significance of social problems.

Meta theory–the way ahead?

The most cohesive attempt at an overall framework, if not theory, remains based on Alderson's work, which seems to have all the more relevance today. Thus, Dawson develops 'the Human Concept'. Quoting P. A. Sorokim's belief that the developed world is reorienting itself from materialism to a spiritually based form of culture, Dawson suggests we are entering the 'human era' where marketing executives must cope with other than market considerations. Referring to Alderson, he writes 'at least one business scholar has suggested that cultural ecology, the study of the adaptation of a social system to its environment, provides a more meaningful perspective from which to study business activity than economics or any other science'.[14] Departing little from Alderson's constructs, he points out that cultural ecology focuses on the capacity of an organised behaviour system to sustain itself by drawing upon the resources of its environment. Survival is the ultimate goal but the system can only exist by adapting to environmental change and maintaining a dynamic ecological equilibrium.

Similar concepts incorporating the wider environmental implications include Rothe and Benson's 'Intelligent Consumption Concept'[15] and Fisk's 'Criteria for a Theory of Responsible Consumption'. Both call for ecological implications and a broad perspective to be taken into consideration by management. 'Responsible consumption refers to rational and efficient use of resources with respect to the global human population'.[16]

Perspectives would therefore seem to be broadening in response to fundamental problems in marketing's macro-environment. To incorporate all its aspects, as well as the individual theoretical strands relating to specific areas to produce one definitive overall theory of marketing that would have relevance to developing nations and communist countries alike, would seem to be an ambitious objective. It might be achieved one day.

In the shorter term, however, the answer would seem to lie with meta theory, which can provide both an overview and some standardisation of method within which the theoretical constructs already incorporated in the discipline can be analysed and refined. Being concerned with the conceptual procedure of science, it offers a thinking practical methodology for all aspects of marketing, as it does for all social sciences. It involves the operationalisation of scientific concepts, the logic of testing theories, the use of theory, the nature of causality and the procedures for making predictions. By encouraging the researcher to make his assumptions specific, and appreciate the limitations of his instruments while sharpening his research strategy, and by minimising dogmatism in scientific thinking and systematising existing philosophical outlooks, it ensures that fundamental scientific and philosophic questions are asked in the correct way and the correct procedures are followed.

The scientific process involves describing, ordering, recording, understanding and explaining, with the aim of predicting and controlling the phenomena under study. The way in which one attempts this process is shrouded in controversy. Bacon's classic model adopts the position of a raw empiricist and suggests the sequence is perceptual experience–unordered facts–definition, classification, measurement–ordered facts–inductive generalisation–laws, theory construction and finally explanation. Harvey[17] introduces the initial image of real-world structures which are used as models in the formulation of hypotheses that can then be tested by experimental design, while Bunge[18] emphasises the notion of testable hypotheses more and stresses the importance of scientific knowledge being gauged by the changes it induces in the body of knowledge and the problems it poses. Wherever the emphasis, the objective is to assess existing knowledge and extend it through the formulation of concepts, testing of hypotheses, acquiring new data and critically evaluating the original concepts and premises. Scientific enquiry thus allows the use of sharp tools like objectivity, reliability, precision, coherence and comprehensiveness.

Some have argued that meta theory is too normative to be useful, the standards set being too rigorous to be adhered to for practical purposes in marketing. Others have suggested that a different scientific method is required for the social sciences than that used for the physical sciences. These are negative arguments and confuse techniques with methodology. Certainly there are limitations to meta theory as a standard model of explanation, but, nevertheless, it possibly remains the only equipment so far invented for developing empirically true statements that have wide applicability. The most limiting factor is whether marketers are willing to accept that marketing is a science. If they are, meta theory fills the gap resulting from the absence of an overall theory of marketing, while at the same time promoting the refinement and optimal development of theory on the specific level and shortening the time period likely to be required for the formulation of an overall theory of marketing.

In the past marketers may have lacked the humility to go back to first principles and collect raw data as the basis for developing their own theory, or have placed too much reliance upon themes borrowed from other disciplines. In the future marketers, it is hoped, will concentrate on developing good theory, especially if they are prepared to accept marketing as a science.

Theory is essential to organise the complex, dynamic field of marketing through its role of simplifying and providing the basis for explanation, prediction and solution of problems. Yet theory presently embodied within marketing is immature and inadequate. It suffers from lack of cohesion, an incorporation of various approaches, a state of minimal practical utility, lack of sophistication and too much reliance on other disciplines. It has been dependent upon the function of marketing which has evolved from (i) discovering and satisfying unmet wants, to (ii) stimulating and serving demand, to (iii) offering a universal behaviour undertaken by everyone at some time. Equally, it has reflected the approach used, whether managerial, societal, institutional, commodity or functional. There remains a need, especially in today's intensified environmental issues, greater complexity and rapid change, to improve our understanding of the manner in which the system works. This underlies the need to develop a *workable* theory of exchange. It must be stressed that the key word in the preceding sentence is 'workable', for clearly there are well-developed theories of exchange in economics and behavioural sciences. However, from our point of view they are inadequate, being an oversimplified and stylised representation of real-world behaviour. Further, it is our opinion that a theory of marketing demands a synthesising of concepts from both the economic and the behavioural sciences if it is to constitute an adequate explanation of the true nature of exchange.

The short-term solution would seem to be the adoption of meta theory as an overall framework. Although partialism would seem to be essential before holism, meta theory will ensure a standardised scientific methodology is used. There remains the problem of the 'relationship' between academics and the 'real world'. It is often assumed that academics think great thoughts which then trickle down to marketing practice. This is unlikely. For too long there has been a gap between descriptive/exploratory research and a normative approach for marketing decision-making. The delicate but necessary link between theory-driven research and normative practice must be strengthened, and its practitioners' co-operation will prevent theory that is of limited utility being developed. In this way present theory can be refined and new theory incorporated.

Whether the perspective adopted is that of the marketer in the profit-oriented firm, or the marketer who is concerned with social marketing, theory originating from and specific to marketing can be developed from which ultimately an overall theory may emerge. If theories need to be discarded or refined to correspond with changes in the broader environment, this does not reduce the utility or significance of theory, for the final justification of theory must be in marketing's ability to improve the lives and environments of mankind. By considering marketing as a science, this goal is likely to be more quickly and effectively achieved.

To conclude Part I of the book, therefore, we would defend marketing's borrowing from other disciplines on the grounds that the emergence of a study of marketing stems largely from a failure of these disciplines to borrow from each other and to integrate economic and behavioural concepts into an acceptable explanation of the real world. Marketing may not have achieved this–and may never achieve it–but it is clearly a goal worth pursuing.

PART II

EVOLUTION OF MARKETING THOUGHT

_____ CHAPTER 4 _____

Consumer behaviour

Contents

Introduction

A republic made up of many states, each with its own culture and
tongue, federated to achieve a common purpose. So might one
describe consumer behaviour, with its foundation of contributions
from the diverse sources of psychology, economics, sociology, statistics, anthropology and cybernetics. While this melange may offer a
fertile ground for theoretical exploration, the marketing practitioner
can be forgiven for querying the relevance of such an apparent
miscellany of ideas and concepts to the attainment of corporate goals.

55

Esoteric theory or corporate relevance? That is the question this chapter examines.

Consumer behaviour as a field of study is but a child, compared to the stature and longevity of the source disciplines. The ensuing pages therefore extend a rationale for the creation of this republic, and the development of marketing interest in the area.

A consideration of the eclectic approach that has been taken to assembling a general framework within which consumer actions can be set follows, with the borrowing from source disciplines recognised. This leads on to an exposition of the major comprehensive models which represent the present frontier of the still-growing theory.

So much for theory: corporate relevance is now the issue. Empirical testing of consumer behaviour concepts is presented, with the implications drawn for effective marketing programmes.

Ultimately, with the impetuousness of youth, the chapter entreats theoreticians and practitioners to combine in developing that consumer understanding that is central to business activities, and so to enrich theory and practice together.

Historical perspectives

Marketing as a management function emerged from a realisation by business that the consumer is the *sine qua non* of every activity of the business–that consumer orientation which forms the substance of the marketing concept has as its objective the direction of the efforts of the enterprise towards the service of customers at a profit.

The need for a marketing function, separate and defined, was a consequence of the changing structure of the economy. Small localised industries gave way to large-scale production plants. An intimate and personal knowledge of the customer had characterised the craftsman era, enabling products to be tailored to meet the known requirements of the individual consumer. The mass production techniques of the large-scale enterprises demanded product consistency and standardisation, so that the craftsman's instinctive appreciation of his customers' unique representation of what constituted satisfaction was an apparent anachronism, and as such was neglected during the early stages of modern industrial society. So long as a sellers' market prevailed in the consumer goods market, the intricacies and complexities associated with producing to meet consumer desires could indeed be ignored with equanimity. Any reversal of economic conditions, however, which would allow for the buyer to exercise personal preferences by making choices between fiercely competing brands within a product range, or indeed between products themselves, would inevitably re-establish as a meaningful competitive tool a business philosophy aimed at producing goods to meet customers' requirements.

Just such a volte-face did in fact come about in most Western economies in the 1950s. During the preceding war period fundamental and permanent changes had been brought about in the economic structure. Income patterns had been reshaped, with a consequent expansion in that section of the consuming public with a level of income in excess of their subsistence needs. Greater discretionary income was not the only distinguishing trait of the post-war consumer. Modes and availability of credit raised access to funds above the level of current income; at the same time, mass-media channels were disseminating product information on a large scale. The 1950s consumer was both wealthier and more knowledgeable than his pre-war counterpart. The element of discretion he was able to introduce into his consumption patterns changed his role from a largely passive spectator to a very active participant in the economic scene.

On the production side the effect of the large-scale units, geared to take advantage of the economic advantages associated with size, had been to widen the gap between the individual producer and the individual consumer. Markets for the manufacturer's output were no longer local and personal; communications had become distant and impersonal; competitive activity flourished. Such an economic situation provided the impetus for the revival of business interests in the actions of the consumer.

A logical progression from the need for marketing as a management function, to replace the craftsman's intuitive knowledge of his customers and his flexibility in meeting individual requirements, was the need to formalise an understanding of consumer actions in the market-place as the cynosure for the efforts of the enterprise adopting a marketing orientation.

Consumer behaviour emerged from this need as a legitimate field of study in the 1960s with the recognition that the functions of an economic system–production and selling: buying and consumption–are not a discrete set of human actions but are part of the total life of the individual. The buying and consumption functions were acknowledged to have a more personalised meaning, representing a quintessence of life in developed countries, and an aspiration in less-developed countries. Could economic models alone explain and predict this wider meaning of consumption activity?

In 1960 Katona,[1] based on empirical work with longitudinal consumer surveys at the University of Michigan, suggested that consumer purchase decisions appeared to be based on a combination of economic and psychological factors, and could therefore be the better understood if the concepts of the two disciplines were also combined for the purposes of analysis. As a starting-point, a theory of psychological economics must encompass the concept of 'willingness to buy' as a determinant of purchase action: 'discretionary demand is a function of both ability to buy and willingness to buy'. Katona set out his basic concept as 'Income, previously accumulated financial assets and access to credit constitute ability to buy, and thereby the conditions without which inclinations to buy cannot be transformed into demand. Willingness to buy is represented by psychological predispositions in the individual who makes the purchase.'

In 1971, assessing the performance of British industry, Andrew Shonfield similarly emphasised the inadequacy of applying an unqualified economic aproach to business activity. 'It is arguable that the disappointment with our current performance in the management of the economy is the result of expecting economics to do on its own a job that requires a joint and massive effort by the whole range of social sciences.'[2] Again, a statement that while the functions of an economic system can be identified, they cannot be isolated.

The consumer surveys undertaken by the University of Michigan have demonstrated the influence of past experience and of future expectations on a purchase decision. Further, these surveys have amply disclosed evidence of the gradual process of social learning, as well as the impact of changing social attitudes on consumption patterns. Credit usage, as a case in point, has detached itself completely from the old stigma attached to hire purchase, with the use of many forms of credit now being an overt and socially acceptable method of planning the timing of purchases.[3]

The 1960s also saw the dawn of a new and potentially powerful consumer movement–an obvious incentive to take an interest in the consumer. Resulting from public awareness of the importance of the consumer in the business game, governments in all Western countries have openly declared that the system does not always operate to the benefit of the individual consumer. Statutory agencies with a variety of areas of authority and power have been created.

Legislation in the beginning was almost entirely protective in nature, aimed at redressing what was seen as the imbalance between the large-scale, impersonal production units and the individual consumer, upholding consumer sovereignty by supporting competition and choice. Later, recognising that choice in the market-place can be negated by lack of knowledge, and the decision thereby disrupted, both legislation and consumerist philosophy extended to the need for accurate, reliable and comprehensive information in the market-place to enable the consumer to exercise his sovereign rights. Experiments in information provision, and subsequent research into the use made of such information, have added new dimensions to consumer behaviour theory.

Methods of communicating product information that is accurate, comprehensive and often technical, have come under scrutiny, revealing the limitations of such deceptively simple schemes as informative product labelling.[4] The notion that more information is better has been both defended and challenged by researchers into consumer behaviour, causing a good deal of controversy.[5] There is a tenable argument that although a minimum level of information is necessary for good consumer decision, there is likewise an upper limit of information at which consumers will become confused and turn to alternative cues for decision aids.

General framework for the analysis of consumer actions

Development of the initial framework within which the various conceptual contributions can be set to unify the disparate elements into a theory of consumer behaviour began with wide-scale borrowing from the source disciplines. The purpose of the free borrowing has been to relate these existing concepts to the purchase decision process of the individual consumer. The accent is on the purchase decision-making process, with the underlying rationale that those variables which can be identified as being salient to the decision process can be applied to the design of more effective marketing programmes.

This introductory fragmented approach has been superseded as the main line of advancement in consumer research by the attempts by academic marketers to construct general and experimental models depicting the interrelationships between those variables that impinge upon the individual consumer before, during and even after, the act of purchase. The influences concerned are those that have been drawn from behavioural science sources. What is new is the conceptualisation of the manner in which these pre-identified factors affect the outcome of the purchase decision process by the manipulation of the informational input.

Models generally provide a useful framework and guide to further research by the clarification of relevant relationships within a graphical representation. Consumer behaviour models particularise the relationships between inputs into the buying situation, the social and individual motivations that are present in the situation, and the resultant outcome. This outcome may be positive or negative–a decision to make a purchase or a decision to reject a product or brand. There are, therefore, obvious advantages to the construction of models at this point in the evolution of a theory of consumer behaviour. The measure of logic in the construct highlights the total picture of a decision process, as well as indicating the contribution of each portion of the model to the whole picture. A frame of reference is created against which consumer problems can be set, with all the major variables classified. Against that, however, are the disadvantages associated with modelling techniques related to human behaviour. One danger is that complex situations may be oversimplified in terms of the model, with the less intricate representation of the model being substituted in marketing planning for the more complicated reality.

Psychology and economics are frequently perceived as located at opposite ends of the spectrum of source disciplines, with the one concentrating upon the uniqueness of the individual and the other working in aggregates.

Theories of consumer choice from both of these disciplines serve to illustrate the problems encountered in drawing together the separate strands into an explanatory and predictive model.

A psychological theory of consumer choice would start from three necessary conditions:[6]

(a) there must be two or more choice alternatives;
(b) the choice alternatives must arouse some conflict;
(c) cognitive processes aimed at reducing the conflict must occur.

Consumer choice then is characterised by conflict, uncertainty and cognitive activity. Figure 4.1 shows a framework commonly used when looking at psychological models of choice.

Two different types of outcome may result from this model. First, a behavioural or external response may occur, in which the individual modifies the environment in which the choice is made. In consumer behaviour this may imply that a brand or product is selected for purchase and consumption, or it may be that an information choice is made.

Second, internal responses may occur, taking the form of firm commitments regarding future behaviour; or they may be less specific in terms of changes in beliefs, values, attitudes, etc. The internal response serves to influence behaviour in future situations.

The relationship between present and future choice situations is depicted in Figure 4.2.

The economic theory of consumer behaviour has two strands, both based on the assumption that the individual has unlimited wants, which therefore cannot be totally satisfied. Faced with this challenge,

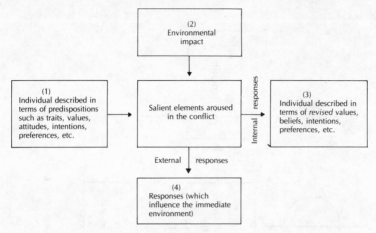

Figure 4.1   Systematic representation of conflict situation

Source: Flemming Hansen, 'Psychological Theories of Consumer Choice', *Journal of Consumer Research*, vol. 3 (Dec. 1976) p. 118.

consumer choice is guided by a schedule of preferences set against a framework of constraints.[7]

The constraints include budgetary limitations, laws, customs, codes of conduct, etc.: satisfaction is obtained from the whole range of amenities that accrue from consumption activity. All such amenities have been combined into the homogeneous abstraction termed 'utility'.

The informed, rational, self-interested consumer solves the basic economic problem by an optimisation process. The two lines of analysis of optimising behaviour stress (i) utility, (ii) preference implementation. In the former type of analysis, utility is assumed to accrue from the use of goods and services, or in more recent formulations from activities, with goods and services becoming inputs into those activities. Preference implementation examines optimisation behaviour within a rank-ordering of consumer wants, the rank-ordering relating to the intensity of the wants.

The difference between the two extreme perspectives, psychology and economics, shows in the economist's abstract definition of consumer activity, whether measured by utility maximisation or by preference implementation. 'There is no need for a more precise definition of any consumer act; indeed a more precise definition would violate the commodity-neutral character of hedonic behaviour theory.'

By contrast the psychologist has a more focused view of both 'consumer' and 'behaviour': the interest lies in the chain of causes and effects within the choice process. The economist is interested in

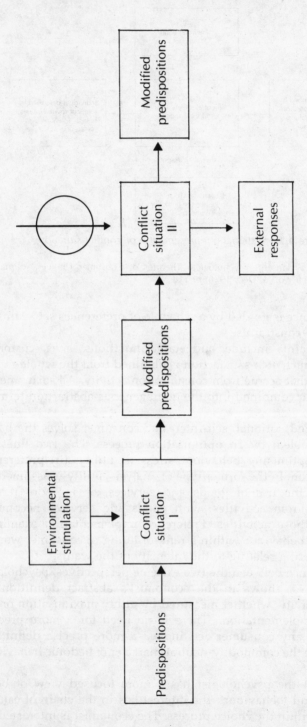

Figure 4.2 The relationship between environmental stimulation at one point in time and a choice made in a subsequent conflict situation

Source: Flemming Hansen, 'Psychological Theories of Consumer Choice', *Journal of Consumer Research*, vol. 3 (Dec. 1976) p. 119.

analysing expressions of consumer preference, whereas the psychologist is also interested in the process of preference formation.

Comprehensive models of consumer behaviour

Virtually every textbook now contains a verbal or flow chart model of the consumer decision process, bearing witness to the most pervasive and influential assumption in consumer behaviour theory–that pre-purchase activity precedes a purchase. In constructing models of the decision process, writers seem to be in general agreement that:

1. Two or more alternative actions exist and, therefore, choice must occur.
2. Evaluative criteria facilitate the forecasting of each alternative's consequences for the consumer's goals or objectives.
3. The chosen alternative is determined by a decision rule or evaluative procedure.
4. Information sought from external sources and/or retrieved from memory is processed in the application of the decision rule or evaluation procedure.

Contemporary consumer models owe much of their basic structure to contributions drawn from models of human behaviour previously hypothesised by the various branches of the social sciences. Traces of these pioneering thoughts are readily discernible in the major experimental consumer models presently extant.

Allport's[8] investigations into prejudice illuminated areas of influence, both from within the individual and also occasioned by his contacts with his social environment, which can be shown to affect the perception of an object stimulus. Prejudice was defined by Allport as 'a feeling, favorable or unfavorable, toward a person or thing, prior to, or not based on actual experience', which equates closely with current opinions on the effect of subjective predispositions upon the outcome of the purchase decision process.

The well-known psychoanalytic perspective of human behaviour is attributable to the efforts of Freud[9] in revealing the different levels of consciousness which make up the individual psyche. Emphasis here was placed upon the impact of the deeper levels of consciousness upon the decision process, motivated by a need structure which the individual is striving to satisfy. Motivation can be understood as the driving force input into the decision process, with output being described as the attainment of the specific goal towards which the individual is propelled by an unsatisfied need operating at a subconscious level.

Veblen's[10] model concentrates upon the interaction of the individual with his social environment by stressing that all human behaviour takes place within the wider social context. Individual behaviour can best be understood as being aimed at a desire for social satisfaction. Veblen's viewpoint has stimulated research into the pressures upon the individual to conform to the norms of family and friends composing his social world. Social conformity has been shown to be of value as an explanatory element of some of the manipulative processes which informational input undergoes as the individual moves towards a decision outcome.

The suggestion that human behaviour is learned rather than innate was propounded by Pavlov[11] as the basis for a theory of classical conditioning. Experimenting with dogs, he established that any two things presented together will be permanently associated together in the cognitive system. With the constant reinforcement of consecutive presentation of the associated objects, a given stimulus will elicit the expected behavioural response.

A final pioneering area in extending knowledge of human behaviour stems from the work undertaken by psychologists of the Gestalt school.[12] Gestalt psychology recognises that a major function of the cognitive system is to relate perceptual stimuli to each other and to the environment in order to create an organised and comprehensible world. This is the setting used by Lewin in advancing an explanatory model of human behaviour. The individual decision process operates within a total situation which includes an individual need structure and interaction between the individual and the external environment. Needs can be satisfied through a range of actions and behaviour results from the evaluation of the positive and negative aspects (as perceived by the individual) related to each possible course of action.

A wider discussion of the contribution of behaviour models to the understanding of consumer actions has been developed by Kotler,[13] from whom the above analysis is largely derived.

The building of the more comprehensive models of consumer behaviour has been stimulated by the combination of these observed behavioural factors with the microeconomic constructs of classical utility theory as proposed by Marshall.[14]

Figure 4.3 is a simplified graphical representation of those factors that have been identified from these sources as exerting pressure at some point in the decision process. Relative strengths and the interrelationships that undoubtedly exist between the variables are not within the compass of this figure.

In the first instance, these factors can be dichotomised into internal

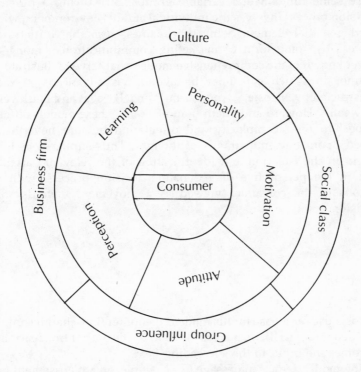

Figure 4.3   Internal and external influences on the consumer decision process

Source: Adopted from C. Glenn Walters, *Consumer Behavior: Theory and Practice* (Glencoe, Ill.: Irwin, 1974) p. 213.

and external influences upon the individual that affect the outcome of a purchase decision. Internal factors refer to those arising from within the individual's unique psychological make-up. Personality and attitude, motivation and perception, the total cognitive system can be expected to be brought into play to produce a purchase action.

External factors, which are sometimes referred to as the environmental forces to which the individual is perpetually subjected, exist in terms of aggregates rather than in the individual sense. It is obvious that consumption patterns are affected by culture, or by social class belonging, by group affiliations and the impact of personal influence. These influences have been shown to be capable of producing extreme distortion of business communications both in the receptivity of the individual and in his method of processing the inputs.

The comprehensive models now to be presented all have as a basis these same fundamental variable groups. Structuring a purchase decision process involves the individual and his environment, with a third essential element being the business firm that initiates the process by some form of marketing communication. Among the better known of the comprehensive models that serve to illustrate the manner in which consumer behaviour has advanced are those constructed by Nicosia,[15] Andreasen,[16] Engel, Kollat and Blackwell,[17] Clawson,[18] Howard and Sheth,[19] and Baker.[20] These models differ in respect to their complexity and orientation but are nevertheless based upon the same strands of thought. Thus similarity is to be found in the isolation and identification of the relevant variables, and in the perspective of a dynamic decision process, with the actions of the consumer viewed as a movement towards some decision point.

Nicosia

Nicosia uses as a base for his model a computer flow chart technique, divided into four distinct areas, or 'fields'. The output from each field becomes the input to the succeeding field.

The model depicts a message (for example, an advertisement for a new product) flowing from its source (in this case, the business firm) in the direction of an eventual decision outcome by the consumer. In Field One the consumer is exposed to and receives the message, with an outcome of the development of some predisposition, or attitude, towards the product. Field Two is concerned with the search and evaluation process, which has as its output the arousal of the individual's motivation, leading to Field Three which is defined as 'possible transformation of the motivation into an act of purchase'. If purchase occurs, Field Four becomes the area of storage and use of the product, with a related output of experience.

In each of the fields, the relevant influences upon the eventual outcome are delineated. As the message flows from the business firm to the formation of a consumer attitude, it will be modified or distorted by internal subjective perceptual elements. During the period of 'search and evaluation' (Field Two) the internal and external forces are differentiated in terms of additional information input. Internally initiated data are concerned with the associations, conscious or unconscious, with the firm, the brand or the product, while external data are culled from the environment in the form of word of mouth communication, or an increased receptivity to advertising in the product area.

Andreasen

Andreasen has developed the concepts of 'attitude formation' and 'attitude change', contributed by social psychologists, to construct a consumer decision model as an information-processing cycle. This model indicates that attitude change can be achieved via exposure to information. Change of attitude is assumed to be a logical preliminary to change in behaviour, an assumption that is lacking in verification since the complexity of the attitude behaviour relationship remains a controversial topic in social psychology studies. It is as yet far from certain that influence in this area is a one-way flow from attitude to behaviour as the model suggests.

Andreasen's model centres upon the individual utilising a message input to reach a decision outcome, with attitude formation and change as the central concepts. The predispositional nature of attitudes (that is, 'not based on actual experience') is shown to impinge upon the individual's perceptions, which operate as a filter through which the information must pass to reach the cognitive system. Thus attitudes to message source or channel may effectively alter the character of the original communication.

Engel, Kollat and Blackwell

Described as a complete model of buying behaviour, these researchers have produced a sequential approach to the purchase decision, using as a base the five steps in decision-making suggested by Dewey—problem recognition, search, alternative evaluation, choice and outcomes. It is proposed as a general model, giving a framework for examining the diversity of influences to which the buyer is subject as the decision process moves from its initial stage of the beginnings of need awareness through its subsequent steps to the final stage of after-the-event evaluation and rationalisation. The contributions of the three basic internal processes—perception, learning and motivation—represent major steps in the model, while personality and attitudes are seen to exert pressure upon the movement through the steps. The social and cultural aspects of the possible purchase decision are also depicted as an influence, either impeding or accelerating movement through the stages.

Clawson

Clawson has extended the views put forward by Lewin in his behavioural studies, with the contribution of Gestalt theories clearly in evidence.

The analysis is concentrated in some depth upon the tension element in a purchase decision as the individual assesses the positive and the negative aspects attached to the decision outcome, producing a situation of psychic conflict. The fact that both the positive and the negative features are perceived subjectively by the consumer is also stressed, indicating that the conflict cannot be resolved on the grounds of objective product characteristics or information. These objective criteria may not penetrate the net of selective perception, or may be distorted on the way.

Howard and Sheth

Howard and Sheth have based their approach to the formulation of a general consumer model on the standpoint of the consumer playing an active role in the business transaction. He is not merely exposed to communications but is portrayed as vigorously collecting and processing information.

Fundamentally, the model is constructed around a series of stimulus variables passing into the individual's processing system and being acted upon by the internal factors of perception and learning, termed by the researchers 'the hypothetical constructs'. A response variable ends the process, with the whole being surrounded by the exogenous variables of social class, culture and personality, plus such constraints as time and income availability.

Inputs are separated out into three groups which distinguish source differences. The first group of inputs relates to the actual product communications of price, quality, availability, distinctiveness and service. The second group derives from indirect and impersonal sources, such as salesmen or the mass media. The third group of stimulus variables identifies the activities of the consumer in collecting data from his social environment via the personal influence of word-of-mouth communication. Thus the interaction between the consumer and his social environment is distinguished and extended, showing the external forces in the decision process not only as a constraint upon behaviour, but also as a reference point for the gathering of credible information. Interaction between man and his social environment is seen to be a two-way function.

The hypothetical constructs of perception and learning detail the manipulation of the information gathered from the various sources, affecting the amount and quality of objective information that reaches the system.

Howard and Sheth have acknowledged that these hypothetical constructs and their interrelationships are a consequence of the integration of a number of well-known theories–Hull's learning theory, Osgood's cognitive theory and Berlyne's theory of exploratory behaviour.

Baker

As an alternative to a flow chart approach, Baker puts forward a sequential decision-making process. Given that the buyer has the necessary resources, economic or otherwise, to transform inclination to buy into real demand, and additionally that circumstances demand that a purchase be made, the objective economic and performance features of the products under review are evaluated. If this comparative appraisal is not conclusive, behavioural factors determine the outcome.

The Baker model is expressed notationally:

$$P\ f[EC,\ PC,\ (E_A - E_D),\ (P_A - P_D),\ BR]$$

where

P = purchase
EC = enabling conditions
PC = precipitating circumstances
E_A = economic advantages
E_D = economic disadvantages
P_A = performance advantages
P_D = performance disadvantages
BR = behavioural response

These models, elaborate and sophisticated as they are, have been welcomed for their descriptive and explanatory qualities. Rigorous empirical testing has been limited: where undertaken its aim has been more to refine an existing model than to exhibit its practical value.

The Howard and Sheth model has been modified in this manner as a result of a continuous body of research which attempts to validate the previously developed model by using a variety of techniques.[21]

An evaluation of the major models of consumer behaviour and their appropriateness to the marketing practitioner at the present state of the art has been undertaken by Foxall.[22] He finds such models to be 'premature, over-ambitious and pre-scientific'.

Consumer behaviour can offer but an immature general theory as yet, with a wide chasm between those separate elements that appear to have a bearing on consumer action and the comprehensive modelling approaches. The lack of practical application associated with such models presents an opportune situation for the 'theory–practice' dilemma to flourish.

Marketing applications of consumer behaviour theory

The relationship between the good theory and its practical application is not a simple one-way flow. Theory progresses as its foundational concepts receive empirical verification–a theory–practice tradition to which consumer behaviour presents no exception. In the context of consumer research, the testing of many of the factors that have been identified conceptually as being influential in moulding the individual decision process has extended alike the insight of both practitioners and theoreticians. The major areas of application that have been suggested can best be illustrated by the presentation of a selection of these empirical studies.

Perception

That perception is subjective, and therefore individual in nature, is a theme common to all consumer behaviour models. Whether implicitly or explicitly, the individual's ability to 'choose' which stimuli he will perceive has been portrayed as a filter through which all marketing communications must pass. Behaviourists have established that it is humanly impossible to absorb all the stimulus objects to which an individual is exposed. An unconscious filtration process therefore comes into operation, with the individual choosing for attention from the plethora of sensory stimuli around him those that appear to be the most relevant to his interests. Such selected stimuli must then be related to the individual's own world by a personalised organisation and interpretation process.

Perception has been defined by social psychologists as the 'complex process by which people select, organise and interpret sensory stimulation into a meaningful and coherent picture of the world.'[23] In the modern industrial economy characterised by distant markets and impersonal communications, the tools of the marketer become a part of that broad spectrum of sensory stimulation. The message broadcast by the marketer, if it penetrates the perceptual filter at all, will be modified by the forces of perceptual interpretation to conform to the personalised perspective of the individual.

Empirical work in the application of the knowledge of perceptual operation to the marketing effort has centred upon:

(a) differential perception—the consumer versus the marketer;
(b) perception of objective physical product attributes; and
(c) perceptual selectivity and its impact on advertising.

In the first of these categories, reference can be made to two studies that highlight the differences in perception between groups of businessmen and their customers. McClure and Ryans[24] studied various product features of heavy domestic appliances from the perspective of both a consumer group and a retailer group. Retailers were found to view products on sale at competitive outlets as being lower in price but less trouble-free in use, leading them to 'stress the trouble-free performance and quietly worry about price'. The comparative data collected from the group of consumers, however, suggested that retailers exaggerated the perceived price differences and consistently underestimated the strength with which consumers view the importance of service and warranty, ease of use and style. It is of some import that such perceptual differences were revealed even within this relatively personalised retailer–customer relationship.

Consumer versus marketer perceptions of a new package design was the focus of Blum and Appel's[25] study, with a wide discrepancy apparent between the two perspectives on the basis of consumer and management reaction to eighteen different package designs. It was concluded that if the package decision had been made by management 'the net effect would have been to select designs which would have had the least appeal so far as the consumers sampled were concerned'.

That non-objective phenomena can be expected to influence consumer perception of physical product attributes is axiomatic in the light of the universal consensus of the subjective nature of perception. A proliferation of studies has been conducted around this concept of perceived product characteristics, including a number of taste tests designed to disclose the effect of a well-known brand name upon perceived quality. Makens[26] found that when identical samples of turkey meat were labelled with a well-known and unknown brand, the sample with the known label was perceived as being of higher quality. Continuing the experiment with two un-marked samples, this time of differing quality, the superior meat was recognised as the well-known brand. A similar type of experiment by Brown[27] used identically fresh loaves of bread, some wrapped in cellophane and some in wax paper. Those loaves wrapped in cellophane were judged to be the fresher.

Some of the earliest studies into recognition of brand without its surrounding cues were undertaken by Pronko and Bowles,[28] who researched consumers' ability to identify brands of cola beverages in a series of projects spanning a period of two years. Allison and Uhl[29] later studied brand identification in the beer market.

That social values influence perception was exposed by Haire's enquiry into the meaning attached by housewives to instant and regular coffee.[30] Users of instant coffee were perceived at that time as 'lazy', and as failing to measure up to a socially determined and socially accepted good-housewife standard.

Social psychologists have observed, as previously noted, that it is not possible for the human being to perceive and internalise the multiplicty of sensory stimulation with which he is surrounded. Bauer and Greyser[31] applied this concept to the field of advertising. Out of a potential exposure of some 1,500 advertisements per day, the consumer was found in this study to perceive only 76, and perhaps 12 of these could be related to his subsequent behaviour.

The existence of the perceptual field has a further implication for the marketing practitioner in view of the growing body of opinion that indicates that brand choice is not merely a matter of brand awareness, but also of the consumer's evaluation of the brand into a set, or group, of products within the perceptual field. It is argued that consumers select from the brands of which they are aware a smaller group of brands from which eventual choice will be made. This eventual choice group has been termed 'evoked set'.[32]

Parallel to the positively evaluated 'evoked set', it has also been suggested that within the brands included in a consumer's overall awareness set are negatively evaluated brands—'inept set'—and a third group, 'inert set', towards which the consumer is neither negative nor positive.[33] This recognition of 'set' relationships is relevant to the marketing tools of product positioning and market segmentation. Product positioning was the subject of a three-part series in *Advertising Age*, which concluded: 'The big breakthrough came when people started thinking of positioning not as something the client does before the advertising is prepared, but as the very objective of advertising itself. External, rather than internal positioning.'[34]

This viewpoint ignores consumer perceptions of brands, and the existence of preferred brands by different groups of consumers. It was a viewpoint that met with criticism, and an insistence that 'the concept of positioning is a poor marketing tool unless it is accompanied by an understanding of market segmentation'.[35]

Learning

Interest in learning theories stems from Pavlov's early work in classical conditioning, which broadly established that much human behaviour is learned behaviour. Learning in this context can be defined formally as 'all changes in behaviour that result from previous behaviour in similar situations'.[36] Learning theory becomes applicable in the context of consumer action, where in numerous purchasing situations the behavioural outcome can be related to past experience.

Although there has been some dispute in the source discipline regarding the simple form of learning theory—a temporal contiguity of stimulus and response leading to the formation of an associative bond—the application of the concept of behavioural learning resulting from past experience to the repetitive buying situation, and to the development of brand loyalty, has generated an interesting segment of empirical research effort.

Reinforcement of stimulus was a central feature of the classical conditioning model, and it is this area of message repetition that has been the most assiduously examined, giving rise to the general observation that distribution of an advertisement over a period of time is more effective in achieving perception and retention than a heavy concentration of the same advertisement in a limited time period.

This generalisation has, however, been subject to modification. Myers and Reynolds[37] conclude from their research studies that continuity of an advertising campaign over a period of time is more effective for an established product, while for a new product, which requires some thought on the part of the consumer, a greater impact can be achieved through concentrating the message repetition into a short time span, which is in accord with the views of psychologists regarding established patterns of behaviour (that is previously learned behaviour), and the formation of new patterns of behaviour.

Krugman[38] studied the effects of repeated exposure to packaging in order to establish the frequency with which an object must be seen to become familiar. He drew attention to the tendency for consumer research to be 'based on responses to single rather than

repeated exposure to products, packaging and advertising copy–
despite an enormous body of evidence indicating that such responses change with experience and the passage of time'.

A major consideration to emerge from the study of message
repetition is the determination of the critical point at which any
further repetition appears to lead to a negative response, or negative
learning taking place. That this critical point exists has been indicated by Cox[39] and by Bogart.[40] Attempts to determine and generalise
the exact location of this critical point have proved inconclusive.
While for one product repetition of the message up to eight times
continued to have an accelerating effect, at the other extreme the
point of decay occurred after only four exposures for a different
product.[41] Clearly, exposure to the advertisement is not the sole
factor affecting the level of interest of the consumer. Variations in
creative presentation have been suggested as a major element; the
particular product groups concerned may also be a determinant of
the critical point.

A long-standing proposition in this sphere of retention and
learning is that 'the greater the complexity and length of the message
the greater will be the amount of repetition necessary for it to be
perceived and retained'.[42] Confirmation of this proposition has been
provided, notably by communications psychologists Hovland, Janis
and Kelley,[43] and by advertising researcher Bogart.[44]

Competition and its effect upon the required measure of message
reinforcement extend the application of learning theory into the
reality of the business world. Underwood's[45] findings indicate that
interference from competing messages may be the major factor in an
advertisement being forgotten.

The phenomenon of forgetting might be described as a passive
influence. The pioneer experiments in this area were carried out
nearly a century ago by Hermann Ebbinghaus;[46] his work remains
the classic in its field, and its essential findings have been verified
many times over in practice. Ebbinghaus used nonsense syllables to
nullify any familiarity effect, and calculated a rate of forgetting on the
basis of the time it took between learning and relearning the
nonsense words. This produced a curve of forgetting.

That the factor of forgetting cannot be ignored is underlined by the
results of a study undertaken by Jenkins and Corbin Jr.[47] Investigating the validity of 'last brand bought' responses, customers of a store
that kept detailed sales slips were interviewed within forty-eight
hours of their last shopping trip.

The questionnaire covered a list of thirteen frequently purchased
products–bread, coffee, cereal, soap, etc. Each shopper was asked to
name the brand bought most recently. Matching the questionnaires
to the sales slips, it was found that on average the correct brand had

been named only 77.5 per cent of the time. In other words, even for products that were used almost everyday in the household, wrong answers were obtained almost one time out of four only two days after the purchase of those products.

Reinforcement of stimulus is also achieved, although only partly in some sales promotions schemes, such as competitions.

The practical value of ascertaining the most effective repetition level and time period for a specific promotional campaign needs no elaboration.

Probabilistic models have evolved to provide a wider description of the learning process, using two fundamental assumptions:

1. Present behaviour is influenced by past behaviour,
2. Recent events are more influential than less recent events.

Kuehn[48] used a stochastic learning model technique to predict purchases of orange juice. The conclusions from this study indicate that brand loyalty is at its strongest among the most frequent purchasers of orange juice, and that brand preference weakens as time between purchases increases. Furthermore, for this particular product it was found that brand loyalties are never so strong that complete acceptance or rejection of any one brand can be assumed automatically.

Personality

Empirical studies verifying the impact of personality upon the consumer decision process have been indecisive, and the use of personality as a predictive variable in consumer actions has proved to be unsatisfactory. Kassarjian has pointed out the inconclusive nature of studies that have been undertaken in a review of personality and consumer behaviour.

All the evidence points to a confusion of mainly negative and contradictory findings. One reason for such discouraging results may well be the surfeit of measuring instruments, which all purport to measure the personality variable. As a consequence research in this area has been atomistic and non-comparable.

A comment by Hall and Lindzey[49] confirms this lack of uniformity in defining personality: 'no substantive definition of personality can be applied with any generality...personality is defined by the particular empirical concepts which are a part of the theory of personality applied by the observer'. Turning to the source area, it is noticeable that, in their classic review of behavioural theory and research, Berelson and Steiner[50] do not include a separate section on personality.

However, Tucker[51] has stated that it would be premature at this stage for marketers to minimise the role of personality in the consumer decision process. He suggests rather that this variable warrants more vigorous attention, perhaps including the development of personality measures that are more closely related to purchase behaviour. Brody and Cunningham[52] are in agreement with this suggestion. As a result of their studies in this area, they argue that the current lack of any revealed relationship between personality and consumer actions is not an indicator that no such relationships exist. Rather it pinpoints the lack of any adequate framework within which to analyse this relationship. Further support is offered by Villani and Wind,[53] who provide evidence that a modification of standard personality tests to reflect greater relevance to marketing could prove worth while.

Motivation

Motivation, as conceptualised by Nicosia,[54] acts as a driving force in the flow towards purchase action; but as an empirical research variable it has been found difficult to render operational. Lindzey[55] outlines the problem in his comment that 'the conceptual nature of motivational variables has remained so murky that even the clear distinction of these variables from other classes of concepts employed in psychological theory is yet to be accomplished'.

Research into the role of motivation has attempted to discover the underlying and subconscious reasons for purchase actions, analysed within a framework of Freudian theory. Businessmen particularly have expressed doubt about the practical applicability of the conclusions from these studies.

The main proponents of motivation research have been Dichter[56] and Henry;[57] the major contribution from their work has been the expansion of the tools of traditional market research to include the use of indirect and unstructured techniques.

As yet, then, motivation must be viewed as a non-operational variable.

Attitude

Attitude is a concept that has been contributed to the theory of consumer behaviour by social psychology. It is commonly considered to represent a predisposition on the part of the individual towards some action. Since attitude research has commanded a significant investment of resources, there is clearly an expectation that attitudes will in fact prove to be reliable predictors of consumer action.

Whether such faith is warranted is a matter of dissent between researchers in the area. An energetic researcher into this area of attitudes is Fishbein.[58] Basing his views upon an exhaustive study of the seventy-five years of attitudinal research, he questions the validity of the underlying assumption of this research area–namely that attitudes towards a product or an object have a direct link with behaviour. Similar misgivings are affirmed by Bird and Ehrenberg: 'the interplay between attitude change and behavioural change is as yet very unclear despite the large and increasing amounts of money and effort put into the assessment of consumer attitudes and motives. There is in fact little data available on the relation between change in attitude and changes in behaviour.'[59]

A mutual causal relationship between attitude and behaviour has been suggested by Joyce[60] and by Kelman,[61] with attitudes influencing behaviour, and behaviour in turn influencing attitudes. In other words, a reciprocal causation is indicated.

An examination of the current state of developments in attitude-behaviour research is presented by Foxall,[62] and serves to confirm the variations in the conceptualisation of attitudes. Essentially, the issue here is the evidence that methodological considerations are impelling investigators towards a particular conceptualisation of attitude, that is, the probability conception of attitude.

Practical findings from attitude reearch are limited. However, a study undertaken by Barclay[63] used a semantic differential scale to examine how well brand attitudes compared with a measure of purchasing behaviour. The product category was a typical mass-consumption food item with the general characteristics of high purchase frequency, relatively low unit price, and a large number of apparently homogeneous competing brands. The measured attitudes to brands were not found to relate to actual purchasing behaviour (that is, brands purchased in the past month). Barclay comments on this result: 'it should not be expected that brand attitudes alone would be strongly associated with purchasing behaviour. Such market place variables as temporary out-of-stock of the favored brand, price dealing of competitive brands, etc., surely exert a critical influence on actual purchasing.'

Udell,[64] on the basis of his research, is inclined to refute this view and to restate Allport's original view that attitudes exert a strong influence upon behaviour, observing that 'attitude research offers a potentially useful device for explaining and predicting consumer behavior. Furthermore, a knowledge of consumer attitudes may provide a sound basis for improving products, redesigning packages and developing and evaluating promotional programs.' Udell's study was designed to determine the public's attitude towards trading stamps. More important, though, the research sought to add to the vexed relationship between attitudes and behaviour by determining 'consumer's attitudes and their behavior concerning trading stamps'.

Culture

As an influential factor in the decision process, and in the formation of consumption patterns, the study of culture has presented peculiar difficulties. Anthropologists have agreed that culture is not easy to define in specific discernible and measurable components since the term represents an overall social heritage, a distinctive form of environmental adaptation by a whole society of people. The pervasive nature of cultural influence is a force shaping both patterns of consumption and patterns of decision-making from infancy; it both describes and prescribes the way of life of the specific society. Actions and thoughts are shaped and limited by the pertinent culture which, by permitting certain actions, thoughts and feelings, makes increasingly unlikely contradictory or tangential behaviour.

Owing to this relative indefinability in operational terms, research efforts aimed at isolating the existence of a cultural impact upon consumer actions has focused upon examinations of the clear-cut variations between consumption habits in different societies and countries.

In addition, the effects of culture upon perception have been revealed. White[65] has related this concept of culturally bound perception to advertising, stressing the initial need for advertising to understand, reflect and accept the value structure of society before setting about its creative task of organising the numerous stimulations a product contains for a particular customer. Advertising, concludes White, 'can operate within the limits of culture to create new expectations for the consumer'.

In a general way, marketers are increasingly aware that although there exist universally acceptable marketing practices, yet there are still substantial differences in the behaviour of the people, which are rooted in their different cultural backgrounds.

An important facet of the cultural variable lies in the existence of subcultures. Subcultures are groups within known and identifiable societies with distinctive characteristics of their own, some of which may be very different from the total pattern of that society. Subcultures are of significance to the marketer because of their influence upon the mainstream, and because of the different types of products and services which they might demand, opening up sometimes unexpected opportunities.

Social class

Sociology has established that relationships exist between social class and consumption patterns. Witness this summary by Kahl:[66]

> Prestige tends to be bestowed through consumption behaviour rather than income. Consumption patterns and interaction networks are intimately linked; people spend their leisure time with others who share their tastes and recreational activities, and they learn new tastes from those with whom they associate.

As a predictor of consumption patterns social class has long been familiar to the practitioner in marketing, offering market segments that are accessible, measurable and have a discernible life-style. However, changes in the post-war economy cast doubt upon the reliability of socioeconomic variables as a guide to consumer habits. That social class is in itself dynamic has been suggested from a variety of sources, giving rise to much theoretical interest and speculation during the 1960s. This outbreak of attention to a variable that had been considered static and clearly defined induced an empirical study into women's shopping behaviour to ascertain the present value of social class and the life-cycle as predictive variables.[67] The findings tended to support the view of the theoreticians that social class distinctions were being obscured by rising incomes and educational levels.

Although doubt was cast upon the reliability of social class as a predictor in the post-war world, the study did show a relationship between store prestige and social class, confirming an earlier proposition by Martineau.[68] Levy's[69] findings also show that, although variations in consumption choices between social classes appear to be diminishing, differences are still evident in shopping ability and methods.

An early statement by Max Weber[70] relating consumption to life-style and social stratification introduced the concept of social status rather than 'class':

> With some over-simplification, one might thus say that 'classes' are stratified according to their relations with the production and acquisition of goods: whereas 'status groups' are stratified according to the principles of their consumption of goods as represented by special 'styles of life'.

Both social class and social status variables are used in the investigation of purchasing and consumption patterns, but measures of social class are probably more representative of status factors than of class positions. One of the most useful developments in measurement of social class was the Index of Status Characteristics of Lloyd Warner.[71]

Group influence

Closer and more personalised than social class or culture is the influence exerted upon individual behaviour by the social groups to which he or she belongs. Man, the social animal of Veblen's theories, spends much of his life in group situations, exposed to the norms of his particular social world and motivated to conform to the identity of the group. Conformity, expressed in terms of an individual's willingness to modify information or perception, to fit the stated view of the social group to which he belongs, has been studied most notably by Asch,[72] using experimental conditions.

A laboratory situation was also used by Venkatesan[73] to evaluate the effects of group influence upon individual perception of the quality of men's suits. From this study it was concluded:

> The acceptance of social influence implied that consumers accept information provided by their peer groups on the quality of a product, of a style, etc., which is hard to evaluate objectively. More generally, the group norm or the prevailing group standard directs attention of its members to a new style or a product. It provides a frame of reference which is the first stage in the consumer decision-making process. In many buying situations there exists no objective standard independent of others' opinions.

Stafford[74] undertook a field study with the aim of relating empirically the theories of reference group influence and consumer behaviour. The study produced some interesting pointers to the existence of group influence on brand preferences, together with findings relating brand choice to group cohesiveness and leadership:

'In more cohesive groups, the probability was much higher that the members would prefer the same brand as the group leader.'

Conclusions

The early days of wholesale borrowing and unqualified transfer of behavioural concepts are over as consumer behaviour theory moves into a period of consolidation. Examination of the single variable set into a market situation, useful though it has been, is no longer a primary concern: at the other end of the scale, the ideal of the comprehensive model remains an ideal, with an insufficiency of precisely focused conceptualisation to give the necessary support.

Meantime, of practical use are tools of consumer marketing with roots in behavioural theory, for example brand identification, product differentiation, positioning, segmentation.

Academic researchers continue to apply and to develop the present theories, and to strengthen the methodological considerations by introducing new techniques. Research into the underlying assumption of a pre-purchase decision process, and the nature of that process, continues in a variety of forms:

multidimensional scaling and conjoint measurement[75]
different processing rules: compensatory, disjunctive, conjunctive, lexicographic[76]
sequence and extent of information utilisation[77]
correlational methods[78]
information integration techniques[79]

In the 1960s consumer behaviour theorists set out with the question: 'What kind of behavioural models exist that could be used in the study of consumer choice?'

At this stage of development the question has changed shape. No longer is observed behaviour 'fitted into' an existing model.

It is at this stage that consumer behaviour theory most needs the input of practical feedback: it is at this stage that the complementary development of theory and practice can be of mutual benefit.

Buyer behaviour

Contents

Introduction

There is a general assumption, among marketing theorists, that consumer buyer behaviour has been the subject of a far greater number of research studies than has the field of organisational–industrial buyer behaviour.

It could be argued that such a viewpoint was incepted from the earliest research in organisational buying behaviour which tended to be practice-oriented rather than academically oriented. Furthermore, research in this area has been scattered across several schools of thought. Numerous disciplines (for example, economics, behavioural and management sciences), and various professions (for example, purchasing, materials management and marketing), have all contributed directly or indirectly to the growth and consolidation of the field. This research tradition has tended to enhance and propagate the notion that the study of organisational buying behaviour has been scarce, nonscholarly and trade-oriented. As this review will demonstrate, a careful examination of extant knowledge does not substantiate this conceptualisation of the state-of-the-art of buyer behaviour.

Organisational buying behaviour has a tradition of prolific empirical and practice-oriented research. In recent times, there have been significant movements towards the development of theories and models of organisational buying behaviour, paralleling comparable efforts in consumer behaviour. A significant number of researchers[1] have argued that there are strong similarities between organisational and household buying behaviour, with particular regard to buyers' expectations, perceptions and mixture of rational versus emotional choice criteria. There are also identifiable analogies between the determinants of joint decisions and the resolution of conflict in such decisions. On the other hand, it can be postulated that the field of organisational buying behaviour presents a special challenge to the researcher. Although there are areas of commonality between the study of individual consumers and organisational buyers, the differences between them create special research problems. Most consumers are not subject to the influence of formal organisational variables and joint decision processes to the same extent as the organisational buyer.

In the pursuit of a coherent review of buyer behaviour research, this chapter intends to discuss the subject area in a generic manner as opposed to attempting any strict dichotomisation into consumer versus organisational buyer behaviour. However, in order to structure previous knowledge in thie field of study, it would appear to be practical to consider issues that are particularly relevant to consumer buyer behaviour, and then to examine considerations in the field of organisational buyer behaviour. It is recognised, however, that there is a degree of inherent interdependence between the two spheres of study. Consequently, if one accepts the notion that all organisational buyers are, in the final analysis, individual consumers, then theories of individual behaviour become relevant. Similarly, the study of group decision-taking can be applicable to consumer choices in, for example, family or collective environments. Hence there is overlap and, indeed, synergism between studies in consumer and organisational buying behaviour.

This chapter, recognising this latter fact, will seek to outline past and current salient research in the field of buyer behaviour, identifying and enumerating deficiencies in previous research and delineating guidelines for prescriptive research studies.

The research tradition

In this section, the notion of customer-orientation in both consumer and industrial markets will be discussed. Issues in both consumer and organisational buyer behaviour literature will be reviewed, together with an examination of the progress to date in the pursuit of comprehensive models of buyer behaviour.

The emerging trend towards customer-orientation

During the past twenty years, there has been a growing recognition that the consumer, not the manufacturer, is the centre of the economic universe. This development has heralded acceptance of the marketing concept–an idea commonly known for its emphasis on the achievement of profit maximisation through the coupling of an organisation's products to existing consumer desires.

However, the marketing concept, when applied to the industrial or organisational field of study, would appear to be in a state of limbo. Thus, it is accepted, but not implemented as a way of life with an identifiable impact on the industrial organisation.

A number of authors[2] have suggested that the majority of industrial goods and services manufacturers would appear to be somewhat preoccupied with the technology itself which surrounds their product offerings. Moreover, two earlier studies[3] have established that industrial manufacturers most frequently cite inadequate market knowledge as the most significant reason for the failure of a large percentage of new products to reach successful market commercialisation. More recent evidence to support this notion comes from the work undertaken by Cooper.[4]

As a consequence of this lack of information on consumer or user activities, industrial marketing practices and procedures are very often characterised by a lack of customer-orientation. Contemporary marketing thinking revolves around the marketing concept which stresses, as its central issue, the satisfaction of consumer needs and wants. Indeed, past comprehensive models[5] of consumer buyer behaviour have incorporated the notion of consumer need as an intrinsic element in their core construct. Indeed, Sheth's[6] model of industrial buyer behaviour has been developed along similar lines.

Hence, there is a relationship between developments and refinements of buyer behaviour theory and the more widespread adoption of the marketing concept as a basis for strategy decisions. Consequently, attention is being increasingly focused on the need to promote customer-orientation across both consumer and industrial product categories. Indeed, there has been an extensive body of research[7] that has examined the role of the customer in the new product development process–the concept of a 'need-pull' approach to marketing strategy as opposed to the more traditional, production-oriented approach of 'technology push'.

A particular consequence of this move to customer-orientation has been the convergence of research efforts on the study of buyer behaviour. The following sections of this chapter will attempt to outline research issues and problems relevant to the analysis of buyer behaviour.

Issues in consumer buyer behaviour

As Mehrotra and Wells[8] have recently commented: 'Traditional efforts at understanding consumers have been as successful as those of the three blind men of Hindustan. Depending on which characteristics of the marketplace the marketers have grasped they have perceived the tail, the trunk, or the feet but never the elephant.'

A review of the literature relating to the behaviour of individual consumers indicates that the vast majority of this literature has developed as a direct result of social psychological studies. Two techniques used extensively by psychologists for understanding human behaviour have found application in the marketing context. The use of standardised personality inventories to understand purchase behaviour was pioneered by Arthur Koponen in 1960.[9] At almost the same time (1959) Dichter[10] was beginning to apply the theories and methods of clinical psychology through motivation research. During the later years of the 1960s researchers had begun to integrate motivation and personality into what has been commonly termed psychographic research. Hence psychographics replaced demographics as a method of consumer market segmentation. A number of research studies were then directed at the examination of a combined demographic, psychographic and motivational approach to analysing consumer behaviour. For example, the research reported by Pernica,[11] on segmenting the stomach medicine market, demonstrated that psychographics, personality attributes and demographics can be effectively combined to provide integrated consumer profiles. Moreover Wells[12] estimated that a comparison of psychographic and demographic descriptors provided an opportunity for the determination of the internal consistency and validity of psychographic variables.

However, in the past, authors have tended to focus on several specific variables (for example social class or income[13]), rather than attempting to systematise approaches to theory development.

During the 1970s the focus of research on consumer buyer behaviour moved to the development of multi-attribute models of attitude. The popularity of these models was enhanced by their association with the basic psychological processes of the individual and to the earlier works in psychology by Fishbein[14] and Rosenberg[15] and, at an even earlier stage in the emergence of the discipline, by Lewin.[16] This strong research tradition renders these models as particularly effective tools for the prediction and quantification of consumer behaviour.

Up to 1973 virtually all tests of the multi-attribute model had adopted a static, correlational approach wherein attributes were combined in some manner and then related to a dependent variable.

However, in order to establish the multi-attribute model as a diagnostic and prescriptive device, it had to be shown that changes in brand attribute perceptions led to or caused changes in brand attitudes. Correlational designs could assess only predictive power, not explanatory value.

In order to validate multi-attribute models, research was directed to the incorporation of multi-method approaches so as to assess the causal influence of attributes on attitude. For example, Bettman, Capon and Lutz[17] used cross-sectional correlation, individual level correlation and analysis of variance to investigate multi-attribute model formats.

There is a fairly recent body of research[18] that indicates that individuals process information according to attribute–particularly subjective information. To the extent that the multi-attribute model can be adapted to solve consumer choice problems, it becomes a useful contribution to the understanding of consumer behaviour.

In the late 1970s, multi-attribute utility models became the subject of increased research efforts. In 1980, Ryan and Bonfield[19] attempted to provide further empirical evidence to confirm the validity of a specific model–the Fishbein Intentions Model.[20] This model states that an individual's intention and subsequent performance of a given behaviour is a function of the weighted sum of the individual's attitude towards the performance of a specific behaviour in a particular situation and the social norms influencing the individual's performance of the behaviour. These cognitive components combine in the form of the well-known additive, multiplicative utility model. The extended Fishbein model has appeal to both marketing theorists and practitioners since it links behaviour to underlying causes, an attitudinal and normative component, through mediator-intentions. Consequently, it promises the prediction and explanation of behaviour that has significance in the market-place.

Ryan and Bonfield's studies[21] have added correlational evidence, in support of external validity, to the body of research investigating Fishbein's Intentions Model. In their empirical, real-life testing of the model, the patterns of association among the model's variables were supported. Although the magnitude of these associations was lower than that obtained in studies that had been conducted in more artificial settings, their evidence confirms the theoretical validity of the model.

As their results[22] show:

> Specifically, the model has been shown to have predictive validity in a real-world marketing application; questions of response set bias have been reduced; the individual and joint relative contributions of the attitudinal and normative components to the explanation of variations in behavioural intentions have been demonstrated; the development

of a more parsimonious model based on referent dimensionality has been shown to be possible and intentions have been shown to be a managerially useful substitute for behaviour in model application.

However, the future direction of research into multi-attribute utility models remains questionable. The methodologies for determining the saliency and relative importance of individual outcomes and referents require to be refined. Moreover, the theoretical forms of the models will continue through the process of evolution. For example, in the case of Fishbein, the discovery of a normative variable validating construct would increase the pragmatic utility and application of the model.

Several approaches can be used to model the formation of individual preferences. The nature of multi-attribute utility models has been examined. However, Hauser and Urban[23] distinguish four additional categories: expectancy value models, preference regression models, conjoint analysis models and logit models. Each of these models relate the evaluation of product characteristics to preferences for each category of decision participant. Consequently, the models permit the analysis of market response–both consumer and industrial–to changes in product positioning.

Considerable research[24] has been undertaken on the ways to abstract the evaluation dimensions along which individuals perceive and assess products using factor analysis and non-metric multidimensional scaling. Sheth[25] has contended that individuals, whose task orientation and educational backgrounds are similar, tend to have common expectations about products and suppliers. Recently, Choffray and Lilien[26] have undertaken new, formal tests to assess whether various categories of participants differ in the number and/or composition of their evaluation criteria. Their results suggested that meaningful differences exist in both the number and the nature of the evaluation criteria used by various decision participant categories. Although their work has been undertaken in the industrial buying field, it has application to the study of consumer choice.

The application of conjoint analysis, in addition to or in place of multi-attribute utility models, is also increasingly relevant to the identification of consumer evaluation criteria.

Essentially, the techniques attempt to separate the appeals of a product or concept into a set of factors, assign utility values to the individual levels of each factor and finally, under the assumption of separability, determine the utility value of any product or concept by adding (or multiplying) the utility values of the individual levels of each of the factors embodied in the product or concept. A concise, expository description of conjoint analysis is presented in Green and Srinivasan[27] and Madansky.[28] The technique has applications to the study of both consumer and organisational buyer behaviour.

However, although it can be seen that evaluation criteria models have practical utility for the study of buyer behaviour, that is, they determine the product attributes that the consumer considers important in the decision to purchase, their predictive validity is suspect. It remains to be confirmed, even at this late stage in the development of buyer behaviour theory, as to whether attitudes are consistent determinants of behaviour or vice versa.

In a review[29] of twenty-four experiments dealing with the effect of an appeal on attitude and behaviour, it was concluded that attitudes changed behaviour to a significant extent. In only two of the twenty-four experiments did behaviour and attitude change significantly in the same direction. A further review,[30] using both experimental and correlational evidence, confirmed the existence of a gap in the attitude–behaviour relationship. Sternthal *et al*[31] also concluded that, although significant, the attitude–behaviour relationship was quite low and the direction of causality remained unspecified. In fact, a large number of researches[32] have concluded that rather than attitude causing behaviour, behaviour causes attitude.

Attitudes and behaviour have generally been studied using one-way determinate models of their relationships. The results of these studies have been disappointing. Wicker,[33] as early as 1969, after a review of the more rigorous research studies, sums up their collective results: 'Taken as a whole, these studies suggest that it is considerably more likely that attitudes will be unrelated or only slightly related to overt behaviour than that attitudes will be closely related to actions.'

Hence, an expressed attitude or intention to buy is an ambiguous piece of information. It could reflect either an ingrained regularity of behaviour or an evanescent summary of behaviour. Both views of the attitude–behaviour relationship have considerable theoretical problems. Moreover, each concept can be too closely identified with either side of the perpetual debate between behaviourism–which perceives man as a bundle of reinforced habits–and humanism–which considers man to be consciously deliberating and choosing.

Dholakia[34] has recently argued that attitudes and behaviour (and their interrelationship) can be influenced by the 'persuasion paradigm': a set of arguments advanced by the communication which are cognitively processed, evaluated and, accepted, rejected, or distorted, stored in the memory, forgotten or acted upon. The basic assumption of the persuasion paradigm is that the creation of a favourable attitude will lead to behaviour which is consistent with that attitude.

The procedure of inferring attitude from one's behaviour can be explained by the use of attribution theory.[35] According to this particular theory, individual behaviour is examined in relation to the conditions in which behaviour takes place and the information inputs at that particular time. The use of external and internal sources of information has important implications. The theoretical difference between persuasion based on information from an external source and behaviour-based persuasion is the conceptualisation of the relationship between attitude and behaviour. While the former is based on models of attitudes causing behaviour, behaviour-based persuasion reverses this relationship. Hence, under the latter conditions behaviour is recognised as causing attitude which becomes the dependent variable.

Attribution theory offers an explanation of the subjective process which occurs after behaviour and assists in the design and presentaton of variables such as incentives, and choice structuring which may lead to inference of internal disposition. The theory is most directly relevant to marketing situations which involve repeat purchase behaviour. However, the available evidence is particularly limited in terms of marketing contexts which represent relatively more complex situations.

The feasibility of the persuasion paradigm is largely dependent on the credibility and ability of the source to create acceptance of external communication. Several studies[36] have demonstrated that the level of persuasiveness which can be achieved is directly related to the credibility of the source. The majority of these studies, however, have been reluctant to investigate the effect of source credibility on eventual behaviour.

In the area of communication in general, considerable emphasis in buyer behaviour research has been placed on the study of consumer information processing. For an overview of work in this area, consult Gronhaug and Zaltman[37], Chestnut and Jacoby[38] and Bettman *et al.*[39]

Parallel to, and in conjunction with the development of middle-range theories of consumer buyer behaviour, an information processing perspective to consumer decision-making surfaced in the form of 'decision matrices',[40] and 'information load'.[41] More recently, the data and methodologies that contributed to the early definition of the consumer information processing system have been the subject of an extensive amount of revision.[42] As empirical evidence has accumulated, the resultant need for concomitant theoretical development has become apparent.

As noted by Newal and Simon,[43] an information-processing perspective must extend beyond specific rules and heuristics involved in choice. To comprehend and adequately predict buyer behaviour, there should be analysis of the unconscious structures (e.g. memories and encoding), upon which our higher-level processing is based. An identifiable need exists for directing research towards the more fundamental problems of perception and memory, as opposed to merely accepting information as is given in the decision-making context. Analysis of issues such as the way in which information is perceived, comprehended, and stored for later use should facilitate our understanding of the consumer information processing system and should provide the basis for accurate prediction of consumer buyer behaviour.

A related field of study to information processing is apparent from the research that has been conducted in the consumer field into the perception of risk. The extent and nature of the perceived risk component can be affected by the amount and type of information generated and communicated to the consumer.

Hall[44] has further emphasised that all purchase decisions are not without their associated risks. Yet, despite the prevalence of recognition of this fact, little research of a pragmatic nature is evident. The paucity of empirical studies in this area has also been noted by Shoemaker and Shoaf.[45] They contend that a considerable effort should be made with respect to the impact of perceived risk upon the manner in which new product purchases are made. More recently, Newall[46] has urged researchers to undertake more work on the unexplored role of perceived risk especially in the area of industrial buying behaviour.

The term 'perceived risk' has been adopted in response to the work of Cunningham[47] and Cox[48] who have argued that the degree of risk is likely to differ from one person to another according to his subjective interpretation of that risk.

This definition has also been confirmed by McFarlane and Horowitz[49] who suggest that risk will remain a subjective concept, 'even when [it] is endowed with numerical precision'.

Since individual risk perception is central to decision-making, factors affecting risk perception are most apparent in studies of individual behaviour. Kaplan *et al*'s[50] results have been validated by later studies[51] of perceived risk in consumer products. The means, standard deviations, ranges and rank orders of the risk ratings by individual product category were highly similar to those obtained in the first study. The data indicated that performance consequences were most predictive of the overall perceived risk for most kinds of products. It also reconfirms that analogous types of products and processes possess similar risk–consequences hierarchies.

The influence of risk-taking behaviour has also been noted with respect to the adoption of new products. Donnelly and Etzel[52] found that individuals with a high degree of risk taking (measured by Pettigrew's Category Width Scale) more frequently respond to a 'genuinely new product'.

Ostlund[53] also found perceived risk to be among the variables correlating most highly with innovativeness. In an examination of the discriminating power of ten variables between buyers and non-buyers of six testable products (i.e. not yet on the market), perceived risk ranked third and acted as a significant predictor of consumer-product purchasing.

Risk is recognised as having a considerable influence on the industrial purchase decision, especially in the area of new products. Peters and Venkatesan[54] found from a study of the adoption of an inhouse computer that 'perceived risk and self-confidence' were the only two variables that significantly differentiated among early and later adopters. Parkinson[55] later confirmed this. His study of the adoption of an innovation in the earth-moving industry indicated that the elapsed time to adoption could be explained partly on the basis of perceived risk.

The concept of group risk-taking behaviour is relevant to the study of both consumer and organisational buyer behaviour. Perhaps a brief summary of research in this area would be expedient.

Experiments by Bern, Wallach and Kogan,[56] Kogan and Zaleska,[57] Marquis and Rietz,[58] Pruitt and Teger,[59] Zajonc, Wolosin, Wolosin and Shermann[60] produce quite heterogeneous results. Sometimes groups are riskier than individuals; sometimes more cautious, and sometimes there is no difference. Stoner,[61] however, proposes that group consensus on the level of risk that should be tolerated is frequently greater than the level of risk which each of the individual members of the group could tolerate on his own without consultation.

Hence, there is no conclusive evidence to show that groups create a 'safer' and thus less risky environment. There is a more general consensus of individual characteristics affecting risk perception, but most research results do concur on the fact that perception of risk is somewhat situational, depending on a fusion of product characteristics, individual perception and precipitating circumstances.

In the main, past studies stress the fact that risk is very much a function of perception. Theories of consumer risk have discussed the individual personality as an influence on risk perception. The trend in contemporary work, however, is to relate these characteristics to past experience, and also to the inherent characteristics of the product to be purchased.

Industrial research findings have emphasised the role of risk tolerance in adoptive behaviour, but is this risk individual or organisational? Both categories of risk–to the firm and to the individual–are interrelated and, as Baker and Parkinson[62] argued, 'their perceived magnitude would seem to be a function of the quality and quantity of information available to the decision maker'.

This chapter has outlined several (perhaps not totally comprehensive) areas of research that have been significant in the historical development of consumer buyer behaviour theory. The role of psychographic and demographic variables in explaining and predicting buyer behaviour has been touched on, albeit briefly. For a further discussion of personal characteristics associated with consumer purchase decision, the author would recommend a fairly recent Strathclyde Departmental Working Paper.[63]

Consumer behaviour has historically focused on personality theory. Consequently, when a simple, bivariate correlation between a personality characteristic and a type of action, such as brand choice or product usage, is hypothesised then an assumption is made that the individual is, in some way, irrevocably predetermined to act in that specific way. There is no recognition that the nature and extent of external information has any impact on the decision-making process. In fact Kassarjian[64] summarises his comprehensive review of personality studies with the general conclusion that most of the studies demonstrate no significant relationships between personality and consumer behaviour. Moreover, there is clearly a very strong case indeed for the conclusion that theories of both personality and attitudes have no useful connection at all with buying behaviour. Similar arguments can be proposed against Freudian psychology, which is essentially unscientific, and the theory of stimulus–response learning.

Hence it could be argued that the direction of consumer behaviour research is essentially turning away from the traditional issues (e.g. attitude versus behaviour discussion; personality theory: multi-attribute utility models; perception of risk etc.) to new considerations.

At present, the topical area of study would appear to be the field of information-processing theory and consumer search procedures. At the recent Association for Consumer Research Meetings, the vast majority of papers presented were related to the question[65] of both external and internal information search. Moreover, the need to utilise innovative measurement techniques to increase the validity and reliability of research findings was also the subject of a significant number of presentations.[66] However, a number of researchers have expressed some concern about the fact that there is no concerted and coherent move towards a defined set of research needs in consumer buyer behaviour. At most, a particular field of study becomes topical for a specific period of time. It then enjoys an era of relative popularity, only to fade into insignificance when another, presumably more vital, issue arises.

Issues in organisational buyer behaviour

One of the most significant research projects in the history of research into industrial buying behaviour was the publication of the Marketing Science Institute study, which was based on the observation of buying decisions in three companies.[67] This rather limited data base was supplemented by analysis of a fourth company's buying decisions, with special attention to the question of source loyalty.[68] Levitt's[69] study of the effects of company reputation and salesman presentations on industrial buying decisions was equally significant and there have been other small-scale studies of communication phenomena in an industrial marketing context.[70] Earlier case studies of industrial buying have not been succeeded by more systematic analysis of buying decisions.[71] The majority of the studies referred to are exploratory in nature; the principal methodologies have been the unstructured interview and the use of self-reporting, both with the consequent problems of subjectivity and bias and a general lack of rigour.

In 1965 Industrial Market Research Limited and the Institute of Marketing undertook a survey[72] across a broad spectrum of industries. This pioneering work demonstrated that an industrial purchase was the result of not one decision, but of many decisions taken by different groups of people, and that the pattern varied according to the nature of the purchase and the nature of the company making the purchase.

Since then, there have been numerous studies that have established the lateral co-ordinates of the members of the buying centre. In the United Kingdom there have been surveys of 'How British Industry Buys' in 1967[73] and 1974[74] and in the United States similar studies were carried out in 1955[75] and 1970[76]. Comparable research has also been conducted in Canada in 1959[77] and in West Germany.[78]

More recently, a number of studies[79] have attempted to examine both the composition of the buying group and the role of multiple decision participants in the procurement process. The following sections attempt to enumerate the principal conclusions and implications of these previous studies.

As Wind[80] points out: 'the basic concept of a buying centre suggests that it is a temporary organisation unit, which may change in components and functions from one purchase to another'. The selection of a particular decision will consequently dictate the nature of the decision-making unit.

Spekman[81] confirms this and suggests that, unlike a formal structural sub-unit (i.e. a marketing or purchasing department), the buying group is a more nebulous construct which permeates diverse func-

tions of the organisation. He suggests that the buying unit's composition, hierarchical levels, lines of communication, etc. are not
strictly prescribed by an organisation chart or official document: 'The
buying group evolves as an informal communication network which
does not derive its structural configuration from the formal organisation *per se*, but rather from the regularised patterning of interpersonal communication flows among the various group members.'

Both Spekman and Wind stress a purposive involvement in the
procurement process as a primary consideration for buying group
membership as well as the non-permanent nature of the buying
group which may change composition from one purchase situation
to another. One of the most significant points that should be noted is
the fact that buying group membership evolves during the procurement process and is a function of the information requirements and
needs of a particular buying context.

In a sense, the work of Spekman and Wind has been of a
pioneering nature. In the past, marketers seeking to influence the
industrial procurement process have had to rely heavily on individual level research regarding the decision inputs of purchasing
departments. This dependence on simplistic data arises from the fact
that little systematic study has been undertaken to comprehend the
structure of the multiperson buying groups' responsibility for major
purchase decisions, a deficiency also noted by Nicosia and Wind
who established that buying is a process which is very diffused
throughout the organisation: 'That is, much information, many
activities, and many people are crucial parts of the buying process
yet are not parts of the purchasing department. The more diffuse a
process is, in this sense, the less appropriate it may be to think of the
"buyer" only as a decision maker in a narrow sense.'[82]

Past research has tended to explore the participation or otherwise
of a number of functional departments and hierarchical levels in the
buying decision. For example, the *Financial Times* surveys[83] examined the activity, in terms of contribution to purchasing decision-
making, of the various functional departments of an organisation at
diverse levels of responsibility. A more recent study by Doyle *et al.*[84]
has also attempted to locate the participants in the buying decision.
Their research proposed that top management, the production manager, regional functions, the board of directors and purchasing agents
were reported most often as temporary or permanent members of the
buying centre. Although this study suggested that the number of
participants in the buying centre was smaller in size for firms
operating in straight rebuy situations, they do propose that further
research is required to establish whether the buying centre composition remains static across all the 'buying classes' identified by
Robinson, Faris and Wind.[85]

The composition of the buying group has also been determined according to the 'role' behaviour of members of the decision-making unit. Attempts have been made to devise a classification system that categorises the roles of these participants.

These roles have been denoted as: users, influencers, deciders and gatekeepers,[86] as contributors, participants, responsibles and directors;[87] and as those who make major buying decisions, make recommendations, must approve purchases, affect the conditions of use and conduct the buying negotiations.[88]

Operationally, conceptualisation of the buying centre by role definition is of little use to a researcher wishing to study the purchasing decision-making process. Specifically, the notion of generalised role relationships within the buying centre does not accommodate a method for ascertaining the individual membership of the buying task group, nor its decision-making potential. What is required is a move towards a macro-sociological approach, emanating from organisational theory, to examine structural variables in conjunction with interpersonal relations within the buying group. Thus, we should seek to apply organisational behaviour concepts to the study of buying centre behaviour and composition. The contingency view of organisations, for example, attempts to conceptualise and analyse the interrelationships within and among sub-sytems as well as between the organisations and its environment. It also seeks to define patterns of relationships.[89] If applied to the phenomenon of the buying group, the complex nature of its structure and composition become more apparent. Contingency theory also facilitates analysis of communication patterns within the decision unit, the evaluation of conflict within the particular organisational sub-unit and the significance of the 'climate' of the buying group.

Hence, it would appear to be relevant and expedient to begin to examine the structural nature of the buying group. Past work in this area has tended to centre on an analysis of the role of the purchasing function *vis-à-vis* others in the decision-making unit. Perhaps a brief summary of research to date on the role of purchasing would provide the basis on which to outline our future research directions.

The extent of purchasing's involvement in buying decision-taking is a result of the following variables:

1. The nature and status of purchasing within the organisation.
2. The purchasing agent's perception of his function.
3. Task versus non-task behaviour.
4. Environmental and extraneous market conditions.

1. The role of the purchasing function within the organisation is generally viewed as being inherently significant to the firm's financial viability. However, disparity (across functional boundaries of

the organisation) can occur in perceptions of the buying role. The corporate management problem, in such cases, is to optimise the overall position and achieve a balance of co-ordination and autonomy.

The responsibility of purchasing will perhaps be affected by the size of the purchasing function and its importance relative to the firm as a unified entity—has it merely an order-processing function?

Gronhaug[90] established that the use of a separate department for purchasing correlated positively with organisational size. The status of purchasing within the organisation influences the status of the individuals and groups involved in the decision-making unit. Webster[91] has commented on the influence of the purchasing function on the actual purchasing decision. He notes that the relative importance of the central purchasing department's influence on the buying decision increases as:

(a) market variables become more important in relation to product variables;
(b) the size of firm and spatial separation of activities increase;
(c) the organisation formally assigns specific responsibility to the purchasing department.

2. The status and position of purchasing within the organisation does influence the purchasing agent's perception of his role and involvement in the buying decision.

The purchasing agent, consequently, often views his position and status within the firm as being more vital than other departments would believe. If a buyer takes a passive role and waits until he receives a requisition before commencing action, valuable opportunities may be lost. His market information on new products, alternative sources of supply, likely price rises, supply difficulties or new transportation methods could be important as far as the company's own marketing efforts are concerned. Clearly, one of the principal tasks of the buyer is to work with his colleagues to help overcome problems while, at the same time, enabling himself to perform more effectively. Yet, there is evidence to suggest that the buyer's organisational status is not as highly regarded as he, himself, would prefer. Research by Weigand,[92] from a non-random sample of 144 manufacturers, concluded that management in these organisations viewed buyers as having far less influence in the areas examined than the buyers perceived themselves to have. He emphasises that this amorphous locus of responsibility for decision-taking implies a disparity in the perception of buying responsibility in industrial firms. Differing perceptions of what is required can result. For example, there can be discrepancies in specific product attributes encompassing such features as:

(a) the design of the product;
(b) the cost of its application;
(c) the product's performance life;
(d) the name of the specific supplier;
(e) the assessment of engineering possibility.

Allen[93] has argued that the attitude of top management to the purchasing function can influence the perceived responsibility of the purchasing officer:

> The professional pressures will be exerted through the demands of his job in terms of problem-solving behaviour, operating through the search for information on products and the state of supplies. It will also be exerted by his relationships with the other people in purchasing and in his relationships with other functions, especially production. If the company policy is to relegate the purchasing function to one of buying against instructions, on blocking access by salesmen to technical people, his role will be under less pressure than if he has a responsibility for exploring new products or seeking innovation in production or maintenance supplies.

Bonfield and Speh[94] have reported the results of research that assessed the opinions of both top management and purchasing management in relation to the current and future role of purchasing. Their data suggest that the corporate role of the purchasing function will expand. However, purchasing management clearly expected to be more involved in production control than top management predicted.

It can therefore be assumed that the nature and status of buying within the organisation is perceived differently according to management level.

Feldman and Cardozo[95] have confirmed that a buyer's general influence will vary in accordanc with the prevailing managerial philosophy towards the buying function. Through their classical or simplistic model which they describe as the 'oldest and crudest conception of industrial buying behaviour', the buyer's role is that of a clerk, whose principal function is the purchase of goods specified by other departments at the lowest price per unit. They postulated that the situation would alter. Buyers today have generally gained managerial status and widely broadened responsibility. Lister[96] echoes this view:

> The essence of what I am saying is that the role and influence of the purchasing executive have not only been undervalued, but that the development and enhancement of his role will fit logically into a more sophisticated and scientific pattern. As marketing attains keener techniques, becomes more sophisticated and scientific, so buying itself must adapt and develop. It is logical for a number of reasons that this

development of purchasing techniques, skills and expertise will not only enhance the status and calibre of the purchasing departments themselves, but will open up new vistas on this side of the marketing exercise.

In a recent article, Browning and Zabriskie[97] examine literature covering nearly two decades and provide evidence of the growing interest in professionalising the purchasing occupation.

Strauss[98] also examined purchasing behaviour, with particular reference to the perceived role of the buyer. He attempted to relate the buyer's motivation to various categories of behaviour. His research was conducted among 142 purchasing agents, mainly in large engineering companies, and the information was collected by observation, interviews and written questionnaires. The study examined the methods by which purchasing agents handled the interdepartmental conflicts that arose during the buying process. The results suggested that agents have plenty of power externally, but much less internally: 'The new breed of educated, ambitious purchasing executives are intending to reverse the traditional order flow from engineering to scheduling to purchasing and to exercise purchasing's authority even at the design state.'

In order to achieve this recognition of increased status and responsibility, Strauss suggests that the purchasing officer will use a mixture of tactics both subconsciously and consciously to obviate any apparent conflict.

This concept of tactical role manoeuvres has also been examined in the early work of James[99] and Marrian.[100] They propose that where the buyer's status is low, he will perform as an interventionist in the buying process in order to raise and enhance his status.

The use of these tactics involved in the role of the buyer is an intrinsic part of the departmental and individual response to the organisational environment and is one component in the decision-making process.

A further two specific influences on the role of the purchasing agent in the behaviour of the buying centre are mentioned briefly below. These are the nature of the product and the stage in the buying process. Both of these factors are examined in greater detail at a later stage. They are included here only to illustrate their relevance to the individual behaviour of the purchasing agent.

A study by Lister[101] stressed the importance of product-specific factors in determining the degree of buyer (*per se*) involvement in the buying decision. He established that the greatest degree of influence was evident in the acquisition of products that could generally be classified as low value straight or modified rebuys.[102] Perhaps the increased professional nature of the purchasing function has served to change this situation.

Luffman[103] examined the buying of steel castings and forgings (classified as raw materials) and found that the influence of specialist buyers dominated the patronage decision. In comparison to this, from a study of fifty-one machine tool purchases, White[104] established that other members of the buying centre were involved at most stages to a greater extent than the person named as buyer. However, once the buying decision had been taken, White discovered that the buyer was a major influence in determining the terms of the commercial agreement.

In a more recent study, Woodside and Sherrell[105] describe the buying problems, activities and persons in organisational buying centres for equipment parts within a specific industry–the paper-milling industry. They established that the purchasing agent was the only individual in the paper mill who was likely to be actively involved in all phases of the buying decision process. These findings may, however, be a particular feature of the industry sector studied.

Two research needs are suggested by this work: Has the increased professionalism in purchasing in recent times implied the involvement of the buyer at the specification stage in the buying process? Does this involvement vary according to industry and product variables, and, if so, does the buyer's self-perception also vary? Hopefully, future research designs will incorporate provision for the solution of these questions.

3. The 13 January 1975 issue of *Business Week*[106] reported that, since 1973, the purchasing executive has been receiving increased corporate recognition, status and compensation as evidenced by his movement into top management ranks. Along with this increased recognition, purchasing managers are acquiring many new duties as they progress into every aspect of the firm's operations, such as forecasting, planning, product design and capital spending. This view is also substantiated by later work.[107]

Purchasing management in private industry has, in recent years, not only developed a body of knowledge on techniques and tools but has more clearly defined its role in the organisation.

The basic responsibility of purchasing executives is to acquire sufficient amounts of quality materials, equipment and services from suppliers at relatively low prices. These incoming items either become 'part and parcel' of the finished product or assist in its manufacture. Consequently, Rink[108] believes that purchasing executives should be directly involved with the needs and wants of the firm's customers. Acceptance of this fact necessitates the buyer's participation in the purchasing process at the outset.

The components of 'task' behaviour (which are expounded below) are vital to efficient purchasing. Consequently, an analysis of their influence on buying centre decision-taking is essential. They can affect the participative roles of the individuals in the buying task group. The components of task behaviour normally relate to the activities which are directly related to the purchase process (e.g. source seeking, supplier appraisal and evaluation, value engineering and analysis, purchase price analysis, source marketing and product cost management).

There has been limited attention focused on the economic or 'task' variables of the buying decision. In recent times, marketers have perhaps been more eager to research the possibility of quantification of or at least recognition of the behavioural or irrational components of purchasing decisions. In some ways, the results of such studies are often of little practical use to industrial marketers. There is an identifiable need to examine the mechanistic criteria which buyers apply during the processes of tender evaluation and vendor selection. Previously, such factors as the manufacturer's credit rating, financial strength, management ability, years in business, size and quality of production facilities, quality control and performance test standards have been considered in this context. Do these criteria still apply? Can the list be extended? How do buyers rate the importance of these factors? What has been the impact of increasing professionalism on purchasing of these 'task' variables. Answers to these questions would surely provide practical insights into the purchasing process, and, particularly, the influence of these factors on the buying group structure and behaviour. It is likely that participants will place differing emphasis on the importance of certain variables– what control does the purchasing agent have on this? Solutions to these problems may, in part, provide a body of knowledge not only on the task motivations of purchasing behaviour, but may also suggest practical guidelines for future professionalisation of purchasing tasks.

4. External environmental conditions can influence the structure and composition of the buying group, although there is very little documented evidence to substantiate this view. Spekman[109] has noted the influence of the environment on the nature and status of the purchasing function in buying group decisions. He established that the more dynamic and complex the buying group's environment, the more likely it is that the purchasing agent's influence heightens as he/she assumes increased data gathering (i.e. uncertainty reduction) activities for the buying group as a whole. However, this situation is only usually apparent when the decision to purchase is non-routine. In such cases, the information needs of the buying group increase dramatically in response to conditions of higher environmental uncertainty. The various group tasks become

less routine and less differentiated and the resultant increase in shared purchasing responsibility contributes to a more flexible organisational design, thereby permitting buying group members to react more quickly to increased possibilities of contingency. The need for acquisition of more extensive purchasing related information increases, facilitating the replacement of rigid vertical paths by lateral communication networks. Further research is required in this area, especially to determine whether this situation is industry specific.

With regard to the wider environmental context, Guillet de Monthoux[110] has undertaken some research into industrial buying in manufacturing companies in Sweden. He has some evidence that suggests that in times of recession, the degree of formalisation within the firm seems to increase: 'A decision which in a boom time might have been taken in a more informal atmosphere now is taken in a formalised way.'

External trends within the general structure of industry can also influence purchasing behaviour, albeit indirectly. Phenomena such as the growing incidence of larger industrial organisations and the increased concentration of buying power are, to a certain extent, the result of extraneous variables beyond the control of purchasing institutions. Blois[111] has shown that with fewer and larger purchasing units in some industries, only about six customers in his study accounted for over 90 per cent of all items purchased. Another example of the influence of sporadic trends is the concept of materials management. Recognition of this idea can have specific relevance to the purchasing behaviour within industrial organisations. Again, in this instance, professionalisation of the purchasing function has accelerated the adoption of this concept.

The previous paragraphs have attempted to explore the influences on the role of the purchasing function in buying centre decision-taking.

A number of specific research needs have been identified within this area. However, there is a general requirement for a research study that analyses the status of purchasing *vis-à-vis* other functional areas of the organisation. The incidence of increasing purchasing professionalisation should be examined with respect to the role of buying in corporate behaviour. There is also a need to identify the nature of purchasing influence across a broad spectrum of industry.

The following paragraphs discuss the relationship between specific, product-related characteristics of the buying decision and the consequent behaviour. It can be recognised that the buying group composition and, in effect, generic buyer behaviour is influenced by particular characteristics of the product to be purchased.

The research of Luffman[112] and White[113] highlights the importance

that should be attributed to product-related variables when determining influences on buying behaviour. They argue that the inherent attributes of the product will influence the nature of the buying
group, by involving certain functional groups in the purchasing
decision.

Abdelrehim[114] and Wallace[115] support the contention that product-
oriented factors have a bearing on buying centre. They cite the
following variables:

(a) the technical complexity of the product;
(b) the value of the item to be purchased;
(c) the frequency of purchase;
(d) the product's essentiality to the production process;
(e) the potential consequences of making a wrong decision.

This list has been extended by a number of authors to include a
further two factors:

(f) the degree of inherent innovation or novelty in the product;[116]
(g) the product's complexity itself.[117]

Woodside and Taylor[118] have suggested that the degree of inherent
'newness' in the product should be a fundamental basis for product
differentiation. They propose the incorporation of Robinson, Faris
and Wind's[119] 'buying-class' framework as a predictor of buying-
class composition.

The research needs in this area are outlined in detail later in this
chapter. However, it would appear advisable to recognise the importance of product-related variables on purchasing decisions and,
to a certain extent, these factors are more easily quantified than the
more nebulous variables of buyer self-perception. The same comment could be made of the next specific influence on buying centre
behaviour–the stage in the purchasing process.

The purchase of an industrial product does not take place at one
discrete point in time. It is normally the culmination of a number of
activities that may, in some instances, span a considerable time
period. An analysis of the product purchase process should enable
the location and identification of those stages in the buying process
at which critical decisions are made. By definition, some of these
stages are intra-company and others inter-company. Intra-company
activities tend to predominate in the early stages of the process and
inter-company activities in the latter stages.

Many classifications for the stages or phases in the purchase
process have been proposed, most based on empirical research.
Although there is no standard system of classification for any buying
situation, there will be a number of key decision points.

The most widely quoted and used classification is the Robinson *et al.*[120] buy phases. This includes eight activity stages as follows:

1. Anticipation or recognition of a problem (need) and a general solution.
2. Determination of characteristics and quantity of required item.
3. Description of characteristics and quantity of needed item.
4. Search for and qualification of potential sources.
5. Acquisition and analysis of proposals.
6. Evaluation of proposals and selection of supplier(s).
7. Selection of an order routine.
8. Performance feedback and evaluation.

Research by Hillier[121] combined some of these stages. He recorded the buying process for over forty purchases of capital equipment by various organisations in the United Kingdom, and suggested that there exist four key decision areas:

1. The precipitation decision stage–when a definite course of action to solve problem is confirmed.
2. The product specification stage–when broad solutions to a problem are translated into specific hardware and software requirements.
3. The supplier selection stage–when potential suppliers are identified and one or more selected.
4. The commitment decision stage–when a customer decides to what extent a supplier has fulfilled its expectations.

The role of participants at various stages has also been explored by Brand.[122] He identifies these stages as the following:

1. Problem recognition.
2. Determine characteristics of needed items.
3. Specific description.
4. Search for potential supplier.
5. Evaluate sources and products.
6. Select supplier.
7. Establish order routine.
8. Evaluate feedback.

Webster[123] condenses these into four fundamental steps:

1. Problem recognition.
2. Organisational assignment of buying responsibility and authority.
3. Search procedures for identifying product offerings and for establishing selection criteria.
4. Choice procedures for evaluating and selecting among alternatives.

His studies also reflect the concept of a changing locus of responsibility for purchasing at diverse stages in the process.

This latter point has been the focus of the majority of studies[124] of purchasing behaviour. The *Financial Times* Survey,[125] for example, has been concerned with the influence and role of individual participants in the buying decision throughout the sequential stages of the process.

It can be concluded from the evidence presented by these studies that the purchasing process has identifiable time-series components and, through these diverse stages, the composition of the buying centre changes.

Decisions are incremental in nature, and hence each major decision consists of several corollaries, and does itself constitute the basis for further decisions. When this concept is applied to the buying process then it can be seen that the precipitating decisions will form the basis for product decisions, the product for the supplier decisions and the supplier for the commitment decisions. At this stage, the purchasing cycle is completed, but, should further products be required from the same supplier, then the end of the first cycle forms the basis for the start of the second cycle. At each stage, there is a buying centre and the locus of responsibility may vary from one stage to another. The decisions made by members of the buying centre in the early part of the buying process will inevitably limit the freedom of the decision-making activities for buying centres involved in the later stages of the process; it also usually follows that the formality of the decision-making activities increases as the process progresses.

There is a need to substantiate (by providing a further empirical base of evidence) the recent conclusions of Wind[126] that buying centre composition is dictated by the stage in the purchasing process. The concept of increasing formality towards the conclusion of the purchase is in its infancy. This point may suggest the increased involvement of professional purchasing in the latter stages. What must be done, however, is to establish whether there is any evidence to suggest the role of purchasing at the initiation stages. If this situation does arise, could it imply increased formalisation of the total purchasing process? Such vital issues demand the attention of those engaged in both marketing and purchasing research.

Further research is also necessary to investigate the frequency of the instance of individual versus group decision-taking. Webster and Wind[127] have shown, for example, that buying committees are used where the judgements of several organisational members are felt necessary to evaluate alternative buying situations, usually where the element of risk is high, a phenomenon confirmed by Sheth.[128] Our current ignorance regarding group behaviour stems from our inability to observe the interactions, always in a state of flux, among the four major components of the group decision process–task, activities, subject and structure of activities. MacKenzie,[129] for example, has suggested that we should begin to identify carefully all atomistic tasks and all subjects involved in the process.

Moreover, the concept of group relationships and communication is directly relevant to the notion of inter-organisational relationships in addition to intra-organisational exchange processes. Currently, a major field of research investigation is emerging which specifically analyses the interaction process between supplier and customer organisations. Hakansson *et al.*[130] have reported the results of extensive research study in this area.

Traditionally, the transaction between 'buyer' and 'seller' has been the focal point of interest of much microeconomic theory and empirical research, for example, through considerations of supply and demand. In other studies, interaction between buying and selling functions has been reduced, in a somewhat myopic manner, to interaction between two persons–the dyadic approaches of Busch and Wilson.[131]

Other research has related the process to the development of a union similar to marriage between the two parties.[132] There is further evidence[133] to suggest that extensive interaction between supplier and user often leads to a very solid commitment between the two, i.e. they tend to build up lasting power-dependence relationships. Gemunden[134] has also commented on the strong influence of these relationships on buying decisions. Recent work at Strathclyde by Parkinson[135] has extended work in this area which would appear to be a potentially viable field of investigation.

One of the major problems in organisational buying behaviour *per se* is simply that much descriptive work has not yet been conducted on a large scale. Investigators have preferred to send large sample surveys to a number of different purchasing managers in a large variety of organisations, ignoring both the buying centre concept and the fact that the buying process itself involves two parties–buyers and sellers. A more fruitful research attack might be to study fewer organisations across more industries according to whatever intuitive classifications or segmentation strategies initially suggest themselves.

Although Sheth[136] cites over 1,000 bibliographic items on organisational buying in a recent literature review, the ultimate impact of this work has been small. Sheth explains that most researchers have felt more comfortable applying concepts from individual psychology (to consumers) than they have in applying concepts from organisation theory to organisational buying. As Zaltman[137] has noted, 'the study of industrial marketing is basically the study of the behaviour of formal organisations'. Perhaps our future research interests should emphasise the *organisational* aspects of buying behaviour.

However, perhaps the most contentious issue that consistently haunts those involved in the study of both consumer and organisational buyer behaviour is the struggle to develop comprehensive and yet pragmatic models of buyer behaviour.

Models of buyer behaviour

Contemporary consumer models owe much of their basic structure to contributions drawn from models of human behaviour previously hypothesised by a variety of branches of the social sciences. For example, Veblen's[138] model concentrates upon the interaction of the individual with his social environment by stressing that all human behaviour takes place within the wider social context. Similarly, a final pioneering field of study which attempted to extend knowledge on human behaviour was derived from the work undertaken by psychologists of the Gestalt school. Essentially, Gestalt psychology recognises that a major function of the cognitive system is to relate perceptual stimuli to each other and to the environment. Against this background of thought, Lewin[139] advanced his explanatory model of human behaviour. The individual decision process operates within a total situation which includes an individual need structure and interaction between the individual and the external environment. Consequently, needs are satisfied through a range of actions and behaviour results from the evaluation of the positive and negative aspects (as perceived by the individual) related to each possible course of action.

These, largely behavioural, models have been gradually superseded by contemporary models of consumer buyer behaviour that strive to be more comprehensive in nature.

Among the better known of these comprehensive models are those developed by Nicosia,[140] Andreasen,[141] Engel, Kollat, and Blackwell,[142] Clawson,[143] and Howard and Sheth.[144] Although the models differ in respect to their complexity and orientation, they are nevertheless formulated along similar patterns of thought. Hence, analogies (between the models) can be found in terms of the methods by which they isolate and identify relevant variables and their perception of dynamic decision processes.

These particular theories of buyer behaviour, however, are generally considered to be impractical for the purposes of rigorous testing and validation. One precursory attempt at empirical assessment of the predictive ability of the Howard and Sheth model was undertaken in a specific market.[145]

A development parallel to the trend towards comprehensive models has been the development of specific multi-attribute utility models of attitude. Such research,[146] although model-oriented, is essentially limited in its potential for application.

By contrast, more complex models for choice behaviour have been developed which show less detailed concern with constructs and greater concern with relationships among the constructs. Large-scale behavioural models,[147] have gained considerable attention in marketing, particularly those outlined above. Lehmann *et al.*[148] have commented on the contribution of such models to buyer behaviour theory:

> While quite different in content and structure, these are models of decision processes which attempt to describe the flows between various constructs relevant to decision making by the consumer. At their present stage of development, these 'buyer behaviour' models are generally in flow chart form which indicate which constructs are asumed to influence other constructs. The parameters governing the relationships among the constructs and explicit mathematical forms of the relationships are generally unspecified.

However, the authors do contend that the inherent value of these models is that they present a means of considering information processing, attitude formation and choice in one concise model. By doing so, buyer-behaviour models provide an organising framework in which research in areas such as the relation of intentions to purchase,[149] Fishbein attitude models[150] and word of mouth communications[151] can be integrated. They present the view that buyer-behaviour models are an extremely useful tool for planning and co-ordinating research studies. Nevertheless, it is important to recognise that buyer-behaviour models are highly developmental and that they should not be viewed as rigid.

In a recent article, Foxall[152] takes further issue with the apparent limited applicability of comprehensive buyer-behaviour models. He proposes that: 'the main drawback to the flow-chart models is that they assume too rational a consumer (particularly at the search and evaluation stages of the decision-making process).... Sequential, discrete stages of the decision process are not viewed as realistic.

He continues by suggesting that the flow-chart models are:

> essentially descriptive rather than explicative, do not delimit the field of human behaviour to which they apply, fail to integrate, except in the widest possible terms, the relevant behavioural variables and approaches and offer no improvement over a cursory, unsystematic

knowledge of shopping activity as far as the generation of definite hypotheses for empirical testing is concerned.

Foxall's article also contains a description of a more interdisciplinary model of buyer behaviour that has been proposed by Baker.[153] For a review of my own comments on this particular model, the reader is referred elsewhere.[154]

To conclude, therefore, developments in consumer buyer behaviour modelling are progressing towards the refinement of comprehensive models. However, as has been demonstrated, in order to achieve an accurate prediction of behaviour, the relationships between the constituent variables must somehow be made sufficiently specific so as to permit their measurement and numeric values must be assigned to each relationship. Needless to say, this phase of development for the field of organisational buying modelling remains, as yet, in the future, as our brief summary of work in this area will show.

Webster's[155] model identified four stages of the organisational buying process. Although the model is not predictive, it does begin to suggest that there are influences from organisational behaviour (e.g. company rewards systems, company buying procedures and organisational structure) which are incumbent upon decision process. The work of Cyert and March[156] was pioneering in this area, recognising the interaction of organisational, social, individual and environmental forces as influences upon the decision processes in goal-setting organisations. Their four concepts have been tested[157] in industrial settings and have generally been supported. The work of Webster and Wind[158] stresses the fact that the specific organisational buying variables–the buying task, structure, technology and people– are affected by the overall organisational variables–task, structure, technology and people. Subscribing, therefore, to a systems approach to organisational buying requires an understanding of the specific limits between the organisational buying variables and the overall organisational variables.

Examination of comprehensive models of buyer behaviour shows that they are comprised of essentially the same basic elements: environmental task or situational, organisational, individual and social factors. There may be particular semantic differences between the models but they all recognise the complex set of interactions that constitute organisational buying behaviour. Hence, attempts to develop conceptual models of organisational buyer behaviour have been valuable in providing a focus for study but have fallen short of expectations in several respects. For example, Robinson, Faris and Wind's model[159] identifies eight stages through which organisations move in purchasing deliberations. However, it has little predictive ability and offers little insight into the nature of the complex interplay between task and non-task variables. Webster and Wind's[160] model is also loosely constructed and offers no testable propositions. Sheth's[161] model may provide a basic classification system for existing literature in industrial marketing, but it is little more than a 'shopping list' of factors that are considered to be important in the study of buying behaviour.

The preceding models may provide the foundation for serious research into the intricate nature of organisational buying behaviour by dispelling common academic misconceptions of what are the relevant influences and behaviours in organisational purchasing. However, our future research strategies must move forward to permit empirical verification of hypotheses. More importantly, one consideration that has been ignored in the published literature is the notion of managerial use. Existing models give little attention to the influence by controllable marketing variables on buyer response. The industrial market response model proposed by Choffray and Lilien[162] is a step towards eliminating deficiencies currently experienced in applying models of buyer behaviour to the industrial setting.

Recommendations for future research directions are proposed in greater detail in the following section. Briefly, however, it would appear that our present need is not for more comprehensive models of buyer behaviour, but rather empirical testing and refinement of the constituents of the grand models that currently exist.

Future considerations

Nearly all of the approaches to the study of both consumer and organisational buyer behaviour that have been outlined above have focused on the individual member of the group and his or her relationships to other members. A few studies have also investigated communication and structural patterns of small groups.

The determination of the unit of analysis of behaviour is perhaps most particularly relevant to the study of industrial buyer behaviour and this is a crucial factor in the development of viable research strategies for the future.

Industrial buying behaviour may be examined on other levels of analysis in comparison to those that have been the traditional focus of study, that is, at the level of the structure of the organisation itself and its interactions with other organisations or aspects of its environment. Two alternative methods of analysis present themselves. Either:

(a) Investigate the impact of macro variables on the behaviour of the decision-making group, e.g. organisational technology, size, complexity, centralisation, formalisation or even environmental variables such as uncertainty.
(b) Investigate relationships and structure within the buying centre, e.g. authority patterns, lateral communication.

Consequently, the focus of study may range from the individual consumer or purchasing agent, the buying centre, the entire organisation to an aggregate analysis at the total market level. The choice of an appropriate unit of analysis affects the subsequent and critical choices of variables, their measurement and analytical procedures. Current research often chooses only one organisational unit (e.g. the purchasing department), thus ignoring the implications of intra-organisational heterogeneity and the multiplicity of influences and conflicts. Hence, a major deficiency of past research has been the neglect of the concept of group decision-taking; past research has tended to 'personify' the organisational decision-making processes by postulating that the purchase decision is made by one person, or it has, on the other hand, collapsed the entire process into an anthropomorphic abstraction by proposing that the 'purchasing department' decides.

Concurrent with the need to examine and determine the unit of analysis on which to examine buyer behaviour, there is also an inherent requirement for researchers to consider the problem of measurement and quantification of the buying decision. From an organisational theory point of view, the more diffused the information–activities–persons process, the more pressing the need to find a structural method of analysing and measuring the decision-making process.

The field of consumer behaviour study has perhaps been more advanced in the area of measurement of behaviour than have researchers in organisational buyer behaviour. Data on buying behaviour can be generated by survey, observation and experimentation and should be analysed by the appropriate analytical techniques. Such procedures have been used extensively in the study of consumer behaviour, but only rarely in organisational buying behaviour research. Similarly, multivariate statistical techniques (e.g. multiple classification analysis, regression and correlation analysis, multiple discriminant analysis and factor analysis), can be utilised in the measurement of non-experimental (observational and survey) data in organisational buying behaviour. A similar situation exists with respect to multi-dimensional scaling techniques and evaluation function procedures. The only exceptions are a number of exploratory and pilot studies conducted by Choffray and Lilien.[163]

Choffray's study[164] also gives consideration to the practical utility of studies of buyer behaviour. He addresses the problem of using analysis of buyer behaviour as the basis for segmentation of, in his particular case, the industrial market. His study also provides a methodology, based on cluster analysis, which uses this information to identify 'microsegments' of potential customers who are relatively homogeneous in the composition of their buying centres. Within each microsegment, the general structure of the buying centre's composition is statistically assessed. Choffray and Lilien also use this information as the basis for formulating a model of buyer behaviour, or 'industrial market response' in their terminology, which is linked to a measurement methodology. Their model focuses on the links between the characteristics of an organisation's buying centre and the three major stages in the industrial purchasing decision process through:

(a) Elimination of alternatives that do not meet organisational requirements.
(b) Formation of decision participants' preferences.
(c) Formation of organisational preferences.

Thus, the model provides tools through which it is possible to measure involvement in the purchasing decision process and uses this information to abstract microsegments of organisations that are homogeneous in their decision-making structure. Consequently, industrial market segmentation becomes more meaningful (and practically possible) to industrial market manufacturers. Their work is a significant improvement on previous study of segmentation classes in industrial marketing. A brief note on past work in this area is presented in the following paragraphs, principally to outline the deficiencies of previous research and to suggest that future efforts at modelling buyer behaviour should consider the need for the ability to predict and identify meaningful market segments.

Past bases for industrial segmentation have fundamental weaknesses. While there is contradictory evidence about the usefulness of some bases (e.g. demographics), it has appeared almost impossible to use other bases, e.g. the decision-maker's characteristics in particular. This is owing to the nature of the inherent difficulty involved in evaluating an industrial buyer on such variables as, for example, personality/decision-making styles, values and value systems and role commitments. Most empirical research that has been carried out in this area has claimed that an individual's need for certainty may be a good predictor of his decision-making style. Cardozo and Cagley,[165] in an experimental study of industrial buying behaviour, observed the possibility of segmenting industrial markets on the basis of purchasing strategies and preference patterns that individual buyers consistently hold. Also Cunningham and White,[166] Lehmann and O'Shaughnessy[167] and Hakansson *et al.*[168] have attempted segmentation and prediction of behaviour on these variables. They all observed, however, that buyers tend to vary in terms of the importance they attach to different attributes for different industrial products. Choffray and Lilien have advanced this earlier work by demonstrating that meaningful differences exist in both the number and nature of the evaluation criteria used by various decision participant *categories.*

From a scientific point of view, the model of Choffray and Lilien[169] can accommodate changes in variables or parameter values and can ultimately serve as a simulator of the effects of changes in marketing inputs or environmental conditions. This should be our objective in developing and refining models of buyer behaviour–to define theories explicitly which will have the essential characteristic of being empirically testifiable.

Moreover, in the context of past research, a number of areas of potential for future work can be suggested.

The recent work of Bellizzi[170] has shown that purchasing behaviour should be studied across new industry sectors. He analysed choice criteria in the commercial construction industry and has emphasised that study of organisational buying behaviour should not be limited to manufacturing organisations, but that the concepts have application in professional and technical organisations as well. Hence, comparative research of procurement processes of public and private sector organisations, profit and non-profit, and product and service-oriented organisations is necessary. Moreover, in contrast to household consumer satisfaction research, there has been very little attention paid to the notion of dissatisfaction among industrial buyers. The subject of reciprocity has been the subject of very little systematic study.[171]

In general, research studies have tended to analyse behaviour in two or three sectors of industry. Perhaps this phenomenon stems from the industrial marketers' characteristic concentration on specific buying situations. Industrial marketers have always been customer-oriented with an emphasis on the needs of specific individual customers and less on the 'market' consisting of all potential customers.

Attempts should also be made to broaden the concept of buying, with particular reference to the contribution that can be made from the organisational behaviour schools of thought. Hence, we should concentrate on organisational buying behaviour as opposed to industrial buying behaviour and focus our analysis on the fundamental processes of information acquisition, analysis and decision-making in industrial, institutional and other formal organisational settings that are all basically similar in their essential characteristics.

More recently, some authors have proposed the use of new methods of data collection. Wind[172] and Crow *et al.*[173] advocate a fresh perspective on methodology:

> However, a need remains for research involving a detailed analysis of the decision strategies used by industrial buyers in requesting quotations and in selecting a final supplier. Such research suggests the development of models that are highly descriptive of industrial buyers' decision processes as well as being predictive of the purchase decision outcome.

It could be argued that, in the search for valid conclusions on buying behaviour which hold for more than one industry, it is expedient to utilize more than one data collection method, thus documenting contacts with several persons per firm. As a consequence of this, the study of buyer behaviour is beginning to apply a diverse range of methodological techniques in the hope of facilitating more accurate measurement of the purchasing function. Content analysis,[174] open-ended interviews, both participant and non-participant observation, and protocol analysis are being applied. A number of authors have suggested that this latter methodology affords the optimum means of permitting direct observation of decision processes. For example, Bettman,[175] Payne,[176] and Russo and Rosen[177] have demonstrated its effectiveness in experimental settings. It remains to be seen, however, whether the methodology has validity in external field settings.

It is the author's contention that the use of such novel methodologies will enhance the pragmatic value of buyer-behaviour models. Essentially, it becomes possible to develop measures that permit systematic description and comparison of decision processes at both the inter-decisional and inter-organisational levels. Recent work[178] that has been undertaken in the Department of Marketing at Strathclyde University as part of a general programme of study that is currently being undertaken by an international group of researchers, confirms the contention that the descriptive research methodology offers an impressively practical, but valid approach to theoretical model-building in buyer behaviour, confirming the earlier findings of Cyert, Simon and Trow[179] and others.[180]

Our focus in the future should be on the decision process, as opposed to the individuals involved in the decision-making process. The recent work of Braun[181] and Cohen[182] has developed the idea that individuals who are involved in decisions are essentially 'actors' who precipitate events. There is a sound argument for our attempts in the future to begin to rationalise the process of buyer behaviour, analysing and measuring those influences that have specific effects on buying decisions at particular stages in the purchasing process. Our efforts in the future must be on attempts to measure and quantify behaviour. Our progress to date in formulating viable and reliable models and predictors of buyer behaviour has been relatively slow. It is time that we transcended the notion that buyer behaviour has both rational and irrational components–we must do something to operationalise our hypotheses and facilitate their measurement and validation: 'When you cannot measure what you are speaking about, when you cannot express it in numbers; your knowledge is of a meagre and unsatisfactory kind' (Lord Kelvin).

Marketing communications

Contents

Introduction: what is 'marketing communications'?

The term 'marketing communications' was chosen deliberately and carefully as the title of this chapter, despite the unarguable fact that it is not yet widely used in marketing practice, because it defines the subject matter as precisely as possible.

First, 'marketing' limits the scope of the topic by telling us what kinds are *not* under consideraton. Marketing communication is quite different from *mass communication*, in which an organisation addresses a largely undifferentiated mass audience (hence the term) for a non-commercial purpose by such means as press editorials, radio news, television documentaries, drama or political propaganda. The organisation would instead be aiming at a deliberately differentiated audience for a commercial purpose, and would employ such vehicles as advertising, sales presentations or pack design. This distinction may seem almost too obvious to need making, but is not always clearly enough observed in the specialist theoretical literature, as we shall see later.

Corporate communications also decribes the use of such vehicles to address a differentiated audience for a commercial purpose, but that audience does not exclusively consist of potential consumers. Many authors have observed that business firms, especially larger corporations, have a considerable number of recognisably separate 'publics' and may need to address all of them at one time or another. However, the impetus for communicating with the financial community, the workforce, the local community or suppliers (only four out of seventeen identified by Britt[1]) is unlikely to be a specific *marketing* imperative, but rather a corporate one. This particular distinction firmly categorises *public relations*, a familiar communication activity practised by many commercial firms, as corporate and not marketing communication because its aim is to foster relationships with the public at large, not to promote products or services to markets. PR may play an important role in creating favourable conditions for subsequent marketing conditions, but that is beyond the scope of this chapter.

Having established that the simple criterion of a *marketing purpose* establishes the boundaries of the 'marketing communications' concept, it is next necessary to define more precisely the communication practices within those boundaries. Let us start with the fundamental notion of a *marketing mix*–those variables in the marketing equation that are capable of manipulation by executive action–conveniently summarised by McCarthy's 'four Ps':[2]

P1 = product
P2 = place
P3 = promotion
P4 = price

The most communicative element in this mix is clearly 'promotion'. (The other three are certainly capable of communicating something about a firm and its offerings in particular circumstances, as many authors have pointed out, but the constraints of space dictate that we focus here on typical rather than special practices.)

This element itself comprises a mix of at least five major strategic-tactical actions:

P3.1 advertising
P3.2 publicity
P3.3 sales promotion
P3.4 personal selling
P3.5 packaging, display

To all intents and purposes, these are the ingredients of 'marketing communications'.

Since the prime purpose of this chapter is to explain the theoretical underpinnings of practice, it would be inappropriate to dwell unduly on definition and description of the five ingredients of this *marketing communications mix*. Readers interested in clarification can refer to Gilligan and Crowther[3] or Dunn and Barban[4] for British and American explanations respectively. But one issue that does warrant our attention here is the careless and confusing use of the terms 'advertising' and 'publicity' in Britain.

Advertising entails the placing of pre-prepared advertisements in definable advertising media at a published advertising rate, whereas *publicity* entails the delivery of information to the news media in the hope that it will be judged newsworthy and therefore mentioned editorially at no charge. The two are clearly quite distinct and complementary alternative tactics, and yet a cursory inspection of the *Advertiser's Annual* shows that a significant fraction of all British advertisers use 'publicity department' and 'publicity manager' to describe what are in fact advertising departments and managers, or a combination of both. The error is particularly characteristic of industrial rather than consumer marketing and readers may need to be alert to the consequent possibility of real confusion in practice. Fortunately, it is seldom if ever perpetrated on the advertising agency side of the business.

'Communications' in the chapter title is an explicit clue to the nature of the effects following a *marketing communications* initiative, such as an advertising campaign or sales call. In everyday usage, according to the *Oxford Dictionary*, 'communication' describes the act of *imparting* or *transmitting*. For thirty years now, however, theorists have been stressing that communication is not simply transmission of a message or sign from one party to another, but rather an *exchange* between them. Schramm, a highly influential academic writer on mass communications whose basic theoretical propositions have been accepted and re-used by succeeding generations of marketing authors, defined it as 'the process of establishing a commonness or oneness of thought between a sender and a receiver'.[5] While few would dispute the transactional nature of person-to-person communication, there is a definite tendency among textbook practitioners and authors to take a far more unilateral view of marketing communication. It is a central tenet of this chapter, in contrast, that firms equally communicate *with* potential customers and not *at* them.

The dictionary furthermore defines communication as the transmission of *information*. In the marketing context, this is not always so. An advertisement, for instance, may provide its audience with entertainment or a feeling about the advertiser and the offering as well as hard information. To imply that its informative function is the only valid or important one of these three, as textbooks also frequently do, is to take too unilateral a view again–this time by undervaluing the audience's discretion in how it chooses to *use* the advertisement. As used in this chapter title, 'communications' is intended to remind us that individuals in a marketing communicator's audience are not passive recipients but *active participants.*

While it is quite true that the firm makes the first move by taking a marketing communications initiative, the audience's co-operation in responding to it is required, and their response may even so not be what the initiator intended. Indeed, the impetus may come from the audience (if not the initiative), in the sense that they deliberately expose themselves to marketing communications relevant to their present needs. The communicator's 'initiative' is thus the audience's 'message', a point that re-emphasises our central tenet that marketing communication is a *transaction*.

The consequences of this important proposition appear not to have been fully assimilated by the authors of most current textbooks, by marketing practitioners or by commentators on (in particular) advertising. One receives a very strong impression that they believe all forms of marketing communications to be what powerful firms do to powerless, though sometimes stubborn, audiences and not something that the latter can choose to consume and use, or not to. It is not enough to build a 'feedback loop' into diagrams of the process or to stress the need to monitor public reaction to marketing communications initiatives; this is a *post-hoc* concession and not at all the same as treating the whole process as a *mutually beneficial exchange from the outset*. The balance of power in this transaction is thus a crucial issue which we will be considering in detail later.

For all the reasons implicit in the term 'communications' in its title, the remainder of this chapter will therefore approach the process of marketing communication as both a planned initiative by the communicator and a purposeful act of consumption behaviour by the audience. Before doing so, however, it may be useful to establish an agreed vocabulary.

Working definitions

1. *Marketing communication*, in the singular, is shorthand for 'communication for a marketing purpose'.
2. *Marketing communications*, in the plural, concerns the transactional processes by which such communication is or is not achieved.
3. *Marketing communications mix* describes the full range of actions by means of which a firm (or other type of organisation) can initiate the exchange.
4. *Marketing communications initiative* describes either (a) a single corresponding tactical action on the part of a firm, or (b) the purposeful act of consuming the resulting message or sign on the part of an individual.

In the first edition of *Marketing: Theory and Practice*, the chapter corresponding to this made significant use of the term 'persuasive communications'. The phrase does not occur here because it would not be correct to assume that marketing communications initiatives–in sense (a) above–must necessarily always have persuasion as their prime short-term objective, or that–in sense (b) above–they will always be used for self-persuasion. 'Marketing communications' strongly suggests persuasive intent, while permitting us to acknowledge the possibility of other motivations.

Marketing communications as a consumption transaction

Figure 6.1 presents a simplified interpretation of the classic flowchart models of consumer behaviour, explained in very much more detail in Chapter 4. The cycle of behaviour is initiated by conscious or subconscious awareness of a need which seems capable of eventual satisfaction by the acquisition of a consumer product or service. (For the sake of convenience, we will continue to speak of consumers and consumer products, but there is in fact no reason to believe that the model is inapplicable to industrial purchasing officers or the target audiences for public service advertising, for instance; the respective behaviour presumably varies in degree rather than in kind.) The felt need is next modified by a set of internal and external influences. The former comprise such modifiers as the consumer's own values, attitudes, beliefs and priorities; the latter consist of such factors as the consumer's perception of his or her social position, subcultural norms or family consensus. In its thus revised form, the original need now becomes a *drive* to find a satisfaction, which in turn stimulates a

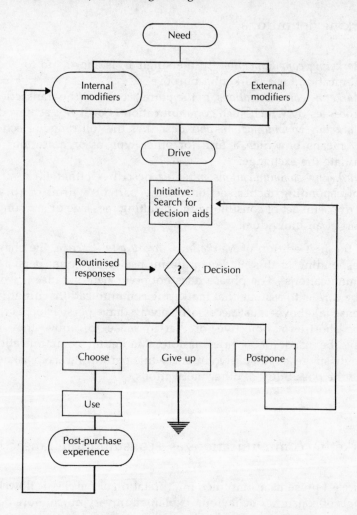

Figure 6.1   A simplification of the classic models of consumer behaviour

deliberate–perhaps mostly subconscious–*search* for aids to decision-making. Two central tenets of orthodox consumer behaviour theory are (i) that a need demands satisfaction and cannot simply be ignored, and (ii) that consumers are not helpless or haphazard in their consumption behaviour, but actively search for aids to systematic decision-making.

In due course, the search operation will be terminated by one or more of three circumstances arising: a decision deadline has arrived; the effort demanded to pursue the search further does not seem to match the probable benefits of doing so; the mass of data already

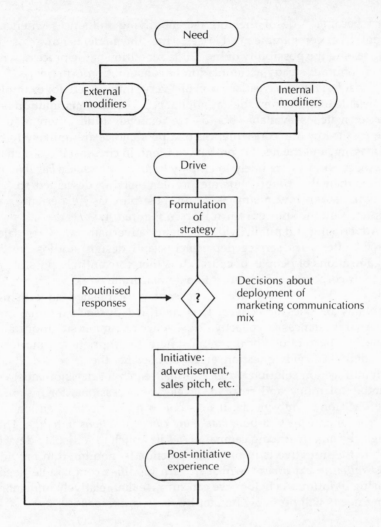

Figure 6.2   Marketing communications practitioners' behaviour

acquired threatens to overload the capacity to handle it. The *decision* must now be made. Generally, it will be to make a choice among available products or services which deliver acceptable satisfactions. Instead, it could be to postpone the choice, for lack of a clear solution, in which case the sequence of actions can be expected to loop back to the search stage and continue to cycle until a solution is found. Theory predicts that the third depicted possibility, to give up with the need unsatisfied, is an extremely unlikely outcome. The process does not end with a choice among alternatives, however. *Use* of the product or service is the basis of *post-purchase experience*, which in turn becomes one of the internal modifying influences when an identical or comparable need arises. Thus, the model is now 'closed', suggesting the possibility of indefinite repetition of the process, with a concomitant steady accumulation of consumption experience.

Consider, however, satisfaction of a very simple need–for example, to be able to light domestic gas appliances. The obvious solution is a box of matches–available brands are relatively little differentiated, the cost is low, the consequences of a poor choice are unlikely to be damaging, and the need is probably urgent. In circumstances such as these, consumers are likely to employ *'routinised response behaviour'*[6] rather than the more deliberate problem-solving described so far. The basis for routinising is again post-purchase experience, as depicted by the shorter return loop in Figure 6.1.

Advertising and publicity departments, advertising agencies, sales forces, after-sales service departments and design studios are all organisations of people, of course. It is therefore entirely possible to fit their corporate behaviour into a similar framework, as Figure 6.2 does. In this case, the need is to satisfy established advertising, publicity or sales objectives. It is modified by such internal and external influences as collective experience of similar situations and collective perceptions of the 'atmosphere' appropriate to output on behalf of the firm in question, and then becomes the drive to devise a communication solution. After a formal search for decision aids, via strategy planning and creative development sessions, for instance, the decision is duly made. If it is not to postpone or abandon the project, the result will be a *marketing communications initiative*. This might be an advertising campaign, a sales pitch or a display device. While the initiative is in progress, reaction is monitored to provide *post-initiative experience*, which in turn modifies comparable needs arising in future. As before, we can surmise that relatively undemanding needs will probably be met by *routinised responses*.

A 'synapse'

The crucial step in building a model of marketing communication as a *transaction* is to join the two flowcharts together. Figure 6.3 introduces the notion of a *synapse*. Borrowed from zoology, this term defines the place where nerve cells meet but are not fused together. At the marketing communications synapse, user and originator of marketing communications initiatives come in contact while remaining in their own distinct domains. This analogy reminds us that consumers are not passive recipients, as so many marketing com-

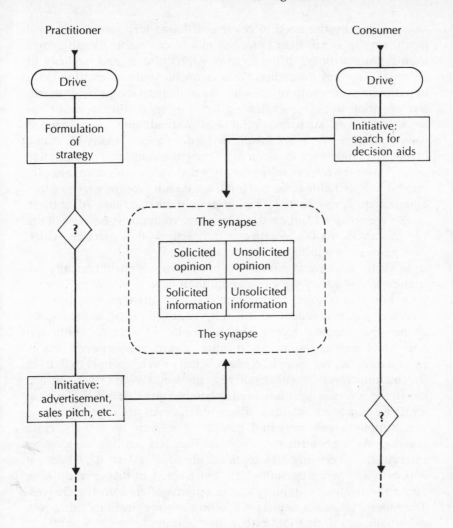

Practitioner

Consumer

Drive

Drive

Formulation
of
strategy

Initiative:
search for
decision aids

?

The synapse

Solicited opinion	Unsolicited opinion
Solicited information	Unsolicited information

The synapse

Initiative:
advertisement,
sales pitch, etc.

?

Figure 6.3   The marketing communications 'synapse'

munications practitioners give the appearance of believing, but
participants. They initiate the transaction by choosing to expose
themselves to marketing communications initiatives–and other inputs: that is their 'marketing communications initiative'. Among the
models of consumer behaviour from which Figures 6.1 and 6.2
ultimately derive, the Howard–Sheth–Ostlund variant[7] is most
obviously consistent with this theoretical proposition.

The decision aids commonly available to the searching consumer
can be broadly categorised into a fourfold scheme: information or
opinion; solicited or unsolicited. Driven to search for aids to deci-

sion-making by the need to cover our floors, for example, we will become more aware than before of manufacturers' marketing communications activity, in the form of *advertisements* and *publicity* in editorial pages of magazines; this is unsolicited information. In a department store, with our sensitivity to floorcoverings heightened, our attention is perhaps attracted by other marketing communications initiatives, such as special *display* stands and the associated colourful *packaging*: more unsolicited information. Finally visiting a carpet showroom, we expect a marketing communications initiative in response: the offer of *sales promotion* material, a *sales pitch*, or both. Indeed, we are liable to be put out if we do not promptly receive this attention, having solicited it by loitering in the sales area. All of these inputs are accepted and used, actively and voluntarily, because of the circumstances. At the synapse, a transaction takes place in which *both* parties are willing participants.

As for the seeking and receiving of opinions, we will typically ask friends whose advice we value about their experiences with flooring materials; this is solicited opinion. If we simultaneously happen to mention our preoccupation to neighbours, there is a very good chance that we will receive much unsolicited opinion. Although opinion is thus as important an input to consumption decisions as information, we are more likely to solicit it from lay people than from the manufacturers' representatives; presumably, we feel we can already guess the opinion of the latter. Furthermore, the typical structure of modern retailing, discussed in detail in Chapter 9, means that suppliers and potential customers seldom come very close together. As the chairman of Beecham Products put it in a television interview, 'advertising has replaced the shop assistant'. Checkout and cash-and-wrap personnel are not trained to dispense opinion about the relative suitability of the options offered on the shelves. Therefore, Figure 6.3 depicts marketing communications initiatives essentially as information, rather than opinion.

Before leaving the distinction between information and opinion, however, it is worth reporting a proposition from the more specialist literature: that there is a change in emphasis between the two as search behaviour continues. This originated with sociologists studying the uptake of agricultural innovations in America in the 1940s,[8] who found that while farmers were simply thinking about a new practice or device in the early stages of the decision process, they sought mainly *information* from formal sources such as government advisers (salespeople) and publications (sales promotion), whereas when the eventual decision became imminent, they turned to the *opinions* of neighbouring farmers and other influential personal contacts. It was not until the 1960s that marketing theorists took up this observation and put it to the test in more conventional marketing settings. A study of convenience-food buying reported by Day in 1971, for instance, confirmed that brand information culled from advertising created the 'preconditions of success' but that the eventual choice decision rested on 'word-of-mouth communications'[9]–in other words, the opinions of personal contacts who already used the brands under consideration.

Other theorists have further speculated that the likelihood of recourse to peer-group opinion varies with the degree of risk perceived to be inherent in the decision. These findings suggest that the role of marketing communications initiatives could be seen as to prompt the solicitation of opinion from peers, while conveying basic information, rather than to precipitate choice directly. This possibility has obvious strategic implications, which observation suggests are not widely recognised.

The balance of power

To postulate that audiences are willing participants with marketing communicators in a transaction poses an important question: how is the balance of power distributed between the two parties? We have already remarked on the apparent belief of marketing commentators that advertising (the most commonly discussed form of marketing communication) is something which relatively powerful advertisers do to relatively powerless audiences. This is not to say they believe that advertisers can sell anything to anybody. On the contrary, whenever charged by critics with 'making people buy things they don't need and shouldn't want', advertising people are quick to point out the very numerous, well-documented cases of heavily advertised new-product failures. Nevertheless, observation of advertisers at work leads to the inescapable conclusion that, to be blunt, they believe they are practising a form of *sorcery*: given auspicious circumstances, copywriters and art directors can weave spells that will bewitch a significant proportion of the audience. This is sorcery rather than science because the sorcerers do not actually know how the effect is achieved. Indeed this very fact explains why researchers have not yet found a dependable way to test the effectiveness of advertising campaigns, as we shall see later. Thoughtful advertising practitioners acknowledge the lack of a sound theoretical base to practice, while the less scrupulous hide behind the trappings of sorcery: bizarre uniforms, arcane jargon and a closed brotherhood. But even those who do not believe their power over the consumer to be absolute, likewise do not really believe that the balance of power is equal. Fundamentally, they expect to do something *to* the audience, not *with* it. To return to the previous analogy: if the spell fails to work, that is because it was cast wrongly, not because the magic is in doubt.

If this deliberately provocative statement of the case seems too extreme, consider the evidence that interested parties on the other side of the fence also subscribe to the view that the advertiser has the whip hand. The Independent Broadcasting Authority's Code of Advertising Standards and Practice forbids the advertising on television of products and services which may be openly sold and promoted in other ways: for instance, 'betting (including pools)', 'fortune tellers and the like' and cigarettes (but not cigars or pipe tobacco). These prohibitions rest on the assumption that television advertising, to a captive audience with its defences down in the security of its own home, could induce normal people to make rash buying decisions with potentially serious consequences. The Advertising Standards Authority cannot similarly prevent non-broadcasting advertisements from appearing, but subjects them to scrutiny against the British Code of Advertising Practice, a document very similar to the IBA's Code, after the event. Consumer activists lobby for the strengthening of direct legislative control over advertising in all media. Their case rests on the assumption, often explicitly stated, that advertising can 'manipulate' ordinary shoppers. In the same vein, political opinion-leaders have claimed that advertising has a 'tendency to over-encourage gross materialism and dissatisfaction',[10] going on to call for tighter controls on the grounds that it causes, rather than encourages, antisocial attitudes.

Thus, a fundamental assumption about the mechanism of marketing communication can be seen to be widely held, though seldom made explicit. Its prevalence among both practitioners and marketing academics was remarked upon twenty years ago by Cox, who dubbed it the 'egotistical view' and forcefully stated his own view that to think of the audience as an inert mass that can be persuaded at will 'exaggerates the power of advertisers and underrates the power and initiative of audiences'.[11] Today, it is apparent that the implicit assumption of a straightforward stimulus–response learning relationship between marketing communicators and their audiences can be severely challenged by a growing body of experimental evidence.

Learning the rules of the game

'Socialisation' is the process by which individuals learn to cope effectively with the challenges of everyday life and thus become competent participants in their own culture, society and community. Ward has coined the term 'consumer socialisation' to express the idea that, throughout life, people steadily 'acquire skills, knowledge and attitudes relevant to their functioning as consumers in the market place',[12] and thereby become effective participants in contemporary consumer society. One of the challenges of everyday consumer life is, of course, to cope with marketing communications initiatives. Ward's thesis is that we all learn–from our parents, our peers, our teachers, the media and many other influences–how to handle advertisements, salespeople, and so on. One might add to his analysis the observation that all such manifestations of marketing communications at work have been part of our collective cultural experience for so long that society has had ample opportunity to learn to cope with them confidently. Posters were advertising booksellers' latest offers to the literate on the temple columns of ancient Greece; medieval town criers habitually inserted paid-for commercial announcements into their 'programme', as radio and television presenters do in the United States today; and commercial television, the advertising medium that most regularly arouses fears of manipulation, celebrated its twenty-fifth anniversary in 1980.

Consumer socialisation is *not* a long process that leaves us vulnerable to marketing communications initiatives throughout childhood and adolescence. Both Ward[13] in the United States and Smith[14] in Britain found, in field investigations, that children begin to discriminate between advertisements and editorial in television programming, evaluate the intent and reliability of the commercials, and resist persuasion at a much earlier age than is generally assumed. The consensus is that discrimination begins at seven or eight years old and the ability to cope with advertising reaches adult standards by the age of fourteen or fifteen. These findings are repeatedly supported and confirmed in an extensive review of the literature by ten American researchers on behalf of the National Science Foundation.[15]

One of the skills that young consumers thus acquire is to 'use' marketing communicators and their initiatives, rather than be used by them. As Figure 6.3 depicted, the communicator is one source of information that can help in decision-making. The skill consists of both recognising that fact and learning to cope with the partisan nature of the communicated information.

Credibility weightings must be allocated to each of the sources of opinion and information exploited at the 'search' stage. Advertising, being perceived as wholly partisan and persuasive in intent, is obviously discounted heavily; sales pitches perhaps even more so. But the unsolicited opinions of friends and neighbours cannot necessarily be taken at face value either. By the process of consumer socialisation, consumers learn not only to use marketing communications but also to erect the barriers of *selective attention and perception* against them when the information is irrelevant or unwelcome. These defence mechanisms are explained more fully in Chapter 4.

Consumers use marketing communications initiatives as more than just decision aids, however. Advertisements, in particular, are used for three other purposes: *entertainment, warranty* and *value-addition*. Though many commentators suggest that we resent the intrusion of advertising into editorial and programme material, casual enquiry soon reveals that people are just as likely to welcome television commercials as cleverly conceived and well-executed relief from the tedium of predictable programmes. Formal surveys over the last two decades[16] have shown that between two-thirds and three-quarters of all respondents in Britain and the United States 'approve' of advertising, and that 'interesting' or 'entertaining' are consistently third among their reasons for doing so. The British surveys also show that respectively about 40 per cent and 50 per cent claim to 'like' press advertisements and television commercials. As for warranty, economists have long recognised that, far from invariably choosing stores' own brands or unbranded goods because they cost less, consumers may prefer the 'tremendous spiritual satisfaction in buying a trusted brand of cocoa–not a shovelful of brown powder of uncertain origin'.[17] Finally, there are good precedents in economic theory for arguing that advertising adds value to many types of product while they are in use. Intuition suggests that the drivers of certain car models, for instance, wish to be seen to be associated with the aura projected to user and non-user alike in the advertisements.

Thus, ordinary people can cope satisfactorily if not perfectly with marketing communications, and initiate the transaction themselves. Advertisers or salespeople do not enjoy the persuasive advantage so often imputed to them by practitioners and commentators. The spectre of manipulation, so frequently raised by critics, is difficult to accept in the light of theory and experimental evidence (except in the important special cases of audiences disadvantaged by lack of education, culture or old age).

We might summarise the argument developed in this section by picturing marketing communications as a form of *game* for two players. There are well-established *rules*, which we learn at an early age. Cheating on the part of the server (the marketing communicator) is detected by a variety of judges, referees and *umpires*–such as the Independent Broadcasting Authority, the Advertising Standards Authority and the many industry trade associations. Consumer-players enjoy the benefit of a *team trainer*, in the shape of the Consumers' Association, and have the option of joining a *club*–their local consumer group. As a last resort, they have recourse to the *law*, via the local government consumer protection service and the Office of Fair Trading. As in all games, *practice* improves performance. The advantage may lie to a certain degree with the server, it is true; but, in this game, the receiver has the option of ignoring the service without losing the game. In all, then, the two parties in the marketing communications transaction are in fact more evenly matched than is generally implied in the literature.

Models of marketing communication

Our finished model of the marketing communication process, re-duced to its simplest form in Figure 6.4, is essentially descriptive; it explains *what* is thought to happen, but not *how*. To be complete, it should attempt verbal and mathematical representation of the mechanisms by which internal and external modifiers operate, the audience processes information and opinion received at the synapse, and the decision is made once the search process is terminated. The first of those considerations is somewhat beyond the scope of this chapter; the basis for answers to that particular question 'how?' will be found in Chapter 4. This section investigates the latter two.

A hierarchy of effects

Textbooks of advertising almost invariably explain what happens at the synapse by describing one or more members of a family of seven *hierarchical models of advertising effect*. These can be thought of as micro-model located within the macro-model just concluded, at the synapse. Table 6.1 presents them in chronological order.[18] Strong's AIDA appeared in his textbook *The Psychology of Selling* and De-Lozier's model in his *The Marketing Communications Process*, remind-ing us that all seven can be seen as general models of marketing communication effect, not specific to advertising. Collectively, they represent an attempt to extend the *stimulus–response model of* adver-

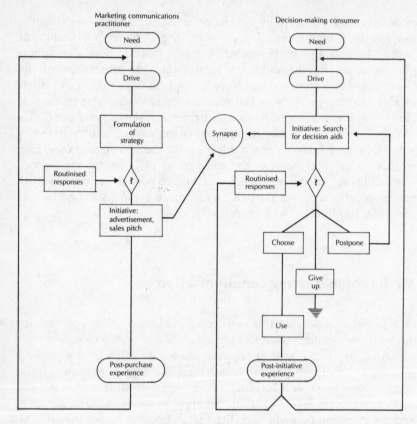

Figure 6.4   The marketing communications transaction

tising effect, by postulating a series of intermediate states between awareness (stimulus) and action (response).

In the original versions, the models were not arranged horizontally, as in Table 6.1, but vertically, to emphasise the concept of a hierarchical series of events. McGuire's took the especially step-wise form of a staircase. Some ran from awareness upwards to action, while others were in exactly the opposite sequence. Table 6.2 rearranges them all into the first of these two vertical models and manipulates the spaces between the steps in the individual hierarchies, to demonstrate unequivocally that they do belong to a single family. It also incorporates the notion, explicitly stated by some of the originators but not the others, that such hierarchies can be related to the three principal categories of mental activity recognised by general psychological theory: *cognitive*, to do with knowledge; *affective*, to do with attitudes; *conative*, to do with motives (alternatively labelled 'behavioural' or 'instrumental'). In this rearrangement, McGuire's and DeLozier's 'retention' steps have been placed at

Table 6.1 Hierarchical models of advertising effect

STARCH, 1923: *to be effective, an advertisement must be...*
seen→read→believed→remembered→acted upon

STRONG, 1925: *AIDA* (a) (b)
attention→interest→desire→action

SANDAGE and FRYBURGER, 1935: *Interaction Model*
exposure→perception→integration→action

LAVIDGE and STEINER, 1961: *Hierarchy of Effects*
awareness→knowledge→liking→preference→conviction→purchase

COLLEY, 1961: *DAGMAR* (c)
unawareness→awareness→comprehension→conviction→action

McGUIRE, 1969: *Information Processing Model*
presentation→attention→comprehension→yielding→retention→behaviour

DeLOZIER, 1976: *Psychological Responses to Advertising*
attention→perception→retention→conviction→action (d)

Notes:
(a) The initials of the four steps.
(b) It is an interesting comment upon the intellectual condition of marketing communications practice that this model was found to be the most widely quoted of the seven in a range of current British, American and French textbooks, despite being first published almost sixty years ago.
(c) Colley's model is always called 'Dagmar', actually the initials of the monograph in which it was first proposed: Defining Advertising Goals for Measured Advertising Results.
(d) DeLozier's model includes a final step, 'post-purchase behaviour', which is omitted here—partly for purposes of comparison and partly because it is not actually a response to advertising but a consequence of action.

different levels because they do not mean the same thing. In describing one task of advertising as 'to facilitate consumer retention of the advertised brand', DeLozier implies the view that retention of the message must precede formation of the intention to purchase. McGuire's model was proposed in a symposium paper which is difficult to trace, but Robertson[19] reports that the term refers in his case to retention of impetus towards action; this is a quite distinct usage.

Critical inspection of Table 6.2 will reveal that terminology, while compatible except for the case just noted, is inconsistent across and within the schemes: labels assigned to steps describe two different sorts of phenomena, which may be indiscriminately mixed within one hierarchy. Therefore, Table 6.3 proposes a distinction between *performance characteristics*, relating to marketing communications initiatives, on the one hand, and *target responses*, relating to the audience, on the other. Simultaneously, it synthesises the twenty-

Table 6.2 The hierarchies as a family of models

Strong	Starch	Sandage and Fryburger	Lavidge and Steiner	Colley	McGuire	DeLozier	
Action	Acted upon	Action	Purchase	Action	Behaviour	Action	Conative
	Remembered				Retention		
Desire	Believed	Integration	Conviction	Conviction	Yielding	Conviction	Affective
			Preference				
			Liking				
Interest	Read	Perception	Knowledge	Comprehension	Comprehension	Retention	Cognitive
						Perception	
Attention	Seen	Exposure	Awareness	Awareness	Attention	Attention	
				Unawareness	Presentation		

Table 6.3 A consolidated hierarchical model of advertising effect

Level	Performance Characteristic	Target Response
VI	Motivation	Action
V	Persuasion	Conviction
IV	Empathy	Sympathy
III	Communication	Comprehension
II	Involvement	Interest
I	Impact	Attention

three separate terminological labels into two sets of six and attaches to those the level numbers I to VI. It is our working model of the models.

Conceptual criticisms

Since the 1960s, hierarchical models of advertising effect have been subject to more or less continuous criticism. Most influential among the critics is Palda,[20] who published a widely reported evaluation of the Lavidge and Steiner model five years after its promulgation. The first of his three most fundamental objections, all based on *a priori* reasoning, is that progression from one step in a hierarchy to the next does not necessarily mean a greater probability of eventual action. His second is that, in particular circumstances such as impulse-buying, the deliberate step-by-step progression implied by the model may actually be 'telescoped'. In similar vein, Copland[21] had earlier reasoned that intermediate steps might well be 'skipped' under certain conditions. Palda's third objection is that he could find no conclusive evidence in the literature for the proposition that affective changes (Level IV responses) necessarily preceded change in behaviour, rather than resulting from it. By thus exposing an untested assumption, he calls into question the very sequence of the hierarchical progression, and hence the stimulus–response basis of the models; his third criticism is certainly the most important of the three.

Throughout the last two decades, Ehrenberg has published empirical findings and theoretical analyses that support Palda's doubts about sequence; Murray[22] provides a useful summary. The field research has been careful and extensive, although it involves a limited range of product categories–commodities such as bread and petrol, and fast-moving consumer goods–and no services. Ehrenberg's view is that, once the decision to try a new product has been arrived at, probably somewhat arbitrarily, and provided the first trial is not an unsatisfactory experience, a stable pattern of reselection develops. The user then deliberately pays attention to advertising for the product (and presumably other marketing communications initiatives), which in turn reinforces the choice. Thus, action (Level VI) determines attention (Level I), which reinforces conviction (Level V). The hierarchy is violated. Ehrenberg and his co-workers have derived a series of mathematical models from their empirical data to express this view more rigorously, and summarised them in a simple verbal model: attention→trial→reinforcement.

Ray[23] takes the argument further by proposing that three variations in hierarchical sequence are possible, according to circumstances:

'Learning'	:	cognitive→affective→conative
'Dissonance-attribution'	:	conative→affective→cognitive
'Low involvement'	:	cognitive→conative→affective

The learning version corresponds to the conventional hierarchical models. He argues that it holds true when the advertising is salient for the audience and there are clear differences among the options available. The dissonance-attribution version, exactly the reverse of the learning version, will apply when the advertising is salient and the differences are small. In such circumstances, choice has to be based on some factor other than advertising; thereafter, attitudes modify in order to reduce dissonance if satisfaction is not delivered in use; finally, cognitive responses to the advertising are rearranged. This is close to Ehrenberg's view. Ray believes the low involvement version applies if salience is low and the differences are small. Low involvement implies lowered perceptual defences, permitting advertising to rearrange cognitions (awareness, recall); when a choice is due, the best remembered option is selected; thereafter, attitudes steadily modify to reinforce the choice. In laboratory experiments, Ray could find evidence for only the first and third variants; the conventional hierarchies thus received some support and the Ehrenbergian version was rejected. A decade earlier, Krugman[24] had argued that what was in fact a 'low involvement' sequence best explained responses to television advertising in particular.

As a final criticism of the seven prevalent hierarchical models (and, indeed, the variants proposed), we might object that they tend to contradict the hypothesis that marketing communication is a transaction, formulated and defended earlier in this chapter. Even with the refinements suggested in Table 6.3, there remains a strong implication that marketing communications initiatives propel passive targets inexorably up a hierarchy of responses and through a sequence of altered behaviour states.

Despite the many objections and variations reported, the conventional 'learning' hierarchies–in particular AIDA, Dagmar and Lavidge and Steiner's–still dominate the frame of reference of typical practitioners and the conceptual frameworks of the better-known textbooks. This is a fact of *practice* which, however questionable on theoretical grounds, has to be accepted as such until a better alternative explanation, sufficiently straightforward and robust to hold the promise of applicability, can be offered to practitioners. For the meantime, the hierarchy of effects at least provides a common, codified and consistent conceptual framework for practitioners. But its ultimate value is determined by degree to which performance characteristics derived from it can be made operational: what do impact, involvement, communication, empathy, persuasion and motivation consist of? The answer must for the present remain, as Palda first recognised, that followers of hierarchical principle do not really know. On balance, then, the consolidated version presented in Table 6.3 may be considered a *useful* conceptual aid but not necessarily a *valid* model.

People as information processors

The preamble to this section stated the intention to investigate how audiences 'process' information and opinion received at the synapse. As we have just seen, the conceptual framework prevailing in the marketing communications business does not actually do that. However, the term itself is a signpost to another direction in social psychology which holds the promise of explaining what the hierarchy only describes: *information processing theory*, in which 'purchase and consumption decisions are viewed in terms of how individuals acquire, organise, and use information'.[25] It is inherent in this approach that consumers–who consume marketing communications as well as products–are not passive 'target audiences' but active seekers and users of information. This reinforces the position already emphatically adopted by this chapter.

Figure 6.5 is a simplified representation of information-processing behaviour, synthesised from several sources. Like Table 6.3, it is a micro-model within the macro-model, located at the synapse. The sequence of information-processing operations is triggered by the

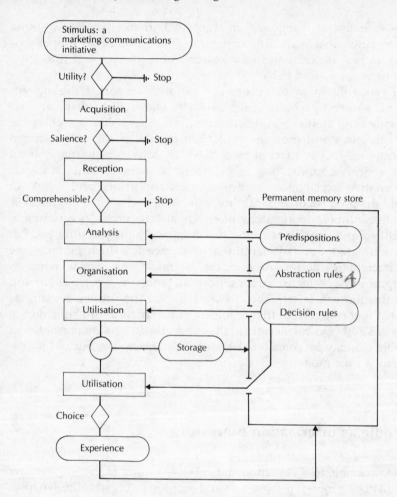

Figure 6.5 Information-processing behaviour

stimulus of a marketing communications initiative. '*Acquisition*' of the available information does not ensue, however, unless its perceived utility is sufficiently high; otherwise, it is simply rejected. The next event in the sequence, '*reception*', follows only if a further criterion is satisfied: that the information is sufficiently salient. If both acquisition and reception are achieved, '*analysis*' can follow provided that the information is in the first place comprehensible; if not, the whole sequence will again be summarily abandoned.

The process of analysis is explained mainly in terms of an operation described as 'rehearsal', which entails association of the comprehended information with previously processed information held in the memory, in order to frame 'support arguments' and 'counterarguments' with respect to the proposition contained in the communication. In other words, the individual is now prepared to self-persuade—or not, as the case may be. The arguments deployed are not developed wholly objectively, but are modulated by 'predispositions' stored in the memory, which are in turn formed by combinations of attitudes, beliefs, personal values and socially conditioned norms of behaviour, and by previous experience relevant to the current communication.

Relevant predispositions may not in fact be available to perform this modulation, for lack of related prior experience or for some other reason. In that case, according to Sternthal and Craig,[26] the information-processing consumer may decide to try the advocated product or service without passing through the remaining stages of the ideal sequence, in order to acquire the necessary experience. This recognition of exceptional situations recalls the variations on the hierarchy-of-effects sequence proposed by Palda, Copland, Ray and Ehrenberg, discussed in the previous section. Presumably, the full cycle of information-processing behaviour will be short-circuited in this way only in conditions of comparatively low risk and price. If short-circuiting does not occur, 'rehearsal' is followed by 'organisation' of the acquired, received and analysed information. The main component of this operation is the process of 'abstraction' in which the mental picture of the product under consideration is enriched by the use of soft cues in the information to infer hard attributes. For example, colour may be used to infer exclusivity or price to infer cheapness in all senses of the word.

'Utilisation' of the organised information follows, the stage at which the totality of processed information held in the memory is manipulated to produce a choice. This is accomplished by the subconscious deployment of a set of four decision rules, which are an innate constituent of human intellectual ability. The 'linear compensatory' rule is an optimising procedure, which consists of scoring all options on every collective attribute judged relevant to the choice. Though easy enough to represent algebraically, this would presumably be an extremely taxing mental task in practice, bearing in mind that it could only be allocated a limited period of mental real-time. The remaining three rules are all satisficing routines and therefore perhaps more realistic. In the 'conjunctive' variant, the total range of attributes is reduced to a manageable number and all options rated on each remaining dimension. The 'disjunctive' rule reduces the number of options to be considered by fixing a threshold level on each dimension and summarily rejecting any which fails to reach that level on any one of them. The most simplified variant, the 'lexicographic' rule, selects one attribute as a more salient criterion than all others and then scores the options on that single dimension only.

When 'utilisation' has been accomplished, the decision-maker proceeds to 'behaviour', according to the textbook expositions of information theory. This implies that the act of consumption inevitably and immediately concludes a single cycle of information processing. But let us now remind ourselves that this chapter is concerned with the consumption of marketing communications initiatives, not of products or services. The former is a prelude to the latter, certainly; but equally the latter is not an immediate consequence of the former. Marketing communications initiatives may be processed and utilised in their own right several times before they are finally used to make a choice among the range of products or services available. Practitioners acknowledge this fact implicitly; for instance, the notion of a necessary minimum number of repeat exposures is one of the main planks of advertising campaign scheduling strategy. Thus, Figure 6.5 shows that 'utilisation' of processed information may result in its *storage* in the memory in its aggregated form, but subsequent retrieval when needed. It is this second utilisation, after a time lapse of indefinite duration, which finally leads to purchase and use of the chosen product or service.

Use provides *experience*, which is in turn stored in the memory and updates the *predispositions* which will influence the process of 'rehearsal' when comparable information is next 'acquired' from a marketing communications initiative. This feedback loop closes and completes our diagrammatic model of information-processing behaviour.

The information-processing model enhances the explanatory power of the hierarchy-of-effects, by suggesting how and why individuals move through a sequence of altered mental states in response to marketing communications messages, but remains entirely compatible with it in so doing. Table 6.4 proposes direct correspondence between four of the five stages in the information-processing model and all six levels of the consolidated hierarchy of effects introduced in Table 6.3. *Acquisition* and *attention* can both be seen as the result of a stimulus satisfying the information-processing criterion of 'utility'; similarly, *reception* and *interest* both imply satisfaction of the criterion of 'salience'. (Sternthal and Craig actually define the reception stage as comprising both 'arousal' and 'attention',[27] the former being a familiar alternative to 'interest' in discussions of the hierarchical principle.) At the *analysis* stage of information processing, the message must first satisfy a 'comprehensibility' criterion, unequivocally relating this stage to the *comprehension* level of the hierarchy. If this test is passed, the process of 'rehearsal' can follow, in which the individual marshals arguments and counterarguments, stimulated by the message, in order to self-persuade (or not); this operation seems clearly enough to correspond to both *sympathy* and *conviction*

Table 6.4 Relationship between information-processing theory and the hierarchy of effects

Stage in information-processing sequence (Figure 6.5)	Level and target response: hierarchy of effects (Table 6.3)
Acquisition	I Attention
Reception	II Interest
Analysis ⎱ (i) Comprehension	III Comprehension
⎰ (ii) Rehearsal	IV Sympathy
	V Conviction
Organisation	
Utilisation	VI Action

in the hierarchical scheme. *Organisation*, in particular the mechanism of 'abstraction', has no direct equivalent in the hierarchy of effects. Finally, *utilisation* corresponds exactly to *action*–provided we recall that the act in question is the consumption and use of marketing communications messages rather than of the product or service to which they refer.

It is now clear that even the most sophisticated available representation of the transaction occurring at the synapse is still firmly rooted in the stimulus–response explanation of human behaviour. What information–processing theory *does* offer is a more complete conceptual framework, more prospect of rendering the constituent concepts operational, a better chance of valid prediction and measurement, and hence more effective strategic planning of marketing communications initiatives. There is one important proviso, however. Audiences do not necessarily use marketing communications only to derive *information*; as we have already seen, they may equally use them for entertainment, warranty or value-addition. In those cases, an alternative explanation of their *modus operandi* is required (and has not so far been offered by marketing communication theorists).

Coping with complexity

When the foundations of present-day practice were being laid, during the 'age of bold enterprise' at the end of the last century, mass consumption was not yet established and the second information explosion (Gutenberg having started the first) had not yet happened. Today, product choice is greatly increased and marketing communications initiatives proliferate relentlessly. Despite all advances in education, the capacity of the human mind has not expanded commensurately; we are intellectually scarcely any better equipped than our grandparents. About twenty years ago, Miller[28] was struck by the fact that human ability to discriminate among related stimuli or memorise inventories was highly consistent across a range of experiments reported by other psychologists: the ceiling on performance was always close to seven separate 'pieces' of information. He was further intrigued by the amount of circumstantial evidence to suggest a general rule. We can distinguish seven colours in the visible spectrum and seven tones in the musical scale; we have fixed the week at seven days; we sort objects into dozens and half-dozens; market researchers' rating scales seldom have more than seven positions; there are ten commandments and seven deadly sins; there are seven examples in this list, which would seem to be too long if it were continued any further. Thus, Miller proposed that the upper limit to the amount of information the mind can handle in any one context is fixed by 'the magical number of seven, plus or minus two'. Despite his excellent academic reputation, we may feel intuitively that the figure is too pessimistic to apply in the marketing situation, when the audience voluntarily seeks out information for decision-making purposes rather than being asked to memorise irrelevant inventories. However, Wright points out that present-day consumers have to operate under considerable general pressure and amid unprecedented communicative hubbub: they are 'harassed decision-makers'.[29] Consequently, they must either go mad or devise some ploy to enable themselves to *cope*. It is an observable fact that the great majority do cope, and information-processing theory provides the framework for explaining how.

The audience's coping strategy is, first, to ignore information that cannot satisfy the criterion of utility, already explained, to reject and forget any 'acquired' information that does not meet the salience criterion, and then to reject any 'received' information that cannot be comprehended. To phrase this in hierarchy-of-effects terms, only a proportion of all marketing communications initiatives will produce the responses of attention, interest and comprehension; to use another familiar terminology, selective attention and perception are at work. These tactics reduce sensory overload to an amount of information that can be stored in the permanent memory and periodically retrieved for the purposes of rehearsal and abstraction. When the time comes for decision-making by aggregation, however, the implication of Miller's and Wright's hypotheses is that the amount of part-processed and stored information will exceed the capacity of the 'current file', and further coping tactics will be needed. The key to their nature lies in how the aggregation rules are deployed: the more complex the decision and the more harassed the decision-maker, the more simple the operation. Indeed, Wright seems to suggest that the marketing situation will almost invariably invoke the brutally simplified *lexicographic* rule, in which choice hinges on how options rate with respect to one attribute only among all those retailed by the competing marketing communications.

Two American advertising practitioners have coined the vivid and highly descriptive phrase 'a ladder in the mind' to describe the outcome.[30] The ladder is labelled with the single product attribute subconsciously rated most important, the competing options are placed on the rungs on the basis of received and organised information, and the one on the top rung is chosen. If it happens not to be available locally or in the preferred colour, the second-rung ocupant will simply be promoted. This explanation is perhaps too draconian for most real situations, however. There is ample evidence that consumers view brands not as unidimensional entities, but as multidimensional. It seems more likely, in that case, that the *conjunctive* aggregation rule will be employed first: the mind will create a limited number of separate ladders, each labelled with one of the attributes common to the brands under consideration, and the options will be independently ranked on all of them. Figure 6.6

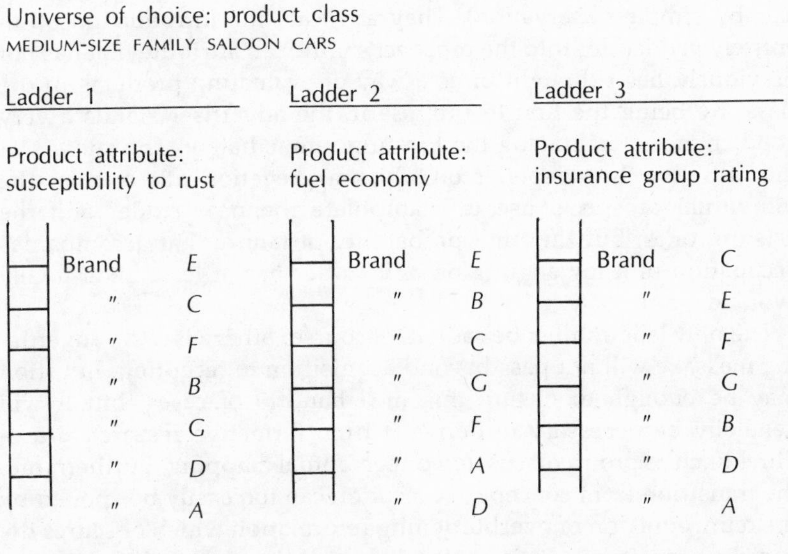

Universe of choice: product class
MEDIUM-SIZE FAMILY SALOON CARS

Ladder 1		Ladder 2		Ladder 3	
Product attribute: susceptibility to rust		Product attribute: fuel economy		Product attribute: insurance group rating	
Brand	E	Brand	E	Brand	C
"	C	"	B	"	E
"	F	"	C	"	F
"	B	"	G	"	G
"	G	"	F	"	B
"	D	"	A	"	D
"	A	"	D	"	A

Figure 6.6   Coping with information overload: 'ladders in the mind'

illustrates the hypothetical case of choosing among competing car models. The 'ladders' configuration may be held in the permanent memory store and revised periodically as salient information is newly received, or it may be used immediately. In either event, the final choice seems likely to be made by employing either the *disjunctive* rule, which reduces the complexity by removing from contention the contenders on the lower rungs of the existing ladders, or the *lexicographic*. We can intuitively agree with Wright that, given the surfeit of information available to prospective car purchasers, *linear compensatory* aggregation is out of the question. This analysis has thus added to the previous description of information-processing theory the notion that aggregation rules may be deployed in combination and episodically.

The general principles of information processing are not straight-forwardly applicable to marketing communications practice. General cognitive theory predicts that rank order of preference, once estab-lished, will be highly resistant to reordering by outside agencies such as marketing communications initiatives. Case history repe-atedly supports this prediction: several examples are reported in a recent journal article on advertising strategy, which is implicitly based on information-processing theory.[31] This being so, head-on competition as a marketing communications tactic is unlikely to persuade individual prospects to rearrange the ladders in their minds. Lateral thinking on the part of the originators of the concept has suggested a radical alternative to the locked-horns school of advertising strategy (which can readily be confirmed as very preva-lent by simple observation). They advocate the introduction of an entirely *new* ladder into the prospect's mind: an attribute that has not previously been thought of as a way of evaluating products in the class. By being the first to propose it, the advertiser stands a very good chance of capturing the top rung immediately. The success of the initiative then depends on which aggregation rule or rules the individual prospects use to manipulate the new ladder and the existing ones, but the high probability of failure that accompanies occupation of a lower rung on any ladder has at least been totally avoided.

The new ladder must be salient, of course; otherwise, the advertis-ing message will not pass beyond acquisition to reception. Intuition may be enough to ensure this in a handful of cases, but it will generally be necessary to derive it from formative research proce-dures such as group discussion or perceptual mapping. Furthermore, the transition from concept to execution can too easily be spoiled by the reintroduction of overburdening information which obscures the basic proposition. It is a fundamental lesson of information-processing theory that advertising (or a sales pitch, for that matter) should be used like a rapier, not as a blunt instrument with which to batter the audience senseless. This conclusion clearly contradicts the conventional wisdom of the advertising business with respect to our working example, cars.

The Avis Rent-a-Car advertising campaign of the 1970s provides an instructive case example of an implemented new-ladders strategy.[32]

In this section we have seen that the hierarchy of effects is the almost universal conceptual model, among practitioners, of what happens at the communicator–audience synapse. On its own, it encourages the 'egotistical' view of marketing communications and does not adequately explain how consumers use the practitioners' initiatives. Information-processing theory elaborates the hierarchical concept and renders much of it potentially operational. It is thus a promising underpinning for marketing communications strategy and deserves to be more widely studied by practitioners.

Recent texts: another model

Until recently, advertising and sales management texts generally explained the process of persuasion in straightforward stimulus–response terms. One or more of the familiar hierarchical models would be described and discussed; explanations of attention, perception, cognition and learning were usually inconclusively bolted on to the basic framework. In the last half-dozen years, specialist texts have appeared that are devoted to theoretical explanation of persuasive effect as a basis for the formulation of strategy, rather than to simple description of the tasks of advertising or sales management. Very recently, the generalist texts of advertising management have begun to follow the lead of the specialist texts. To serve as an organising principle in place of the hierarchy of effects, these have resuscitated early models of mass communication, summed up well by Laswell's verbal version: 'who says what in which channels to whom and with what effect?'.[33] The result has been chapter schemes such as the selection, drawn from three texts of this type,[34] in Table 6.5. It is interesting that these ostensibly academic treatments in fact adopt a markedly practitioner-oriented stance. In none of them does the 'receiver' figure as anything other than a target; the implicit assumption that advertisers impose communications on audiences is once again very clear.

Table 6.5   Framework for explanation of advertising effect, post–1976

Lasswell 1960	DeLozier 1976	Percy and Rossiter 1980	Aaker and Myers 1982
	'A Marketing Communications Model' and 'Communicator Parameters'	'Advertising Communication Variables'	'A Model of the Advertising Communication System'
Who?	Source	Source factors	Source
Says what?	Message	Message strategy	Message
In which channels?	Channel variation parameter	Media selection	Channel
To whom?	Receiver	Receiver selection	Receiver
	Temporal parameter	Scheduling strategy	

For present purposes, let us consolidate the schemes in the table into five factors that influence audience response to a marketing communications initiative:

audience effects
message effects
source effects
channel effects
time effects

Audience effects

Under the first of these headings, the texts typically first draw upon the literature of general social psychology for a list of determinants of *attention*. Selectivity of attention is then treated in some detail because, from the firm's point of view, it represents an obstacle to effective communication; Schramm's formula[35] is widely reported as an operational means of assessing the probability that an initiative will or will not win attention. Span of attention is also discussed, in relation to the longstanding conflict in practice among proponents of long and short copy. They do not subject to scrutiny the equally durable assumption among practitioners that the audience's natural predisposition during television commercial breaks is to leave the room in order to perform a variety of routine tasks. This is unfortunate, since British survey findings that contradict it have been available since 1977.[36]

After attention, the texts typically list determinants of *perception* and then explain the concepts of perceptual set, perceptual defence and perceptual vigilance. After that, the determinants of *cognitive* performance are usually discussed. Emphasis on perception and cognition does have direct practical applicability. Creative strategists recognise the possibility that their audience may perceive the content and treatment of their initiatives in an unexpected way, or may not *decode* the message as was intended. They should therefore be interested in the factors responsible for such gaps between intent and outcome. To take one example, consider the effect of social class on the reception of advertisements. Advertising people are mostly male and belong to the top two grades of the sixfold socioeconomic scale: they are 'ABs' in marketing parlance, or grades I and II to sociologists. Their target audience, on the other hand, is very often female and typically belongs to the next three grades: C1, C2 and D. These realities are reflected in authentic reports of quite startling gaps between conception and perception.[37] Unfortunately, the general principles enunciated in the texts are seldom rendered operational; that task is left to the reader.

The next 'audience effect' to receive attention is generally *persuasibility*. This is another vital topic, since practice is noticeably based on half-explicit assumptions about the relative susceptibility of different target audiences to persuasion. Two determinants, sex and age, figure prominently in the discussion. Research studies are reported that found women to be more persuasible than men. Examination of the original sources reveals two serious shortcomings, however: first, the studies were all conducted twenty or more years ago; second, they all involved persuasion in a social setting, not a marketing context. But advertisers seem to accept the proposition without question, whether as a result of reading the texts or intuitively, to judge by the almost universal practice of using male 'voice-over' in television and radio commercials directed at women. Where age is concerned, the texts are likely to take three studies in social communication conducted more than fifty years ago (plus, perhaps, the more recent research into the susceptibility of children mentioned earlier in this chapter) as the basis for a bold assertion that persuasibility decreases steadily with age. Common sense suggests that a plateau is in fact reached early in adulthood and that the elderly may well be more rather than less persuasible. Relevant new research is needed.

The lists of factors determining attention, perception and persuasibility can be divided in each case into one category relating to characteristics of the marketing communications initiative in question (stimulus variables) and another to characteristics of the audience (individual variables). Sex and age are clearly examples of the latter. The complete lists of individual variables for each of the three phenomena are in fact very similar; one could certainly deduce from the text treatment of various rag-bags of psychological concepts—such as needs, attitudes, beliefs, personality, IQ, self-esteem and many others—that a general-purpose inventory of determinants of human behaviour can be compiled and used in practice. The most recent text of the three under review here tentatively acknowledges the fundamental precept of information-processing theory by suggesting as an individual variable 'willingness to search for and/or process information'.[38] This chapter has taken the view, of course, that such willingness is axiomatic; it is ability that will vary. The determinants of that variability might usefully be deduced from the general-purpose inventory and experimentally tested.

Finally, treatment of audience effect typically discusses demographic and psychographic *segmentation*. It is far from clear to the casual reader how this topic fits into the overall scheme. We may presume the authors have in mind that the procedure provides an operational means for reducing the possibility that an initiative will fail to gain a target audience's attention because of inappropriate choice of channel, and of increasing the probability that it will—to use information-processing theory terminology—satisfy the criteria of utility and salience.

The length of this sub-section may suggest that the treatment of audience effects by contemporary texts is thorough, albeit disorganised and susceptible to conceptual criticisms. On the contrary, the ingredients are typically integrated very weakly into the general frameworks and hardly related to one another at all.

Message effects

Message formulation is the only part of the marketing communication process that is wholly under the sender's control, and is thus dealt with in considerable detail by the managerially oriented texts. This is all to the good; too often, in practice, ignorance of theoretical principles permits this aspect of the creative process to develop a logic of its own, with the consequence that the resulting formulations do not transmit the message accurately, completely or, perhaps, even at all. The constituent topics are normally message codes, message appeals and message structure.

(A) CODING

Drawing upon the abundant literature of social communication, the various authors describe the principles of verbal and 'nonverbal' or 'paralinguistic' coding. The former entails study of denotative and connotative meanings of words and phrases; the latter concerns modulation of verbal meaning by such agencies as tone of voice, cadence, personal appearance and 'body language'. Manifestly absent from text treatments are three non-human coding elements: typography, colour and sound-effects (including music). The omission is almost certainly accounted for by the fact that the source literature concerns itself exclusively with social persuasion, in which those elements are either absent altogether or relatively insignificant. A field experiment reported in the marketing literature compares recall and intention-to-purchase in test subjects exposed to respectively black-and-white and colour-monochrome press advertisements for a canned food,[39] and a paper on advertisements directed at children theorises that jingles work by enhancing participation.[40] Otherwise, empirical evidence is not easily found.

There is a serious need for examination of the literature of graphic design and musical composition, to suggest preliminary hypotheses about the *modus operandi* of these *adjunctive* codes, and marketing-specific experiments to test them. The lack of a theoretical basis for this aspect of message formulation has two unsatisfactory practical consequences: first, strikingly arbitrary use of typography and music in many advertisements and television commercials (less obvious in the case of radio); second, a marked bias towards copy at the expense of design in many advertising agencies' creative departments.

(b) APPEALS

The texts deal with this topic in terms of the very familiar dichotomy between 'rational' and 'emotional', with its roots in the Aristotelean concepts of pathos and logos. Evidence for the relative effectiveness of the two turns out to be equivocal, to say the least. Only four empirical investigations are cited by the three texts collectively. These were conducted between 1935 and 1960, all in a non-marketing context. Two contradict one another and the other two come to no firm conclusion. It is observable that advertisers and salespeople can seldom resist the temptation to deploy an emotion appeal, even within an ostensibly rational argument. Yet there is a general problem with this strategy, explained by Percy and Rossiter[41] with particular respect to the fear, that the relationship between the strength of an emotional appeal and its effectiveness is non-linear;

both weaker and stronger expressions of the appeal are less effective, for different reasons.

Only two categories of emotional appeal are discussed in the texts: fear and humour. Sex-appeal and snob-appeal, both easily observable in advertisements and sales promotion material, are not acknowledged. Where fear appeals are concerned, a study by Janis and Feshbach[42] seems to have found a permanent place in advertising folklore, despite a far more recent investigation by Ray and Wilkie[43] that contradicted it. The former concluded, on the basis of experiments involving messages about dental hygiene delivered by 'live' presenters to a student audience, that effectiveness had an inverse linear relationship to the strength of the appeal. Advertising-specific experiments by the latter led them to conclude that 'moderate' fear appeals would be most effective. A conceptual weakness of any such studies, not generally mentioned in the authors' reviews, is the difficulty of grading the strength of a fear appeal objectively. There is certainly room for doubt that Janis and Feshbach's 'strong' appeals were in fact any stronger than Ray and Wilkie's 'moderate' appeals.

Many case examples that have been widely disseminated verbally demonstrate remarkably convoluted efforts to avoid any hint of an appeal to fear in advertisements for toothpaste, air travel and life assurance. In contrast, the Scottish Health Education Group used an unarguably strong fear appeal in a 1979 anti-smoking advertisement: 'ashes to ashes', with reinforcing graphics. Pre-testing showed that the appeal evoked correspondingly strong perceptual defences of selective misperception or, if that was countered by changing some elements of the design, wilful rationalisation. The researchers note that the negative nature of the action demanded—'stop smoking' instead of, for example, 'brush your teeth'—complicate the conclusions to be drawn.[44]

In the case of humour as an appeal, the texts report a careful review of the literature by Sternthal and Craig,[45] which led them to mainly negative conclusions: that humorous treatments are no more persuasive than serious versions of the same message and may detrimentally affect comprehension. Their only definitely positive finding was some evidence that humour could 'distract' the audience from rehearsing counterarguments. Despite this, humour remains a very popular ingredient of marketing communications in practice—including sales pitches, if in moderation.

The Scottish Health Education Group adopted a humorous approach for its first 'general life style' advertising campaign in 1978. This was a deliberate decision, based not on the notion of distraction but on the accepted psychological explanation of laughter as a means of releasing tension. Their researchers conceded that conceptualisation of the mechanism is again rendered more complicated by the fact that the message is negative: don't behave this way if you value your health.[46]

Although sex-appeal is not treated by the texts under review, some relevant studies have been conducted.[47] (A great deal more has been written, neither based on empirical research nor deduced from theory.) Most researchers set out to relate sex-appeals of graded intensity in advertisements to audience responses such as awareness, recall, perceived quality of the product and perceived reputability of the advertiser; a few tried to identify the components of sex-appeal; none successfully addressed the question of how the appeal achieved its effect. This lack of applicable knowledge notwithstanding, it can easily be observed that sex-appeals are at least as usual in practice as fear or humour appeal. They are especially common in advertising and sales promotion for industrial products and services, where relevance to their nature and use is not part of the rationale.

(c) Structure

Message effect is not only a question of content but also of structure. Under this heading, the texts under review examine 'polarity', 'order' and 'completion'. *Polarity* is treated in terms of the relative persuasiveness of one-sided versus two-sided arguments. Research studies conducted almost forty years ago by Hovland and his colleagues[48] are cited in support of the proposition that persuasiveness is mediated by audience characteristics such as general intellectual capacity and initial stance on the issue in question. What is seldom made clear enough is that the original experiments involved arguments about military tactics and an audience of soldiers. A more recent study, reported by one text only, did involve advertisements for cars, cookers and floor polishes.[49] But the test audience was students, who would not normally be experienced users of such products. In any case, observation of current advertising suggests that the two-sided variant is almost never used in practice; presumably the fear of being seen to own up to weaknesses outweighs any knowledge of the possible benefits of two-sided argumentation. This objection can be expected to apply equally to sales pitches.

Order concerns 'recency' versus 'primacy', or the relative persuasiveness of 'climax' and 'anticlimax' order: respectively saving the best argument to the end or putting it at the beginning. The authors report that 'Lund's Law of Primacy in Persuasion' ruled unchallenged from 1925 until the 1950s, when a burst of experimentation identified such intervening variables as interest, familiarity, salience and the nature of the topic. Rosnow and Robinson[50] finally concluded, on the basis of all available evidence, that climax order is indicated if the intervening variables are positive, anticlimax order if not. In practice, one suspects that advertising copy is conceived by copywriters as a 'story' rather than an 'argument'. Stories conventionally build to a climax or denouement; advertising copy does likewise in imitation and not because of Rosnow and Robinson. Sales pitches, on the other hand, probably can be thought of as arguments, and the classic experiments will have more relevance.

It is noticeable that the texts devote no attention at all to visual order–that is, disposition of the graphic elements of an advertise-ment or sales promotion piece. This unfortunately reinforces the verbal bias of practitioners, already noted. As in the case of visual coding, exploitation of source literature in the graphic design field is urgently needed.

Completion concerns the relative persuasive merits of leaving an argument open-ended and drawing an explicit conclusion. Several experimental studies conducted between the 1950s and the 1970s are cited, including a second series by Hovland and colleagues;[51] again, none took place in a marketing context. The general conclusion is, as before, that intervening variables mediate the response. A 'rule' is offered, that arguments should be closed when intellectual capacity is low, complexity high and salience low.

One is obliged to be sceptical about the applicability of the reported empirical evidence to marketing communications practice, because almost all the experiments involved neither marketing communications initiatives as stimuli nor typical consumers as audiences. Two further objections relate especially to advertisements and may not invalidate transfer of the general findings to the formulation of sales pitches, publicity releases or sales promotion pieces. First, they do not typically deploy arguments of the sort presented on such topics as military tactics or dental hygiene; the concepts of polarity, order and completion prove difficult to apply in practice. Second, a high proportion of all advertisements contain relatively little 'copy'. Posters generally rely on headlines only, and one famous campaign of the last four years has used no words at all (Benson & Hedges Special Filter). In these cases, the concepts are wholly inapplicable. Even in real examples with more wording, practical exercises with our own students have shown that message structures defy analysis according to theoretical principles. The practical relevance to advertising copywriting of the texts under consideration must therefore be severely limited. For the present, there is no body of theoretical knowledge that might permit scientific evaluation of such prevalent structural fashions as: ultra-short sent-ences, artificially punctuated; 'clever' headlines; boastful straplines; introverted style; arbitrary line-breaks.

Before finally leaving the subject of message effects, let us take note of a new development in *coding* practice, too recent to be yet in the texts but reported in a management journal.[52] In France, a computer program has been used to analyse the linguistic content of (i) product descriptions in advertising copy (ii) users' descriptions of the same products (iii) non-users' descriptions, and thereby to identify 'core words', 'plus words' and 'minus words'. Advertising copy and sales representatives' pitches relating to the product in question are then modified by removing minus words altogether, maximising plus words and substituting core words for alternative descriptions throughout. It is claimed by the originator that this 'language analysis' procedure can 'develop a sure-fire selling message'. Judgement of its practical feasibility and usefulness must be suspended for the present through lack of crucial details, except to express the serious reservation that the computer cannot take account of connotations conferred by context, the mediating influence of non-verbal codes or the effect of structure on cognition.

Source effects

Under this heading, the three texts introduce the intuitively reasonable proposition that an audience's response is determined not only by its own characteristics and those of the message but also by its perception of the source of the message. Most of the empirical evidence cited in support of generalisations about source effect consists of experiments in persuasive *social* communication. In these cases, the source of the message is always clearly either a person or an organisation represented by a speaker. In marketing communication, the source can be ambiguous, even compound. It may perhaps be seen as a firm, a presenter (or sales representative), an actor playing a part, the brand itself, or some combination of these. Counterproductive interaction is a distinct possibility in practice. Social-communication experimenters furthermore assume that a target audience will rate a source either credible or not. In the marketing context, the audience can be expected to rate the source neither wholly credible nor wholly non-credible, and a sliding scale of credibility must be visualised. The literature does not recognise this shortcoming of its source material.

There is general agreement that source effect has three components, though terminological confusion can make it seem that more are postulated. These are 'credibility', 'attractiveness' and 'power'. It is argued that source *credibility* operates by evoking a response of 'internalisation' on the audience's part: the source's perceived values and behaviour are accepted and in part adopted. The consensus of an extensive literature, in which Hovland and various fellow-researchers again figure prominently, is that credibility is determined by perceived 'expertise' and perceived 'objectivity' (often called 'trustworthiness').

Expertise must be relevant, of course. When a company or salesperson is seen to be the source, this will not generally pose a problem; when a presenter intervenes, as in much television advertising, there is a strong chance that it will. For instance, in class analysis of recent press and television advertising, our students perceived Stirling Moss (Audi) fully expert, did not accept at all that David Niven (Maxwell House) was the expert he explicitly claimed to be, and perceived Andre Previn (Ferguson) to be expert in music but not in electronic systems for producing it. Perceptions of financial vested interest further 'muddied' judgements in these and other case examples. Thus, this credibility dimension is by no means as straightforward in practice as it appears in social communication theory.

Where objectivity is concerned, the reported finding of empirical studies (not conducted in a marketing setting) is that sometimes 'blatant attempts to persuade are more effective in producing change in attitude or behavior than the more "commonsense" notion of minimising persuasive intent'.[53] This is just as well for the formulators of sales pitches, of course, and good news for advertisers. Three experiments from the 1960s are further reported to have surprisingly found that generally low-credibility sources were more effective persuaders than high-credibility sources.[54] They were not conducted in a marketing context either, however, and it would be a rash marketing communicator who adopted a deliberate low-credibility strategy.

Source *attractiveness* is thought to operate by evoking a response of 'identification' on the audience's part. Reported empirical investigations concern the attractiveness of persons, not organisations. It is a moot question whether or not people in fact assess companies as attractive or unattractive and will identify with them or not, but there is evidence that advertisers do think so: 'friendly' building societies and 'caring' stores. The use of presenters may also be interpreted as a tactic to provide the audience with a human surrogate with which to identify. The consensus of an extensive literature, again exclusively non-marketing, is that source attractiveness is determined by perceived 'similarity' and 'familiarity'. Observation suggests that presenters and endorsers are seldom similar to the target audience. We may therefore extend the original argument by postulating that they represent an ideal self or fantasy self. As for familiarity, the evidence contradicts the old adage that it breeds contempt; this is an encouraging rationale for recall as an advertising objective, repetition as a scheduling strategy and persistence in a salesperson. A study by Zimbardo and others[55] which unexpectedly showed that an unattractive source is more persuasive is widely quoted. Before this is taken as vindication of the Procter and Gamble school of television advertising, it should be noted that the experiment actually involved 'persuasion' to eat fried grasshoppers by strong authority figures.

Source *power* evokes the response of compliance. At first sight, it seems unlikely that advertisers or salespeople could wield power over an audience, but the instruments of power are punishment and reward, and it is the latter that can be relevant in the marketing context. Furthermore, the almost universal use of male presenters to female advertising audiences may be a subconsciously executed power ploy, given the power accorded to men by the social conditioning of women in many sections of society.

There is an evident possibility of conflict among the components of source effect in practice; high credibility might coincide with low attractiveness, for instance. If so, there is non-marketing empirical evidence that attractiveness prevails.[56] On the other hand, it seems equally reasonable to expect synergy if the combinations are right.

Before finally leaving the topic of source effect, it will be as well to re-emphasise a caveat introduced into the discussion at several stages: virtually every one of the empirical studies on which the authors under review have based their theoretical explanations of marketing communication and their consequent strategic frameworks was concerned with *social* persuasion. Percy and Rossiter's 363-item bibliography contains only thirty-six references specific to *marketing* persuasion, or exactly 10 per cent, for instance. The texts thus rest extremely heavily on an assumption of the transferability of findings from the one context to the other.

Triads

Interaction between audience and source, as explained in the texts under review, does not take place *in vacuo*, but is modified by reactions to the product or service that the source advocates. The interaction is 'triadic' rather than 'dyadic'. Indeed, the picture can be further complicated by perceptions of the vehicle in which the message is conveyed (the subject of the next section) or by the introduction of an endorser into the equation. The texts do not deal with this complication well, if at all. The key to understanding the resolution of these many forces lies in *cognitive consistency theory*. We lack the space to explain it adequately here, but Lowe Watson[57] provides a complete and conveniently accessible explanation, specifically related to advertising.

Channel effects

If it can be shown that an audience's response to a marketing communications initiative is affected by perceptions of the credibility, attractiveness and power of the source, it is reasonable to propose that it will similarly be mediated by perceptions of the channel through which it is transmitted–for example, the media vehicle or the sales representative. Indeed, some authors regard these channels as one of several sources recognised by the audience, or alternate between treating them as channels and as sources.[58] Channel effect is also one main theme of McLuhan's essay, 'The Medium is the Message',[59] a cult success of the 1960s that has been surprisingly neglected by marketing academics. A recent survey of American practitioners demonstrated strong majority agreement with the statement that 'the attitudes of readers toward a magazine can greatly influence their reaction to advertisements in it'.[60] In practice, British media planners certainly accept the message-modifying potential of vehicles in the channel, implicitly, when they use such adjectives as 'relaxed', 'urgent' or 'chatty' to describe types of newspaper,[61] or discuss 'media values' and 'rub-off effects' in their professional journals.[62] Nevertheless, the virtual absence of an organised body of formalised knowledge, such as does exist in the case of source effect, obliges practitioners to make media selections 'on the basis of intuition and folklore'.[63]

Authors who do discuss the components of media effect generally deduce them by analogy with source effect. Aaker and Myers suggest 'unbiasedness', 'expertise', 'prestige' and 'mood created',[64] while Percy and Rossiter offer 'identification', which is the response corresponding to 'attractiveness' as a dimension of source credibility.[65] McLuhan's celebrated 'hot/cool' categorisation refers to the degree to which media involve their audience, from which a 'power' component might be deduced. Consolidating, we find a familiar trio: credibility (unbiasedness, expertise, prestige), attractiveness and power. There is empirical evidence only for the first of these. It has been found that: doctors were more influenced by editorial in technical journals than by the same material in general magazines, a finding relevant to publicity initiatives; media planners rated medical journals very differently on sixteen attributes related to media effect; high-prestige magazines had a more positive effect on 'consumers' evaluations of promotional messages' than low-prestige magazines; housewives' perceptions of the expertise and prestige of general magazines affected their perceptions of the expected price, quality and reliability of advertised products.[66] All four studies relate to press advertising or editorial, but it is reasonable to suggest that response to television or radio commercials could be similarly mediated by perceptions of surrounding programmes or by the images of the respective television stations (sixteen in Britain as we go to press–fourteen ITV stations plus Channel 4 and TV-am–but many more soon, with the arrival of widescale cable television and dish-receiver reception of continental stations). Only the former variable has been investigated, in the United States; a marked effect was measured.[67] Much more field research is needed before generalisations are possible.

The dearth of experimental support for the reviewed explanations of source effect is explained by the fact, becoming a tiresome truism in this chapter, that the authors have drawn mostly upon the literature of *social* persuasion. In that context, no channel vehicles intervene–or, at least, none with obvious mediating potential. It is not entirely clear whether no marketing-specific research has in fact been carried out, or whether it has but is not yet reported in the texts and journals.

Time effects

Advertisements do not normally appear once only, but in *campaigns*; this is even true of most recruitment advertising and 'small ads'. The object may be to maximise numbers in the audience who have a chance to see the advertisement at least once, to expose at least some of them to it more than once, or to present a series of different treatments of the message in sequence. In all typical situations, then, part of the audience will be exposed more than once during a given period. Furthermore, although retail sales assistants may expect to close the sale or lose it in a single transaction, field sales representatives normally expect to make more than one call on each prospect. Consider two more facts: that sales promotion initiatives, such as calendars or bookmarks, may well be referred to repeatedly over a period, and that editorial resulting from a publicity initiative is very often kept for future reference if the topic is especially salient. For all these reasons, a single marketing communications initiative must be conceptualised as one episode in a series of events, and it is reasonable to postulate that audience response will therefore be subject to *time* effects, as well as being mediated by audience, message, source and channel characteristics. The mechanics of learning, remembering and forgetting thus assume theoretical importance. While the texts under review do recognise the time effect and deal with the relevant phenomena, it is the least successfully integrated of the five effects in all three cases.

One way to describe the objective of a marketing communications initiative is that the audience should *learn* new behaviour as a result. Therefore, the texts devote a good deal of attention to learning theory, on which there is an abundant source literature. One factor worth singling out from a mass of detail is the theoretical principle that rewards reinforce learning. In the advertising context, this may provide a straightforward rationale for two particular creative strategies which always precipitate prolonged and usually inconclusive discussion. The rewards offered by 'teaser' campaigns and 'puzzle' advertisements[68] are participation and, upon successful decoding, self-esteem. Similarly, humorous advertisements may offer the reward of entertainment, an alternative to the explanation put forward in the discussion of message appeals. It is a moot point whether or not purchase is the change of behaviour learned as a result of being rewarded, however.

The texts explain that learned responses are not permanent, because of simple forgetting ('decay', in advertising terminology) and the retroactive inhibiting effect of intervening events. Marketing communication strategies for gaining repeat exposure can thus be seen as having the fundamental purpose of reinforcing learning by counteracting the effect of both phenomena. This statement is slightly complicated by the findings of field experiments into perceptions of source credibility by Hovland and various colleagues in the 1940s and 1950s,[69] in the context of social persuasion, which are reported in detail in two of the three texts. These compared initial audience agreement with high- and low-credibility presenters to agreement after an elapsed period, with and without re-exposure. A second exposure had the predictable effect of comparatively increasing sympathy with the high-credibility source and comparatively reducing agreement with the low-credibility source. This so-called 'sleeper effect' leads DeLozier to the astonishing conclusion that 'companies with less financial resources may be just as well off to use a low-credibility source (who presumably would cost less to hire)...and to advertise less frequently'.[70] It would be a foolhardy advertiser who deliberately chose these tactics, rather than making the effort to improve credibility by corrective operations on other marketing mix variables and following up with frequent affirmative marketing communications initiatives.

Returning to the effects of repetition, uncomplicated by considerations of source or message effect, we find that the first attempt to relate the *scheduling* of advertisements to learning theory was made as long ago as 1912 by Strong,[71] later to originate the AIDA hierarchy-of-effects model. The principal finding of his laboratory experiments was that an optimum scheduling interval could be identified, beyond which forgetting would occur between exposures but below which no improvement in recall (his measure of learning) could be detected. This pioneering work was eventually taken up forty-seven years later by Zielske,[72] whose carefully controlled field experiment initiated a whole series of related studies and led ultimately to formulation of the concepts of *threshold* and *wearout*. It is postulated that no learning takes place until a threshold level of 'advertising pressure'–number of repetitions within a given period. Thereafter, learning is progressive and new behaviour patterns–such as search, trial and purchase–may result, until a saturation level is reached beyond which each repeat exposure produces fewer new learned responses than the previous one. This is the wearout phenomenon. It is easily confused with simple forgetting, but the latter is a function of the passage of time alone, while the former is related to advertising pressure.

The twin concepts are clarified diagrammatically in a thorough literature review by Corkindale and Newall,[73] who also undertook a field survey to investigate their applicability to media scheduling practice in Britain in the mid-1970s. They found that both concepts were seen as salient by more than 80 per cent of respondents, most of whom nevertheless seemed to use informed guesses to fix advertising pressure in terms of OTS or TVRs (measures of potential exposure), or cost. The majority did not think they would ever enjoy a budget large enough to run the risk of wearout; the researchers disagree, believing that the onset of wearout is earlier than their respondents' guesses, and suggest that many advertisers actually waste a significant fraction of their budgets on counterproductive repetition.

Sixty-two years after E. K. Strong's initial impetus, E. C. Strong[74] combined Zielske's data with his own, devised a set of regression equations, ran a computer simulation of various scheduling patterns and concluded that recall was highest when repetitions were spaced in 'flights' rather than in a continuous series. These two patterns correspond to media planners' alternative strategies, 'burst' and 'drip'.

Since the early 1970s, several computer programs have been developed for scheduling media campaigns, the best known probably being the earliest: MEDIAC.[75] It is important to be clear that the scheduling decision should in practice take account of several variables, among which are competitors' past and future schedules, seasonality, media owners' discount terms, creative treatment and conventional practice. Since none of the software packages in fact incorporates all of these, they should be used only as an aid to decision-making and not as decision-makers. With that caveat, and supposing that computer assistance is a feasible option, it certainly enhances the traditional practices: drawing on past experience, imitating or adapting conventional practice, buying media owners' off-the-peg solutions, or making symmetrical patterns on a scheduling grid.

Five-way interaction

It is intuitively reasonable to hypothesise that audience, message, source, channel and time effects interact–perhaps synergistically, perhaps destructively. The texts do not consider this possibility at all, and there seem to be no experimental findings that might suggest relative weighting coefficients for the five variables in such an equation.

Measuring effectiveness

To conclude a long chapter on a complex subject, we turn to a final important issue: the measurement of effectiveness. The discussion that follows relates mainly to the considerable inventory of techniques used to evaluate advertising; by comparison, other classes of marketing communications initiative are hardly tested for effectiveness at all.

As in any field of activity, this should be a matter of comparing actual results with *criteria* derived from pre-determined *objectives*. Advertising effectiveness is seldom measured so scientifically, however, despite Colley's famous 'DAGMAR' statement more than twenty years ago.[76] This is quite simply the consequence of a very widespread failure among practitioners to state relevant and measurable objectives in the first place, which is often reported in the literature[77] and can be readily verified by informal survey. Without objectives, there are no criteria. In their absence, practitioners use a limited number of off-the-peg, standardised procedures.

Inspection of the inventories of advertisement testing procedures listed in a typical text[78] reveals to the quizzical reader that they can all be related to an implicit *hierarchical model* of advertising effect. Neither authors of texts nor research practitioners make explicit that quite fundamental conceptual underpinning, but this section will shortly demonstrate that advertisement testing procedures in common use do indeed correspond to one of the hierarchical *performance characteristics* set out in Table 6.3. The advertisements in question are thus required to 'pass a test', quite literally, rather than to satisfy specific criteria of effectiveness derived from specific objectives. (The celebrated American advertising agency chief, Bill Bernbach, is reputed to have said: 'The client wants some research, so cut him a yard of it'.) If this proposition is valid and advertisement testing is in fact presented as being much more precise and scientific than it actually is, that is a highly critical shortcoming of advertising practice–which the great majority of practitioners either do not or will not recognise.

At the lowest level of the hierarchy of effects, we find the performance characteristic *impact*, with the accompanying target response of *attention*. Much advertising research effort is directed in practice at measuring these qualities. In advertising parlance, 'pre-testing' measures the reaction of a sample of the target audience to almost-finished treatments of the proposed advertisements before the campaign is due to start. Pre-testing for impact consists of assessing by questionnaire the amount and quality of attention paid to such treatments presented in folders with other existing advertisements ('folder test'), in dummy magazines, as 'storyboards' (cartoon-strip summaries of television commercials) or 'animatics' (videotaped storyboards, electronically edited to simulate continuity, with integral sound-track), even as semi-finished artwork for poster designs optically superimposed on a photograph of a real poster site and film-projected. Such pre-tests are often conducted on a paired-comparison basis. This is ingenious and valid assessment of a useful performance characteristic, *provided that* those who make decisions on the basis of the results understand that 'effectiveness' has been measured only at the lowest level of the hierarchy of effects. This may well be so in the cases so far described, but the 'post-testing' of impact (that is, measuring attention paid to the actual advertising in real conditions) is a quite different matter. The criterion chosen for this purpose is almost invariably recall, as typified by 'reading-and-noting' tests in the case of press advertisements and 'day-after recall' testing of television commercials.[79] As before, one cannot disagree that the simple fact of recall does demonstrate impact. However, recall figures are customarily presented in practice as far more general indicators of effectiveness. Researchers imply, and advertisers seem willing to believe, that a respondent who can remember particular ingredients of an advertising message or treatment is significantly more likely to follow the advocated course of action than otherwise. But this is in reality a highly debatable proposition. It is equally possible to argue that recall represents nothing more than 'repeat attention' (voluntarily recalling the original to mind), in which case it simply measures impact or, perhaps, a certain amount of *involvement*. If so, the procedure is being invested with a diagnostic power out of all proportion to reality by the implication that it can test motivational effectiveness, a Level VI performance characteristic. Furthermore, recall testing is typically used as a criterion of effectiveness quite regardless of the nature of the advertising objective in question, which might in fact have been related to comprehension, for example.

Effectiveness is generally measured at the next level of the hierarchy-of-effects, *involvement*, by a battery of laboratory tests. Most record physiological measures of arousal when sample members of the target audience are exposed to the advertisement: psychogalvanometer, EEG, pupillometer, blink-rate meter, polygraph (the 'lie detector'). While there is no doubt that the arousal level of the subjects can be measured, since these techniques are long established in experimental psychology, their value as indicators of involvement with the advertisement is severely limited by the fact that they do not show what form the arousal takes. Does a sweating palm mean fear or pleasure? Despite this, they are regularly offered and accepted as valid measures of 'effectiveness'. Four laboratory tests were developed specifically for the evaluation of advertising, and measure respondent-indicated interest: ASL interest dial, Alpha quiz chair, CONPAAD and Sync. While these are unquestionably valid indicators of a specific performance characteristic, the fact remains that they measure only at a very low hierarchical level and may therefore fail to demonstrate that an advertisement has in fact met other intended objectives.

Typical texts describe no test procedures specifically directed at measuring performance at the middle-order levels of the hierarchy: *communication, empathy* and *persuasion*. In the case of the latter two, one can perhaps guess why not, but communication–or its corresponding target response, *comprehension*–is a criterion that figures with great regularity in statements of advertising objectives, either explicitly or implicitly. It is therefore surprising that the non-expert but inquisitive reader is obliged to deduce from the literature, in the absence of direct explanation, that middle-order performance characteristics are measured by means of *ad hoc* depth interviews and group discussions, and that such measurement seems to be infrequently attempted. (A notable exception to this rule is the case of public-service advertising on themes such as smoking and drinking; because these are sensitive and complex issues, comprehension is an especially important criterion of effectiveness which is carefully measured by such procedures.)

The remainder of the commonly reported pre- and post-testing procedures all correspond to the performance characteristic at the highest hierarchical level: *motivation*. Into this category fit such 'intention-to-purchase' measures as the Sherman Group's 'Buy Test', controlled experiments such as ASL theatre tests (formerly more familiar as Schwerin Tests), attitude measurement and sales monitoring. These are presented as complete tests of advertising effectiveness, understandably, because they measure probable or actual *action* on the audience's part. The latter two require special comment, however.

Readers may be surprised to find *attitude* measurement included in this list. Indeed, it is normal for texts to treat attitude scaling as though it were quite unrelated to the hierarchy of effects. It is here placed at Level VI because psychologists define an attitude as (among other things) a 'predisposition to act'. It is therefore reasonable to suppose that advertising researchers believe they are testing motivation by measuring attitudes, even though they do not say so explicitly. Unfortunately, the cause-and-effect relationship between attitude and action has never been conclusively proved, however reasonable it may seem intuitively; attitudes are predispositions, not precipitators. Practitioners seem unaware of this complication, or reluctant to recognise it. Because attitude-measurement techniques are easily available for borrowing from social psychology, they are widely and regularly used as criteria in practice–but without due regard to their surrogate nature.

The *sales* criterion has the appeal that it is easily measured, either by in-house monitoring or by subscribing to syndicated services such as the Nielsen Indexes, TCA or TGI. But serious methodological problems are concealed in the apparently straightforward procedure. For instance, the criterion is invalid if some other dimension of effectiveness was in fact called for by the campaign objectives. It is tempting to insist that sales are what advertising is all about, as the 'hard school' often does, but the fact is that it would be foolish to condemn a corporate image campaign, for instance, because increased sales did not result within the time horizon of the post-test. This example also raises the question of response-lag. Advertising takes time to make its effect felt, especially in the case of less frequently repeat-purchased products. If the sales criterion is applied too soon after the event, it may produce excessively pessimistic results. Moreover, there is a problem of seasonality: sales are not always constant throughout a period. If the timing of the test happens to coincide with either a peak or a trough, misleading conclusions may again be drawn. Sales monitoring needs to be repeated at intervals over a suitable period if this problem is to be avoided. Finally, there is the quite fundamental methodological drawback that, unless all intervening variables (other marketing mix elements or environmental factors such as weather, for example) can be controlled, a cause–effect relationship between advertising and sales change cannot be assumed, let alone proved. However tempting it may be to credit advertising or blame it, according to circumstances, the fact remains that any one of several other factors could have outweighed its effect.

This necessarily incomplete survey of common advertisement procedures confirms the proposition that they are indeed implicitly founded on a hierarchical model of advertising effect. Furthermore, the techniques most usually reported in the literature are confined to the bottom and top ends of the hierarchy-of-effects, capable of measuring only either impact and involvement or motivation. Valid performance criteria, such as communication, cannot therefore be tested unless advertisers are alert enough to insist that the criteria implicit in the proposed test procedures bear some relationship to the objectives the advertising is intended to meet, and researchers are willing to construct purpose-designed measuring instruments accordingly. Otherwise, it will continue to be counter-productively typical that advertising budgets are slashed or swollen on such test criteria as sales movements, attitude shifts or recall scores, which are not only off-the-peg surrogates but also too often conceptually dubious in themselves.

Summary

'Marketing communications' is a transaction between firms and people. While we may think of marketing communications initiatives as originating with firms, the fact is that people often initiate the transaction in the process of a deliberate search for information which can help with their consumption decisions. At other times, they consume and use such marketing communications as advertisements for several other purposes, including entertainment. People are active participants in the transaction, not passive recipients.

The balance of power is less weighted in favour of the firms than is generally believed–both outside and inside the marketing communications business. The transaction can be likened to a game for two players. People learn the rules at an early age, by the process of 'socialisation', and social institutions of various kinds exist to be arbiters of fair play.

The heart of the marketing communication transaction is typically described in terms of a 'hierarchy of effects'. Although this model is distinctly elderly, does not explain how people 'use' marketing communications and has been subject to continuous conceptual criticism from influential quarters, it still forms a day-to-day frame of reference for the majority of practitioners. A key to better understanding of what happens in the transaction is offered by information-processing theory, not yet integrated into the familiar texts and still unfamiliar to most practitioners. This theory has the further potential to explain how people manage to cope with the information overload that characterises the contemporary market-place.

Very recently, authors of marketing communications texts have abandoned the simplistic hierarchical model, but not in favour of information-processing theory or any other more sophisticated explanation. Instead, they have resurrected an equally elderly model of mass communications: source-message-channel-receiver. Under each heading in turn, they derive principles of marketing communication from laboratory and field experiments in interpersonal and mass communication, without demonstrating the validity of transfer from one context to the other, and raise as many questions as they answer. One valuable contribution, however, is to draw attention to the fact that marketing communication transactions do not happen once-and-for-all, but can recur as people are exposed to repeated initiatives by firms.

Measurement of effectiveness continues to be dominated by the hierarchy-of-effects framework, seldom made explicit. Instead of being required to satisfy criteria derived specifically from marketing communication objectives, initiatives (mostly advertisements, in practice) have only to pass a set of ready-made tests relating to levels in the hierarchy. Three particular surrogate criteria, popular in practice–recall, attitudes and sales–do not in fact measure what they purport to.

A great deal has been written about marketing communications. Much of it can unquestionably be helpful in practice, if cautiously interpreted, but much more remains to be verified or is yet to be discussed.

CHAPTER 7

New-product development

Contents

Introduction

Developing new products, modifying existing ones, and eliminating those that no longer make a positive contribution to the company's marketing performance, are key activities for marketing management. In Levitt's original terms[1] every major industry was once a growth industry, based on a new technology embodied in new product or service. Eventually major industries also became decline industries because of a failure to introduce new products or services to replace those on which their original success was based.

Because of the obvious importance of the product variable in the marketing mix, a considerable amount of attention has been given to the determinants of success in product management, especially in the area of new-product development. This research tends to have a pragmatic orientation. If new-product development can be managed successfully at the individual company level, then the firm is not left behind by competitors who have successfully introduced new products. A considerable amount of resources may also be saved (for example, introducing better screening mechanisms to reduce the chances of new product failure).

In the economy as a whole product development is also crucial to international competitiveness. The market share of British companies in many international markets (for example, engineering products) has declined because of a failure to introduce new and better-quality products to meet competition from overseas sources.[2]

This chapter reviews the literature that has addressed the problems of product development examining its potential for marketing practice. The review begins by considering the general importance of new products. This section establishes that new products do make an important contribution to a company's marketing success, but that the process is inherently difficult and risky, with many products failing to live up to the expectations of the company developing the product (innovator).

The review then examines the new-product development process itself, and identifies the principal techniques associated with the individual (idealised) process. The management sciences literature has placed considerable stress on the quantification of decisions at different stages in the process, and this review briefly considers the types of decision that may be taken, and the extent to which formal techniques appear to be used. This part of the literature is essentially prescriptive in that it suggests what should be done to improve the chances of success. It does not show whether the use of such techniques actually leads to success or failure.

The next section of the review considers this issue. Here the findings of a large number of research studies into the process of new-product development are summarised. These studies have examined success and failure in detail, and this literature provides some firm indicators as to how to manage product development successfully.

The final section of this chapter examines the basic problem of organising for product development and managing technical change. From this final part of the review it is clear that the attitudes of management themselves may play the most important role in influencing the success or failure of new-product development.

The importance of success

The extent to which companies are dependent on new products varies considerably from sector to sector. In some industries, the pace of technical change tends to be slow with the largest proportion of sales coming from products that have been on the market for a considerable time. These industries include the extractive industries

Table 7.1   Inter-industry variations in dependence on new products

Question: Where does the largest proportion of your own sales come from?

Industry	Products launched within the last five years %		Products launched more than five years ago %		Totals %	
Building and construction	45	13	55	16	100	29
Chemicals/allied products	29	12	71	30	100	42
Clothing	67	19	33	9	100	28
Electrical machinery	38	13	62	21	100	34
Engineering/general machinery	41	71	59	102	100	173
Fabricated metal	21	8	79	30	100	38
Food, drink, tobacco	11	6	89	49	100	55
Furniture and fixtures	57	8	43	6	100	14
Iron and steel	21	6	79	22	100	28
Leather	54	7	46	6	100	13
Paper	24	5	76	16	100	21
Plastics	50	9	50	9	100	18
Printing and publishing	38	8	62	13	100	21
Textiles	50	33	50	33	100	66
Miscellaneous	64	9	36	5	100	14
Stone, glass, clay	24	5	76	16	100	21
Total	38	232	62	383	100	615

(Significant at 99 per cent level of confidence.)

To be read: 45 per cent of the firms in the building and construction industry replying to this question indicated that the largest proportion of their own sales came from products launched within the last five years. (The interpretation of what consitutes a 'product' will vary depending on the nature of the industry. It is this element that creates a somewhat arbitrary result. These figures should be taken solely as a rough indication of the rate of technical progress in the industry.)

Table 7.1 indicates that there are significant differences in the contribution of new products to overall sales volume in different industries. New products would appear to make the most important contribution in what might be termed the 'fashion' industries, clothing and furniture and fixtures, and least important contribution in those industries where the basic product changes little from one year to the next (food, drink and tobacco, fabricated metal, iron and steel, stone clay and glass and paper).

Source: M. J. Baker and S. T. Parkinson, 'An Analysis of the Significance of Innovation', Appendix to SSRC Report *Predicting the Adoption and Diffusion of Industrial Innovation* (University of Strathclyde, 1974).

Table 7.2   Cost of research and development: analysis by sector (1978)

	£ million	%
Central government		
Defence	331.0	9.4
Research councils	152.3	4.3
Other	271.8	7.8
Local government	3	0.1
Total	758.1	21.6
Universities and other places of further education	317.3	9
Public corporations	212.5	6.1
Research associations	50.8	1.4
Private industry	2,061.0	58.7
Other	110.6	3.2
Total	3,510.3	100

Source: *Annual Abstract of Statistics* (London: HMSO, 1982).

such as quarrying as well as process industries such as chemicals and allied products. However, in many industries the pace of technical change is rapid and companies are increasingly dependent on products launched recently to maintain their competitive position (Table 7.1).

The volume of research and development expenditure provides a second indicator of the importance of product development. Table 7.2 shows the volume of expenditure on research and development in the United Kingdom. From this table it is clear that private industry is the major source of research and development funds, spending over £2,000 million in 1978 (or approximately 59 per cent of the total expenditure on research and development in the United Kingdom in that year). The next major spenders were central government for defence (9 per cent) and universities and other higher education institutions (9 per cent). These figures do not include the costs of commercialisation which are likely to be even greater than development costs.[3] This level of investment indicates a high level of commitment in both private and public sector to research and development activity (and illustrates the importance of success in product development to recoup such investment).

The importance of product development can also be illustrated by referring to specific industries. For example, Nielsen[4] reports that in 1981 a total of 664 new grocery products were introduced into the

United Kingdom market. This in itself gives a limited view of the volume of product development activity in this industry. According to one advertising agency representative: 'If you start with 500 concepts, you may come up with 25 which are worth testing. Perhaps a third of these go national, and maybe produce a turnover rate the client is happy with. But after 10 years in the market only one of them may still be making money.'[5]

Thus, a far larger number of product ideas would have been put forward at earlier stages in the development.

In the electronics industry the West German Siemens Group, one of the world's five leading companies in the electrical and electronics industry in terms of sales turnover, spent more than 3 billion Deutschmark on research and development in 1980–1, representing nearly 9 per cent of its world sales turnover for that year. New products launched within the last five years accounted for 49 per cent of its sales turnover, while products under ten years old accounted for 78 per cent of sales turnover. With this scale of investment in new products in both consumer and industrial markets it is clear that failure can have a disastrous impact on the companies involved. Despite this it is apparent that many new products do fail. This paradox has been referred to as the product development dilemma.[6]

It is difficult to give precise statistics on the incidence of failure of new products since definitions of failure tend to vary considerably between studies. Schon commented pessimistically: 'In the absence of any clear criteria of success and failure and of adequate statistics, it is not very useful to attempt a quantitative analysis. It is, at any rate, more accurate to say "almost nothing new works", than to say "most new developments succeed."'[7]

Booz, Allen and Hamilton's survey[8] suggests that of every fifty-eight product ideas that enter the product development process, only two reach the commercialisation stage and only one is commercially successful.

Crawford's summary of the position in 1977[9] reported estimates of failure ranging from 40–80 per cent in food and drug items, 37–80 per cent for new consumer goods, and 20–40 per cent for new industrial goods.

Ramsay[10] examined the relative success of new brands launched into the United Kingdom grocery market during the 1970s. His study focused on eighty-four product classes, whose sales accounted for about a third of total grocery business. Defining success arbitrarily in terms of reaching a sales target of £4 million by 1980, he found on average only four successful new products were launched per year into this market. For every one new product that was successful in terms of reaching the sales target of £4 million, three other new products failed to reach the target.

Finally, Project New Prod[11] data show that for every 100 new industrial products that are developed, approximately twenty-two are killed prior to launch, nineteen fail commercially, and fifty-nine are successes. These data exclude a large number of product ideas that were not developed to the final stage of finished product, but nevertheless had a considerable amount of money spent on them before the project was shelved.

The strategic importance of new-product development, and the high probability of failure, has generated a considerable amount of research into the process in recent years, and the review that follows provides an overview of the major dimensions of this literature, and its contributions to marketing practice.

The process of new-product development

The process of new-product development has been stylised in the literature into a sequence of stages which it is suggested that companies tend to proceed through when developing new product ideas. The product development process as such is usually conceptualised as Figure 7.1, with minor variations depending on the author. At the first stage in this process management is concerned with generating new ideas. At all subsequent stages the number of ideas is gradually reduced as a series of checks are made on the potential of the product idea. Most writers would tend to view this model as an idealised representation of product development which is rarely encountered in reality. In practice it is recognised that there will be considerable reiteration within this cycle, as for example will occur when a company discards all its ideas by the business analysis stage. Some companies will also miss stages out, or approach the process in a completely *ad hoc* manner, perhaps starting with the product development stage itself (actually building a prototype product before screening the idea's potential). Large consumer products companies may have the resources to execute each of these stages more thoroughly. Companies serving industrial markets may never go through any of these stages formally but simply respond to individual customer requests. The variety of forms of product development makes it difficult to use one general model to represent a wide range of circumstances. The model's main usefulness lies in the framework it provides for analysing the product development process.

The management science literature contains a wide range of techniques that have been prescribed for different stages in this

Figure 7.1   Stages in the product development process

Source: Booz, Allen & Hamilton, *Management of New Products* (New York, 1968).

process.[12] In this literature writers have addressed the major problems of each stage and have made recommendations on how to improve the firm's actions in each area. Table 7.3 identifies some of the principal techniques that have been suggested. The underlying assumption of this part of the literature has been that the success rate of new products can be improved if the techniques themselves are improved. This would appear to be only partly correct. As subsequent sections of this chapter will show, the process of product development is not readily amenable to the application of clear-cut formulae.

Baker and Pound[13] and more recently Clarke[14] have concluded that although there is a large literature from management writers offering systems and models to be used in decision-making, few, if any, of the managers who they studied actually used such techniques, either before or during the innovation process.

Robertson and Fox[15] comment on this in their study of innovation processes in 'real-time'. Talking about their own research and the earlier results of the Sappho programme at Sussex University they comment that:[16]

> No such techniques were applied by the managers we observed, and in the 38 projects examined in detail during the Sappho project (1971) there was a marked absence of evidence that such techniques had been used. To this extent it can be concluded that formal decision making techniques are not among the systems used by managers in arriving at the decisions which initiate and guide industrial innovations.

As a consequence therefore it may be of relatively limited use to look for specific techniques in isolation of other more general aspects of the innovating firms. The general qualities of management and the organisational conditions favouring innovation may have an equal if not more important role to play in the success or failure of new products.[17] The following section moves from the normative or prescriptive view to consider what firms actually appear to do in practice, and how this correlates with success or failure in innovation.

Product development in practice

The continuing high rate of failure of new products suggests that there is not yet one prescriptive approach to the management of the new-product development process. However, a considerable number of researchers have attempted to identify factors that are associated with success or failure.

For example, Myers and Marquis[18] found that demand-related or market-pull innovations were more likely to be successful than product-related or technology-push innovations. Successful innovation appeared to be more likely to be related to meeting the market's requirements than developing a new technology. A National Industrial Conference Board study of why eighty-seven new industrial products failed identified the following reasons for failure: inadequate market analysis (33 per cent of cases), product defects (25 per cent) and higher costs than expected (15 per cent).[19] A follow-up study that replicated this approach identified inadequate market analysis (45 per cent), product technical problems (29 per cent), lack of effective marketing (25 per cent), higher costs than expected (19 per cent), competitive reaction (17 per cent), poor timing (14 per cent) and technical/production problems (12 per cent).[20]

Table 7.3   Principal techniques appropriate to new-product development process

(A summary of techniques suggested by the literature.)

Idea generation

(a)   Consider product planning as part of corporate strategy.
   –Are there 'gaps' perceived in company's present or future offerings?

(b)   Systematic review of technology.
   –Monitor scientific literature, attend conferences, seminars, participate in trade associations, sponsor university research.
   –Forecast new technologies using forecasting techniques, e.g. Delphi, trend extrapolation, morphological analyses.
   –Set R and D budgets.
   –Run creativity sessions to 'create' new ideas–or 'buzz' sessions.
   –Monitor changes in supply markets.
   –Review patents and new licence possibilities.
   –Monitor competition.

(c)   Analyse market.
   –Systematic 'lost order analysis' of sales trip reports.
   –Continuous data collection from identified market segments.
   –Special *ad hoc* surveys of consumer groups/individual consumers.
   –Run creativity sessions to 'create' new ideas.

Initial screening

Measure consistency of product idea with overall objectives of company.

Produce summary product appraisals that:
(a)   estimate profitability;
(b)   estimate sales performance;

The Science Policy Research Unit[21] at Sussex University concluded that successful new-product development was most likely where:

(a) close attention was given to user needs as the major source of ideas;
(b) there was commitment on the part of key managers (Product Champion) prepared to sponsor the innovation through the major stages in its development;
(c) the appropriate organisational framework existed flexible enough to adapt to innovation, with well established and effective communication between managers in different functions;
(d) there was a deliberate search for ideas.

Table 7.3 *cont.*

Initial screening

(c) estimate capital requirements;
(d) estimate demands on resources;
(e) evaluate technical opportunity;
(f) evaluate patent protection;
(g) estimate production load;
(h) evaluate impact on existing products and similarity to major business.

Business analysis

Use various techniques to estimate:

(a) development costs;
(b) manufacturing costs (including prime costs and additional capital);
(c) market price, sales volume, break-even point, duration of sales;
(d) sales and launch costs;
(e) cash flows out of and into company;
(f) use sensitivity analysis to compare effect of different assumptions on (a)–(e).

Product development

Ensure value for money in design by:

(a) value engineering of product;
(b) continuing tests of consumer response as product develops;
(c) prototype evaluation and testing.

Market launch

(a) pre-identify target market/test market.

Since the early Project Sappho research, Rothwell has produced several studies of the textile machinery industry, principally using a case study-based approach to examine the problems of the management of new technology. In 1976, in a study of twenty textile machinery manufacturers, he concluded that successful manufacturers paid greater attention to user needs, and managed the marketing function more effectively.[22]

In an overview of the main findings of studies since Carter and Williams,[23] Rothwell concluded that the importance of good marketing was evident throughout,[24] and in a later review of problems of technology transfer into industry, based on the textile industry,[25] he concluded that innovation that failed could have succeeded if there had been better communication between managers, better under-standing of user needs, and better-quality management.

In consumer products these same general factors also appear to be related to success, although there are far fewer documented studies. There is some evidence to suggest that in this area the company's advertising agency may often play a crucial role. According to research by Lindsey Dale and Partners, an agency specialising in new-product work, agencies were closely involved in the develop-ment of nine out of ten of the most successful new products of the 1970s.[26]

A second major difference is the role of the intermediary in most consumer markets, that is, the multiple buyer. In a survey of the retail trade Kraushar commented: 'Apart from misjudgment of the market and poor implementation, the most important reason for failure is related to distribution and trade attitudes. Retail buyers are clearly becoming more sophisticated, and have hardened their attitudes.'[27]

The main reasons given by respondents representing major retail buyers for refusing products were lack of real product advantage (74 per cent of respondents), no shelf space (58 per cent), declining market (56 per cent), poor quality (53 per cent), little advertising support (48 per cent), and no introductory terms (15 per cent). From these findings it is clear that distinctiveness or significant innovation was required to gain trade acceptance.

Project New Prod[28] also identified the importance of the distinc-tiveness of the innovation as a key factor in success. In this project Cooper identified three composite factors or dimensions that domin-ated the 'success equation'. These were product, market and technic-al strength. Each of these factors could be split into a number of different elements which were associated with success in product development.

Under the product factor the crucial elements were meeting customer needs better than competing products, offering unique features that competitive products did not offer, being of higher quality, and permitting the customer to reduce his costs. This work stresses the importance of customer perception of the new product. An innovation will only be significant in the eyes of the market if it has improvements that are valued by the potential buyer. Innovation that offers technical changes not valued by the potential buyer will not be seen as significant.

Under the market discussion Cooper's findings stress the import-ance of effective market research, having a well-targeted sales force at launch (pre-identifying the most likely early purchasers), and pro-ficiently executing the launch. These elements indicate the import-ance of developing a thorough understanding of consumer or organisational buying behaviour, in order to determine the likely response to the product. Baker[29] has also stressed the importance of understanding the behaviour of potential customers at the pre-launch stage. In his view the key problem of marketing new industrial products is that of accelerating the rate of acceptance of the product. He argues that this can be done most effectively by pre-identifying the most likely early buyers, understanding their purchasing behaviour, and building a marketing strategy around this understanding.

Project New Prod also showed that technical competence was an important factor in success in product development. According to Cooper engineering skills, product technology and design and production resources all have to be organised and used effectively for success in product development. Parkinson's[30] study of British and West German machine tool manufacturers supports this view. West German manufacturers appeared to be more successful in developing new products for international markets because, among other factors, they gave greater resources to the design and development function, emphasised technical skills more in general management recruitment and training, and put more emphasis on value engineering at the product design stage.

Summarising the literature in this area, success would appear to depend upon achieving the right blend of product, market and technology factors over time in an integrated manner. However, this view has to be tempered by the need to take account of other more elusive factors, such as the attitude of management to risk, or situation-specific factors related to individual projects. These factors make it difficult to apply generalised models to the process of new-product development and produce prescriptions for individual product-market situations. As Project New Prod showed, the outcome of a project may lie more in the hands of the management involved than might otherwise be assumed. Therefore, it is relevant to examine what is known about the management of new-product development, and to determine whether this knowledge can be of use in managing the process better.

The management of new-product development

The new-product development cycle is usually seen as one of gradual risk reduction where each stage is seen as reducing the chance of product failure. However, while such models may create the impression that the process is manageable, there is considerable evidence to suggest that the process is far from being so. The demands of new-product development place a considerable strain on different parts of the organisation, and some appear better organised to deal with the problem than others.

Alternative organisational forms suggested for new-product development include 'venture management', new-product committee, and matrix management.

In the venture management approach a 'mini business' is in effect created within the firm with its own staff, budget and clearly defined objectives. Venture management is seen as providing the necessary degree of flexibility allowing managers scope for quick response to changing conditions, while at the same time allowing such 'mini-businesses' access to the funds of the parent corporation for commercialisation or development costs.[31]

The new-product development committee is an approach chosen to bring together specialists from different functions within the organisation on a regular basis to plan new products, and control their development. It is in effect likely to be a periodic version of the new-product department, but unlike the new-product department managers have other line responsibilities in their respective functions.

The matrix management approach is an organisational form deliberately designed to give managers from different organisational functions responsibility for different aspects of the same problem. For example, Ames[32] suggested that a firm should employ product managers, responsible for the sales of individual product lines, and market managers responsible for the sales to individual markets. Working together such managers could provide a useful understanding of both products and markets.

These techniques are examples of 'integrating' devices used by management to co-ordinate the activities of the individual departments. New-product development puts a particular strain on organisations because the contribution of each of the individual departments has to be co-ordinated effectively. However, each department is likely to evolve its own structure and orientation to perform its own task effectively necessarily. Thus, specialisation within departments is likely to lead to problems of integration between departments.

Lorsch and Lawrence[33] reviewed this problem in a study of product development in five selected companies. Table 7.4 illustrates their findings on the patterns of specialisation that they found in three basic departments.

These findings indicate the problems of integrating the activities of the managers involved from different functions.

Table 7.4   Patterns of functional specialisation

	Departmental structure	Orientation to time	Orientation to others	Orientation to environment
Research	Low	Long	Permissive	Science
Sales	Medium	Short	Permissive	Market
Production	High	Short	Directive	Plant

Source: J. W. Lorsch and P. R. Lawrence, 'Organising for Product Innovation', *Harvard Business Review* (Jan.–Feb. 1965).

Where innovation is marginal then only minor adjustments may be needed in the organisation to accept and develop the new idea. However, major changes in products are likely to lead to greater demands on the organisation. For example, microprocessor-led developments in control technologies have forced some machine-tool companies to set up special project groups with their own 'dedicated' staff. In general, as the rate and degree of change in the company's products increases, so the need for integrating devices such as the product-development committee appears to increase.

Attention has also been given to those factors that are conducive to new-product development in the firm. In particular, attention has been focused on those characteristics of the organisation that facilitate change. In this area marketing has drawn heavily upon findings from other disciplines, in particular from the administrative sciences and the study of organisational behaviour.

Burns and Stalker[34] defined two types of organisation, labelled mechanistic and organic. The mechanistic organisation was typified by task specialisation, clear and stable definitions of tasks, rules, and responsibilities through job description, and authority coming from above with most communication being in the form of vertical commands. Such organisations were also characterised by a short time span for review of the organisation's performance, and a narrow average span of control. By contrast, the organic organisation tended to be run on the basis of common experience and team work, tasks were continually redefined according to the individuals' interaction with other participants. Authority came from the group and communication was both horizontal and vertical. There were relatively few levels in the hierarchy and there was a long time span for reviewing the organisation's performance. The organic organisation also had a wide average span of control and provided detailed knowledge to all organisational members according to their roles.

Burns and Stalker suggested that the features of the mechanistic organisation were such that it tended to restrict the introduction of new technologies whereas the organic system was likely to be more responsive and a better climate for new-product development. However, as they commented, any one organisation was likely to have some elements of both mechanistic and organic features. In their view an organisation could be positioned on a continuum from mechanistic to organic, and its general position would thus be a measure of its innovativeness.

A more considered view of their work suggests that greater consideration could have been given to the degree of organic or mechanistic influences at different stages in the innovation sequence. As Zaltman has commented:[35]

> their theory is somewhat limited in that it does not note both the initiation and implementation stages of the innovation process...we are less clear as to how the organisation became aware of the innovation and then decided to develop it using the type of structure it did.

In other words, one form of organisation, organic, would have been suited to the idea-generation stage, whereas a mechanistic organisation would then be suitable to the development phases. Since innovation requires a constant input of new ideas and an initial flexibility to adjust to such ideas, but then needs some kind of formal system to evaluate the suitability of such ideas, a combination of both systems might be more appropriate.

There is more recent evidence to suggest that those companies that are most active in product development have evolved a management style which facilitates the product development process. Johne[36] has shown that the most aggressive innovators in a sample of electronics companies tend to have a relatively loose or 'organic' climate which facilitated the initiation phases of product development, and a relatively tight or 'mechanistic' climate which facilitated the idea implementation stages of product development. Such companies appear to be able to achieve a 'shift' from organic to mechanistic climate to suit different stages in the process. Product development strategy and management structure were clearly interrelated.

The majority of researchers tend to agree that a flexible organisational structure is needed to provide a favourable atmosphere for technological innovation. Shanks, for example, has commented that innovation has flourished more often:[37]

> where there is a certain fluidity, and flexibility in the company structure, which permits the interplay of personality and ideas, and where management is psychologically ready to alter existing plans and patterns to accommodate change and innovation.

Ismail[38] has reviewed this literature extensively. From this review Ismail concludes that innovations are likely to be more successful in organisations that have the following characteristics:

1. A lower degree of formalisation (measured by the absence of written-down rules and procedures to prescribe task performance and interaction with other members of the organisation).
2. Good systems of communication encouraging lateral as well as vertical contact.
3. Close integration between the members of different departments.

From the research that has been done in this area it is clear that the organisation's climate can have a marked effect on its chances of success in product development. However, it is also evident that the attitude of management towards new-product development can have as much if not more influence on the chances of success. Given the appropriate commitment and quality of management then the precise form of the organisation may become a secondary consideration. This is the view of Carter and Williams whose work has become one of the standard references in this area. They commented:[39]

> We have examined many patterns of organisation that have been evolved to facilitate change. Given a basic ability in the senior management, it is clear that consciousness of the problem and due attention to it are of more importance than a particular management structure.

Carter and Williams's research marks one of the first detailed studies of the relationship between the general quality of management and innovativeness. Their work was conducted under the aegis of the Science and Industry Committee. This committee was set up in 1952 by the British Association for the Advancement of Science 'to study the problems of speeding up in industry the application of the results of scientific research'. Its terms of reference were:

> To identify those factors which determine, in different industries and in different types of firm, the speed of application of new scientific and technical knowledge; to examine their relative importance, their inter-relations, and their correlation with characteristics of the firm or industry; to obtain evidence of the effectiveness of measures already taken to speed up the application of science in industry, or to remove hindrances to such application; and to examine the possible results of other proposed measures.

Their work was concentrated on fifty firms in the north-west of England, and they sought to identify the characteristics of the technically progressive firm. Such a firm was defined as 'a firm which is in the forefront of discovery in applied science and technology, and which is quick to master new ideas and to perceive the relevance of work in other areas'.

From their work they identified twenty-four factors that were present in technically progressive firms and not present in unprogressive firms. These are listed in Table 7.5.

Since the publication of Carter and Williams's study other researchers have replicated the original research in different situations, and come to broadly similar conclusions. Success in new-product development appears to be related to the overall quality of manage-

Table 7.5   Characteristics of technically progressive firms

1. High quality of incoming information—the more progressive a firm, the higher quality of the technical literature that it takes, and the better its contacts with scientists and technologists in other firms and other institutions and universities.

2. A deliberate survey of potential ideas—the progressive firm deliberately searches for new product ideas unlike the parochial firm.

3. A willingness to share knowledge—the progressive firm is more willing to share its knowledge with other firms and contribute to journals and conferences.

4. A willingness to take new knowledge on licence and to enter joint ventures.

5. A readiness to look outside the firm—the progressive firm is more likely to set its standards of performance by what it sees in its competitors rather than relying on internal standards.

6. Effective internal communication and co-ordination—unlike the backward firm, the progressive firm is characterised by:
   (a) Effective teamwork between departments when new developments are being planned. Thus evaluation of the potential market, of the costs of production, and of the capital position of the firm is made by various departments well before a decision to continue with development is made.
   (b) Responsibility, authority and the objectives of the company are so specified and understood that individuals and departments work effectively.
   (c) Differences in outlook in research and development, production, and sales do not hold up projects.

7. High status of science and technology in the firm—there are not only more research and design and development staff in the progressive firm, but these staff also play a more important role and are represented by an important and powerful voice on the Board.

8. A consciousness of costs and profits in the research and development departments (if any)—the progressive firms give more attention to economic justification in choosing projects for research and development and in deciding which are worth continuing with.

9. Rapid machine replacement—progressive firms replace machines more rapidly.

ment. As the authors themselves state: 'To a great extent the receptiveness of a firm to technical change must depend upon the understanding and appreciation of science and technology to be found in the various ranks of management; and this in turn depends on the training and exprience of individual managers.'[40]

Recent research has shown that the attitudes of managers in the purchasing organisation may also play a major role in influencing the success or failure of an innovation. The final section of this chapter briefly examines the role of the customer in product development.

Table 7.5 *cont.*

10. A sound policy for recruitment for management–the progressive firm tends to recruit people with considerable training, unlike the unprogressive firm.
11. An ability to attract talented people–the progressive firms have on the whole a greater ability, as well as a greater desire to attract trained and able staff.
12. A willingness to arrange for the effective training of staff–the more progressive firms have a greater interest in arranging for the training of their staff.
13. Use of management techniques–the progressive firms tend to use such techniques as method study, work measurement, production planning and control, standard costing and budgetary control, unlike unprogressive firms.
14. Identifying the outcome of investment decisions–the technically progressive firm is more likely to attempt to identify the outcome of investment decisions, unlike the non-progressive firm.
15. High quality in the chief executive.
16. Adequate provision for intermediate management.
17. Good quality in intermediate managers.
18. An ability to bring the best out of managers.
19. Use of scientists and technologists on the Board–a characteristic frequently found in progressive firms and absent in unprogressive firms.
20. A readiness to look ahead–progressive firms generally tend to look further ahead than unprogressive firms.
21. A high rate of expansion.
22. Greater ingenuity in getting round material and equipment shortages.
23. An effective selling policy.
24. Good technical service to customers–progressive firms tend to help their customers to understand the properties and right use of their products, and to overcome any difficulties that the customer might find. This often involves using scarce technological skills either in a technical sales force, or by a readiness to send design or production staff to help customers. By contrast, unprogressive firms often had to be pressed very hard before they would give any help. Such firms not only failed to help customers, they failed to derive information that would have helped them to improve their product.

Source: C. F. Carter and B. R. Williams. *Industry and Technical Progress* (Oxford University Press, 1957).

The role of the customer

The consensus of a large number of studies of factors associated with success in new-product development is that the identification of user needs is one of the most important aspects of the process. It is often stressed that suppliers should be active in identifying the needs of their potential customers and consciously design new products or services to satisfy them. Such a view puts the responsibility for new-product development squarely upon the supplier, and this has been the orientation of many reports in recent years that have made recommendations on how British companies might improve their product development success.[41]

However, recent research findings suggest that the quality of a company's customers and the extent to which they are receptive to innovation or demand it from their suppliers is an important determinant of success. In short, success in product development may also be related to the quality of the customer. This is likely to be particularly the case in areas of complex technology where the user may identify the need for a new product or process and often specify part or all of the technical solution. Von Hippel[42] reported a study of forty-nine companies, where 67 per cent of the innovations examined were developed by users, not equipment manufacturers. In 20 per cent of the cases users needed an outside supplier to manufacture the innovation in question and initiated manufacture through a customer request. Parkinson and Avlonitis[43] came to similar conclusions in a study of the adoption of flexible manufacturing system technologies in West Germany and the United Kingdom. In their study it was engineers in the user organisations who identified the need for this type of manufacturing system, drew up the specifications and discussed these with equipment suppliers. The equipment suppliers, predominantly machine-tool manufacturers, responded to the initiative of their customers.

Von Hippel[44] identified three alternative models for industrial product idea generation. In the 'customer active' model a product request from a customer leads to a 'customised' product which may thus be marketed to other customers. In the 'manufacture active' model, customer needs are researched by the manufacturer, ideas generated and tested, and the product finally marketed. In his final model an unfilled known need exists, which an advance in technology fills, leading to a product innovation. For example, an electronics manufacturer may anticipate that there is a known need for components that are smaller, lighter, faster in operation or cheaper. Any development meeting these criteria has a guaranteed market.

Parkinson[45] reported a study that suggests that success or failure in areas of complex technology may well depend on the extent to which the supplier's own customers are receptive to and demanding of new technologies. Firms that failed to identify and actively cultivate continuous contact with progressive customers found themselves left behind by competitors who did have such contacts.

Concluding remarks

The area of new-product development has been one of the most extensively researched areas in marketing in recent years. As a result there is a large volume of literature addressing a wide range of issues, and it is possible to pursue several themes in the study of the process. From the practitioner's point of view the results of this work may initially appear confusing because of the volume of research findings, often based on different research methodologies and frequently contradictory.

However, the literature is beginning to come together in a coherent manner, and certain basic generalisations now have operational usefulness. For instance, it is apparent that despite the use of formal techniques in project appraisal and prototype development, many new products continue to fail. As this review has suggested, the onus is on the management involved in the process to establish the right organisational climate for product development. Much has been written about establishing such a climate and how to manage the process more effectively; much has also been written about the importance of establishing user needs, and effective marketing planning at the launch stage. This literature provides firm guidelines for product development work.

It is unlikely that new-product development will ever become a wholly predictable process. There are too many situational factors that will influence the individual project's chances of success or failure. However, the process is now sufficiently well understood for some firm guidelines to be put forward to improve the chances of success of individual projects. The next step in the process is to diffuse this information to managers involved in product development work.

CHAPTER 8

Diffusion theory and marketing

Contents

Introduction

As we saw in the previous chapter, a natural consequence of the marketing concept, with its emphasis upon the determination of consumer wants and the deployment of resources to match these wants, is that the marketing function places particular stress upon new-product development. In this chapter we will attempt to demonstrate that the problems associated with introducing new products into the market-place appear to be remarkably similar to those experienced in gaining acceptance for innovations in other areas of activity. This being so, one might reasonably anticipate that there are considerable benefits to be gained by studying the process by which other innovations appear to secure acceptance as a basis for enhancing consumer reaction to new products.

The process by which innovations spread through a population of users or adopters is generally termed 'diffusion'. Accordingly, in this chapter we first consider the evolution of the diffusion research tradition as a preliminary to examining the marketing variant which is normally referred to as the 'product-life-cycle concept'. In turn, this examination leads us to enquire whether it is possible to operational-ise the product-life-cycle concept and thereby make it a useful tool for marketing managers concerned with new-product development. To this end we describe briefly our own model of the adoption process which attempts to synthesise both economic and behaviou-ral variables and so suggests how marketing may usefully borrow from other disciplines in developing valid theory of its own.

The evolution of the diffusion research tradition[1]

The earliest research into the process of diffusion appears to have been triggered off by the interest of anthropologists in the spread of ideas between societies. This interest, which began to gather momentum at the beginning of this century, set out to determine whether particular ideas, activities and patterns of behaviour were transferred from society to society or were the result of parallel thought development. Essentially, the thrust of this work was historical and descriptive and laid greater emphasis upon the social consequences of the innovation. None the less certain important generalisations were advanced including one that has formed the foundation for much subsequent research–namely that acceptance of an innovation depends very much upon the prospective adopter's culture. Thus closed or traditional systems were found to hinder diffusion while open or modern social systems appear to stimulate it.

One of the earliest contributors to social theories of diffusion was Gabriel Tarde, whose *Laws of Imitations* was published in 1903.[2] In this work Tarde makes several novel proposals which have been very influential in shaping the development of diffusion theory, including the proposition that if adoptions of an innovation are plotted against time from introduction to complete diffusion they will assume the characteristics of a normal distribution, or if plotted cumulatively assume the familiar S-shaped curve which characterises the product-life-cycle. Tarde is also to be credited with identifying the rela-tionship between cosmopoliteness and early adoption and of formu-lating the concept of the 'opinion leader' as a member of a social system to whom others look for advice.

During the 1920s a large number of studies were undertaken by empirically minded sociologists most of which were concerned with the tracing of a specific innovation through a population of adopters.

With the benefit of hindsight one of the surprising features of this period of development of diffusion theory is that there was very little, if any, transfer of ideas from one branch of research to another. Thus only recently has any attempt been made to integrate the various findings into a single theory of diffusion.[3]

One of the major foundations of this newly emergent integrated theory are the findings of the rural sociologists. By the early 1960s contributions from this area numbered several hundred, many of which replicate the classic study of Ryan and Gross.[4] Among the many contributions of this study three have had a lasting impact:

1. the concept of adopter classification into categories;
2. the determination of the social characteristics which identified the earliest and latest adopters; and
3. recognition and statement of the deliberate nature of the decision to adopt an innovation.

A second major source of contributions to diffusion theory was provided by the area of medical sociology. Perhaps the most famous study in this area was that undertaken by Coleman, Katz and Menzel which is often identified as the Columbia University Drug Study or the 'Gammamyn' Study.[5] Perhaps the most significant contribution from this study was the establishment of a positive relationship between opinion leadership and innovativeness.

A survey of contributions from other areas such as that undertaken by Rogers[6] would seem to suggest that they have made very little original contribution to major concepts developed in rural and medical sociology. Thus, while educationists have been responsible for very large numbers of studies, these tend to have built upon, and confirmed, the findings of other researchers. Similarly in the marketing area the main thrust has been in the application of extant concepts in an attempt to reduce the high failure rate associated with the introduction of new products. More recently, however, there have been indications that this research is making an original contribution of its own in the field of what might be termed the 'characteristics of innovation area'.

As mentioned earlier, Everett Rogers made an invaluable contribution to diffusion research by summarising and pulling together contributions of the various and diverse research traditions. Certainly it is to Rogers that we owe a major debt for singling out the definitions and major concepts which now enjoy such wide currency among marketers. Particularly worthy of mention are his definition of diffusion, the stages in the adoption process, the five dimensions of an innovation and development of the concept of 'adoptive categories' in pursuit of an attempt to define an innovator profile. We review briefly these concepts below.

The diffusion process

The characteristics of the diffusion process may be summed up as: (i) acceptance (ii) over time (iii) of some specific item (iv) by adopting units–individuals or groups–(v) linked to communication channels (vi) to a social structure (vii) to a given system of values. In this context acceptance is probably best defined as 'continued use'. Thus, while purchase of a durable good would count as acceptance or adoption, first purchase of a low-price consumable item might only amount to a trial such that adoption would only be assumed given repeated purchase of the item.

Time of adoption is central to the whole concept of diffusion and underlies all attempts to describe the diffusion process in mathematical terms. In the case of most industrial and consumer-durable goods usually it is possible to establish the date of purchase and therefore the elapsed time since first introduction, and thereby identify the sequence in which organisations or individuals adopted the item. Unfortunately measurement of elapsed time from first introduction usually depends upon recall in the case of smaller consumable items and is a much less reliable guide to the sequence in which individuals actually adopted an innovation than is the case with industrial goods.

The specific item in our definition is the innovation under study while the unit of adoption has traditionally been conceived of as an individual. However, in recent years the role of joint-buying decisions in both the industrial- and household-buying situations has been increasingly recognised and may be expected to play a more important role in future studies. Clearly in the case of joint adoption decisions identification of the roles played by the respective parties to that decision should have a significant effect upon the promotional and selling tactics adopted by an innovator.

The role of channels of communication, social structure and its attendant value system have all been demonstrated to have a major influence upon the diffusion process. It follows, therefore, that in diffusion studies great importance is attached to identifying both the formal and informal channels of communication used by adopters. Similarly, from a marketing viewpoint the social structure defines the boundaries within which items diffuse and so constitute a statement of the total population of potential adopters. Finally, value systems have a major impact on the way in which a given innovation will be viewed by prospective adopters, and the need to achieve consonance between an innovation and a value system in order to achieve adoption is obvious.

Stages in the adoption process

The assumption underlying the formulation of adoption-process schemes is that consumer acceptance of a product is not an instantaneous or random event, but a distinct mental and behavioural sequence through which the consumer must progress if adoption of a product is to occur.

Various representations of the adoption process have been suggested but all have a common aim of dividing up the adoption process into comprehensible parts in order to provide a conceptual framework for the analysis of how and why adopters move from first knowledge of a new idea, to its trial, to a decision as to whether to adopt or reject that idea. In 1955 a committee of rural sociologists defined a sequence of five stages through which an individual passes in coming to an adoption decision, namely: awareness, interest, evaluation, trial and adoption. In a marketing context Lavidge and Steiner[7] propose a six-stage sequence related to three basic psychological states:

Awareness Knowledge	the cognitive dimension
Liking Preference	the affective dimension
Conviction Purchase	the conative dimension

As noted earlier, the purpose of models of the adoption process is to provide an analytical framework, and it is not intended that one should consider the stages as necessarily being equidistant, as the importance attached to each will tend to vary in relation to both product and consumer characteristics. Similarly, while some researchers have suggested that individual stages in the sequence may be omitted in real life, our own preference is to accept the alternative hypothesis that stages cannot be omitted but that the individual adopter may move up several steps simultaneously, thereby collapsing the hierarchy of effects into a shorter time period. This latter explanation enables us to account for deviations such as impulse buying and also for the different weight attached to different stages dependent upon variations in product and consumer characteristics.

A number of other alternative models of the adoption process have been put forward of which perhaps the best known is the marketer's

AIDA (Attention, Interest, Desire, Action) model which identifies four stages consisting of attention, interest, desire and action.

The basic adoption-process and hierarchy-of-effects models have been criticised on the grounds that the only certain indication from analysis of many diffusion studies is that awareness always precedes adoption.[8] As a consequence of these criticisms a number of more sophisticated models have been proposed, *inter alia*, by Robertson and Andreasen and Nicosia.[9] Space limitations preclude analysis of these alternative models and the reader should consult the original sources for a discussion of these.[10]

Dimensions of an innovation

Another important component of Rogers's model is identification and classification of the five dimensions of an innovation–relative advantage, compatibility, complexity, divisibility and communicability. These dimensions may be defined as follows:

(a) relative advantage is the degree to which an innovation is superior to the idea it supersedes;
(b) compatibility is the degree to which innovation is consistent with existing values and past experiences of adopters;
(c) complexity is the degree to which an innovation is relatively difficult to understand and use;
(d) divisibility is the degree to which an innovation may be tried on a limited basis; and
(e) communicability is the degree to which the results of innovation may be diffused to others.

It is important to note that these characteristics must be defined in relative terms depending upon the potential adopter's status, knowledge and perception of the information concerning the innovation that is presented to him. With this proviso it is clear that the greater the relative advantage an innovation possesses, the more compatible it is with a potential adopter's status and beliefs; the less complex it is, the more readily it can be tried without risk to the trialist, and the easier it is to communicate information concerning the nature and effect of an innovation then the more readily it will be understood. At least two observations may be made about this statement. First, the more radical an innovation, the less will be its perceived compatibility, divisibility and communicability and the greater its perceived complexity, and therefore the more uncertain its relative advantage; and, second, any predictions concerning the reaction of a given potential adopter will depend very heavily upon our level of knowledge concerning the status of that adopter at the time that he becomes aware of the innovation.

Adopter categories

Earlier in this chapter it was noted that if one plots the number of adoptions against time from first introduction of an innovation, the resulting distribution is normal. The observed regularity of this distribution led to the use of the parameters of the normal distribution as a basis for classifying adopters into categories. Using standard deviation from the mean, adopters are divided into five groupings as indicated in Figure 8.1, namely innovators, early adopters, early majority, late majority and laggards.

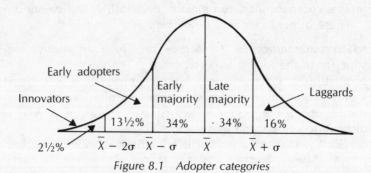

Figure 8.1   Adopter categories

By definition it is tautological that innovators should precede early adopters, that early adopters must precede the majority and so on. In consequence it follows that if we can pre-identify the characteristics of innovators for any given category of innovation, then we may concentrate our marketing efforts upon these individuals. Clearly the potential benefits of such an ability have not been lost upon either the marketing practitioner or his academic colleague. However, while a great deal of empirical work has been undertaken in trying to develop an innovator profile–the results to date of such studies have been both inconclusive and inconsistent–in large measure this inconsistency would seem to stem very largely from a failure to add marketing insights to borrowed concepts. Thus the product, for example, has become almost an adjunct to the researches undertaken rather than being recognised as a key variable *vis-à-vis* the individual consumer characteristics.

Despite some of the deficiencies noted, there can be no doubt that diffusion research has provided a fruitful source of ideas for marketers. Further, having recognised the deficiencies of existing ideas when translated into the marketing context, it becomes possible to see how modification may make such concepts even more useful to the marketing practitioner. In the remainder of this chapter we summarise briefly a modest attempt of our own to make use of diffusion concepts to improve performance when introducing new products into the market-place.

The product life-cycle

Earlier in this chapter we noted that the manner in which successful innovations diffuse through a population of adopters is sufficiently consistent to encourage the use of the parameters of the normal distribution to classify users into different adopter categories. If instead of plotting the number of adoptions against elapsed time from first introduction of an innovation we were to plot the cumulative adoptions, then our bell-shaped normal-distribution curve would be transformed into a symmetrical S-shaped curve. Such S-shape curves are particularly familiar to marketers for this is the shape asumed by the curve used to represent the life-cycle of a product. Such a life-cycle curve is reproduced in Figure 8.2 and is traditionally divided into the four phases indicated, namely introduction, growth, maturity and decay.

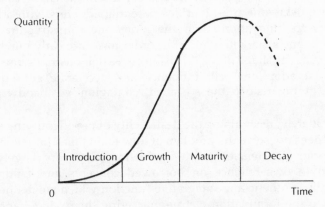

Figure 8.2   The product life-cycle

While most practitioners would readily agree that the product-life-cycle is an accurate reflection of the manner in which sales of a new product develop, many would question whether the concept has any practical or operational utility. Essentially, such doubts would seem to stem from the observation that in advance one very rarely can predefine the scales appropriate to the plotting of a diffusion curve. Thus if one does not know whether a population of adopters will be numbered in tens, hundreds, thousands or tens of thousands, or whether the appropriate unit of time is to be minutes, hours, weeks or even years, one hardly knows how to interpret the early perform-ance of the new product as a basis for predicting the final sales volume and time to complete diffusion. For this reason many practitioners tend to confine the product-life-cycle concept to the category reserved for many other theoretical constructs which can be labelled as academic, namely 'interesting but irrelevant'.

Our own view, which we develop at some length elsewhere,[11] is that while accepting the possible deficiencies of exponential curves as a forecasting device, the concept does provide one with an enormously useful strategic insight; namely, that the final shape of an exponential function is a direct consequence of its early shape. For example, if one assumes one of the more simple exponential func-tions, namely a geometric progression, then we would project a doubling of sales for each unit of elapsed time. This being so it follows that if the elapsed time to first purchase from introduction is six months, then we would forecast sales of two more units in the succeeding six-month period, four units in the six months after that, eight units in the following six months, and so on. If, however, the time to first adoption were halved to three months, then sales of fifteen units would be achieved in half the time, that is one year instead of two. Clearly the insight that underlines the search for a consumer innovator profile referred to earlier in this chapter is that the more quickly one pre-identifies potential adopters with a high receptivity to innovation, then the more one can structure and concentrate one's marketing effort in order to secure early purchase. Thereafter, as the shape of the diffusion curve demonstrates, the very fact of first adoptions will influence and accelerate subsequent adoption giving rise to the so-called 'contagion' or 'bandwagon' effect.

Unfortunately, recognising the desirability of pre-identifying early adopters does not solve the problem of how to do this. Our own view is that prior deficiencies in this direction may very largely be attributed to over-reliance on borrowed concepts and failure to perform the synthetic and integrative function which we defined as essential to the formulation of true marketing theory in Chapter 2. Specifically, we feel it is essential to pull together economic and behavioural concepts of buying behaviour in order to approximate the real-world situation.

A composite model of buyer behaviour[12]

While recognising the dangers of over-generalisation, the study of the literature of buyer behaviour would seem to warrant division into two distinct categories: a rational/economic model which is strongly associated with the marketing of industrial goods; and a behaviourist model commonly used to describe individual buying behaviour.

Notationally the economic model may be simply represented as:

$$A = f[EC, PC, (I-D)]$$

where A = adoption decision, EC = enabling conditions, PC = precipitating circumstances, I = economic incentives, D = economic disincentives.

The enabling conditions encompass all those factors that might conceivably be necessary to permit adoption. In both the industrial and the consumer context an obvious precondition is possession of, or access to, sufficient finance to cover purchase or lease of the new product. Other examples of EC in the industrial situation would be relevance to the prospective adopter's current or proposed area of activity, compatibility with the extant production system, and possession of the necessary technical and organisational ability to incorporate the innovation to the firm's operations. In a consumer context, sex, religion, age, physical condition, and so on, may all be highly specific determinants of an innovation's relevance to a potential adopter, and the absence of such an enabling condition would completely preclude any possibility of adoption. Operationally, therefore, we may regard EC as the first coarse screen in distinguishing between possible adopters and obvious non-adopters.

Having defined the population of potential adopters, logic dictates that among them some will be in a much more receptive state than others and so will perceive the stimulus (new product) as much stronger than other less receptive prospects. In our model, factors that predispose active consideration of an innovation are identified as precipitating circumstances. Given the existence of the necessary enabling conditions, PC may be thought of as encompassing all these factors which predispose the firm or individual to consider the adoption of an innovation. In terms of the hierarchy-of-effects model of the adoption process, *PC* coincides with the interest stage as it includes those instants or elements that move the prospective adopter from a possibly passive awareness to an active consideration. In an industrial context the breakdown of plant and equipment, a shortage of fabricated or raw materials, components or subassemblies, loss of market share due to price and/or quality differentials, or the opportunity to enter new markets, are but a few of the factors that might precipitate active consideration of an innovation.

Economic incentives and disincentives are specified separately in our model because it is believed that by doing so a better picture of the net economic benefit will emerge than by using a composite variable such as relative advantage. In a purely objective world economic logic would seem to demand that if one has a clearly identified need and is presented with a solution that offers a net improvement in one's economic status then one cannot refuse. In reality of course we all know of many instances where such apparently irresistible offers have been flatly rejected for subjective reasons; for example, the works manager who turns down a piece of labour-saving equipment of proven performance on the grounds that attempts to substitute capital equipment for labour would lead to trouble with unions.

Because of the role of such subjective factors one might be led to believe that the behaviourist explanation would be more satisfactory than that proposed by the economist. However, as we have already noted earlier in this chapter, a major deficiency of the behaviourist approach to buying decisions is an almost complete neglect of the product characteristics as an influence on the decision. In other words, the behaviourists ignore objective data that clearly are of importance in much the same way as economists neglect the importance of perception. Thus in order to operationalise our economic model of buyer behaviour we need to incorporate in it an additional variable which represents the behavioural response of the potential adopter.

In *Marketing New Industrial Products* we describe at some length a research study undertaken to try and identify the sort of factors that collectively might make up the behavioural response of industrial buying units. While modest success was achieved in terms of defining specific variables which influence the adoption of the two innovations under study, our overall results clearly indicated a strong probability that these were situation-related. In other words, while our general model of buying behaviour combining both economic and behavioural variables appears to be an acceptable reflection of the real-world situation, it will be incumbent upon individual marketers to define and specify the nature of the sub-variables which comprise the aggregated variable if they are to be able to use the model to assist them with their own new-product marketing programmes. Certainly it seems unlikely that any researcher without direct knowledge and experience of a particular situation in a given market at a given point in time would have the information necessary to operationalise the model.

Since the publication of *Marketing New Industrial Products* extensive research has been undertaken at Strathclyde (and elsewhere) which confirms the situation-specific nature of the adoption decision. For the most recent review of many of these factors the reader should refer to *Market Development* by Michael J. Baker (Harmondsworth: Penguin, 1983).

Summary

As in the other chapters in this part of the book, we have attempted to show how concepts and ideas from other disciplines may be used as a basis for thinking about marketing problems. However, our consideration has also indicated that it is unlikely that such ideas will be immediately useful without suitable modification and adaptation.

CHAPTER 9

The distributive trades

Contents

Overview of concept

Claims to be the oldest profession in the world have been made by a number of disciplines, and the merchant is no exception. The merchant, some would claim, was the medieval fount of the Industrial Revolution, maker of kings and princes, exploiter of commodity movements, shaper of empires and the mainspring of a colonial system that covered the world. His function is generally described as commerce, and its effect is to allow the manufacturer to communicate with distant markets. This, as Adam Smith[1] pointed out, allowed the manufacturer to benefit from the division of labour, or, in today's terms, large-scale operations.

His function in general terms is to buy from producers of primary and secondary products and resell in the most suitable markets to other buyers or consumers. Sometimes referred to as the commercial channel, the wholesaler and retailer when combined with the manufacturer's marketing and distribution departments make up the channels of distribution, or, in American terminology, the marketing channels. The starting point of the channel varies with the occasion from the final product producer, to the primary main commodity producer, while the final destination varies from the retailer to the customer, or the consumer.

The functions of the channel of distribution have in the course of time shifted backwards and forwards in the channel as changes occurred in the economics of the industry. This can be seen by comparing the views of earlier writers (Simmat;[2] Jeffreys[3]) with modern writers as to the functions performed.

Simmat (1940)		*Jeffreys (1950)*
Selling	1.(a)	Selling and sales promotion
Advertising	(b)	Market research
Marketing	(c)	Invoicing, stock control
Warehousing	2.(a)	Warehousing and storage
Packing	(b)	Packing
Transport	(c)	Transport
	3.(a)	General administration
	(b)	Credit and finance

Definitions of the marketing channels

The problem with definitions is that they tend to incorporate the attitude of the inventor to economic activity. Bucklin[4] considered that the start point was the producer of the final product, that is a product to which no further form change would be made, and the final point the consumer, and that the channel consisted of all the business entities in between. Rushton[5] considered the channel stopped at 'the final point of sale'. Guirdham[6] adopts Breyer's[7] definition which avoids the concept of a collection of institutions, namely: 'A distribution channel is formed when trading relations

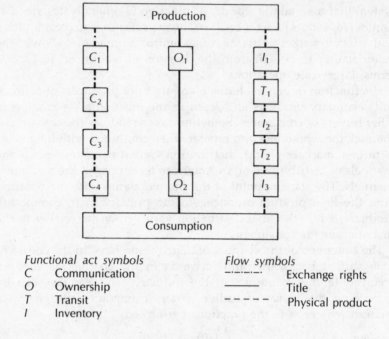

Functional act symbols

C   Communication
O   Ownership
T   Transit
I   Inventory

Flow symbols

—·—·—·   Exchange rights
————   Title
— — — —   Physical product

Figure 9.1   Functional structure flow chart

Source: L.P. Bucklin, 'The Classification of Channel Structures', in Bucklin (ed.), *Vertical Market Systems* (Glenview, Ill.: Scott, Foresman, 1970).

making possible the passage of title and/or posession (usually both) of goods from the producer to the ultimate consumer is consummated by the elements of the system.' This renames the business entities as elements, and emphasises the trading relationship and takes a functional rather than an institutional view. A functional view concentrates on what is done in the channels no matter who performs the task and tends to lead to concepts associated with efficiency rather than economic description.

When Jeffreys listed the costs of distribution it showed the production orientation prevalent at the time, and reflected the traditional cost accounting approach.

Similarly, Stacey and Wilson[8] were functionally oriented when they acknowledged the growing 'intervention of manufacturers in the distributive process' and recommended that decisions as to the best distribution channels should be based on the criteria of the costs of the functions to be performed.

By the 1960s the functions of the channels were being re-examined and redefined as flows on the basis that they could be performed in whole or in part at different levels in the channel. The number of flows and the role of the institutions varied from author to author. Bucklin's[9] scheme of four functions, excluding production, simplified earlier and longer lists to four: communications, ownership, inventory and transport. Each function when operationalised became a flow so communications became exchange rights, ownership became the movement of title, inventory and transport became the physical flow. Dommermuth and Anderson[10] classify channels as a 'sytem of functions', prompting the study of channels as a system with all the characteristics of a system, a view expanded recently by Gattorna.[11] The channel as a system lacks the main attribute that many people associate with a system, that is a central decision-making point to co-ordinate the sub-systems. The idea of the similarity of living systems was fully explored by Miller[12] who demonstrated their universality from the simplest to the most complex while Reidenbach and Oliva[13] showed how the Miller concept could as well describe the functioning of a channel of distribution as it could a whole society. It seems possible to avoid the enumeration of functions by defining channels of distribution as one of the sub-systems of the economic environment which links producers and consumers. The sub-system need not have a beginning point nor an end point but exists as a system whose function is to bridge the gap between production and consumption in a symbiotic relationship, each supplying part of the needs of the other. Those agencies who perform the functions may, in whole or in part, be members of that system while they perform their function, in the same way that an academic is a member of the system of education, but is also a member of a family system, or a political system. Such a sub-system is present whenever production and consumption are separated between two individuals irrespective of the type of economy in which it is embedded.

The economist is interested, following Alderson and Martin,[14] in the reason for the separation, the relationship of exchange, the interpolation of intermediaries, their number and function, the development of routinisation, and the location of the decisions, and control in the system, and these aspects will be explored.

Parts of the system

In a market-oriented society the parts of the system of distribution are under independent ownership and control rather than the central control of a centrally planned economy. The functions performed by each part may therefore alter with changes in the economic environment. Producers at some stage in their growth may 'spin off' some of their functions in the manner described by Stigler[15] when lower unit costs can be obtained by a specialist achieving the economies of larger scale. Many of the wholesalers and retailers owe their existence to farmers and tradesmen spinning off the function of dealing with customers which prevented them from achieving economies of scale in farming or in their trade.

This chapter describes those parts of the system which continue to do that for today's producers and are generally referred to as the *intermediaries*. The next chapter explores relationships between the parts of the system, or the channel members, as they are usually called, as they try to co-operate with one another in the pursuit of their individual objectives. Of course, these individual objectives may not always be in harmony, particularly when a growth orientation may lead to conflict.

Finally, the next chapter will review the methods used by producers to organise and maintain relationships with selected intermediaries as part of the management of their marketing channels.

The intermediaries

This allows therefore the inclusion of the study of the retail and wholesale trades, the physical distribution industries of transport and warehousing that share the physical movement with the producers, and occasionally some of the other distributors such as the hotel and catering industries, the advertising industry, and the market research agencies. A few explain how these intermediaries manage their business, but most are content with description.

Inter-organisational relationships

This is usually a group of studies that explore the relationships between the channel members in their operating as a system. For some this means the economic relationships, for others the behavioural relationships of communications, structure, process, control. The second aspect depends heavily on the language of administrative science and social science, and on the disciplines of psychology and anthropology.

It is in this area that the channel as a sub-system is most closely examined in its system parts with few studies properly relating the area of study to the whole sub-system. For example, one popular area of study whose origin can be traced to Palamountain[16] dealt with conflict and co-operation, out of which came studies of power as a means of influencing relationships, thus ignoring the symbiotic relationship of the whole. Many other aspects of the sociopolitical framework devised by Boddewyn as reported in Baker[17] did not receive the same attention. Indeed, Boddewyn's framework which sets out to redress the lack of importance given to the 'environment' is also lacking in the information processes by which the parts learn what is happening in the environment.

This aspect of marketing channels study has mostly been concentrated in the USA with the danger that, since the environment differs, the sub-system may also operate differently when compared with other countries. That subject, comparative marketing, is as yet relatively untouched, and there is a hope that comparative studies can open up new insights into the production–consumer linking sub-system.

Channel management

Some writers specialise in texts aimed at a wider market than that of academics with their interest in how things work, and instead write for those who are interested in making things work. They concentrate therefore on the business policy of the firm and in particular on marketing policy. As part of that policy area channel strategy deals with the decisions concerning the target market, the allocation of functions, the analysis of opportunities and the results. It is generally a normative approach based on the latest academic opinion of how things work, prescriptive in terms of a step-by-step approach, with recommendations of systems to be applied in collecting and processing information. This last is generally not based on research, but on dialectical materialism by which one proceeds to develop processes from generalisations that seem to be true in other situations. These generalisations originate in the auditing practices of accountants, the diagnostic of the surgery, or the rules of thumb of the investment analyst.

The intermediaries

The retail trade

With the decision by the government to discontinue the decennial census of distribution and its intermediate sample survey, a source of great detail has been lost. It is replaced by an annual Retail Enquiry, the most recent being 1979 published in 1981. The Retail Enquiry is based on a sample of retail firms drawn from a standing register based on VAT records, which excludes shops with turnover limits below the level required for registration for VAT purposes.

Supplementing this, the *Business Monitor* provides monthly index numbers of total sales for retail and catering organisations by form of organisation and kind of business.

In addition to these government official sources, two Quangos also had an interest in statistical data. One, the Distributive Industry Training Board, closed down on 31 March 1983, handing its training function back to the industry, while the other, the Distributive Trades Economic Development Committee, examines ways of improving efficiency and performance through improved organisation and management. They were responsible for producing a model of the retail trade in 1978 and for setting up the Unit for Retail Planning Information which narrowly escaped closure in 1981 because of an 'unprecedented fall' in research and consultancy from the public sector. This organisation performs a valuable service to the trade, to local authorities, and the government in providing recommendations on retail facilities provision by means of surveys, research, analysis, and library facilities.

Private sector organisations who collect and publish data are either organisations of the trade, such as trade associations or groups of associations such as the Institute of Grocery Distribution,[18] or they are market research organisations who regularly publish market data. Some examples of this are:

Retail Trade Developments in Great Britain (London: Gower Press, 1979).
Research provided by Cambridge Information and Research Services (CIRS).
Retail Trade in the UK (London: Euromonitor, 1981).
Mintel Reports.
Economist Intelligence Unit Reports.

Typical data provided by these sources are too voluminous to do more than provide a sample here (Tables 9.1–9.5), and these figures are usually accompanied by some comments on the trends.

Table 9.1   UK consumer expenditure (1971–9)

	1971	*1976*	*1978*	*1979*
Income pre-tax (£m)	47,952	112,216	141,984	166,868
	%	%	%	%
Taxes, National Insurance, etc.	19.3	23.2	21.2	20.1
Savings	6.9	11.3	11.4	11.5
Consumer expenditure	73.8	65.5	67.4	68.4
Proportion of expenditure taken by retail shops	44.1	42.5	42.0	40.7

Source: Central Statistical Office and Department of Industry as adapted in the *Nielsen Researcher No. 3* (Oxford: A. C. Nielsen, 1980) p. 7.

Table 9.2   Retail trading in Great Britain

	1971 %	*1976* %	*1978* %	*1979* %
Type of shop				
Grocers and prov. dealers	26.6	28.0	28.0	28.3
Other food retailers	16.7	16.6	16.1	15.9
Clothing and footwear	15.2	14.4	15.1	15.1
Durable goods	10.0	9.5	9.4	9.5
Misc. non-food	25.4	25.3	25.1	25.0
Dept stores	6.1	6.2	6.3	6.2

Source: as Table 9.1.

Table 9.3   Total retail sales by form of organisation

	1961 %	*1971* %	*1976* %	*1977* %	*1978* %	*1979* %	*1980*[e] %	*1985*[e] %
Independents	60	54	39.8	37.3	34.3	31.1	29.0	26.5
Multiples	29	35	40.2	42.9	45.9	49.4	52.4	54.4
Co-ops	11	9	7.1	6.9	6.6	6.4	6.2	6.6
Dept/variety stores			8.4	8.2	8.4	8.1	7.5	7.5
Mail order			4.5	4.7	4.8	5.0	4.9	5.0

e = estimate.
Source: *Retail Trade in the UK* (London: Euromonitor, 1981) p. 28.

Table 9.4   Grocery retail sales by form of organisation

	1971 %	1976 %	1978 %	1979 %	1980 %
Co-ops	13.2	14.0	15.3	15.0	14.2
Major multiples ⎱ Other multiples ⎰	44.3	49.4	38.9 19.0	40.8 18.4	42.8 18.1
Major symbols ⎱ Other indep. ⎰	42.5	36.6	7.5 19.3	7.2 18.6	6.9 18.0

Source: *Nielsen Researcher No. 4* (1981).

Table 9.5   Concentration of buying power in the retail grocery industry

	1975	1976	1977	1978	1979	1980
Number of:						
Co-op societies	227	215	206	201	195	186
Major multiple	6	6	6	6	6	6
Other multiple	56	57	52	47	44	43
Major symbol	55	49	44	43	40	40
Total	344	327	308	297	285	275
	%	%	%	%	%	%
Proportion of grocery business influenced	75	76	77	81	81	82

Source: as Table 9.4.

For the decade 1971–81 one commentator (Walters)[19] has identified the economic and social trends within the nation that have affected the retail trade, the most important being the amount of consumer expenditure taken by retail shops, an amount that is affected by income levels and taxation. The decade was marked by two periods of recession which affected the purchasing power of wages, the first beginning in 1974 and the second in late 1980. Attribution of reasons for each occasion is a matter for the economist or politician but some would suggest the price of oil was one factor. Retailers are somewhat pragmatic and respond quickly to environmental changes rather than try to anticipate them. They can afford to do this since the planning horizon in retailing is at its longest in the development of new retail facilities, and its shortest in merchandising, where flexibility is limited only by the organisational relationships with suppliers, a matter to be taken up in later sections.

The recession had the effect of increasing consumer sensitivity to price appeals and most stores, some more reluctantly than others, developed either *de facto* price-cutting strategies or simulated price-cutting strategies, or a combination of both. The second recession, which found retailers attempting to recover from the effects of the first, put a strain on the cash resources of some.

Social changes, in addition reflected in the shopping behaviour of consumers, have been a combination of changes first noticed in the 1960s, and were summarised by Walters[20] as:

1. Changing population structure:
    zero/low growth rate;
    more elderly shoppers.
2. Earlier marriage, more divorce, more single-parent families.
3. Restricted disposable income.
4. Increased price sensitivity towards food expenditure.
5. Diet changes, more ethnic foods.
6. More leisure, longer holidays.
7. More working wives.
8. More appliances.
9. Increased use of large shopping outlets.
10. Less frequent shopping.

To this might be added changes made by government in laws concerned with consumer protection, in taxation, and in wages regulation. In general there was a tremendous increase in consumer protection laws leading to increased consumer pressure for refunds. Rates increased at a faster rate than rents with some stores reporting 400 per cent increases in one year, and the wages councils pushed up wage levels faster than ever.

This combination of changes made for very difficult trading conditions that were only met by good operational management, appropriate strategy changes, and a general improvement in the productivity of labour, stock, and fixed capital, matters that will be taken up in the next section.

The effect on the structure of the trade was simply to increase the rate at which that structure as expressed in market share, by form of organisation, was changing. The long-term trend is shown in Tables 9.6–9.8, which show a decline in the market share of independents and a growth in the share of multiples. Since the early 1970s this has become more pronounced, being accompanied by a reduction in the numbers of businesses and shops. The corollary of fewer businesses and outlets is that those that remained increased in size, that is, larger organisations and larger shops were developed. Many small shops, the independents, went out of business and those who survived did so by supplying market segments separated by time and

Table 9.6   Estimated shares of total retail trade

Year	Co-ops %	Multiples %	Dept stores %	Independents %
1905	6.0	5.0	2.0	87
1910	7.0	6.5	2.5	84
1915	8.0	9.0	3.5	79.5
1925	8.5	11.0	3.5	77
1930	9.5	13.0	4.0	73.5
1935	10.0	16.0	4.5	69.5
1940	11.0	18.0	5.5	65.5
1950	11.0	20.0	5.5	63.5
1955	11.5	22.0	5.5	61.0
1960	11.0	25.5	5.0	58.5
1965	9.0	33.0	5.5	52.5
1970	7.0	39.0	6.0	48.0
1980[e]	6.2	52.4	7.5	33.9*

* Including mail order
e = estimate

Source: J. B. Jeffreys, *Retail Distribution in Great Britain 1850–1950* (Cambridge University Press, 1954); Censuses of Distribution 1950–71.

Table 9.7   Retail sales by form of organisation and kind of business

Kind of business	Independent	Multiple	Co-op	Dept store	Other*
Grocers	30.2	55.2	14.6		
Other food shops	40.3	47.2	12.5		
Clothing:					
Women's wear	10.0	24.0	3.6	37.0	26.0
Men's wear	12.0	29.0	2.0	28.0	29.0
Furnishings	23.0	43.0	5.0	10.0	9.0

* Mail order, general shops, etc.

Source: as Table 9.3.

Table 9.8   Numbers of businesses and outlets

	Businesses	Change %	Outlets	Change %	Employees	Change %
1971	368,222		509,818		2,852,600	
1979	235,174	−36	351,187	−45	2,429,000	−14.8

Source: as Table 9.3.

Table 9.9   **Retailers having more than 4% of the packaged grocery market***

Retailer	1981 %	1979 %
All co-ops	16.5	17
Sainsbury	14.5	12
Tesco	13.8	14
Asda	8.3	7
Shopper's paradise (1.8) Other Fine Fare (3.6)	5.4	5
Presto (2.8) Other Allied suppliers (1.6)	4.4	5
All members of Symbol groups	6.8	10
Kwiksave	5.6	5
Co-op Retail Services	4.1	N.A.

* Covers 75 packaged grocery fields.

Sources: as Table 9.3; and trade estimates.

locational convenience. They opened at hours different from those of multiples, and catered for customers who did not want to make a long trip to a large shop. They survived in the grocery trade by obtaining supplies from voluntary groups (17 per cent of total grocery trade in 1979) or by using cash and carry wholesalers.

The structural changes were probably most noticed in the grocery trade, but among Other food shops the independents' market share was not so deeply eroded and indeed many continue to meet the competition of the supermarkets and to flourish by being more expert and more specialised. The large multiples' market shares of the grocery trade change every few weeks, of course, but towards the end of 1981 the position was that the co-ops were the market leaders followed by Sainsbury and Tesco.

This broad picture of the trends is a simplification of the pattern in separate sectors. The broad account of multiple growth and independent decline does not describe all the problems. The next few sections describe the circumstances of each category of organisation.

The independent

Several studies have been made of the small shopkeeper[21] which tended to verify their place in the economy as supplying time and place convenience; their problems of finding supplies at competitive prices; their problems of making sufficient profit to finance the inflation of stock values; the problems created for them by urban planners in destroying older, cheaper, property and replacing with more expensive; the problem of achieving improvements in their operating ratios. Most writers are interested in halting the decline in small shop numbers on the basis of maintaining a variety of shopping forms and levels of convenience usually for the sake of the low income and less-able groups who might be isolated from the supermarkets into some kind of shopping 'ghetto' where they cannot obtain competitive prices. Dawson and Kirby suggest that if the small shop cannot survive by changing and broadening their assortment, then the options are closure or belt-tightening.

DEATH OF THE INDEPENDENT

Examining the attempts at closure by food shops, Kirby and Law[22] note the extreme difficulties in attempting to find out *how* they close. Bechofer and Elliott,[23] in examining retailers giving up business found that most (84 per cent) were leaving retailing altogether, 39 per cent were having difficulties in selling their shops, and 23 per cent had tried unsuccessfully to sell their business on a previous occasion. Those who buy a small retail business seem to be largely unsuited to the task with 44 per cent having a previous employment experience unrelated to the task. Of those with some experience, 28 per cent had experience in retail management and 28 per cent as shop assistants. This could explain the short life of many independents.

The department store

Department stores are generally taken to mean multi-level general stores whose main merchandise base is clothing and soft-furnishings. They have partial counter or personal service, and are differentiated from variety stores (e.g. Marks & Spencer) which are situated on not more than two levels with a shallower assortment of merchandise. Since there are many other independent general stores who could be similarly classified, then the group includes both independent and multiple organisations. The method of classifying each store is described in the Retail Enquiry.

Estimated shares of trade in this sector in 1980 were department stores, 4.1 per cent, variety and general stores, 3.4 per cent. The department stores have survived in one form or another in London since 1812 (Swan & Edgar, closed 1982), and in Japan since the sixteenth century. At first built to cater for the upper and middle classes in the first half of the nineteenth century, department stores were repositioned in the second half of the century to deal with the city-centre trade that arose from the development of public transport systems; and in contrast, the variety stores are a product of the 1930s recession, aimed at limited variety and fast turnover. Marks & Spencer's original slogan was 'Don't ask the price, it's a penny'. For most, survival has been achieved by merger, acquisition and, occasionally, new store buildings to give them the advantages of large scale. The acquisition techniques of Clore and Fraser were repeated in 1981 by the Fraser group's new chairman, Rowland Smith, in his sale and lease-back financing to make the assets 'sweat a little more'. Most stores are indeed now doing that by using computers to assist in stock control and sales analysis, as well as in much of the routine processing work, in the rationalisation post-merger period in order to take advantages of large scale.

Table 9.10   Department stores—market shares

	1979 %
House of Fraser	29
Debenham	19
Co-operative Society	15
John Lewis Partnership	17
Sears Holdings (Lewis's)	11
United Drapery Stores	5
Owen-Owen	3
Others	4

Source: as Table 9.3.

The co-operative societies

Individually, many of the co-operative societies are small organisations, often restricted to one town in operation, while others cover large territories and operate many stores of different types. In addition to the retail societies there is also a Co-operative Wholesale Society (CWS) that is owned by the retail societies. At one time a Scottish Wholesale Society, owned by the Scottish Retail Societies, operated in Glasgow in a similar fashion. The Co-op also owns through the CWS a range of other organisations and establishments such as farms, food-processing plants, catering establishments, laundry and dry-cleaning units, garages and travel agencies, and engages in banking, insurance and funeral undertaking. One of the CWS operations is the organisation of the Co-operative Retail Services (CRS) who manage retail shops for co-operative societies who could no longer pay their creditors, mainly the CWS.

The rationalisation process, first proposed in the Gaitskell Independent Commission report,[24] has resulted in the 918 societies of 1958 being reduced to 201 in 1979. Their turnover is divided between food 74.3 per cent (grocery and dairy being the largest section), and 25.7 per cent in non-food of which furnishing and clothing contributes the largest proportion.

Much of the original member orientation of the society has been reduced by the improved performance of other outlets in the retail trade during the 1950s and 1960s. The growth of multiples probably weakened the attraction of the payment of a 'dividend' or rebate on

Table 9.11   Co-operative societies' trade

	1978 %
Food	
Grocery and provisions	38.9
Tobacco and cigarettes	5.9
Bread and confectionery	3.6
Meat	6.0
Green grocery, fruit, and fish	2.1
Wines and spirits	4.2
Dairy	12.9
Restaurant/catering	0.4
Non-food	
Drapery	4.2
Men's wear	1.2
Footwear	1.3
Furnishing, hardware and electrical	10.8
Pharmacy and optical	1.8
Coal and fuel	0.8
Motor trades	2.8
Other	2.8
Total	100.0

Source: as Table 9.3.

Table 9.12   Inter-store price comparison*

Multiple	Index of retail prices 1982 %
Spar	105.9
Co-op	101.4
Fine Fare	101.1
Sainsbury	97.1
Tesco	95.3
Asda	91.8

* 100 equals 1979 average
Source: AGB Index 1979.

total purchases, since multiples generally operated price levels just below those of the co-operative in the 1960s. Inter-store price comparisons for the top grocery multiples confirm this is still so but to a smaller extent (Table 9.12).

Attendance at general meetings of the boards of directors, to which members can be elected, has also slumped and many boards find difficulty in filling all their vacancies. The growth of the average society's turnover has made it necessary to introduce a higher calibre of manager, some trained by the Co-operative College, others from private retail organisations, to improve the operating efficiencies of the Society. Their achievements have been considerable in wholesaling and retailing. They have introduced modern warehousing, computer-controlled automated systems, improved manufacturing specifications and Co-op-labelled products, conducted many research studies to improve their marketing (Seaman, Blamires and Morgan)[25] and advertising programmes, and succeeded in stabilising the market share of the co-ops and possibly even reversed the downward trend.

Mail order

Mail order as a form of organisation is usually taken to mean the companies in Table 9.13, who accounted for 4.1 per cent of the retail trade in 1981.

Table 9.13   Mail-order companies

	1982 Share of trade %
Great Universal Stores (Kays, Great Universal, John Noble, Trafford, John England, Marshall Ward) and John Myers (1981)	40
Littlewoods (Littlewoods, Burlington, Janet Frazer, Brian Mills, Peter Craig, John Moores)	32
Freeman's	12
Grattan Warehouses	8
Empire Stores	6
Others	2

Source: Economist Intelligence Unit. *Retail Business,* 1982.

In spite of the free availability of the same and similar merchandise in stores owned by the companies, these mail-order firms satisfy several needs of particular segments of the market they serve. Mail-order demand has been growing slowly over the last ten years but is expected to level off at about 7.5 per cent of all non-food sales. The needs they satisfy are convenience of place and time, simple credit facilities, and low-stress shopping. The convenience attribute has many dimensions, and includes the avoidance of travelling to city centres, especially for mothers of young children, working wives, and men who dislike shopping anyway; the time dimension for all of these groups is also evident in that the shopping hours are unrestricted, and that garments (51 per cent of sales are in clothing and footwear) are easily returned.

The other mail-order companies consist of specialists in particular product groups like garden and seed catalogues, special clothing, or specialist hi-fi equipment, together with the traditional department stores who offer a mail service to distant customers in the upper social classes.

Direct-mail marketing

Another type of mail selling is used by companies who advertise their products either in the media or by the special-rate direct-mail leaflet deliveries. This system is developing quite rapidly as a channel of distribution for new, or small, firms who find that they are shut out of the retail market owing to their inability to meet the larger firm's requirements of volume, delivery and price. Direct-mail marketing agencies, who will provide such services as advertisement and leaflet design, leaflet delivery or telemarketing, have also formed their own British Direct Mail Association. In 1980 it was estimated that direct mail accounted for 17.4 per cent of the total mail-order market. It now calls for improved management techniques (see *Marketing* (30 September 1981)).

Forms of trade

This section is intended to list all those methods used to retail goods by the organisations just described and begins with the self-service method started in the grocery trade and subsequently disseminated to all other kinds of business.

HYPERMARKETS, SUPERSTORES, SUPERMARKETS, AND SELF-SERVICE

The separation of these types is mainly on the basis of selling area, with some added qualification such as: location, type of building, merchandise, number of checkouts, and car-parking space. The definitions shown in Table 9.14 have been accepted by the Monopolies and Merger Commission[26] while European definitions have been explored by Barnes.[27]

Table 9.14   The Institute of Grocery Distribution (IGD) definitions based on selling space

	Square feet	No. of stores 1979
Self-service	under 2,000	
Supermarket	2,000 and under 25,000	7,130
Superstore	over 25,000	
Hypermarket	related to planning references of stores of 50,000 or over	250

Source: *Retail Grocery Trade Review* (Watford: Institute of Grocery Distribution, 1981).

Table 9.15   Size profile of grocery multiples

Square feet	January 1981 %
Under 2,000	27.9
2,000 and under 4,000	24.7
4,000 and under 10,000	27.0
10,000 and under 15,000	8.7
15,000 and under 20,000	5.4
20,000 and under 25,000	2.2
25,000 and over	4.1

Source: as Table 9.14.

The trend to large scale is more clearly seen in an IGD profile of grocery multiple store size in a sample of 5,600 stores, a pattern referred to by McLaurin of Tesco as polarisation, in which he claims the supermarket is being squeezed out by the hypermarket. The figures (Table 9.15) show little evidence of the movement.

Government control of planning permission, normally a local-authority responsibility, was introduced at the 50,000 square-feet level. Applications over this size were referred to the minister and usually resulted in a planning enquiry, at which the views of neighbouring planning authorities were sought together with other interested parties. The process can be quite lengthy and consideration is given to:

effect on retail trade in surrounding areas;
traffic loading on major and minor roads, especially the effect of
    short trips on motorways;
the effect on rateable values in surrounding areas;
the use of greenfield sites.

Government policy generally appears to prefer that superstores should attempt to use urban areas of dereliction, and that the development should take account of the shopkeepers whose business will suffer. Studies of the post-development effects have been quite extensive, some of the more recent having been completed at Mansfield[28] and Scunthorpe,[29] while Gibbs[30] provides an analysis of fifty-two planning enquiries. Most hypermarket and superstore impact studies are agreed that grocery shops in the immediate vicinity suffer substantial loss of trade to the point of closure; others with more complementary goods or services benefit; while supermarkets up to 30 miles away suffer reductions of around 10 per cent of turnover, which may make them non-viable if demand in that area at that time is affected by recession—smaller units at a distance are less affected.[31]

DISCOUNT STORES

An older retail strategy involving a high rate of stock turnover combined with low prices, low service levels and low-cost locations has been applied with great success to merchandise that traditionally carried mark-ups in the range 25–40 per cent, that is, the higher-order goods like white and brown goods, toys, hardware, carpets, DIY products, bicycles, perambulators and jewellery. Attempted in the food trade it often results in less well-known brands being stocked, and an operational system that only requires shelf pricing, and a limited range.

The key to the non-food stock management is computerised stock control which treats stock in one branch as available in all other branches. Argos and other catalogue stores take the process to its logical conclusion by selling only from catalogues. A corollary of low-cost locations is the need to advertise, so stores like Comet use the catalogue approach in their media advertising.

MARKETS AND STALLS

The 1979 Enquiry no longer lists market stalls so the 1971 census is the main source of data. This estimated that there were 31,790 traders, stalls and mobile shops accounting for 1 per cent of retail trade. Nigel Maby of Spook Erections claims that his Edinburgh (Ingliston) market is the largest in Britain–if not in Europe–and he is typical of the market owners who have increased their operation. In addition to private operators who own anything from one to fifty markets, local councils own and operate the majority of these in England and Wales, sometimes in purpose-built or converted buildings, but sometimes in the open with canvas roofs.

Table 9.16   Number of retail markets in Great Britain (1971)

Public retail markets	*565*
Privately owned or operated	*135*
London street markets	*88*
	788
Covered markets	*275*
Open markets	*425*
London markets	*88*
	788

Source: Markets Year Book, 12th edn (Oldham, 1971).

The *Markets Year Book* (12th edn, Oldham, 1971) as cited by Kirk *et al.*[32], provides a breakdown of markets, as shown in Table 9.16.

They estimated the number of markets to be 86,612 in 1971 and since then the number of private markets appears, from direct observation, to have increased, especially in Scotland.

Retail credit

(a) CHEQUE TRADING COMPANIES

This is one of the earliest forms of financing retail credit. It was originated by Joshua Waddelove of Bradford in 1880[33] and little change has been made in the system since that time, except to adjust discount deducted from the repayment to the shopkeepers. Provident currently charges between 12½ and 13¼ per cent of the sales value. The customer also pays a charge of 15 per cent on the amount borrowed over the repayment period of 23 weeks. This amounts to an Annual Percentage Rate (APR) of 97 per cent.

The major company is the Provident Financial Group Ltd (with 65·7 per cent of the market) which with Cattle's (Holdings) Ltd and Compass Paget Ltd accounted for 82.7 per cent of the turnover of £140.7 million in 1979 and were referred to the Monopolies and Merger Commission.

The main recommendation of the Commission was that the companies abandon the policy of restricting the retailer's freedom to charge cheque customers a price that differs from other customers offering different payment methods.

(b) CREDIT CARDS

The older credit card companies were initially intended as Diner and Traveller Credit Cards to enable the rich to avoid carrying large sums of money. The next wave of cards were originated by banks who issued credit cards to suitable customers or, in some cases, to non-bank customers. The more well known were Visa and Access. Towards the end of the 1970s, retailers began to introduce in-store cards operated by financial institutions; although not a complete list, Table 9.17 gives the known position of the major schemes in 1980.

Table 9.17 In-store credit cards

Company	Operator
Boots	National Westminster
Asda	National Westminster
Tesco	Midland
Marks & Spencer	Citibank Trust
Fine Fare	Unicredit
Woolworth	Unicredit
Lasky's	Unicredit
Harry Fenton	Unicredit
International Superstores	Barclay card
Wallis Fashion Group	Barclay card
Russell & Bromley	Barclay card
International Stores	Barclay card

Source: as Table 9.3.

(c) CONSUMER CREDIT OFFERED BY RETAILERS

Most stores, no matter their size, have traditionally offered some form of credit to customers; the proportion of credit granted is shown in Table 9.18.

Table 9.18 Consumer credit sales (1980)

	%
General Mail order	67
Durable goods shops	20
Department stores	9
Other general stores	4

Source: as Table 9.3.

The use of consumer credit in the decade 1971–81 fluctuated between 6 per cent and 7 per cent of retail sales, going up when consumers were confident about the future, and down when recession gripped the economy. A corollary of the behaviour of credit is that the savings proportion taken from earnings also increases with the recession and falls with confidence in the future. Since mail-order houses trade in credit they experience particularly difficult trading during a recession. In early 1982 credit sales were beginning to rise, causing some to wonder if buyer confidence was returning.

Table 9.19   Method of payment (1979)

	All adults	Current A/C holders	Non-current A/C holders	Credit card holders
% of all adults	100	51	49	17
% of all payments (value)	100	71	29	31
Method of payment (value) of which:	100	100	100	100
Cash	58	45	89	33
Cheque	26	35	4	41
Credit card	1	2	—	5
Standing order				
Direct debit	11	15	—	18
Retail store A/C				
Other	4	3	7	3

Source: AGB Index 1979, cited by S. F. Buck, 'The Changing Business Environment in the 80's', Market Research Society Conference (London, 1980).

The in-store credit cards are usually operated for the retailers by a finance house and Barclaycare, the retail arm of Barclaycard, had about twenty-five schemes in operation. The future prospects for 'plastic money' are thought by some to be improving, but credit-card transactions still only account for a tiny proportion of payment methods,[34] as Table 9.19 (payment methods for items or services valued £3 or more) shows.

Hotel and catering establishments

Not usually included in texts as an outlet for products, this sector accounts for a considerable quantity of food, drink and other products, as indicated by the data produced by the government.

Sources of data in this sector of the distributive trades originate in various censuses and enquiries in 1950, 1960, 1964, 1969, 1977 and 1980. The 1979 enquiry was a large-scale enquiry and published as a *Business Monitor* paper SDO 29, while the 1980 enquiry was published in *British Business* (6 August 1982). The turnover of all businesses in this sector amounted to £12,424m in 1980, compared with £15,278m in retail grocery. It is divided between the types of outlet shown in Table 9.20.

Table 9.20 Hotel and catering sales turnover (1980)

Description	Turnover £m	%	Gross margin %
Hotels and other residential establishments	2,483	19.9	48.1
Holiday camps, camping and holiday caravan sites	405	3.3	46.4
Restaurants, cafes, and snack bars selling food for consumption on premises	1,431	11.5	36.4
Fish and chip shops, sandwich and snack bars, partly take-away	1,103	8.9	37.7
Public houses	4,857	39.0	27.1
Clubs	1,570	12.6	17.2
Catering contractors	575	4.6	39.2

Source: *British Business* (6 Aug. 1982).

Only a few sectors have any significant degree of concentration and this is set out below:

Hotels, etc.   4 firms account for 11.7% of hotel turnover

Restaurants   9 firms account for 17.7% of restaurant turnover

Public houses   10 firms account for 66.4% of public house turnover

This fragmented industry therefore is able to support a considerable specialist wholesale trade including specialist catering wholesalers who offer full service. Smaller establishments also patronise the cash and carry wholesaler whose catering trade customers account for 40 per cent of traffic and 30 per cent of turnover. Catering size packs have been devised for this trade as well as new developments in catering products. The margarine producers, and the sugar and flour processers, produce mixtures with a number of catering applications which are in effect the convenience foods of the catering industry, and result in transferring many of the catering functions closer to the channel starting point, that is up-channel. This allows caterers to rely on less skilled (and less expensive) labour. As well as large-size catering packs, they also produce portion size packs–especially soups, butter, jam and condiments. Specialist plant have also appeared to supply such users of individual catering supplies as airlines and transport firms.

In addition to food, drink and fuel purchases of £5bn, this sector also purchases buildings, vehicles, plant, machinery and land, to a total amount in 1972 of £322m–of which £133m was for plant and machinery.

It has special needs from suppliers who seek to capitalise on these needs with considerable ingenuity, not always in a way the hotel customer appreciates, as anyone who has stayed in a hotel can testify. Wholesalers in this market are more inclined to compete on service than on price since price is a much smaller part of the cost of goods and services supplied by the hotelier, than the retailer.

Retail marketing

The main changes in structure of the retail trade noted in the previous section were...larger organisational size and larger retail outlets.

The larger organisational size is evident in the increased geographical spread of branch organisations throughout the country so

Table 9.21   Numbers and operators of large stores

Superstores (over 25,000 sq.ft)		Large stores (10,000 and under 24,000 sq.ft)	
Operator	No. stores	Operator	No. stores
Allied Suppliers	11	Allied Suppliers	75
Asda	65	Asda	14
Fine Fare	31	Bishops	3
Hillards	7	E. H. Booth	1
Key Markets	4	Fine Fare	40
Linfood Holdings	8	Hillards	16
Wm Low	2	Amos Hinlan	9
Mainstop	18	International	37
Wm Morrison	14	Wm Jackson	6
Safeway	1	Key Markets	28
Sainsbury	10	Linfood Holdings	10
Savoy Centre	5	Wm Low	5
Tesco	70	Mainstop	4
Woolco	11	Safeway	47
		Sainsbury	171
		Tesco	131
		Waitrose	38
Co-ops	47	Co-ops	92
Independents	14	Independents	13
Total	314	Total	739

Source: as Table 9.4.

that multiples who had dominated their own regions now moved into competition with multiples in other areas. They 'invaded' these other regions using new, much larger shop units to compete with the older, smaller units of their competitors, principally in the grocery business. In turn their own region was open to penetration by competitors using the same strategy. This created a defensive need to speed the redevelopment of small units, some being closed, others being amalgamated to provide larger premises, at a higher cost than new units.

Confirmation of the trend is available in two new directories and a poster map, the Large Stores Directory and the Superstores Directory 1982 (Institute of Grocery Distribution) which lists a total of 318 superstores and 739 large stores as at March 1982. So far as the non-food trade is concerned, the growth of organisation size is more evident than the growth of large units (see Table 9.7), but the consequences are similar.

Larger retail outlets were consistent with increased ranges of merchandise and expansion into non-food in which grocery companies were less experienced. Much of the range expansion was experimental with companies dropping lines they found unsuccessful. Many variety chains who added food during this period subsequently dropped the packaged grocery products. New retail warehouses for furniture, DIY, textiles, freezer supplies and horticultural products were developed.

Competition for customers

Whereas previously large retail firms seldom had to face competition from other similar firms in the market they now were forced to consider their marketing strategy, both for growth and for defence against other organisations of the same type, on a scale never before experienced, requiring them to compete for the mind of the consumer at national level as well as shopping centre level resulting in increased retail advertising expenditure. Buck[35] demonstrates the increased importance of advertising in a dramatic fashion by listing the top twenty advertisers for the years 1969 to 1978. The 1969 list has three retailers while the 1978 has fourteen, with twelve of them in the top position.

A more realistic measure is the changing share of advertising devoted to retailing and this is shown in Table 9.22.

Part of the decade was a period of recession and inflation and Walters[36] lists five changes in the retailer's strategy to deal with this.

Table 9.22   Retail advertising as a proportion of total advertising expenditure

	Retail advertising expenditure £m	Manufacturers' consumer advertising £m	Ratio %
1970	56	250	22.4
1971	63	271	23.2
1972	84	311	27.0
1973	114	362	31.4
1974	134	348	38.5
1975	163	387	42.1
1976	206	493	41.7
1977	260	613	42.4
1978	307	745	41.2
1979	354	836	42.3
1980	435	1,072	40.6
1981	487	1,172	41.6

Source: *Advertising Quarterly* (London, 1971–82).

1. They increased sales area productivity.
2. They expanded their markets.
3. They considered customer service and its effect on sales.
4. They restructured their business philosophies.
5. They increased the use of capital equipment in their businesses.

Cook and Doyle[37] summarised the choices open to maintain long-term profitability (Figure 9.2), and from an empirical study comparing retailer strategy with performance, concluded that neither the strategy of aggressive market share expansion, nor productivity improvement separately, were generally very successful. The most successful strategy was an integrated strategy aimed at producing an appropriate (rather than maximum) market share and a matching financial strategy geared to an effective structure of margins, asset turnover and leverage.

The strategy of any firm, whether manufacturer or retailer, is in essence a shorter-term version of the business policy of the firm. The components of that policy as it applies to marketing were summed up by Borden[38] as 'the marketing mix', while for retailers a similar array of components of business policy was described by Stern.[39] The decisions concerning these components are made within the bounds of a long-term planning horizon and are intended to result in a store image whose parts are in harmony and with which the target market is satisfied.

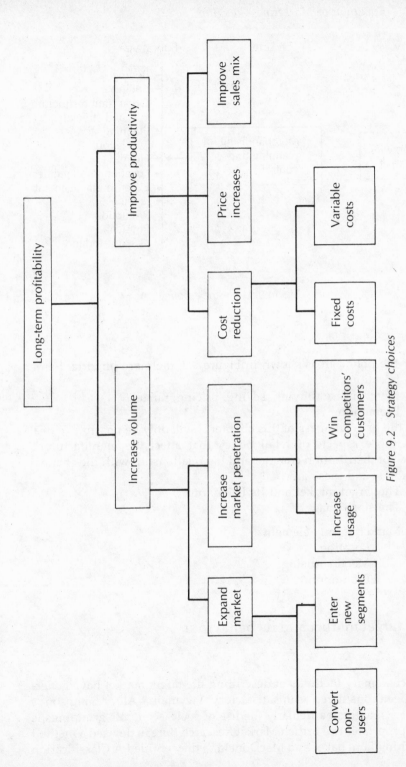

Figure 9.2 Strategy choices

Source: D. Cook and D. Doyle, 'Marketing Strategies, Financial Structure and Innovation in UK Retailing', in Marketing Education Group, *Conference Proceedings* (1978).

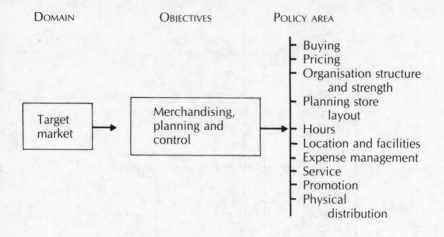

Figure 9.3   Business policy

Of the policy areas shown in Figure 9.3, the more important are:
    Location
    Merchandise (buying, selling, pricing, range)
    Promotion
In the brief compass of this chapter it will only be possible to deal with those aspects of retail policy that affect the manufacturer's choice of distribution channel and his relationship with the channel members, and these are:
    The target market and its behaviour
    The store image

    Marketing mix elements:
        Location
        Merchandising
        Promotion

The target market and its behaviour

The customary methods of describing the target market have generally been considered as unsatisfactory (Twyman;[40] Allt;[41] Sampson[42]) and for retailers particularly the use of socio-economic groupings is inappropriate. The British Market Research Bureau devised a method (Bermingham, Baker and MacDonald[43]) they entitled A Classification of Residential Neighbourhoods (ACORN) based on Webber's[44] system for classifying electoral wards and parishes into thirty-six types of neighbourhood. This seemed particularly appropriate for retailers seeking out new locations for expansion, and was taken on board by URPI to asist their clients in finding suitable areas for expansion. For the purpose of finding out about shopping behaviour patterns there still remains much to do.

The shopping behaviour of the target market affects and is affected by the business philosophy of the retailer as far as the merchandising policy is concerned, and research in this area was relatively sparse in the United Kingdom. In the United States the volume was sufficient to encourage a state of the art review by Granbois[45] which enabled him to classify research into four areas:

1. Theoretical explanations of variables in the pre-purchase information search.
2. The incidence and extent of shopping, the morphology of shopping trips.
3. Store preference and store image in specific areas.
4. Store patronage, i.e. customer profiles, location and distance models, store loyalty.

All of this research is of course based on American consumers and may not be directly applicable in the United Kingdom in the light of life-style differences identified by Douglas and Urban[46] in the United States, the United Kingdom and France. In an earlier article[47] it is also suggested that existing models of consumer behaviour require two sets of transformation:

1. From a model describing the behaviour of the American consumer to one explaining the behaviour of consumers in *any* foreign country.
2. From general models to problem-specific models.

Such cross-cultural studies of shopping decisions as have been done[48] do indeed identify some differences and also similarities. Replication of American studies at times produce different results[49] and at other times similar results[50].

PRE-PURCHASE INFORMATION SEARCH

Models of the buying process are of interest to manufacturers who are concerned to create some predisposition towards their brand by means of pre-purchase information, but the retailer is also interested in the information search process in so far as it affects the consumer's store choice, for much of the exposure occurs within the store as an incidental process as well as on shopping trips for purchase. The retailer is also directly interested in the information search as a prior process to deciding which stores to visit on a shopping trip. The summary of American research by Granbois referred to above suggests that the list of determinants of pre-purchase search are:

The consumer	–Reference map, product importance, purchase frequency, personality and self-perception and salient attributes used to judge the product.
The decision environment	–Availability of information, product assortment available, degree of differentiation between products, frequency of change in prices, styles and technology.
Product characteristics	–Price, size, bulk, life-span relationship between observable and performance characteristics, subjectivity of evaluative criteria, social conspicuousness, and complexity.

The searching process then continues until the consumer reaches a point where further benefit of searching would be suboptimum in the consumer's own value system. Information searching has several purposes in reducing risk and uncertainty, improving knowledge of choice available, and many others. The effect of retail advertising in the present structure of the trade is to attract the more mobile population of the 1980s to visit larger stores in larger catchment area centres, increasing the pull effect of the large centre and large store.

SHOPPING TRIPS–INCIDENCE, EXTENT, AND MORPHOLOGY

Basic to all shopping trip behaviour, is the product or the product groups that have generated the trip, thus many products are grouped together as 'groceries', others as fashion, house renovation, gifts, holiday needs, or life-style maintenance. The consumer's order of preference for these groups is arranged in terms of some scale of higher-order to lower-order goods. Higher-order goods require more analytical decisions than lower-order and these decisions occur less frequently and take longer. Howard classifies the range of decision-making behaviour as Extensive Problem Solving (EPS), Limited Problem Solving (LPS) and Routinised Response Behaviour (RRB).[51]

This in effect means that both information gathering and shopping trips can be classified as associated with these different types of behaviour. It is usually assumed that grocery buying is in the RRB class allowing for the development of habits and eventually loyalty. In today's market loyalty as a concept has tended to be replaced by patronage, that is, the allocation of grocery purchases among diffe-rent stores. Similarly, shopping trip patterns for higher-order groups have also been subjected to change by increased retail advertising, capital investment (in buildings), improved infrastructure and other environmental changes.

The majority of United Kingdom studies have been completed by geographers rather than sociologists or marketers, or have been commissioned by town planners intent on adjusting planning re-quirements to current needs (see Davies;[52] Evans;[53] Garner;[54] Bruce;[55] Holly and Wheeler;[56] Openshaw;[57] Dawson;[58] Thomas;[59] Dawson and Kirby).[60] American researchers found that new resi-dents' behaviour exhibited a shift from EPS to RRB as they settled down in their new area, suggesting a process of investigating the retail facilities before making a choice of regular store, although there was some indication that patronage transfers to local branches of their previous choice also occurred.

Shopping trip behaviour is also affected by income, and most American studies have concentrated on low-income groups who seem particularly prone to restricting shopping trips to local centres.[61] Those who make frequent and extensive trips outside their own area (outshoppers)[62] also exhibit attributes that separate them from other shoppers—being younger, richer and more innovative, and likely to live in smaller towns.

STORE PREFERENCE AND STORE IMAGE

There are many similarities between the concept of brand preference and image, and store preference and image, with consumers typically including in their shopping activities a very small sub-set of the stores available to them. Not surprisingly, retailers are interested in the store attributes that affect store choice. Many of the studies aim to discover and to measure the salient attributes used by shoppers. British researchers have been fairly active in this respect,[63] explain-ing the relationship between store image and store choice. More and more retailers are now applying this type of research to resolve their long-term strategy of developing a store image to appeal to their target market.

The CWS recently gave an account of the research basis for their own long-term strategy,[64] in which a 20-attribute measure of shop image was completed by respondents. The salient attributes for each consumer was then subjected to a trade-off (or conjoint) analysis by each respondent to obtain utility values for each attribute. These utility values then become input for a behavioural micro-model which can be manipulated on the basis of alternative scenarios of shop image. The model can then be used to predict consumer preferences for each alternative, and guide the organisation towards either their image development or their target market. A similar but less powerful approach was also being used by researchers in the United States of America[65] to demonstrate that consumers preferred those stores that most closely reflected their own self-image, confirming the concept of a matching process. The implications for choice of target market, the positioning of the shop in the mind of the consumer, was also explained by Ring[66] concerning men's fashions.

STORE PATRONAGE

Studies of store patronage have focused on the characteristics of patrons in terms of 'profiles' describing their demographic, psychographic, or life-style attributes for particular types of store.[67] Also included in these studies are catchment area definitions and descriptions concerning the proportions of expenditure and shopping-trip behaviour. This frequently leads to the building of alternative models for store location and planning purposes. When segments of the market are identified which have a higher than average patronage of one store this leads to studies that identify the reasons for the development of this loyalty, generally to be found in attributes of the shopper.[68]

THE TARGET MARKET DECISION

The development of the concept of the target market has become more sophisticated with the realisation that society is more complex. New groupings of shoppers have been developed such as the Time Buying Consumer,[69] the Professional Woman,[70] the Recreational Shopper,[71] and the Working Wife.[72] This opportunity to specialise, to create 'boutique'-type stores based on the willingness of shoppers with mobility to shop outside their neighbourhood, depends to a large extent on an improvement in the economy, for if present trends continue, precisely the opposite could result. Given a scenario of more expensive transport costs, population decline, increasing proportion of people aged over 60, declining per capita income, then the trend could change to a more dismal view of retail development.

The target market decision affects all areas of company policy, whether deciding on new branch locations, merchandise range and pricing, promotion and service. It is therefore the first in importance and should be made only in the light of market information. Similarly, decisions in other policy areas should be based on known and verified changes in the behaviour of the target market, otherwise the retailer is likely to be blown off course by the winds of competition.

Marketing mix elements

The salient elements to be examined are location, merchandising and promotion.

Location

The location decision commits a retailer to considerable capital investment, or to a contract from which he may not readily withdraw, and for this reason a planning horizon of several years is involved. Were less permanent arrangements possible, the decision could be taken more lightly. Where it is possible to enter into more flexible arrangements, retailers will sometimes do so. Others, like Marks & Spencer, prefer a longer-term commitment and will only take up a location when they are thoroughly satisfied with the long-term prospect.

One well-known bakery chain solves its location problems successfully by working closely with a property developer who offers them an initial one-year lease with an option to extend to a longer period, when the developer acquires a property he considers would be suitable. Some retailers create a separate property-owning company which operates in virtually the same way. These methods and several others are devices to reduce capital risk and investment while compelling the assets to make merchandising profits. The location function, while it may be spun off, still has to be performed.

Stern and El-Ansary[73] attempted a taxonomy of the types of decision faced by analysts and this could be augmented by new decisions required by urban redevelopment.

The inter-regional analysis decisions are mainly concerned with the target market and company strategy while intra-regional decisions are more concerned with specific sites, but when movements are forced upon the company, then there is a need to re-examine strategy.

The retail location decision is also of interest to central and local government and their rules are likely to affect retailers' decisions.

Table 9.23   Taxonomy of location decisions

Type	First-time acquisition	Additional outlets	Abandonment	Urban relocation
Inter-regional analysis	Which region	Direction of Growth	Re-evaluation of competition	Strategy evaluation
Intra-regional analysis	Which site	Type of centre	Evaluation of strategy	Evaluation of strategy

Source: adapted and extended from L. W. Stern and A. I. El-Ansary, *Marketing Channels* (Englewood Cliffs, N.J.: Prentice-Hall, 1977).

The particular rules are the Town and Country Planning Acts which empower local authorities to control new development. In the case of large stores, central government has reserved the right to call in these applications for planning permission, and may hold a planning enquiry. The result is that there are at shopping-centre level a number of other influences on the retailer's decision. The retailer may also employ a specialist agency to help in the decision-making, allowing the influences to be grouped as follows:

> *Town planners.*   Main interest is in identifying effects of altera-
> tions in the retail structure caused by the addition of new
> premises, population movement, or abandonment of premises.
> *Geographers.*   Academic interest in land use and population set-
> tlement patterns, movement, spatial interaction, and shopping
> hierarchies.
> *Market researchers and location specialists* such as Donaldsons, or
> the Unit for Retail Planning information. Main interest is to
> provide centre and site evaluations in terms of turnover.

Each group of influencers is of course aware of the work of the others and borrows techniques they can adapt to solve the different problems brought to them. There is no single technique that can be adapted to all the different types of problem. Problems may range from straightforward assessments of greenfield site occupation, to predicting the impact of a retail development on neighbouring shopping centres.

PLANNERS AND GEOGRAPHERS

All problems take place within the regional retail structure in so far as a boundary can be drawn around the region. Within the region, one town can be identified as a regional-level shopping centre and a hierarchy of other centres can be distinguished. These centres may be further classified into three or four types following such criteria as sales turnover, range of services provided, forms of organisation, or some combination. A regional shopping expenditure model of the gravity type may then be constructed to show how each centre attracts sales turnover from each of the population areas of that region. This type of model is based on each centre having a power of attraction and is subject to a constraint of distance from (i) the various population centres, and (ii) the competing shopping centres. Calibrating the model, that is making it reflect the real situation, is done by fitting in known expenditures at all the centres to produce parameters which, when the model is run, will generate the known shopping centre sales data. These generalised models[74] have been used in modified forms in the United Kingdom, to predict changes in shopping patterns in local authority areas[75] or are used by URPI[76] as a model which can be adapted to most needs, as in Glasgow's city centre shopping model in 1982.

The model can be used subsequently to predict the allocation of regional shopping expenditure under changed conditions such as the introduction of a new shopping centre, or a hypermarket which requires planning permission. From the retailer's point of view the model can be used to predict hypermarket turnover, but cannot immediately help to predict a single shop's sales in a shopping centre development.

These models ignore aspects of consumer behaviour such as preference for particular centres or individual shops, combined-purpose trips (business and shopping), interrupted journeys, which can also influence expenditure allocations, and have consequently been modified by incorporating the results of household surveys of shopping behaviour during a limited period, and these are reviewed by Shepherd and Thomas.[77]

Since 1974, when a seminar was held in the House of Commons to allow interested parties to air their views before MPs,[78] a number of impact studies that measure the effect of the establishment of a superstore or hypermarket on the surrounding retail structure have been conducted,[79] and those noted are typical. In the case of the Coatbridge ASDA, a town-centre hypermarket, the impact on the immediate retailers was devastating, leading to a number of closures, and two such studies have been carried out there. Similarly the impact of town-centre redevelopment has resulted in changed retailer performance in Newcastle.[80]

CATCHMENT AREA STUDIES

Another geographer approach is to identify the catchment area of a shopping centre or centres by a methodological procedure of shopper interviews to discover trip origins, and expenditure, and to plot these on a map which can then be divided into primary, secondary and tertiary areas.[81] Since the shopper surveys may include store patronage questions, the survey can then be used to produce market shares for particular commodity groups. The methodology of shopper surveys are suspect for two reasons. The sample of the shopper population may not be representative of catchment area expenditure, because the most frequent shoppers may be small spenders while mothers of large families may be less well represented yet be the large spenders on groceries. Older shoppers may be more than proportionately represented. The timing of the survey may also affect representativeness because of the season or the day of the week. Grossing up the sample results is therefore likely to produce inaccuracies.

The need for grossing up could be avoided by purchasing the data from URPI who can produce expenditure zone information. By arrangement with CACI Inc., they can now supply data (population, households, income index and ACORN profiles) at two levels of expenditure zone: (i) regional zones corresponding to Head Post Office areas, and (ii) local expenditure zones corresponding to main or Crown Post Office areas. There are 1,101 such zones. Another kind of analysis is the provision of population, household ownership and income data for 315 major shopping terms, presented in analysis bands from a central point.

Market researchers have extended the concept of catchment area analysis into retailer-specific model-building for the purpose of assessing individual retail sites of which several might be offered to the multiple retailer weekly. This meets the needs of those retailers who are confronted with a constant stream of location decisions which are to be made on the basis of their experience in other branches. Such a model is also useful to identify reasons for existing branch performance. The model consists of multiple attribute discriminant analysis of those exogenous and endogenous factors that seem to affect turnover. The first paper by Heald[82] was followed by Simmons,[83] Clawson[84] and Fenwick,[85] with further applications of the technique to bank branches and building society branches.

Typical lists of data used are:

Exogenous	*Endogenous*
Key traders in the area	The outlet selling area
Direct competition	Selling staff

Car parking facilities
Office accommodation
Public transport
Exterior appearance
Catchment area
Demographics

Rateable value
Appearance of interior
Display space
Supervisor's ability

The dependent variable is, of course, turnover or revenue, and the model is created by the explanatory power of discriminant analysis in selecting those factors that generally account for the sales turnover. Fenwick[86] prefers a model in which competitive activity is market-share related, rather than turnover-volume related. Both of these relationships of course are approximations, because the effect of competition really depends on all the endogenous variables above, but Fenwick's model when tested could account for 62 per cent of variance with a mean absolute error of under 5 per cent of revenue.

URBAN RELOCATION

This problem area appears as yet to have received more attention from geographers than from planners who create the problem, and retailers who discover it. It is the problem originally identified as urban decentralisation, which was the cause, it is said, of department store closures during the late 1960s and early 1970s when some authorities permitted the creation of peripheral shopping centres. This was followed by city-centre 'revitalisation' when traffic engineering solutions to road congestion coupled with the increased use of car parking on gap sites (once occupied by department stores) attracted some retailers back into the city centre. Department stores who established peripheral branches in their expansion now face a decision in location policy for peripheral operations are likely to be quite different in character from those in a Central Business District (CBD).

The general pattern of CBD retail decentralisation appears to be related to the class of goods. Lower-order goods or services are first to move, and are followed by the next higher-order of goods, as the city size increases. Woolworth in 1982 acquired all the stores of Dodge City, the DIY specialist, and this was followed by the closure of twenty-five of Woolworth CBD shops. This could be described as an expensive but convenient transfer of some of its business to a peripheral location. The next logical step is to remove lower-order goods from the CBD shops and replace them with higher-order.

Merchandising

The merchandise planning horizon is probably at its longest in mail-order trading when six months is needed to allow for the production of the catalogue. For most retailers the period is much less, being at its shortest in groceries where three weeks might be the time needed to place orders.

Merchandising is generally regarded as the most important function and is often described as the buying and selling processes. It is more than that for it involves decisions on merchandise range and depth of assortment which can only be reached by relating to the viable demand of the target market. Since the target market is made up of several segments, its viable demand is that sufficiently large section of its demand which can be accommodated and sold in a particular location, at a price which will trade off the range attractiveness against the inconvenience of travel. Merchandise policy and location policy therefore are interactive. A lower than average price can overcome travel inconvenience, and can be compensated by a lower than averge occupancy cost.

Merchandising is therefore defined as the matching of viable target market demand in a particular location with saleable merchandise that will achieve the firm's objectives. The initial decision is called retail positioning.

THE NEW RANGE DECISION

The establishment of a complete range of products for the first time is a relatively small problem compared to the frequency with which decisions concerning the existing range will occur during the life of the store.

The main function of the first decision is to create an image of the store based on a small part of the range. The decision as to what items can be put together and be called a range cannot move far from the expectations of the target group and indeed helps to define the target group. A notable example of this is the development of the DIY retail warehouse whose origins can be traced to the local timber supplier's establishment of a retail outlet. Development based on demand from the DIY segment led to some retail outlets extending their range into ironmongery, hardware and tools. At this point someone discovers that the DIY market has changed and now consists of amateurs rather than semi-skilled customers and that the depth of assortment is now less important than the range of assortment. A new range is needed for this new market segment together with a new location policy.

Changes in the merchandise range occur with relatively little effort on the part of the retailer who is subjected to pressures for addition by suppliers and customers, while his accountant urges him to drop slow-moving or less-profitable lines. Customer pressure for cheaper groceries linked with the appearance of hard times among some less well-known brands produced generics. These changes in the long term can be seen as cycles of response to various business environment pressures described by Stern and El-Ansary.[87] A particularly interesting cycle is that of specialisation/generalisation, which Hall[88] described as a characteristic cycle of evolution in the retail trade, but little application has been found for the identification of these various cycles.

From this point merchandise operations consist of adding or dropping product groups that the existing target market seems to want, with very little in the way of research other than test marketing in representative stores. Obviously the merchandise policy of a store is a salient component of store image, as was mentioned earlier, but there do not appear to be many researches which operationalise store-image research into merchandise policy. Merchandise policy is more likely to be decided operationally by evaluating the return from the allocation of space to different product groups, so as to maximise total return in the store.

SHELF-SPACE ALLOCATION

Much of the research in this area has been in the grocery trade which appears to experience more demands on its shelf or display space from new products than other trades. Studies tended to explore the effect of changes in allocation on sales (value or volume) or the contribution to profit. The first criterion, sales, is attractively simple to measure but does not take account of the cost of space, nor the cost of handling. The second criterion creates problems in allocating these costs. Curhan,[89] in reviewing work up until that point, concluded that the effect of changing space allocation varied with the type of product, type of location and environmental factors. Few retailers have made practical use of such research even when computer packages are available to assist, probably because they are not looking for answers to this problem. The main assortment problem is deciding whether or not to add a new supplier offering. Recent postgraduate work sponsored by Fine Fare suggests that researchers have indeed been looking at the wrong problem and might better spend their time devising methods such as that of Westwood, Palmer and Pymont[90] to help retailers examine new product offerings. Currently retailers are being urged to use Electronic Point of Sales

(EPOS) data capture as the answer to all their problems concerning assortment, space, promotion, and display decisions. Whitaker and Lay[91] believe that some caution will be exercised because of the large capital investment required.

Leeflang[92] and Anderson[93] examined the problem from a viewpoint of portfolio management. They suggested that the store's profits are largely determined by its portfolio of brands and that this portfolio determines the space each should receive. The less sensitive a store's customers are to brands, the more flexibility the store has in its portfolio.

This approach, when related to recent developments in retailer brand groceries[94] and in so-called generic products, would indicate that many brands have been losing ground in their appeal to the consumer when confronted with low prices, to the point where some retailers now restrict their portfolio of brands to the market leaders, while minor brands are relegated to the weaker independents, or disappear to become retailer brand producers. For the manufacturer this reveals a need to include in product research more trade-off analysis which can take account of the competition from future retailer brand developments.

OWN LABEL

The interest of researchers in own label (or distributor) brands has certainly increased during the decade, although the seminal work remains that of Cooke and Schutte.[95] Advertising agencies expressed alarm during their conference[96] at the apparent drop in advertising budgets, while Lind[97] commented that retailers are coming to accept the value of advertised brands, but only if sold at prices that left little room for advertising them in the future.

Manufacturers' policies on own label supply appear to be related to industry excess capacity, industry concentration, the product-life-cycle, the volume of advertising, and the economic environment.

Excess capacity is frequently thought by suppliers to be one of their reasons for supplying own label since there is likely to be more damage to their competitors than to their own brand when supplying an existing customer. The extra volume enables fixed costs to be spread more thinly, and can even allow them to install more productive machinery.

Industry concentration is related to the degree of monopoly possessed by the leaders, and that monopoly enables them to control supply to a degree. Retailers have noticed that where there is no dominant brand, own labels do well.

Protection of producers from own label competition is readily achieved by innovation since there may be few who can legally produce a substitute until the product has been investigated, so own labels tend to occur when maturity has been reached.

Heavy advertising support creates a degree of loyalty, and Broadbent[98] has demonstrated the link between advertising share, market share and price.

The economic environment creates difficulties for some sections of the market, and although most researches are unable to distinguish differences between own label and manufacturer brand customers,[99] one study of baked beans buyers[100] identified family size and age as a differentiating factor.

SUPPLIER SELECTION

The buyer–seller dyad is often researched in the industrial-buying situation but less frequently in the field of commerce. Industrial buying generally recognises different decision rules for different product classifications, with a large number of influencers present in the buyer's organisation. The commercial buyer probably has fewer classifications but many more single buying decisions. There are fewer influencers in their decision and a different balance of importance between product choice and supplier choice. Buyer objectives are also likely to be different. Stern and El-Ansary[101] list ten attributes used in the decision process, while Doyle and Weinberg[102] report that only eight dimensions are examined.

Stern and El-Ansary list:

Demonstrated consumer demand (or projected demand, if a new product)
Projected gross margin
Expected volume
Merchandise suitability
Price and terms
Service level offered
Manufacturer reputation
Quality of the brand
Promotional assistance
Vendor's distribution policy
(national, regional, local; exclusive, selective, intensive)

Once the commercial buyer is satisfied about expected product performance, and supplier's ability to provide continuity, his main concern is to obtain some price and exclusivity advantage over his competitors while the supplier is intent on increasing sales over a long period to provide production expansion. This draws the nego-tiating parties together in co-operation to achieve both objectives.[103]

The purpose of all merchandise control systems is to integrate the several components which will reduce the inventory at all times to that level which will satisfy customer demand, while never running out of stock, or losing supplier discounts.

The components of the control system are:

Sales targets–based on forecasts for each product
A stock plan appropriate to the targets
A buying plan that will support the stock plan
Inventory turnover objectives based on a profit target
A promotional plan to achieve specific sales targets

Once the sales targets and the profit targets have been decided, merchandise policy choice ranges from high mark-up–low stock-turn to low mark-up–high stock-turn in a fashion that has already been decided in selecting the target market and the store location.

Whichever policy is chosen, the resulting stock and buying plans are a matter for programming once the relationships have been identified. This is likely in the future to become more sophisticated as computer applications are extended by retail accountants re-sponsible for calculating the 'open-to-buy', that figure of unused budget for buying that reacts quickly to the prospect of over- or under-performance against target.

Pricing

Far from being an automatic process as might seem to be implied by a policy decision on mark-up, pricing is part of the promotional and image strategy of a retailer. In recent years as the recession deepened, grocery retailers moved gradually from a selected and limited num-ber of price-promoted (that is, reduced) items to an increasingly large number, and did so in spite of earlier evidence that consumers could not remember prices accurately for more than a dozen or so items. The recall ability varied of course with consumer attributes. Some multiples took the policy to its logical conclusion and established specific low-cost operations in separate discount chains, presumably in areas that they believed had a high proportion of price-sensitive customers, thus adapting their policy to a newly identified target market. In some cases price-sensitive customers are also insensitive to brand so stores may follow a policy of using lower-price brands, or, if store loyalty is high, increase generic brand representation throughout their range.

Research on the effects of in-store promotions at the point of sale (POS) followed on the heels of research on space allocation. Related to POS promotions is the trend towards providing unit price information on the shelf, and the effect of shelf edge price marking as a replacement for product price marking when Electronic POS (EPOS) check-outs are introduced[104] has also been researched. Experiments to relate changes in the marketing mix to sales turnover have been conducted at various times in the last ten years, in the USA (Wilkinson, Mason and Paksoy,[105] Chevalier,[106] Doyle and Fenwick).[107] The variables in the marketing mix varied from display changes to combinations of price changes, advertising level, and display level, while increases in the sales turnover level were up to several hundred per cent. These experiments usually required a high cost in labour to count unit sales before, during and after the change. A few reports are now appearing[108] of data collected electronically at the point of sale, being used to research the sales turnover effect of changes being made to the advertising budget and strategy over a wider range of products and larger numbers of stores.

The earlier research work suffered from the drawback of being limited to a few products in one store, and therefore having a limited applicability. The indications which emerged from such studies were that:

(a) price level and display level together have a strong impact on most product sales
(b) price and display appear to be more important than newspaper advertising in the short term
(c) price reduction is the main factor in sales turnover.

Comparative pricing has now become fairly popular as an advertising feature in types of merchandise. In some cases the price comparison is with previous prices in the same store, or with the manufacturer's recommended price, or with price levels generally applicable in the area, so long as the claim complies with the Trades Description Acts 1968–72. Della Bitta, Monroe and McGinnis[109] found in their experiment that price comparisons alone were insufficient to produce purchase motivation; that the information search process ceases more abruptly with increases in the discount level; that the format of discount (value or percentage) appeared to produce different responses; and that the customer tended to trade-off features against price in deciding rather than examining the price alone.

Retail advertising

As was seen earlier, retail media advertising now accounts for over 40 per cent of manufacturers' consumer advertising, with agencies being faced with the need for new approaches, and clients having to develop approaches. Once restricted to provincial media, advertisers, particularly grocery advertisers, have a new-found strength in television advertising. Since retail store image is conveyed mainly through merchandise and price, it is inevitable that catalogue-type advertising is a basic feature. Some stores in fact use only catalogue-type advertising because price is their main appeal. When this style is practised by all competitors then some shoppers make their purchase decision in the comfort of an armchair, thus reducing the traffic-generation effect of the advertisement. Haynes[110] classifies retail advertising as a direct response type and lists four kinds of direct response.

Group I   To sell merchandise from the page
           To get coupons clipped
           To make telephones ring
           To persuade people into shops, showrooms, show homes

The last item, traffic generation, is essential in the grocery trade since the majority of final decisions to purchase are made in the store, so that the merchandise featured in the advertisement serves as a 'call bird' to persuade the consumer to visit the store. Once the consumer has visited the store, in-store promotion and display takes over.

Group II   To encourage them to purchase
           To make them want to come again
           To recommend the store to friends
           To get the store talked about
           To increase the store prestige

Retailers' attitudes to spending money on advertising vary widely according to their view of their own competitive situation. Some stores located in shopping centres that are sufficiently attractive to draw customers, feel that they have little need to persuade people to visit their stores and concentrate on the second group of objectives. Others, particularly those in off-centre locations, rely on advertising to generate traffic. Those in competition with similar stores also feel the need to remind customers of what they offer, so grocery store advertising is usually substantial. Stores also need to advertise when they have some relevant information–such as a change of policy–to communicate to customers.

Ornstein suggests tentatively that a number of retailer attributes can be identified as relating to the size of the promotional budget:[112]

Longevity, time span of reputation
Height of reputation
Quality of location
Frequency of repeat shopping
Width of range
Supplier's contribution to co-operative advertising
Specific promotional effort

Whatever the budget, however, retailers are well aware of the need to co-ordinate all their promotional activities with their merchandising programme so that the merchandise is the dominant influence on the advertising objectives. This finds expression in different ways, as when Mothercare features only standard top-selling lines (a practice followed by many others), and avoids featuring new products, while grocery stores feature volume sellers at low prices. These promotional offers often use national brands as traffic builders.

In recent years some television media users among retailers have included secondary objectives, after the merchandise, as a form of background and these appear to have 'image building' as a major orientation. Woolworth also used an array of personalities, each with quite different images, to support their Christmas advertising while others depend on archetypes of their target market, or select personalities who could be seen as archetypes.

The effect desired by most retailers is usually expressed in relatively simple terms related to traffic generation, or, perhaps mistakenly, unit sales, since unit sales are also affected by conditions inside the store. In Haynes's view the budget should not only be recovered by extra sales but should generate an additional profit, presumably to pay for the investment that could have been diverted to merchandise. Most advertising agents would agree that retailers demand more for their budget than manufacturers.

Although this brief review has not covered all the functions of retailing, or the organisational and financial structures of the emerging giants, it has attempted to highlight the salient features of retail-marketing strategy and to highlight areas of research interest. All retailers are agreed as to the importance of the consumer; however, in the United Kingdom, studies of consumer behaviour are relatively sparse, although they are increasing in number. There will indeed never be an end to the information needed on the changing shopping behaviour of the consumer.

There are few retailers who would now try to be all things to all customers and much more is being done by market research agencies and advertising agencies as to descriptions of target markets which can form the basis for the marketing mix of the retailer.

Just as in any other sector of industry the marketing mix is likely to vary from one firm to another, so in retailing, retailers competing for the same or similar target markets find ways of differentiating their appeal. To compare Sainsbury with Tesco helps to show how differences can emerge in decisions on the marketing mix, and to demonstrate the influence of past reputations.

The wholesale trade

Apart from one year in the decade (1976), the return on capital invested in grocery wholesaling has fallen steadily from 25.5 per cent to 16.7 per cent, reflecting the increased pressure of competition from multiple retailers in the trade of the independent retailers, who are the wholesale customers. Data on the structure of the wholesale trade comes from the Census of Wholesale Distribution (1950, 1965 and 1974). Those have now been replaced by annual sample enquiries, based on the VAT Register, starting in 1977 with the latest for 1980 published in *British Business* (12 August, 1982). This shows an increase in total numbers of wholesalers since 1965, as shown in Table 9.24.

Table 9.24   Wholesalers

	Total business units	Total employees
1965	41,049	778,660
1974	80,104	912,237*
1980	91,692	N/A

* Excluding proprietors

The increase may be attributed generally to the 1965 numbers being low for reasons of failure to make a return, while the 1974 and 1980 returns are based on the VAT registrable businesses and would exclude those below the turnover threshold while there may have been numbers coming over the threshold by 1980. However, it would seem that the average numbers employed per business has reduced between 1965 and 1980, which could be the result of the formation of new businesses and an improvement in labour productivity in the larger businesses. Possibly when more comparable data are pro-

Table 9.25   Change in numbers of wholesale business

Description	1974–80 % change
1. Food and drink	0
2. Petroleum products	−23.6
3. Clothing, furs, textiles and footwear	− 3.7
4. Other goods	+37.9
5. Coal and oil merchants	−22.0
6. Builders merchants	− 7.0
7. Agricultural merchants	−12.4
8. Industrial merchants	+68.7
9. Scrap and waste	− 5.1
10. Industrial and agricultural machinery	+ 9.4
11. Leasing	+93.2

duced in future years the picture will be clarified. The change in numbers of businesses varies with each sector with some sectors stationary and others changing, as shown in Table 9.25.

The 'other goods' classification which apparently contains many dealers who were found difficult to place, accounts for over 10,000 of the increase in the number of businesses, and many of these appear likely to be new businesses so far as the VAT register is concerned. Because of lack of data, it is not possible to say what kind of business they are as to method of trading.

The data classified by method of trading have not yet been published for 1980 and for the reader's convenience, in later comparison, Table 9.26 provides a list of the methods of trading in 1974 with the numbers of businesses. Detail by trade classification is also given in the original report.

The original source also provides a wealth of other data on turnover, stocks, capital expenditure and gross margin, to name but a few. It is impossible to provide further analysis on, for example, trends in cash and carry wholesaling and trading methods (which are dealt with in sources such as the *Nielsen Researcher* (no. 2, 1982), or to comment on the gross margins of those businesses working for HM Government, without expanding this section and losing sight of the objective which is to deal with the development of the system as a whole.

Table 9.26   **Numbers of businesses classified by method of trading**

	1974
Wholesaler or dealer buying outright and selling in the UK	54,506
Wholesaler with own retailing outlet	10,442
Retailer buying group	529
Manufacturer's wholesale organisation	1,924
Import and/or export merchant	7,059
Agent or broker, home or export trade	3,640
Buying, selling or distributing for HM Govt. Purchasing organisation with HO abroad Other	2,004
Total	80,104

The function of the wholesaler within the channel has already been listed as:[113]
Minimising total transactions
Minimising the system costs of stockholding
Minimising delivery costs of assortments
Minimising transaction costs
In addition to these basic functions, some wholesalers are involved in other activities. A survey for the Monopolies and Mergers Commission[114] showed that fifteen out of twenty-nine companies were involved in activities listed as:

Grocery sector:	Grocery retailing
	Food packing
	Electronics
	Property holding
	Vehicle repairing
Pharmaceutical sector:	Pharmaceutical retailing
	Manufacture of pharmaceuticals
	Removals and storage
Drink, tobacco and confectionery sector:	Retailing of drink and tobacco
	Management of off-licences and restaurants
Miscellaneous:	Wide variety of activities in manufacturing, retailing, export and pre-packing, and in construction, engineering and service industries.

The wholesaler is not so much marketing-oriented as merchant-oriented, in that he sees himself as trading between the manufacturer and retailer in any opportunity that allows him to do for the manufacturer what he cannot efficiently do for himself, while he will do for the retailer work that the manufacturer finds troublesome and unprofitable. It calls for a knowledge of the problems of both suppliers and retailers. He understands the problems of the small manufacturer and will, given the opportunity, take all of his output without actually owning the firm. In the textile trade he will use the manufacturer as a subcontractor, supplying him with material to be made up for resale to the retailer. He can energise manufacturers and retailers alike with opportunities to make profits. Indeed he can produce and sell products without ever becoming involved in any activity other than stockholding, by subcontracting the product design, and manufacture, package design, market research, advertising, physical distribution and debt collection. He will normally retain the billing operation. This scenario pictures the wholesaler as a dealer, an arranger after the style of the medieval Italian merchants who organised the French and Flemish weavers to supply them with goods for Italy and the East, while arranging reciprocal trade in the merchandise of the East for Western Europe. The increase in their numbers may in fact be associated with an increase in foreign trade.

The other type of wholesaler, handling the producer to retailer link, providing fewer functions other than breaking bulk and delivery, is currently in competition with manufacturer wholesaling and retailer wholesaling to the point where they complained of being discriminated against in the discount offered by manufacturers to multiple retailers. The Department of Prices and Consumer Protection took up the complaint and the subsequent enquiry substantiated the complaint of discrimination but felt that any remedial legislation might exacerbate the problem for it would require the prohibition of the practice of referring for investigation by the Monopolies and Mergers Commission any alleged Unfair Trading under the Fair Trading Act 1973. They concluded that unfair practices such as discrimination in discounts be dealt with by the same process and each case decided on its merits.

The gloomy view of the position of wholesalers taken by some writers does not seem justified by the information available, for wholesalers are responding to the changing environment and providing service where it is needed. The vast movement to cash and carry trading has spread to many non-food sectors, where improved efficiency has made it desirable for manufacturers to change their channels of distribution. Cash and carries are finding difficulties in the face of multiple retailers and many have been taken over by conglomerates who are mainly manufacturers. Evidence abounds of wholesalers who are finding ways to increase turnover and profits.

CHAPTER 10

Channel management

Contents

Inter-organisational relationships

Overview

The concept of a 'natural' development in channel structure under-lines many of the economic approaches to channel theory. It can be

246

seen in the concept of the life-cycle applied to the firm's channels (Baker),[1] or the view that channels reflect the stage of economic development of a country (Wadinambiaratchi).[2] Bucklin[3] proposed that, in the long run, the members of the commercial channel will be driven to providing desired consumer services at the minimal cost possible, and that this will come about because of competition. This suggests that market forces in a competitive economy are the principal shapers of relationships. At the level of the firm the channels are influenced by the development of the firm or the product, as suggested by Guiltinan.[4] This supposes that perfectly competitive markets can be found in the economy.

In the United Kingdom the Monopolies and Mergers Commission acknowledged that the system of making references, to prevent monopoly abuse, had the result of increased competition in the distributive trades. In the competitive process, the weak and the unlucky retailers went out of business while the efficient increased their market share and acquired a new power over their suppliers, paving the way for a monopoly over whose products reached the market.

If, then, the attempts to control the development of monopoly are difficult, even fruitless, should there not be some form of controlled monopoly when no abuses are allowed? Such controlled monopolies exist in different degrees in many places both in the United Kingdom and abroad.

In another Monopolies and Mergers Commission report[5] the British Gas Corporation (BGC) was found to exercise excessive control over the conduct and performance of manufacturers who were unduly subservient to BGC and that this level of dependence restricted competition between manufacturers, and also restricted competition in retailing.

In command economies, controlled distribution systems appear to be inefficient in other ways–such as providing poor service, and unable to supply the simple essentials of life.[6]

The problem of monopolistic structures is that while the opportunities exist for savings through routinisation, command rather than negotiation, and the use of integrated technology systems in communications, materials handling, and control, the balancing inefficiencies overcome these savings in the long run. The inefficiencies are usually listed as a decrease in innovation, an increase in market price, and a decline in the productivity of labour.

The question emerges then of the direction that should be recommended to firms as they grow in size and develop their distribution systems, to the point where they are tempted to integrate forwards or to organise the retailing of their own products. The same situation faced by the retailer opens the possibility of integrating backwards to ensure supplies. Examples of successful vertical integration are difficult to discover in their pure form, for they are usually a mixture of the vertically integrated channel and the voluntary co-operative channel–multiple channels or multi-marketing.[7] These arrangements result in frequent conflict, charges of discrimination in prices, discounts and supply conditions.

There is therefore no ideal solution, no normative structure that can be recommended to any firm. The only generalisation that seems to apply is that channel development in the firm depends on the intentions of the leadership, that is, on their objectives within the industry to which they are attached as suppliers in relation to other members of the structure. These objectives are then subject to the constraints imposed by other firms' objectives, by economics, by society (including government) and ultimately the culture. This view was taken by Michman,[8] as he attempted to widen the definition of marketing channels.

Seeking for an operational definition of channel management, Cox and Schutte[9] emphasised the inter-organisational aspect when they defined a channel as: 'An organised network of agencies and institutions which in combination perform all the activities required to link producers with users, and users with producers, in order to accomplish the marketing task'.

This definition avoids the academic problem of where the channel starts and finishes, whether it should include changes in the form of the product, and whether it should include suppliers to the end-product producer. These arguments really add little to knowledge, for it is a matter of convenience what is included. On occasion, it may even be useful to include the housewife's store cupboard as part of the system when trying to calculate the effects of rumoured shortages on other channel member behaviour.

The study of channels might begin by looking at behaviour, since the economic aspects really follow from 'the will to do' rather than the other way about, a problem discussed by Scitovsky[10] in his preface. A similar question, 'Are channels of distribution what the textbooks say?' is asked by McVey[11] when he discusses the over-emphasis of the view that all institutions perform similar functions, to the point of ignoring their intentions and objectives. The alternative hypotheses are: either organisations manipulate and control environments, or environments dominate and constrain organisations.

Much of the work on the behaviour of organisations in their working relationship has been concerned with the need for co-operation, in establishing and maintaining a relationship, with the nature and cause of conflict which can disrupt the working arrangements, and with the power which is exerted either to benefit one firm at the expense of another, or to resolve a conflict. These indeed are important elements of behaviour between firms, and in turn are related to the concept of the channel as a behavioural system.

Boddewyn's[12] framework for the study of a behavioural system, which dealt with (i) actors, (ii) processes, (iii) structures, (iv) functions, (v) interaction with environment, has usually been taken up by marketing analysts in relation to structures with a considerable number of studies devoted to co-operation or conflict and power/dependence studies. The functions of channels are often regarded as being in the power of the channel leader (often the manufacturer) to allocate to intermediaries, on the basis of minimum cost, and so have been studied from this viewpoint by accountants.[13]

Those social scientists who contribute to this discussion do very little of their field-work in the marketing relationships of commercial firms so that many of the concepts of domain are borrowed from studies of organisations involved in providing health services or employment services.

Channels as a behavioural system

A behavioural system of firms really must start by examining the organisations of which the system consists, so that the motives and their origins may be understood. Miller[14] describes the organisation as having parts that are common to all living organisms, and are described as:

1. Reproducer. The sub-system that is capable of giving rise to other similar systems.
2. Boundary. The sub-system at the perimeter which holds together the components of the system, protects them from environmental stress, and excludes or permits entry to various sorts of matter–energy and information.
3. Eight-systems which process matter–energy.
4. Nine-systems which process information.

The organisation is thus described as having nineteen sub-systems, of which nine are involved in processing information. Reidenbach and Olivia[15] attempted to place the marketing function into this framework only to discover that marketing decisions were not restricted to the marketing department so that the oversimplification involved in confining decision-making to the Product, Price, Promotion and Place (the Four Ps) was inadequate to describe what was done. Lambert,[16] intent on examining the decision process concerning channel management (one of the Four Ps), points out that information needed for these decisions is often available in some other part of the firm without the marketing manager's knowledge. The original channel decision rationale on the firm's inception could seldom be traced. Modifications were made in response to events, rather than as part of a co-ordinated strategic plan.

Major changes in a firm's channels are often the result of a crisis or catastrophe, for, in Gattorna's[17] view, organisations are structured with a degree of flexibility to adjust to the environment, but each system has a definite upper limit in terms of its capacity to deal with perturbation. It is possible therefore for certain conditions to combine and build up in such a way that a system may become grossly unstable and undergo sudden and catastrophic change.

The ability of the firm to survive such a change really depends on the ability of the information sub-systems to process correctly and route the data to the appropriate decider. Since the frequency of such occurrences depends on the environment, a long period of stable environment seems likely to produce an organisation incapable of processing and routing information. So far as the distribution environment is concerned, it seems that the number of grocery retailers reaching what Walters[18] called the 'critical mass' caught many producers unawares. The changes demanded of them by retailers with buying power were greater than their ability to adjust.

The firm in the market

Domain consists of claims that an organisation stakes out for itself in terms of (i) range of products, (ii) population served, (iii) services rendered. It seeks to establish it, defend it, and expand it. The area of the market within which it does this may be called the task environment, consisting of (i) customers, (ii) suppliers of materials, labour, capital, equipment and work space, (iii) competitors for markets and resources, (iv) regulatory groups such as governments and unions. Beyond the task environment lies the remainder of the influences such as the economic environment and the cultural environment.[19]

In order to maintain its niche, it requires to form a symbiotic relationship with other organisations, that is, a close association such that they become dependent for their existence on each other. This domain acceptance is considered by Carter[20] as a requisite for exchange to take place. In his research on employment organisations he found three predictors of domain acceptance:

1. The goal attainment level of the focal organisation (i.e. the one seeking acceptance).
2. The ability of the focal organisation to deliver its services.
3. The receptivity of client population to the domain claims of the focal organisation.

Non-predictive variables included the internal consensus of the focal organisation. Translated into marketing terminology, this meant that acceptance by channel members depended on:

1. Marketing objectives of the producer.
2. The ability to fulfil these objectives.
3. The receptivity of channel members to the producer's goals.

The corollary of the proposition is that if the dependency of one or the other is weakened then so is domain acceptance. It would appear that conflict is not the only cause of dysfunction–that is, disturbance in the functioning of the symbiosis–but so are changes in the needs of either organisation as a result of internal changes. These internal changes may be the result of organic growth or changes in objectives.

The relationships therefore tend to exist in a condition of co-operation or conflict, as one or other attempts to dominate the network of relationships to achieve their own goals. The ability to dominate is attributed to the possession of power, and it has been the object of various studies to describe it (Etgar),[21] to measure it (Brown and Day),[22] to model it for effect (Lusch;[23] Cadotte and Stern[24]), to account for it (Stern and El-Ansary)[25] and to manage it (Stern and El-Ansary).[26]

Power, arising out of the unequal control of resources, between the exchange partners[27] may be used to specify roles, that is, to get the channel partner to do what he would otherwise not have done, thereby sowing the seeds of future conflict; or it may be used in the event of conflict to help resolve that conflict.[28] A growing number of field studies are now appearing in order to measure power/dependency relationships (Ahmed;[29] Wilkinson;[30] Etgar;[31] and Lusch[32]) and to conclude that in general suppliers attempt to use power in the relationship to their own advantage with various levels of toleration of that abuse. Most of the studies are snapshots of the situation at any point in time and as a result fail to identify action being taken by the dependent member to lessen that dependency by seeking to minimise the power of the task environment elements over them by maintaining alternatives.

In the present struggle for control between packaged grocery producers and retailers, some of the producers are seeking to establish export markets within the EEC to lessen their dependence on United Kingdom retailers, while the retailers in turn are seeking

EEC sources for their own label supplies. Such actions are not easily studied by transient investigations, nor can all the actions of dependent partners be anticipated. The history of business is replete with firms who suffered from the unanticipated.

Confronted with the unanticipated, most managers could conveniently claim that they have no control over environmental change, and that the unanticipated is by its nature incapable of being allowed for. However, Zeitz[33] argues that a new orientation to inter-organisational relations can be provided by dialectical thought, that is, determining objects (events, trends) beyond the limits of experience by use of the principle of understanding. He argues that a dialectical model of social systems can be extended to power and resource relations in inter-organisational networks. In essence he provides a series of hypotheses concerning inter-organisational relationships that hold good in other situations, and says that the principle will apply in business relations. His list covers four main areas:

1. *Resource externalisation*
    (a) *Resource dependency.* To the extent that resources and the manner of securing them remain stable, interactions between organisations tend to fall into repeatable patterns.
    (b) *Active control of environment.* Moments of control are not empirically separable from moments of constraint. Each interaction must be created anew by organisational action, and in the process of reproduction, incremental or drastic changes in the pattern of interaction may occur during periods of crisis.
    (c) *Persistence of structure.* Creative actions are transformed into enduring patterns, because the resources produced by action tend to persist over time and to constrain future interactions. Each resource has its own decay function which is a product of the internal characteristics of the external resource.
2. *Unequal exchange*
    Equal exchange conditions are accepted[34] as characteristic of one aspect of exchange systems but another characteristic develops simultaneously and exists in tension with it.

    Differentiation of function implies differential expropriation of resources by the firms, which leads to inequality in the resources available, and ultimately to unequal control over the procedural conditions of the exchange. Eventually the preconditions of equal exchange are transformed into their dialectical opposites.
3. *Contradictions*
    In dialectical thought contradictions mean a condition of social

systems such that an element is both a necessary condition for the development of another element, and a sufficient condition for its transformation.

4. *Reactivity and consciousness*

Awareness of its environment by an organisation is always less than that of an organism and it has a weaker awareness of patterned relationships. Organisations are therefore constrained by their lack of awareness into selecting portions of the environment on which to focus.

This fourth area has as serious implications for communications between the environment and the organisation, as Lambert's findings have for internal communications.[35]

Communication systems

In spite of the emphasis given by Miller,[36] Forrester[37] and Zeitz[38] to communication systems, few have done more than describe the state of modern communications technology, and adapt information theory to a normative model suitable for inter-organisational communications.

Simmons[39] identified a new need emerging for manufacturers to listen and react to the views of their key retailers, a view expressed by the retailers themselves. Few manufacturers collect data in an organised way, relying on spontaneous comments from their sales force. Few manufacturers regarded this trade feedback as vital to their management decisions. Only one-quarter believed this input to be essential for target setting, account handling, distribution and service policies.

Many manufacturers are looking forward to the spread of Electronic Point of Sale (EPOS) data capture by scanning of bar-codes which, according to Bloom,[40] will be well established by 1987–9, providing data that will be in demand by advertisers. Neilsen takes the more cautious view that retailers will consider the additional investment costs as a constraining factor against existing systems and will only invest when they can count the savings.[41]

Communications *to* retailers is usually regarded as being less important than to customers if judged by budget comparisons, and writers quote many examples of communications failures being the cause of channel strategy failures.[42] By and large, little research in this interesting area has emerged in the United Kingdom.

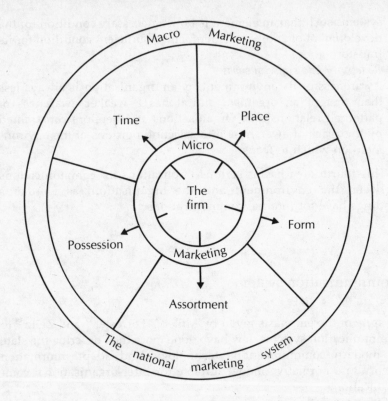

Figure 10.1   Macro and micro marketing
Source: from E.J. McCarthy, *Basic Marketing* (Homewood, Ill.: Irwin, 1971)

Channels as economic systems

The concepts of macro and micro were first applied by McCarthy,[43] who classified micro marketing as the firm's managerial decisions in the market, while macro marketing was the national system that creates and distributes goods and services to satisfy consumer demand. Figure 10.1 will help to explain this concept.

Marketing channels are participants in providing at least three of these utilities, shown in the quadrants in Figure 10.1, and in some views also provide a contribution to changes of form, if the concept of a channel is extended to include suppliers to the final product manufacturer, and the flow of material within the manufacturing plant. An additional utility identified by Alderson[44] was the provision of assortments. These utilities are offered to the consumer in the market-place where exchange may take place under the conditions described by Alderson and Martin.[45]

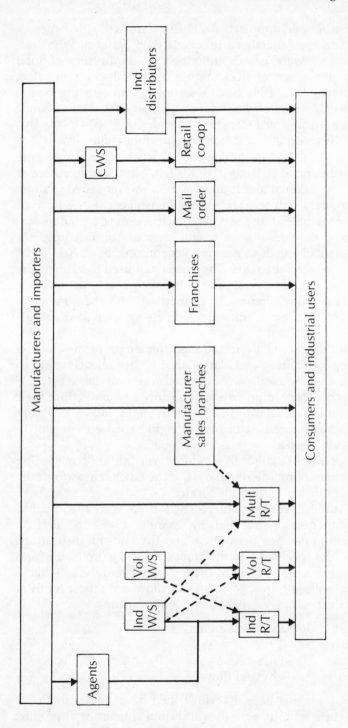

Figure 10.2   *The main institutions in United Kingdom distribution*

Source: M. Guirdham, *Marketing: The Management of Distribution Channels* (Oxford: Pergamon Press, 1972).

The macroeconomic approach deals therefore with the types of institutions and the generalised functions they perform. Wholesalers, for example, were earlier described as minimisers of total transactions, minimisers of stockholding costs, and so on. Retailers provided convenience of location, assortment, and opening hours, etc. A channel of distribution viewed from this concept became a simple listing of the agencies involved and their order of involvement. This system gave rise to simplified structures, shown in Figure 10.2.

Particular commodities or groups of products received treatments such as those described in Baker,[46] or Mallen,[47] or the frontispiece to Cox,[48] when the national distribution system was modelled to show primary, secondary and tertiary sectors, consumers in the form of households, government, the service industries, new capital formation, and exports. These were useful devices for teaching, for describing extant channels to new market entrants, but beyond that added little to research insights. They were also used to support the hypothesis that there is a relationship between economic development and channel development in connection with the number of intermediaries[49] but inconveniently Japan always provided an outstanding exception.

The number of intermediaries affected the length of the channel and, according to Alderson and Martin, the number of levels could go on increasing so long as they contributed to improving efficiency, and then at some stage in growth manufacturers would reduce their dependence on intermediaries. Mallen,[50] taking up Stigler's concept in a micro approach, produced a total of eight hypotheses to explain why this should happen.

The first hypothesis stated: 'A producer will spin off a marketing function to a marketing intermediary(s) if the latter can perform the function more efficiently than the former'.

Some difficulties were encountered by writers who attempted to define the functions performed by channel members, first in agreeing on the functions performed, and then on the institutions involved. Bucklin specified four functions (excluding production and consumption) of communication, ownership, inventory and transport, each specialised in respect of a single flow, with three levels of aggregation (institution, establishment, and function).

> Communication–Exchange rights
> Ownership　　–Title
> Inventory　　–Physical flow
> Transport　　–Physical flow

Expanding from this base, Bucklin[51] then developed a model of channel structure with its partial equilibrium sub-sector of product assortments as a means of predicting the normative economic structure of a channel, were there no behavioural influences. The first contention (there are sixteen) was: 'Competitive pressures will force channel structures to a long run equilibrium position in which the marginal costs to the commercial sector of changing any output are equal to the marginal costs consequently incurred by the buyer sector'.

Gattorna[52] comments that this is a wholly theoretical concept embodying the idea of static conditions and unlikely to occur in practice. The concept of a normative channel ignores also the occurrence of innovation in channels, innovation of technology, of system, of assortment—which can all have far-reaching effects.

Earlier studies had focused on innovation in particular institutional practices, giving rise to new forms of horizontal competition and to descriptions of cycles of behaviour such as these summarised by Stern.[53] This produced studies of the characteristics of both innovator and innovation[54] who introduce system change.[55] Technological innovation also appears to have far-reaching effects, as pointed out by Le Boeuf[56] when he argued that many of the innovations in French food products are unnecessary 'value added' to increase revenue, have the effect of increasing industrial and commercial concentration, and raise the price of food, often with no real benefit. The brewing industry in the United Kingdom, by means of an innovation, pushed the industry into a completely new, more monopolistic channel structure, and some would say an inferior product.

Changes in channel structure, if Buckin's theory is followed, led some to suppose that changes which were induced in the distribution of agricultural products, especially of developing economies, would lead to real benefits in the form of a reduction of spoiled products, handling and storage costs, and negotiation costs,[57] and that this would lead to a real income increase, since such a large proportion of income is spent on food. Food distribution channels in Western Europe were investigated by Barnes[58] to examine the variables that influenced superstore development. He found that his model could only predict accurately at the regional level and could not be used at the national level, because of the wide range of differences in the variables measured. A further issue of measuring the consequences on the food distribution channel efficiency had to be abandoned in the face of measurement difficulties.

The macro approach appeals to those trained in economics but the difficulties of applying any of the knowledge to the national economy, or to an industry, in setting down development guidelines, are as great as trying to persuade the TUC to believe Milton Friedman.

Channel management

The channel decision

When dealing with the behavioural system of marketing channels, firms were compared with organisms who sought out a niche for themselves within their environment in such a way that they could be related to other organisations. This niche was described as the domain. In marketing management terms it would be described as market positioning, and be considered as an aspect of strategy that affects the whole firm in its organisation of products, production and distribution. Market positioning therefore affects the internal structure of the firm, as well as the relationship with other organisations, and is an area of policy that cannot be delegated.

Market positioning determines both the policy of the marketing manager and the production manager. The marketing manager may negotiate for his firm only when the position of the firm has been determined. If he negotiates *in order* to determine the position of the firm then he must persuade the organisation to accept what has been negotiated. There may be difficulties in doing so. The initial channel decision is therefore a chief executive decision, which may be modified subsequently by his delegate but only radically altered by that Chief Executive. The relative permanence of this initial decision was noted by Lambert[59] when he discovered in his survey that many channels never change substantially from their basic structure. The larger and more successful the company, the more likely that inertia exists within the firm. Changes that do occur are the result of problems. Christopher and Wills,[60] in an overview of the use to which market research was put, pointed out that most of the users were manufacturing directors and accountants who must work closely together, and are probably in the best position to appraise marketing data. The channel decisions are most likely to be influenced by the managers responsible for the organisational life than those responsible for the inter-organisational boundaries. Modification to channels are even more fragmented than one might imagine since sales managers make decisions concerning the selling function and distribution managers make changes to the movement function.

Lambert implies that stability, a condition that Burns and Stalker[61] noted as a cause of bureaucratisation, leads to inertia, so then the opposite condition, instability in the environment or in the technology, will lead to an open system perspective when executives take account of the full range of inputs into an organisation. One would expect more frequent reconsideration of marketing channels (as well as other elements) in circumstances where there is a high rate of change, the decisions being intended to reduce the uncertainty felt in decision-making, and to develop some measure of stability even for a brief period. Johnson[62] suggests that one of the strategies frequently used by manufacturers in a rapidly changing market is to seek channel dominance, by developing some power in the channel relationships. He counsels flexibility in strategy, and the adoption of a strategy that suits the environment.

The effect of environmental change in an organisation that is unprepared for change is described in a framework suggested by Fink, Beak, and Taddeo as:[63]

An initial period of *shock*

A period of *defensive retreat*

An *acknowledgement phase*

A process of *adaptation and change*

It would seem, however, that organisations operating in a stable environment are likely to be the least prepared, while organisations in rapidly changing environments and technology are the best prepared.

DECISION NEEDS

Guirdham,[64] Lambert,[65] and Rosenbloom[66] (see Table 10.1) list conditions that make it necessary for the firm to face channel design decisions, most of which reflect changes in technology, design or the market.

Table 10.1   Conditions requiring channel design decisions

Guirdham	Rosenbloom	Lambert
New product	New product developed	(Type 1)
New target market	New target market	Competitive activity
Marketing strategy change	Change in other elements of mix	Major new product or acquisition
New firm	New firm established	Financial considerations
Shift in product- life-cycle	Intermediary's policy change	Costs
Competitive activity	Change in intermediary availability	New activity in the market
Changes in channels		Major shift in volume of business
Market segmentation possibilities	New territories sought	(Type 2)
Sales expansion prospects	Major marketing environment change	Reasons for dropping intermediary
Costs	Inter-organisation conflict	Lack of market share
Legal considerations	Regular review	Failure to pay bills
Periodic review		Low sales

Some of these occasions call for major decisions, and indeed considerable reorientation of the resources of the firm, and are usually considered as separate and special cases. These are:

Export channels
Services channels
Franchise channels

A decision to enter any of these channels would only be taken after extensive investigation of the marketing environment, and of the firm's resources and development needs to meet the demands of a new situation. Similarly, a modification involves a re-examination of company objectives and channel objectives.

LEGAL CONSTRAINTS IN CHANNEL ORGANISATION

Changes in the law can be regarded as one of those changes in the environment to which an organisation must adapt, or the law may be regarded as a constraint affecting the options open to all organisations in its domain. This section appears here since it may be a cause of decision, or a constraint on decision.

The main source of legislation is the national government, who devolves some responsibilities for administering the law to local authorities. In Scotland there may be some differences in the delegation of authority, and some differences in the legislation. The national government is also responsible for enacting laws proposed by the EEC, while exporters with EEC-wide marketing channels are moreover subject to EEC laws in these relationships.

The principal EEC laws are concerned with putting into effect the Treaty of Rome competition rules in Articles 85 (1) and 65 (1) which are intended to prohibit: 'Agreements, decisions, concerted practices, and dominant positions likely to affect trade between member states'. Competition in food pricing is also affected by the Community Agricultural Policy and the establishment of regimes in eleven product groups. In the United Kingdom the prevention of monopoly is regulated by laws on Restrictive Trade Practices, the main being:

1. Restrictive Trade Practices Acts 1956, 1968
2. Resale Prices Acts 1964
3. European Communities Act 1972
4. Fair Trading Act 1973.

The Fair Trading Act created the post of Director General of Fair Trading and the Consumer Protection Advisory Committee, and gives power to control 'unfair consumer trade practices' and to refer cases to the Monopolies and Merger Commission, as they did in the complaint of 'discriminatory discounts to retailers',[67] the refusal by

Raleigh Industries to supply certain retail discounters; or some perfumery manufacturers' refusal to supply grocery multiples such as Sainsbury.

The relationship between manufacturers and their agents is also controlled by the Law of Agency, while a franchise relationship is regulated by the Law of Contract.

Monopoly rights are more or less effectively sustained by the following Acts:

Patents Acts 1949–61
Registered Design Act 1949
Trade Marks Act 1938
Copyright Act 1956
Design Copyright Act 1968

and case law relating to unregistered trade marks. These are intended to give originators of new products or designs the right to exploit their product for sixteen years without competition from copies. Similar rights apply to trade marks, package design, or logo, or a fashion article.

Transport operations in physical distribution are regulated by national statutes as amended by far-reaching EEC regulations. In legal terms the transport industry is divided into Common Carriers and Private Carriers. The Transport Acts of 1962 and 1968 dramatically altered the roles of the Nationalised Road and Rail Industries. The old licensing system that restricted entry to the industry was replaced by quality licensing with the effect of creating a competitive atmosphere. Quality regulations affect the minimum standard of maintenance of the vehicle and its roadworthiness; and the working conditions of the driver, in terms of permitted hours, and daily mileage. The most recent addition to the community-wide controls was the tachometer, a device to record vehicle movement. It was only accepted after a bitter struggle by unions and with many protests about costs from owners.

CHANNEL DESIGN

A number of recommendations on a method of channel design have been made since Berg's[68] contribution, and they have usually followed a logical sequence such as that of Guirdham (see Table 10.2).

Several other paradigms, some of which describe a series of steps in flow-chart form, have also been produced (see Cravens *et al.*;[69] Rosenbloom;[70] Lambert;[71] Michman and Sibley;[72] and Narus[73]).

The essential difference between them is the commencement point. Some, like Berg, assume that the channel objectives and strategy have been noted, and start with the process of defining the

Table 10.2   Paradigms of the channel decision process

Berg	Guirdham
1. Factor the strategic situation 2. Convert key factors into activity requirements 3. Group tasks into work units 4. Allocate tasks to middlemen 5. Designate structural relationship	Phase One—General Marketing Strategy 1. State corporate objectives 2. Prepare forecasts and characteristics of whole product/market 3. Set marketing objectives 4. Identify target market Phase Two—Distribution Strategy 5. Set distribution objectives 6. Identify key customer requirements and create distribution strategy 7. Select alternatives for screening 8. Identify selection criteria 9. Screen out unsuitable channels

target market, the buying situation envisaged, and proceed to identifying the things that need to be done to achieve that condition, given that there are a number of intervening variables such as those listed by Rosenbloom:[74]

1. Market variables
2. Product variables
3. Company variables
4. Middlemen variables
5. Environmental variables
6. Behavioural variables

Obviously not all decisions go through such a laborious and painstaking approach, except in the case of a new company with ample resources to mount large-scale operations. The most frequent occasion for a new channel decision would appear to be in export marketing. Case-study problems of new channel design generally involve small new firms with one new product and limited information.

An interesting research area in this respect is the area of problem-solving or modification in channels where more limited information is used. Lambert[75] suggests that the most important information used in such modifying decisions is cost and revenue data in the form of channel profitability analysis—an idea already mentioned by Simmat.[76] Such recommendations necessarily ignore behavioural and communications aspects which would affect revenue (sales) and therefore the analysis. The most frequently occurring reason offered to Lambert for channel redesign was in fact some aspect of market conditions, with only two companies indicating that changes in profitability was a reason for modification.

Lambert's research suggests that channel design modification is a reaction to a changing market environment. This would require an information system within the company that was capable of accepting and relating marketing data in a form usable by the board as well as the marketing department. Internal communication systems will play a large part in that decision. Communication systems usually incorporate some system of filtering (and interpretation) which modifies the data, and codes them so that they are related to the decision-making process of the board who are concerned about financial consequences.

Most modifications have an effect on the cash flow of the firm, and on the flow of products. A modification may have subsequent effects on the flow of modifications to old products and the design of new products. In some cases, if information flows of internally generated data have a greater influence than market data on the decision process, then channel modifications may originate in production, or accounting–and not, as often supposed, in the environment of the market. The product and price decisions may, for example, be more strongly influenced by the production director rather than the marketing director. The channels decision must accept the product/ price structure as given and adapt channels to that decision.

This situation prevails in much of the United Kingdom textile industry whose existing channels are switching to overseas sources. The industry currently is maintaining production and price policies suited to a rich quality-conscious market rather than developing production skills to suit current channels. The conditions of channel design modification as a reaction to the market environment changes conceals problems that are more complex than the loss of channel members.

SCREENING ALTERNATIVE CHANNELS

Many of the screening paradigms involve multi-stage processes appropriate to different objectives. Kotler,[77] for example, proposed several methods for selecting one from five alternative channels when a manufacturer wishes to expand from being a commodity supplier to a consumer goods supplier. His suggested screening methods are analogous to new product screening, namely:

1. Weighted factor score
2. Hierarchical preference ordering method
3. Strategy simulation method

Kotler's third method has many similarities with those of Guir-dham and Lambert who suggested that investing in a channel should be treated like any other investment and evaluated on its profit-earning capacity. Comparisons based on discounted profit and other financial measures tend to assume a knowledge of cost behaviour beyond the reach of any manager dealing with new situations, and to strain the certainty of forecasting.

A fourth method was proposed by Corstjens and Doyle[78] in an application for a confectionery manufacturer who owned some retail outlets and used other channels, consisting of his own retail outlets, franchised retailers, distributors in Europe, and multiples' own labels. The problem was to decide which channels to develop, the ideal number of outlets per channel and the channel margins, in order to maximise profits subject to certain production constraints.

The operationalising of the problem resulted in a non-convex programming problem which seemed to be an application for signomial programming. The data used originated in management estimates of the behaviour of the functions used in the model which, since it was based on their knowledge of actual operations, seemed reasonable. In other decision circumstances such experience-based estimates may not be available and the model may not predict accurately. In the event, the model recommendations were in line with current management thinking, and confirmed the recommendations from the company's management consultants.

Their solution dealt simultaneously with decisions concerning the number of intermediaries per channel, the margin policy for each channel, and the optimum development for multiple channels. The solution assumes, as do most others, that there is no competition for resources to develop new products that could enhance the desirability of the company as a supplier and therefore make available more intermediaries. The question of intermediaries' availability is usually ignored since it is reasonable to assume that firms who feel they have options are desired suppliers. Few, if any, writers have dealt with the problems of margins, and intermediary numbers (intensity) in spite of their occurring frequently in practice, as was shown by the Monopolies and Merger Committee.[79]

Although these selection methods generally adopt profit as the objective criteria for determining the channel(s) to be used, there are a number of behavioural criteria which management may wish to satisfy in addition, or even in partial substitution for, short-term profitability. Desirable though they may be, behavioural criteria must recognise the need for a long-term profit criteria to be achieved. An optimisation model that incorporates behavioural criteria has been proposed by McAlister[80] which makes an attempt to resolve the problem.

These behavioural criteria are:

1. Management perceptions of risk, and growth of particular channels.
2. Preference for power or dependency in relationships.
3. Preference for distance or proximity to final consumer.
4. Management confidence in firm's product performance.
5. Management attitudes to uncertainty.

The criteria used in selecting channels are based on an expected pattern of organisation and management of each channel; however, every member of that channel is not identical in many important attributes, so it is now necessary to specify some criteria for selection of intermediaries which can be converted into operational criteria for the sales manager.

Negotiating with intermediaries

This part of the process is generally fairly continuous and traditionally has been the function of the sales department, as part of the business of negotiating with intermediaries in the process of arranging sales contracts. Contracts of course are negotiated between buyer and seller in the process of building up a sufficient number to constitute a channel. Both buyer and seller have their own criteria for selecting partners in the contract dyad, a fact that becomes more apparent as the retailer equalises the power structure of the channel. In multi-level channels the intermediary may be negotiating both as buyer and seller resulting in differences of criteria. Viewed from this point of view, the channel of distribution then becomes an equilibrium set of contracts.[81] The criteria used for evaluation by seller and buyer in the contracting dyad typically cover the factors shown in Table 10.3.

The negotiations necessary to the formation of a contract requires that agreement is reached on (i) prices, (ii) terms of payment, and (iii) the obligations and responsibilities of each party to the contract, each party making concessions according to his perception of his negotiating power and desire to achieve agreement. Negotiations therefore may result in adjustments being made on any combination of the three essentials to the contract which can incorporate a wide range of activities covered by responsibilities and obligations.[82] In the bargaining process the parties are usually employees of an organisation who are in effect working to policies and objectives laid down for them and thus their discretion in negotiations is constrained. The heart of bargaining is in not stating the true limits that one is willing to concede while at the same time trying to discover

Table 10.3   Seller/buyer evaluation criteria

Supplier's evaluation of intermediary service (Especially with territorial franchise)	Intermediary evaluation of supplier offer
Product range carried	Demonstrated consumer demand
Types of customer	Projected gross margin
Territory covered	Expected volume
Inventories	Merchandise suitability
Installation and repair services	Price and terms
Prices	Service level offered
Sales quotas	Manufactured reputation
Advertising and sales promotion	Quality of brand
Financial stability	Promotional assistance
	Vendor's distribution policy

Source: Adapted from L. W. Stern and A. I. El-Ansary, *Marketing Channels* (Englewood Cliffs, N.J.: Prentice-Hall, 1979).

the limits to which the other may go. Each party develops techniques in the negotiation process that will create uncertainty in the other without interpreting the information presented as evidence of non-co-operation.[83] A prior condition to the negotiation is the 'image' of the other party, and organisations will take care to present a favourable image to be seen by any potential partner in the dyad. These images are affected by matters outside of the firm's control, in particular the industry or trade classification of which the firm is a member.[84]

The organisational buying behaviour of members of the commercial channel has been largely ignored, apart from fashion buying, with only one recent work[85] listed in a 213-item state of the art review.[86] Given that buyers in this field play different roles in their organisation, having different objectives, it would therefore seem dangerous to generalise the behaviour of other kinds of buyers to the retailer or wholesaler.

Once agreement has been reached the relationship moves into a new phase, in which the manufacturer is interested in the sales performance of his product when offered to consumers. The interest is highest with new products and diminishes as satisfactory levels of performance are reached. The retailer's interest wanes in a similar fashion as other suppliers claim his attention with their offers. The need to maintain the retailer's interest in the supplier's range is the problem of motivating intermediaries.

MOTIVATING INTERMEDIARIES

The primary motivator of economic benefits of the negotiated contract or exchange will only operate if the consumers react by purchasing at the rate anticipated, and this will be reflected in sales levels, and stockturn rates. The fulfilment depends mainly on the effectiveness of the reseller's methods, his identification of customers' needs, and his efficiency as a business entity, as well as on the effectiveness of the suppliers' marketing programme. Some of the things that can happen to frustrate these expectations are:

1. Buyer estimates demand level incorrectly.
2. Target market (of seller) not available in retail area.
3. Unseen disadvantage discovered in the product.
4. Advertising support ineffective.
5. Misunderstanding of consumer benefits.
6. Appearance of competing producer.
7. Failure in servicing support.
8. Disagreement on reasons for product returns.
9. Retailer fails to use essential point of sale material.
10. Inadequate sales training by retailer.

This is not an exhaustive list but it demonstrates the need for identifying causes of failure before applying a remedy that will prevent a deterioration in relationships and more difficult negotiations in the future.

SECONDARY MOTIVATORS

The initial hothouse treatment given by the intermediary to the new line is relaxed as other new products are offered to him, and exposure afforded to older lines is reduced as a result of competitors' efforts. Some continuity of effort is needed to protect the shelf space being gained, so the collection of information on the exposure of the producer's own product and that of competitors is essential.

Currently this type of information can be supplied by a number of agencies who specialise in retail audits, but the future method of such data collection is likely to lie in the scanning of ANA (Bar) Codes by electronic means at the check-out counter.[87] Such data, when supplemented by salesmen's reports, or other more objective market research, can provide the sales manager with information for diagnosis of the retailer's level of satisfaction. The technology of monitoring channel performance is considered in the next section, and at this point it is sufficient to note that secondary motivators need to be adapted to the particular problem that has arisen.

The potential conflict, whose nature and resolution is discussed earlier under the theoretical aspects of behaviour, can be avoided or managed by strategies such as those outlined by Stern and El-Ansary:[88]

Diplomacy
Joint membership in trade associations
Exchange of persons
Cooperation
Mediation
Arbitration
Adopting superordinate goals

The tactics represent different forms of continuing negotiation on the part of two or more members of the channel in which agreement is sought on problems as they arise, with the negotiation being helped along by independent assessors. The idea that conflict could be suppressed by one party using its power to dominate was not acceptable to Lusch[89] as a long-term solution since it simply sowed the seeds of discontent among distributors.

For most firms, motivation consists of a number of carrot and stick measures, characterised as price concessions (discounts etc.), financial assistance or some kind of protection from competition, but Walters[90] suggests that all motivational tactics are reflections of the firm's policies of maintaining the co-operation levels achieved during negotiation, ignoring the concept of a dominant partner. The firm's policy areas are operations, organisation and communication. Operational policies are the rules that have been set out for the establishment of prices, terms, obligations and responsibilities. Organisational policies are the arrangements that are developed within and between firms, while communication policies determine who receives what kind of information. If power has played a part in the original agreement, then the power holder apparently attempts to maintain his advantage, in the face of conflict, to the point where the channel is likely to begin losing members.

DESIGN OF COMMUNICATIONS

Communication takes place as an integral part of the negotiation process with each end of the channel of communication set in the cement of each organisational member of that communications channel. The flow spans the boundary of the organisation and traditionally certain of the functionaries of the channel are cast in the role of gatekeepers. The marketing department, as a representative of the firm to the market, is often regarded as one of the major gatekeepers in regard to inter-organisational relations, with the purchasing department responsible for those inter-organisational links with suppliers.

Inside the organisation, according to the traditional view, communications channels are designed to provide information for decision-makers on the basis of rationality in the decision process. Piercy[91] points out that organisation scholars have shown that information is not neutral but is commonly manipulated to provide power for individuals in the structure, a power used for personal ends. It could be used to create rather than reduce uncertainty, to control resources of the organisation, and to influence the decision process.

Piercy was concerned with information being *collected* by the organisation from its environment, to point out how little research had been completed in this area, but if it is true that information is distorted, filtered, misinterpreted and generally manipulated before it reaches a decision-maker in the organisation, then the scope for similar manipulation also exists for information *issued* by the firm. Governments commonly look at such information directed to consumers with a great deal of suspicion and a considerable Code of Prohibited Practices now exists. However, much of this code does not apply to information presented to channel intermediaries and agencies. Such information will need to comply with other legal requirements, especially where it forms the basis for a contract, or with para. 6.4.1 of the British Code of Sales Promotion Practice.

The scope for using information issued to channel intermediaries as a means of obtaining power and leadership in channels by colouring information is much greater than that of communications through the media. Personal communications can, by innuendo, do much more than formalised information to persuade intermediaries, unless they are experienced in evaluating information.

Much of the material in these areas is presented as case study or, even worse, anecdotal material, which is itself subject to distortion and misinterpretation, as outlined in Stern and El-Ansary[92] who list areas likely to be affected by information. These are:

Inventory levels
Transport and storage
Promotion
Product changes
Pricing, especially discrimination

Alternatively, a normative approach is used to describe an apparently orderly, structured system subject to occasional abnormalities of overload, noise, secrecy, mistiming and perceptual difficulties. The system may be described as a network of communication flows (Figure 10.3); the information classifies by type; the media of

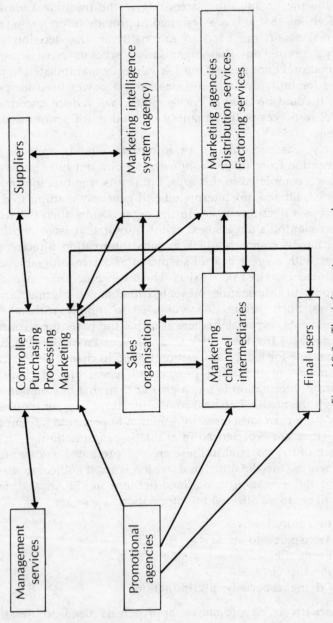

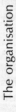

The organisation

Figure 10.3   The information network

Source: Adapted from R.D. Michman and S.D. Sibley, *Marketing Channels and Strategy*, 2nd edn (Columbus, Ohio: Grid, 1980).

communication by its effect, cost, and reader; and the process
involved in the message transmission.

Types of Information:

Inward   Inventory status at other channel locations.
           Sales levels of industry members.
           Market conditions and potentials.
           Promotional data. Costs and effects.
           Distribution changes.
           Competitive offerings.

Outward   Product offering information–characteristics, benefits.
           Pricing structure.
           Organisational changes.
           Services available–technical, financial, advisory.

The Media:

	Direct	*Indirect*
To intermediaries	Salesmen	
	Production specialist	Trade press
	Company magazines	Past and present customers
	Product specifications	
	Catalogues, service manuals	Government sources Specifiers
	Merchandise displays	Market research agencies
	Electronic linkages	
	Labels, tags, etc.	Libraries
		Advertising agencies and their media
To consumers	All advertising and promotional media	Past and present customers
	Individual letters	Consumer associations
	Retail and exhibition displays	Media complaints
	Mail-order catalogues	Programmes
	Labels and tags	Market research agencies
		Advertising agencies

The wide range of media and members of the communications
system underlines the problem of designing and encoding messages
that will be correctly timed to move the other flows in the channel
system in a co-ordinated manner, and to ensure that the predicted
sales levels, inventory levels, costs and profits are achieved on a
continuing basis.

The problems are multiplied by the need to ensure that the message transmission is properly executed, that is to say that encoding and decoding is achieved without loss or distortion, and that all the media used are cost effective in reaching their destination. To avoid problems of disharmony the messages to and from the different members of the system need to be in agreement with each other when decoded.

Channel evaluation and control

MONITORING CHANNEL PERFORMANCE

Measuring channel performance with a view to recording intermittently the state of affairs with regard to the firm's objectives would imply that the firm is interested in the twofold process of cost minimisation and sales maximisation as a basis to survival. Rushton[93] identifies three measures of performance which may be applied:

1. Efficiency (or productivity) measures (input–output)
2. Generalised profit measures (output–input)
3. Effectiveness measures (results *vs* objectives)

on which efficiency is the most commonly used measure by suppliers or retailers. The problem comes in deciding what aspects of input, output and results to measure.

EFFICIENCY MEASURES

Input measures are most easily handled in cost terms, which demand an accountant's services, to produce data. Such data may be used either specifically for channel performance, or for overall company performance. Applied to measuring existing channel profitability, or to other aspects of the firm's distribution system, the first requirement is the conversion of a 'natural' classification of cost to a cost centre of activity. Typically these cost centres consist of personal selling costs, sales administration, advertising and promotion, physical distribution (transport and warehousing), as demonstrated in Table 10.4. The set of cost centres is then redistributed to the aspect of the channels system being measured. In the example the sales performance of different types of customers is examined from the standpoint of sales, and profit, to show that the net profit ratio of some is below and some above the average. In the event that there

Table 10.4   Retail customer group–cost analysis

Function Retail sales value	Small indepen- dents £45,000	Large indepen- dents £145,000	Mul- tiples £500,000	Co-ops £60,000	Total £750,000
Personal selling costs	3,000	8,000	24,000	5,000	40,000
Sales administration:					
Supervision	450	1,200	3,600	750	6,000
Order processing	600	1,000	1,000	400	3,000
Credit and collection	1,100	1,700	3,700	1,000	7,500
Advertising and promotion					
Consumer media	3,600	11,600	40,000	4,800	600
Trade media	120	400	1,320	160	2,000
Point of sale	600	1,000	3,000	400	5,000
Sales deductions					
Retail margins and dis- counts	8,100	29,000	125,000	13,200	175,300
Physical distribution					
Stockholding costs	2,250	7,250	25,000	3,000	37,500
Transport	1,500	2,500	10,500	1,500	16,000
Cost of production (43.03% SP)	19,364	62,393	215,125	25,818	322,700
Total costs	40,684	126,043	452,245	56,128	675,000
Net profit contribution	4,316	18,957	47,755	3,972	75,000
Percentage of retail sales	9.59	13.07	9.55	6.62	10

Source: Michael J. Baker, *Marketing: Theory and Practice*, 1st edn (London: Macmillan, 1976) ch.6.

are non-assignable costs, then the net profit ratio becomes a net profit contribution ratio with the same effect. The low performers (and there will always be low performers) may be a necessary part of the system depending on the channel objectives, but the data for costing the channel objectives makes it possible to re-examine the objectives.

The possibilities of allocating costs by computer makes it possible to improve cost analysis extending to:

Size of customer
Method of sale
Territory
Product group
Salesman

These improve the analysis of the total marketing performance.[94]

Another measure used by intermediaries is the input of the number of persons employed against turnover as a measure of labour productivity since retailing is traditionally labour intensive.

OBJECTIVES EVALUATION

Net profit changes on their own do no more than indicate changes in the performance level without specifying the reasons for the change. It may be sufficient to conduct *ad hoc* investigations when the levels drop, rather than rely on relating the drop to some other significant indicator such as total industry sales levels. Brown and Renton[95] suggested *ad hoc* investigations as a result of their experience of a timber products manufacturer, while Lambert[96] found that regular measurement was the most common procedure. The nature of the measures used appeared to be related to the background of the executive. If he had a marketing background then his reference was likely to involve selling institutions. None of the methods used included net profit contribution analysis or segment profitability analysis.

The most frequently mentioned methods used for formally evaluating the channel were cost, service levels, market coverage, sales, and gross margin. Some of these items measure channel objectives achievement while others measure general levels of profitability. Service levels is a standard of performance in physical distribution, while market coverage and sales performance are channel objectives. Rosenbloom[97] suggests that the sales and distribution performance of channel members should take place under the following headings:

Criteria	Performance measure
Sales performance	1. Gross sales
	2. Sales growth
	3. Sales compared to target
	4. Market share
Inventory maintenance	1. Average inventory maintained
	2. Inventory/sales
	3. Inventory turnover
Selling capability	1. Total number of salesmen
	2. Salesmen assigned to manufacturer's product

Such detailed information on individual intermediaries might be appropriate in the case of franchised distributors, but for other firms only the sales performance data for groups of customers may be used.

OTHER PERFORMANCE MEASURES

Market coverage is a convenient marketing measure that indicates the degree of market exposure achieved and is used frequently by suppliers of groceries and other convenience products. Expressed as a percentage, it is the total product group sales of the firm's intermediaries represented as a percentage of all retail sales of the producer's group. This may be based on value or volume. It has the effect of specifying the extent of the consumer's purchase opportunity. Typically a national packaged grocery brand leader would achieve levels of 85–90 per cent market coverage. Such data are regularly available from retail audit agencies.

MARKET SHARE

The same sources will also provide data on market share by region, and sometimes by type of customer. At least one agency also specialises in reporting share of shelf space gained in a limited number of key retailers.

GENERAL PROFITABILITY

A general measure of profitability developed by McCammon[98] presented an abbreviated form of a financial ratios tree; this is a quick method of diagnosing the general health of a company in terms of its capital management and its margin management. However, while this is of interest to company financial advisers, operational managers are more likely to use financial data that is closer to the ground, in respect of inventory levels, margins, creditors, cash flow, expenses and audit considerations. Recommendations for a system of management controls were made by Highton and Chilcott[99] which would provide sufficient information to retail buyers, managers and auditors to see the performance of their company in sufficient detail for control.

The difficulty of striking a balance between investigations that seek out the rationale behind management decisions, and the presentation of a normative model for decision-making is nowhere better demonstrated than in a section concerned with the management of a function. In this section the relationship between organisations has been explained as a basis for a paradigm of executive action.

The physical distribution decision presents quite a different set of problems. It is a straightforward exercise in achieving optimum efficiency in engineering terms, which is easily understood by a well-trained engineer but less well understood by a marketing manager.

Physical distribution management

Importance of the function

When all other aspects of a relationship between buyer and seller
have been settled, there remains one vital function to be performed:
the physical transfer of the product. Failure in any aspect of the
transfer may lead to serious consequences for both this contract and
those in the future. The performance of British industry in respect of
delivery failure was documented by the Council of British Chambers
of Commerce in Continental Europe (1979). A sample of buyers were
asked 'What are the main factors which limit the expansion of your
sales of goods or services originating in the United Kingdom?' Their
responses are shown in Table 10.5.

**Table 10.5   Factors influencing expansion of United
Kingdom purchases**

Deliveries	16.3
Supplier's prices	13.8
Supplier's support	9.1
Demand	9.1
Value of sterling	7.8
Customs tariff and quotas	7.2
Transport services and costs	6.8
Image, reputation	6.6
Quality, design	6.5
Other	6.1
Finance	5.3
Non-tariff barriers	1.7
None	3.7
	100.0

Within the United Kingdom, Cunningham and Roberts[100] found a
similar story among buyers with regard to their choice of supplier.
All of them put delivery at the top of their list of attributes
influencing suppliers' choice. At the retail level, Christopher[101]
reported that of 29.4 per cent of customers encountering a stock-out
for a particular item, fewer than half were prepared to search any
further, and instead selected a substitute.

Table 10.6   Distribution cost sources

	Kearney %	CPDM %
Transport	48	30
Warehousing	28	
Warehousing and storing		25
Administration and order processing	11	
Administration and other costs		24
Inventory financing	13	
Inventory		21
	100	100

In addition to the effect of failure on sales, physical distribution also incurs a cost in the performance of the function, and any savings that can be made without deterioration in the service level become a direct addition to net profit, having indeed an effect that can be compared to an increase in sales. To put costs in perspective, one survey by distribution consultants A. T. Kearney Ltd[102] estimated that 16.7 per cent of the selling price of goods was accounted for by distribution, while another study by the Centre for Physical Distribution Management (CPDM) put the figure at 12 per cent. The difference is accounted for by the use of different data bases both in the definition of costs and the industries included. A breakdown of the costs is shown in Table 10.6.

Table 10.7   Movement and handling ratios

Cost centre	% of total GDP	% of goods producing GDP
In process	7.7	12.5
Inter process	7.8	12.6
Warehouse	2.2	3.6
Transport	9.9	16.0
Retail	6.7	10.8
Inventory	4.7	7.5
	39.0	63.0

Source: A. Rushton and J. Williams, 'Logistics–Neglected in the National Productivity Debate', *Logistics Today*, vol. 1, no. 1 (Jan. 1982).

Rushton and Williams[103] go even further in a study of sixty-nine firms and allege that 63 per cent of the gross domestic product in manufacturing is attributable to movement and handling (see Table 10.7).

Components of the function

The problem of agreeing on which cost to include originates in the manner in which different organisations allocate responsibilities for the component parts of the function. The function itself is likely to differ according to the manufacturing process, the nature of the market, the size and complexity of the firm and the stage of development of the firm. For some companies, purchasing and distribution may be quite a limited operation, handled by the storekeeper and a driver! In others responsibilities may be allocated as in Figure 10.4, which shows a spread over three departments.

These differences affect the costing allocations, and produce problems in cost centre accounting, a problem that affects the cost information available to both the marketing manager and the distribution manager.

The accounting problem affects decisions as to the 'best' mode of transport, and the 'best' service level, decisions about the number and location of warehouses, the transport mode and operation, inventory investment and management, and the communication network.

The costing problem was explored by Ray, Gattorna and Allen[104] who considered the development of systems that produce cost centres for types of customers, and individual customers, leading to the conclusion that pricing could be differentiated to accommodate different demands made by customers on the distribution service. This aspect is usually recognised by the development of discount structures mentioned earlier, when it was shown that few firms arrive at these discounts in consequence of a cost analysis of distribution services. The author's recommendations, based on an analysis of eight sponsoring firms, distinguish between a distributor's 'profit centre' model and a manufacturer's 'cost centre' model. Manufacturers face the problem of distinguishing distribution costs from production and marketing costs and may come to different conclusions. All of the companies used computer programs but varied in their use of the computer in distribution, as shown in Table 10.8.

In addition to cost data, management also require performance data in order to maintain or improve productivity of the system, and

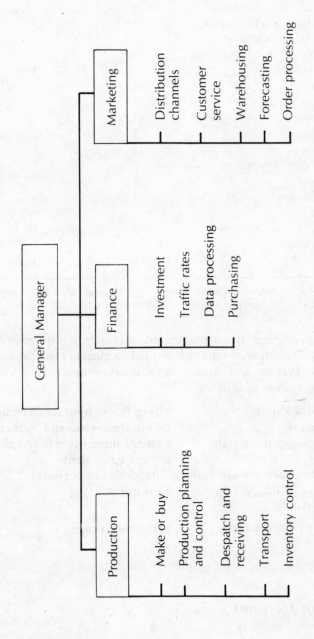

Figure 10.4 Typical allocation of PD responsibilities

Source: A. T. Kearney and C.J. Clarke, *Improving Productivity in Distribution* (London: A.T. Kearney Inc., 1980).

Table 10.8   Use of computer programs in distribution

Computer use	Manufacturers	Distributors
Accounting system (including payroll, invoicing, credit checking)	5	3
Customer pricing		1
Delivery documentation		1
Depot location	1	
Drop size pricing	1	
Incomplete orders	1	
Load analysis	2	1
Order processing	4	1
Stock control/replenishment	4	1
Stock shortages	1	
Vehicle establishment	1	1
Vehicle costing		1
Vehicle routing	2	1
Warehouse packing	2	1
Total firms	5	3

Source: D. Ray et al., 'Handbook of Distribution Costing and Control', *International Journal of Physical Distribution and Materials Management,* vol. 10 (1980).

these two aspects form the management information requirements for decisions. Performance data is intended to measure the capacity usage of the system and incorporates measurements of several aspects of the system as follows:

1. Current throughput measurements — Mix of throughput for all channels in the system and by intrachannel alternatives in weight/volume equivalents
2. Future throughput estimates
3. Distance–between system nodes — Categorised by region if appropriate
   –to customer
4. Drop size deliveries
5. Work study measurements — Manpower usage

Distribution decisions

The need for a physical distribution decision has many similarities with the need for a distribution channel decision. As with channels of distribution, total system overhaul is quite infrequent, with an estimate in the 1970s of an eleven-year interval between major changes. Instead, parts of the system are modified to produce improvements.

Modifications are made most frequently to the transport section of the distribution system, in response to changes in the legal requirements of the government, as to the permitted working conditions, or the safety of road-users. Other changes may be prompted by the development of vehicle systems that offer improved productivity. Modifications are next most frequent in the information system, when order-taking, order-processing, and invoicing are changed to accommodate the use of the computer in the inventory-control system. Telephone selling associated with the order-taking part of the system is naturally absorbed into the total system, since the computer program is written to process data for the inventory control system, the warehouse system, and the order transportation system. Many companies have been able to speed up the order-processing cycle, but few have considered the effect of such a change on other parts of the system.

The concept of total distribution system management is based on the premise that maximising the effect in one part of a system may lead to sub-optimisation in another part. The trade-offs between parts of the system are often described as shown in Figure 10.5.

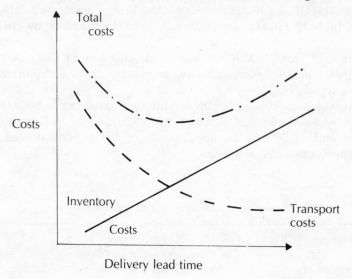

Figure 10.5   The inventory transport cost trade-off

Source: D. Firth *et al., Distribution Management Handbook* (Toronto: McGraw-Hill Ryerson, 1980).

The bottom of the total cost curve in Figure 10.5 is of course quite flat and permits quite a wide band of choice in costs for a given service level but, as other costs than transport are considered, the band narrows. Some managers will also consider the risk of lost sales through stock-outs as an additional cost and this would further affect the decision.

The situation becomes more complex if the inventory held in production is taken into account, together with the effect of purchasing decisions on quantity. Add to this, decisions to buy rather than make, decisions which have been made on information about costs of production which exclude inventory costs, and market prices, and the decision becomes more difficult, because of the lack of knowledge of the intra-system effects.

The total system design

Several paradigms for system design have been published which in most cases commence with the concept of a customer service level, that is, the customer's needs with regard to delivery. Determining these needs is the function of trade research, and A. T. Kearney's view of the United Kingdom customers' service level needs are set out in Table 10.9 in rank order with, for comparison, a list by Firth *et al.*[105]

Gilmour[106] found different needs in Australia in the scientific instrument and supplies industry, suggesting that needs differ by market segments.

Heuristic solutions to the distribution problem have been suggested by several writers, of which two are produced in Table 10.10. These tend to be specific applications of the general procedure; hypothesis, analysis, synthesis.

Table 10.9   Customer service level needs

Kearney	Firth et al.
Speed of delivery	Consistency of delivery
Completeness of orders	Speed of delivery
Frequency of delivery	High levels of order fill
Paperwork efficiency	Good communications
	Flexibility

Table 10.10 Heuristics for the distribution decision

Kearney	Perrault and Russ
1. Segment the market	1. Define important PDS elements
2. Analyse the competitive position	2. Determine customers' viewpoints
3. Quantify the customer service required by each market segment	3. Design a competitive PDS package
4. Determine the commercial objective	4. Develop a promotional programme to 'sell' PDS
5. Analyse the physical distribution movement and costs	5. Market test the PDS package and promotional programme
6. Compare possible alternative arrangements	6. Establish performance controls
7. Develop supporting systems and organisations	
8. Assess whether costs are commercially acceptable	

A combination of these decision models would result in a long process of evaluation, requiring considerable resources, while the recommendation would require capital investment to implement–investment in transport equipment, warehousing, and computer hardware and software. The redesigned system needs therefore to justify itself in cost savings or increases in sales revenue.

The influence of marketing

One of the reasons for such a review is sometimes the discovery that a competitor's service level has become so superior that it is making serious inroads on market share, or cost savings seem likely to be substantial for a relatively small reduction in service level.

On these occasions the firm needs to know the expected behaviour of the customer in response to the changes. The market research techniques of conjoint analysis can be used to determine his preferences. Most improvements in services are made at extra cost, or by forgoing services in other areas. Cash and carry offers poorer services but lower costs. The choices facing a customer consist not only of a service level for a product, but all the other attributes of the product in competition with all the other products. The poorest service level may well be acceptable if the product is uniquely beneficial, so long as that attribute is in the supplier's monopoly. Service levels really need to be decided in the light of the company's total market offering. Some companies may decide that expenditure on price discounts, or developing inter-organisational routines, may be more effective than expenditure on reviewing the physical distribution system.

Main components of a system

Warehouse location

The trade-off between warehouse numbers and transport costs is fairly well known. As warehouse numbers increase, transport costs diminish, mainly because of change in the relationship between low trunking costs and high local delivery costs. In addition, fewer stock-outs lead to possible increased sales revenue. Of course as warehouse numbers increase then so do inventory investment, warehouse investment, communications, and all operating costs, and so the concept of an optimum number of warehouses emerges.

In the early 1970s, prior to the surge in oil prices, reductions in the number of warehouse locations were quite common, following on the wave of mergers that were taking place. The increase in interest rates that had begun at this time provided some incentive to the process, as did the increase in motorway mileage and growth of vehicle/road capacity. In 1968 a change in transport law also freed companies from a number of restrictions on transport growth. It seemed to many that this relatively small island could adequately be served from one or two strategically placed warehouses.

Since that time cost structures have changed again with changes in oil prices and considerable increases in interest rates. Further changes in company law to take account of inflation also made it profitable from an acounting view to hold large stocks rather than minimise investment in inventory. It could therefore be argued that for some companies an increase in the number of warehouses, rather than a reduction, would now provide an optimum distribution network.

Of all the physical distribution decisions this area of warehouse numbers and location has the longest planning horizon and therefore deserves high-level attention, together with the use of operations research specialists and accountants. The operation research specialists bring to the problem model-building skills (see Higby;[107]

Bowersox[108]) which leave room for considering different scenarios of development. Any advantages these skills offer depend on the ability to identify correctly those features likely to have a future impact.

Warehouse management

In the short term, warehouse management makes a direct contribution to fulfilling the objectives of the system in terms of achieving the desired lead time, at the lowest cost. The efficiency of the operation begins with the layout of the warehouse, the design of material handling equipment, and the concept of an integrated packaging policy that can satisfy the demands of many different handling, storage, and movement systems, and finally the information system through which the whole logistics are set in motion. In some cases special requirements exist for 'picking' systems that will meet the needs of mail-order companies who have a large number of Stock Keeping Units (SKUs) and a large number of customers, or of retailers who operate their own warehouses. At the other extreme, some manufacturers may rent warehouse space and adapt the existing premises where their distribution needs are not so demanding.

Warehouse layout and handling systems are usually company specific, although there may be similarities in industries accustomed to handling similar-sized products and orders. One retailer now has facilities for reading bar-coded cartons in its transshipment centres to provide a semi-automated warehouse. Other retailers and manufacturers have developed 'picking' systems that operate on the principle of moving the stock to the staff for picking, while some who handle large quantities of fairly standard-sized 'outers' and a low rate of change in customer needs have developed completely automated picking systems, or warehouses.

It must be stressed that all warehouse systems are designed to solve one company's problems in the warehouse depending on whether the general purpose is transshipment, break-bulk, or assortment.

The main attribute in common is that warehouse management's approach is to minimise operational cost, first on the company's own business and secondly on other business that will assist in maximising building use. Organisations such as SPD Ltd designed originally to handle Unilever Products now find that Unilever business accounts for about half of its revenue, with other companies' products accounting for the remainder.

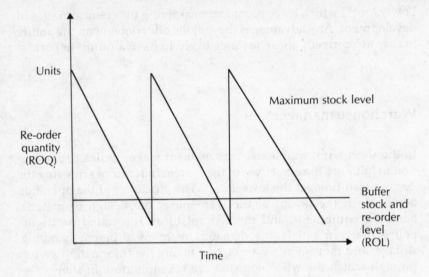

Figure 10.6   Effects of re-order level control

Materials management

Inventories serve many purposes, and on occasion more than one function may be fulfilled by the same inventory. The functions are:

Transit inventory	– the average quantity in transit
Cycle inventory	– the result of batch production and continuous demand and late delivery
Buffer inventory	– balancing level production aganst seasonal peaks and troughs in demand

Figures 10.6 and 10.7 represent typical patterns of stock holdings.

An inventory plan consists of target inventory levels based on time periods, representing the policy of the company with respect to customer service levels, production needs for stability, and financial goals. It takes account of the trade-offs for each function to produce the best course of action to satisfy the different demands of each function of the firm. In order to fulfil the promises of the plan the organisation develops effective materials management techniques.

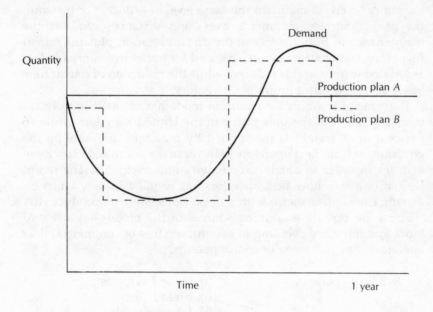

Figure 10.7   Seasonal inventory

The heart of the systems is the choice of the replenishment system to be used. The basic types of system are:

1. Re-order level with fixed ROQ
2. Periodic re-order with ROQ based on forecast
3. Replenishment system for replacing stocks sold

All three systems depend on timely, accurate information on current stock levels, and more companies now use computer-stored processed, and electronically transmitted information, in systems designed to their needs by specialists.

Transport mode

The size of in-transit inventory can be affected by transit time and mode, so that there is a trade-off between transport mode and inventory levels, to maintain the same level of service. For instance, the use of surface shipments over long distances requires the maintenance of buffer stocks at the distant location plus the transit inventory. Using air transport, the need for buffer inventory (and its associated warehouse) is reduced, while the reduction of transit time has a beneficial effect on transit inventory.

The general trend in the choice of mode has resulted in railways receiving much of the bulk traffic in the United Kingdom while 76 per cent of all freight is transported by road with pressure on the government from fleet operators to increase the permitted capacity of vehicles in order to obtain productivity improvements. The recent legislation controlling fleet operators has resulted in new limits on driving time and distance with a deleterious effect on productivity.

Firms are now re-examining sources of the mode they use and more and more are deciding to use the services of commercial fleet operators. The full range of choice open is:

1. Own fleet operation   – (i) owned vehicles
                                 (ii) hired vehicles
                                 (iii) leased vehicles
2. Subcontracted services   – (i) hire trunk transport service
                                 (ii) hire trunk transport and warehousing
                                 (iii) hire distribution service to include local delivery
                                 (iv) groupage services
3. Combination of owned and hired operation to resolve fluctuations in demand for services.

Transportation management

The supervision of all matters affecting the use of the transport fleet is generally regarded as the responsibility of the transport manager with some differences in the control of the routing and scheduling section.

Routing and scheduling concerns the daily planning of work for each driver, who leaves his depot with a full load and returns empty having made his deliveries. Most depots still plan the route, deliveries, and load the vehicles manually, many using some fixed form of planning based on routes or areas.

With rising costs of local delivery there have been attempts, not all successful, to improve the productivity of planning by using computers, either to determine the routes and loads, or to provide assistance in evaluating options. The decision to use the computer was a logical extension of the decision to use it in order-processing and in warehouse management. O'Brien[109] suggests that the computer has now been 'educated' sufficiently to be of use to load planners as an interactive aid able to respond to 'what if?' questioning.

Fleet productivity

Obtaining productivity improvement is the constant ojective of the transport manager in order to ensure that the whole fleet is effectively utilised, with the fleet composition balanced against demand so that he is never short or surplus to requirements. At the same time he has to provide his employees with a work load that will meet agreements with their representatives as to hours and wages.

Since much of the unproductive time is at the customer's 'goods inward' door either waiting or unloading, any scheme to reduce this time is to be welcomed. The improvement may be the result of changes in equipment, customer relations, or training methods. New problems constantly arise in this respect, as for example proposals in 1982 by the Health and Safety Commission to regulate manual handling conditions of work. One of these proposals provides a guideline for manual handling of a maximum of 35 lb.

Finally, the fleet manager is responsible for ensuring that regulations for safety and maintenance are complied with, preparing and presenting vehicles for inspection and certification.

Communications

The final section deals with information used by the physical distribution system and originating in the system for use elsewhere in the firm. Much of this section is attributed to Skjoett-Larson[110] who lists the roles of the logistics information system (LIS) as:

1. A triggering mechanism to drive the system
2. A management monitor and control mechanism
3. A co-ordinator of the sub-systems of logistics and of logistics with other company functions
4. One of the links of the company with suppliers, customers, sub-contracted agencies

The triggering mechanism

This is the mechanism for processing customer orders and dealing with physical distribution agents. The customer's order is first converted into a company usable format before processing. The processing comprises:

> Editing for accuracy
> Screening for credit and integrity
> > Stock availability and backlog.
> Transforming into
> > Picking and packing orders
> > Delivery orders
> > Invoices
> > Control reports
> Transmitting data and orders to the PD
> > sub-systems for updating and action

The technology for the process may be manual, mechanical, electrical or electronic depending on the size of the company, the volume of processing and the need for accuracy and speed. In the technology of the 1970s many companies combined telephone sales and ordering with direct computer entry.

Once processed for the purpose of the logistics system, the data are accumulated as measures of performance of the system and in a longer time span, as measures of the marketing performance and production performance.

The related material systems

The triggering mechanism affects both the production and supply system which receive copies of the picking schedules in order to generate replacement inventory, or to accumulate deliveries to some predetermined batch level.

The accounts department will also match delivery acknowledgements with invoices prepared earlier to stimulate the flow of cash into the business. The speedier the process of invoicing, the better the cash flow. These data when accumulated are then vital to the financial controller in measuring business performance.

Other company functions

Information systems are generally designed to provide data where, when, and in what form they can be used in a function. In many instances within the sub-system, the management decision parameters are part of the structure, and the decision is as automatic as a thermal control valve. Other decisions require managers to access data not normally supplied as a routine. Lambert[111] found that marketing managers were unaware of the availability of distribution cost data they needed to evaluate channel performance.

The source of the required data is either another sub-system within the organisation, or the external environment. The options in the communications system design to answer this need are:

1. Data consolidated in a central file to which all authorised decision-takers have access. Such a system presents security problems.
2. Closely connected activities are grouped together with access offered to all decision-takers in these activities.
3. System 2 supplemented with access offered to selected decision-takers in other functions.

An integrated information system designed to deliver information only where and when it is needed, becomes part of a planning system to reduce 'slack' in the physical capacity of the firm, a slack that could be large buffer stocks to take up forecasting failures, surplus capacity to obviate the need for planning, or any other action to bridge discontinuities and reduce co-ordination needs at the cost of wasted resources.

The effect of such a system for reducing delays in information transmission may not always have only the effects desired, but extend to other aspects of the system. In an order-processing system it could also raise the backlog level which in turn would stimulate the production manager to action, to reduce it. Changes in any system ought not to be made without thorough projection of the likely effects over all other functions connected to it.

CHAPTER 11

Analytical frameworks for strategic market planning

Contents

Introduction

The hallmark of human survival throughout the ages is its biological and cultural adaptation to a changing environment. Evolution has endowed mankind with a 'survival kit' that enables him not only to accept a changing environment, but also to use his sense of foresight to manipulate it.

In the context of the evolution of the firm, an increasingly turbulent business environment predicates the need for underlying adaptability in terms of policies, organisational structure, products, markets and technology. However, the ability to anticipate successfully and prepare for environmental change initiated by social, political, economic or technological events, has so far been elusive, as the history of many firms reveals.

It is a widely held view that strategic planning now assumes an important role in coping with the risk and uncertainty of a turbulent business climate. The recent ascendance of strategic planning can be attributed to the growing concern of industry and commerce with how to manage environmental change by looking ahead and planning for the future. Nevertheless, the emerging interest in the future does not so much herald the dawning of a new era in management philosophy, as indicate a growing concern for the inevitability of decline, as enshrined in Levitt's[1] dictum 'that every declining industry was once a growth industry'.

Table 11.1   Examples of environmental variables beyond the firm's control

Economic conditions	Demographic trends	Techno-logical changes	Social–cultural trends	Political–legal factors
GNP trends	Growth rate of population	Total government spending for R and D	Life-style changes	Anti-monopoly regulations
Interest rates	Age distribution of population		Career expectations	Environmental protection laws
Money supply		Total industry spending for R and D	Consumer activism	Nationalisation of industry
Inflation rates	Regional shifts in population	Focus of technological effort	Rate of family formation	Tax laws
Unemployment levels	Life expectancies			Special incentives
Standard of living	Birth rates	Patent protection		Foreign trade regulations
Wage/price controls	Income distribution			Attitudes towards foreign companies
Exchange rates				
Energy availability				

The emergence of marketing as a business philosophy shows an early concern for the impact on the firm of what Kotler[2] calls 'the external uncontrollable variables' (see Table 11.1), as well as internal forces of change. Moreover, it has always been clear that to maintain a competitive advantage the firm needs to anticipate and respond to changes that affect its products (technology) and markets (customers). Although the orientation of strategic planning can be directed towards longer-term issues of general management concern, its ultimate expression takes the form of product-market strategy decisions.

This chapter considers the evolution of strategic planning and briefly introduces the managerial processes it involves. It also discusses the conceptual foundations of analytical frameworks that have been developed to promote the process of strategic planning, referring in some detail to the work of bodies such as the Boston Consulting Group, General Electric, Shell and the Strategic Planning Institute. By examining the way in which the frameworks address specific issues, it is hoped to reveal the scope and limitations of the guidelines they offer for taking product-market strategy decisions.

Background

There has been an enormous growth in the size and complexity of firms during the post-war period of rapid economic growth and expanding international trade. That multinationals and conglomerates have evolved is known to be a consequence of the merger, acquisition, diversification and transnational expansion of firms during this time. There is evidence[3] to support the view that during the latter part of the post-war period there has occurred a progressive diminution of the degree of control exercised by the firm over its environment. This is attributed to the firms widening exposure to an increasingly turbulent social, political, economic and technological climate.[4]

Drucker labels this era 'the age of discontinuity'. His early work[5] shares with Levitt's a keen understanding of the need to change what was called management's 'myopic' perception of the firm in relation to its environment. Ansoff[6] notes that 'no firm can consider itself immune to threats of product obsolescence and saturation of demand' and, therefore, 'firms in all industries need to make regular periodic reviews of product-market strategy'. Levitt[7] expresses ideas akin to those of Ansoff when he urges management to avoid 'marketing myopia' by recognising that changes in demand, technology and competition call for what he refers to as 'the periodic reorientation of a firm's activities'. Both authors recognised the fundamental importance of making explicit the firm's purpose and cohesion by determining 'what business the firm is in'. Furthermore, the call for a periodic reorientation of the firm's 'business' recognised that the critical success factors in the competitive arena are transient, and that the firm's mix of resources and capabilities must frequently be realigned in order to exploit emerging sources of potential competitive advantage.

In considering the evolution of mankind Bronowski[8] notes that real mastery of the environment does not come from being able to dominate it, but comes from 'understanding and moulding the living environment'. In an analogous fashion, Hofer and Schendel[9] suggest that the success of the firm's strategy is determined by the basic characteristics of the 'match' it seeks to achieve with its environment, by redeploying resources in response to environmental stimuli.

The importance of matching the firm's competences and goals with the opportunities and risks created by the changing environment has been widely discussed by Ansoff[10] with respect to the principle of monitoring and anticipating environmental change. However, the growing incidence of completely novel threats and opportunities has augmented the influence of the unpredictable component of environmental change. In so doing, the time available to the firm for taking and implementing corrective management decisions has been reduced. Consequently, as the disequilibrium of the underlying forces of change grows, the future is becoming more uncertain and less foreseeable. Indeed, the inevitability of change and the difficulty of predicting it qualifies as the subject of one of a group of five marketing maxims recently proposed by Baker.[11]

The process by which US firms adapted to environmental change, during the early part of this century, has been examined by Chandler.[12] He discovered a time lag between the occurrence of events causing change in the firm's environment, for instance market saturation, and the subsequent adaptation of the firm through new policies, organisation structure, products, markets and technology. As Chandler saw it, the majority of firms did not really manage environmental change, but were managed by it. Moreover, the failure to make an early diagnosis of the underlying problems (of, as in the above example of market saturation, declining markets and product substitution) was seen to make the process of repositioning the firm more hazardous. Therefore, since the mid 1950s, as Ansoff[13] notes, 'lag time adaptation became increasingly ineffective, because of the accelerating pace of environmental change'.

In response to the growing diversity and complexity of commercial challenges that are arising, firms are devoting more and more senior management attention to the evolving methods and procedures, or what Ansoff[14] calls the 'know-how and technology' of formalised strategic planning. Ultimately, the aim is to be able to manage change and discontinuity in the firm's environment by anticipating and preparing for it.

Defining strategic planning

Strategic planning has been defined by Kotler[15] as 'the managerial process of developing and maintaining a viable relationship between the organisation and its environment through the development of corporate purpose, objectives and goals, growth strategies, and business portfolio plans for company-wide operations'. But, as Steiner[16] observes, there is no single definition of strategic planning, or of its specialised terminology, that is broadly accepted. A few definitions of strategy and strategic planning are shown below.

1. The answers to two questions were implicit to Drucker's[17] early conceptualisation of an organisation's strategy: 'What is our business? And what should it be?'
2. Chandler[18] defined strategy as 'the determination of the basic long-term goals and objectives of an enterprise, and the adoption of courses of action and the allocation of resources necessary for carrying out these goals'.
3. Andrews's[19] definition of strategy combines the ideas of Drucker and Chandler: 'strategy is the pattern of objectives, purposes or goals and major policies and plans for achieving these goals, stated in such a way as to define what business the company is in or is to be in and the kind of company it is or is to be'.
4. Hofer and Schendel[20] define an organisation's strategy as 'the fundamental pattern of present and planned resource deployments and environmental interactions that indicates how the organisation will achieve its objectives'.
5. According to Abell,[21] strategic planning involves 'the management of any business unit in the dual tasks of anticipating and responding to changes which affect the marketplace for their products'.
6. In 1979, Derek Wynne-Jones,[22] head of the Planning and Strategy division of P.A. Management Consultants, considered that strategic planning 'embraced the overall objectives of an organisation in defining its strategy and preparing and subsequently implementing its detailed plans'.
7. Christopher Lorenz,[23] editor of the Management Page of the

Financial Times, considers processes by which top and senior executives 'decide, direct, delegate and control the generation and allocation of resources within a company'.

This selection of definitions indicates that strategic planning involves two principal concepts: first, that of strategy itself, that is, the goals and objectives (the ends) the firm sets itself; and secondly, that of the process by which strategy is developed (the means). Whether the formalised approaches to strategy formulation (known as strategic planning) include setting goals and objectives is a contentious issue which has been the subject of considerable debate. A dichotomy of views has evolved around the arguments of two principal actors: Ansoff,[24] who holds the 'narrow' view favoured by Hofer and Schendel,[25] considers the two concepts to be separate and distinct; and Andrews,[26] whose holistic view interlinks them.

The value of strategic planning

Several research studies have shown that firms that plan their product-market strategies have a greater chance of achieving commercial success. The work of Thune and House[27] compared the performance of eighteen matched pairs of medium to large firms in the American food, steel, drug, machinery, petroleum and chemical industries: pairs consisted of a firm that used formal strategic planning, and one that did not. Applying performance criteria such as earnings per share growth, return on investment and sales (see Figure 11.1), it was found that the firms that used strategic planning outperformed those that did not. Further findings suggested that the performance of firms had significantly improved after adopting formal strategic planning systems (see Figure 11.2).

The early work of the PIMS[28] researchers at the Marketing Science Institute concluded that strategic planning makes a significant contribution to a firm's profitability. Additional studies conducted by Eastlack and McDonald,[29] Herold,[30] Guth,[31] Ansoff,[32] and Karger and Malik[33] provide further evidence to support the view that firms that practise strategic planning will generally outperform those that do not.

Various reasons are offered for the apparently beneficial influence of strategic planning. As Unni[34] records, two important reasons are that strategic planning 'provides employees with clear goals and directions to the future of the organisation and provides a standard against which future performance can be compared'. Steiner[35] summarises the reasons in the following way.

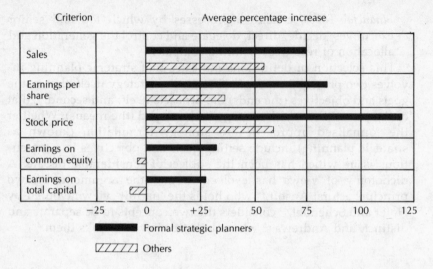

Figure 11.1   Comparing the performance of firms that used formal strategic planning, and those that did not

Source: S. Thune and R. House, 'Where Long Range Planning Pays Off', *Business Horizons*, vol. 13 (1970).

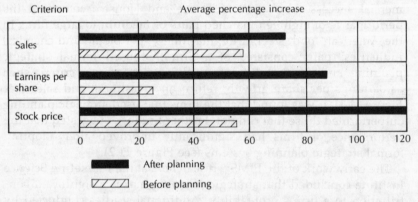

Figure 11.2   Comparing the performance of firms before and after formal strategic planning

Source: S. Thune and R. House, 'Where Long Range Planning Pays Off', *Business Horizons*, vol. 13 (1970).

1. It is indispensable to top management's effective discharging of its responsibilities.
2. It forces managers to ask and answer questions that are of the highest importance to a company and that skilled managers should address.

3. It can simulate the future on paper, a practice that permits a company to make better decisions about what to do about future opportunities and threats now, rather than waiting until events happen. Planning itself classifies the opportunities and threats that lie ahead for a company.
4. It is an effective way to look at a business as a system and thereby prevent suboptimisation of the parts of the system at the expense of the whole organisation.
5. It provides employees with clear objectives and directions to the future of the company and serves as a basis for management control and evaluation.
6. It helps to identify the major strategic issues and to establish priorities for dealing with them.
7. It leads to better co-ordination of company efforts.
8. It assists in the allocation of discretionary strategic resources and the development and training of future general managers.

The impressive body of opinion in support of the apparent benefits of strategic planning is not free from the occasional dissenting voice. Rue and Fulmer[36] examined the planning practices and financial performances of 432 firms in the American services, durable and non-durable industrial sectors. It was found that in the service industries non-planning firms outperformed the 'planners' in all instances, the reverse holding true for firms in the durable and non-durable industries. Sheehan's[37] research into the planning practices of Canadian industry also takes the form of qualified dissension. It indicates that in some instances non-planning firms outperformed those that used formal strategic planning. Doubts concerning the validity of these findings have focused on methodological matters.

Recent criticism has been concerned with what Hunsicker[38] calls 'the malaise of strategic planning', that is, that sophisticated strategic planning systems demand so much effort that senior management often finds itself in a 'paralysis of analysis'. Wensley[39] contends that formal strategic planning deflects the attention of senior management from the search for a sustainable competitive advantage. Nevertheless, despite the growing body of articulate criticism of strategic planning, the need for a means to monitor and anticipate environmental change, and to prepare the firm for the future, is not abrogated. But, as Day[40] has recently written, 'we are now in a period of critical reappraisal of (these) planning approaches, where unqualified enthusiasm has been largely replaced with healthy and thoughtful scepticism'. The fundamental premise on which this chapter is based is that strategic planning has an important role to play in the firm.

The strategic planning process

The strategic planning process has been considered, by both Ansoff[41] and Bower,[42] as a means for solving the special problems that are associated with formulating a firm's strategy. The essence of the envisaged problem-solving process is depicted in Figure 11.3. Prescriptive models of strategic planning develop the principal steps of the problem-solving process in a variety of ways, largely reflecting the experience and background of their originators. Simple models may take the general form depicted in Figure 11.4, this being more useful where the firm is about to begin developing a formal strategic planning system than the complex model shown in Figure 11.5. However, in some circumstances simple models are incapable of yielding meaningful strategies because they embody an insufficiently accurate and detailed representation of the strategic planning process.

Models of the strategic planning process are often similar in many respects,[43] even though much of their content is implicit. They usually involve the following sequence of activities, and differ primarily with respect to the detail and complexity with which each step of the sequence is considered.

1. Defining the business
2. Situation audit.
3. Establishing objectives
4. Strategic alternatives.
5. Selecting portfolio of strategic alternatives.
6. Implementation.
7. Measurement, feedback and control.

Lorange and Vancil[44] state that there are three distinct 'cycles' or hierarchies in the process of strategic planning. The first 'cycle' identifies and assesses strategic alternatives in the perspective provided by the firm's objectives, expressed in terms of sales growth, market share, return on investment, cash flow, or profitability; and by its 'definition'[45] in terms of customers (markets), their different needs (market segments/product functions) and products (technology). The second 'cycle' is concerned with the formulation of strategies for functions such as marketing or production which are consistent with the broad strategic alternatives. The third 'cycle' concentrates on preparing short-term operational plans and budgets, as instruments with which to allocate resources within and between the firm's component businesses.

Hofer and Schendel[46] have proposed a similar three-level hierarchy of the process of strategic planning. It operates at the corporate level, the individual business level, and the functional area level. At the first level (the corporate level) the process is concerned with determining, for example, what set of businesses the firm should be in; how resources should be deployed; what organisational structure is required; and what competitive advantages there are to be gained. At the level of the individual business (the second level) the process focuses on determining the critical success requirements of competing in a particular industry sector, or market segment. It is also concerned with policy issues pertaining to research and development, new product development and market development. At the functional area level the process is primarily concerned with developing distinctive competences with which the firm could establish a dominant market position, or technological leadership in a product-market segment. Consequently, issues such as manufacturing productivity, pricing, distribution and promotion are given considerable attention at this level.

The appealing concept of the three tiers of strategic planning is less expedient where the firm operates across a number of product-market boundaries. Large international conglomerates, frequently the result of mergers, will normally make available a wide variety of products to a number of markets: DuPont, the multinational chemicals giant, currently operates in seventy-five major businesses, with well-known brand names such as Teflon, Kevlar, Lycra, Hypalon, Nomex, Nubain and Glean. But any firm that pursues a strategy of product or market diversification will be increasingly concerned with managing a range of business endeavours: the allocation of resources and the identification and evaluation of threats and opportunities are key areas with which strategic planning is concerned where firms operate in this fashion. Acute problems are also known to occur in discriminating between component businesses with real growth potential, and those that offer, in comparison, a less attractive return on investment; and in directing financial support from mature businesses that generate excess funds to those where growth should be funded.

The problems of marketing a particular product in a given market, and the multifarious environmental factors that affect it, should be the focus of attention for strategic planning. In this context, the concept of the Strategic Business Unit (SBU) has been shown to be particularly relevant.[47] It asserts that multimarket–multiproduct firms should consider their organisation as a collection of discrete business units, capable of achieving dissimilar levels of performance, and worthy of a distinct product-market strategy (see Figure 11.6).

There is no universal definition of what constitutes an SBU, it being largely dependent on circumstances specific to each firm.

A large UK-based multinational electrical engineering conglomer-

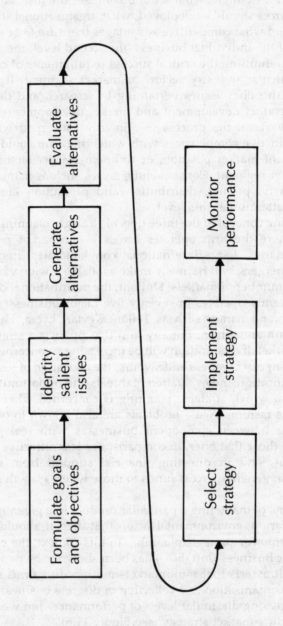

Figure 11.3 Strategic planning as a problem-solving process

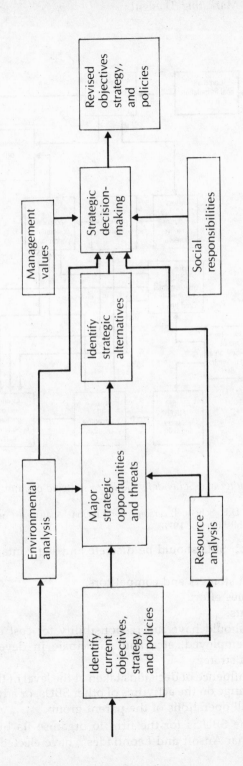

Figure 11.4 Andrews's model of strategic planning

Source: K. Andrews et al., *Business Policy: Text and Cases* (Homewood: Ill.: Irwin, 1965).

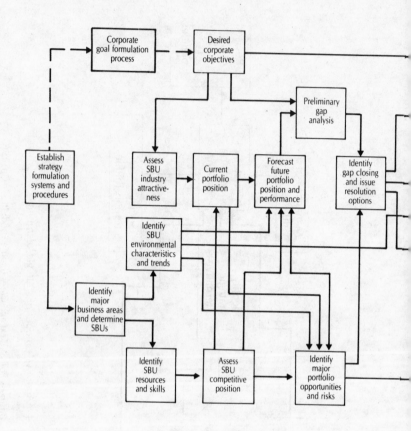

Figure 11.5   Hofer and Schendel's model of strategic planning

Source: C.W. Hofer and D.E. Schendel, *Strategy Formulation: Analytical Concepts* (St Paul, Minnesota: West Publishing Co. 1978).

ate requests that each SBU should be discrete and self-contained in these respects:

Industry sector, customers and competitors.

Marketing and sales effort.

Operating accounts.

Management. It should have full responsibility for cost control, profit, capital employed, etc., and participate in developing product-market strategy.

Autonomy. The influence of decisions taken at the level of the SBU should not impinge on the activities of other SBUs, or adversely affect the overall operations of the parent group.

An alternative to the SBU is for the firm to organise its business activities around what Ansoff and Leontiades[48] have elected to call

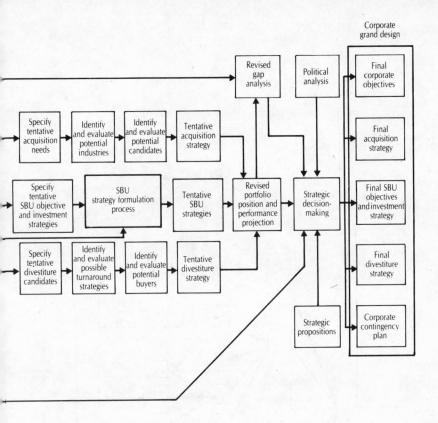

the Strategic Business Area (SBA). Following their recommendations, the firm's environment (social, political, economic, technological) is subdivided into relatively independent segments which contain their own distinctive trends, threats and opportunities: these then become the basic organisation unit within the firm. In brief, an SBA is therefore seen as representing a distinctive area of opportunity in terms of the demand served and technology used. In this scheme the SBU is said to be the unit of the firm responsible for developing one or more coherent areas of opportunity, that is, SBAs. In its role of developing the profit potential of the firm, the SBU is seen to be subservient to the SBA.

Strategic planning at the level of the SBU not only compels the decision-taker to be familiar with the associated product and its

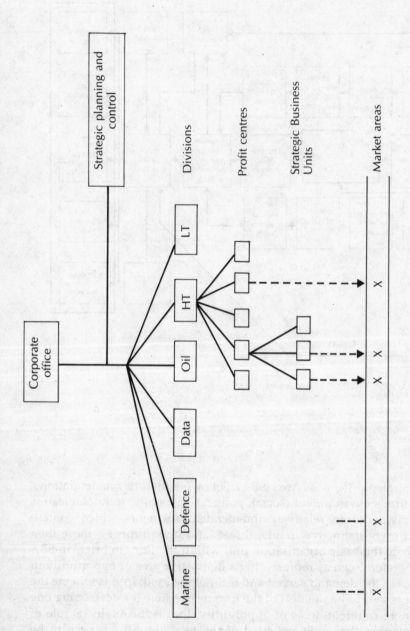

Figure 11.6 Organisational levels for planning and control

market; it also ensures that the interests of each SBU are represented in the firm's broad strategic plans. Nevertheless, the focus of strategic thinking at this level will tend to be biased towards the interests of the SBU. The management of the SBU is also unlikely to have the ability, or the resources, to monitor and anticipate environmental changes which demand a change in marketing strategy to confront opportunities and threats as they evolve. As Drucker[49] suggests, the first task of management is to run the business it has; the second is to ensure its future.

Strategic planning in the previously mentioned electrical engineering conglomerate is the responsibility of a separate, tomorrow-oriented group, reporting at a senior level to the director of personnel and management services. This group is responsible for diagnosing the current strategic position, or 'business posture', of the firm and each of its SBUs; and for conducting a comprehensive analysis of strategic alternatives available to them. The firm is organised in the fashion of Figure 11.6.

Within the strategic planning framework of a large German engineering firm, strategic plans are produced for the parent group as a whole; for its fourteen product lines; and also for its thirty SBUs. Having already defined its business, the process begins with what constitutes a situation audit, that is, an analysis of its customers, competitors, market characteristics, environmental trends and corporate strengths and weaknesses. At the first level of strategic control, product line plans are made, covering a ten-year time horizon. Their main purpose is to spot gaps in the firm's product-market strategies, and to initiate the projects necessary to fill them. At the second level, operational plans for each SBU are devised with a two-year horizon for line management functions such as production and marketing. At the third level, monthly operational plans and budgets are used to allocate resources within each SBU.

Defining the business

A basic tenet of strategic planning requires the firm to identify the 'common thread',[50] or core-competence of its resources and capabilities; then, to attempt to match them to the threats and opportunities in the market-place; and, finally, to make an explicit statement of strategic objectives.

The first step in the strategic planning process determines the purpose and direction of the firm. It also indicates the type of information required to help analyse strategic issues. Answers to the following questions should be provided:

1. What business are we in?
2. What unique features/capabilities does the firm have?
3. What are the interests of the major shareholders?
4. What resources does the firm have?
5. What strengths and weaknesses does the firm have?
6. What threats and opportunities face the firm?

The way a business is defined largely determines the broad areas of activity in which a firm participates. It further provides a frame of reference within which to identify and assess strategic threats and opportunities.

Businesses can be defined in terms of products (technology) or markets (customer groups). Levitt[51] argues that broad market-based definitions, expressed in terms of the customer function that is performed, are preferred to technology-based definitions. Abell[52] contends that businesses should be defined in terms of their 'scope and segmentation/differentiation' according to these three dimensions: customer groups; customer functions; and technologies. The term 'scope' defines the extent to which a business participates in one or more customer groups, customer functions and technologies. Segmentation/differentiation measures the way in which businesses participate in markets along each of the three dimensions.

The situation audit

Drucker[53] notes that 'a business is not defined by the company's name, statutes, or articles of incorporation. It is defined by the want the customer satisfies when he buys a product or a service.' The situation audit begins with an analysis of the customer, it being the basis for identifying salient differences among customer groups. The questions it poses have been summarised by Abell and Hammond.[54] Table 11.2 provides a checklist of the factors to be considered when conducting a customer analysis.

The analysis of competitive posture is a vital part of the situation audit. Indeed, as Richard Lochridge of the Boston Consulting Group recently remarked, 'The strategy requirements of any business are ruled by the competitive environment and the potential for change in that environment'.[55] The actions of competitors must be considered and questions such as these[56] addressed:

Who are the present and potential new entrants?
What are their past and current strategies?
How are they performing?

Table 11.2   Checklist for customer analysis and market evaluation

Customer analysis		Market evaluation
Consumers	Industrial, regulated and government users; OEMs and contractors; distributors and dealers.	
Demographics	Types of users	Total dollars or units
Personal Characteristics	Size/geographic location	What is the best way to segment:
	Buying habits	By customer type
Buying habits	Objectives and expectations	By location of customers
Objectives and expectations		By price levels
How products are used	Product use	By product type and features
Economic factors	Economic factors	By decision-makers or decision criteria
How important is a product?	Importance?	By customer strategy
Pre- and post-sales service required	Service required?	Size of segments
		Dollars
	Financial abilities	Units
Financial abilities		Growth rates
	Business strategy	Total/segments
Personal strategy	Decision-maker loyalty	Dollars
Loyalty of key decision-maker	Quantity	Units
	Frequency	Pricing trends
Quantity	Terms/conditions	Cyclicality/seasonality
Frequency		Sensitivity of demand
Terms/conditions		Price
		Service
		Feature
		External factors
		Captive market, not available to independents

Source: W. Rothschild, *Putting It All Together—A Guide to Strategic Thinking* (New York: AMA COM, 1976) p. 49.

What are their strengths and weaknesses?

What actions can be expected from them in future?

A checklist for analysing the strengths and weaknesses of competitors is shown in Table 11.3 and an example of a simplified competitive analysis is shown in Table 11.4.

The competitive environment in which a firm operates is continually changing so that new threats and opportunities arise frequently. In the long term a prerequisite of strategic success is being able to adapt quickly to new environmental conditions by anticipat-

Table 11.3 Summary of competitor analysis

Conceive/design	Produce	Market	Finance	Manage

Technical resources
  Concepts
  Patents and copyrights
  Technological sophistication
  Technical integration
	Physical resources
	  Capacity
	  Plant
	    Size
	    Location
	    Age
	  Equipment
	    Automation
	    Maintenance
	    Flexibility
	  Processes
	    Uniqueness
	    Flexibility
	    Degree of integration
		Sales force
		  Skills
		  Size
		  Type
		  Location
		
		Distribution network
		
		Research
		  Skills
		  Type
			Long-term
			  Debt/equity ratio
			  Cost of debt
			
			Short-term
			  Line of credit
			  Type of debt
			  Cost of debt
			
			Liquidity
			
			Cash flow
			  Days of receivables
			  Inventory turnover
			  Accounting practices
				Key people
				  Objectives and priorities
				  Values
				  Reward systems
				
				Decision-making
				  Location
				  Type
				  Speed
				
				Planning
				  Type
				  Emphasis
				  Time span

Human resources
  Key people and skills
  Use of external technical groups
	Human resources
	  Key people and skills
	  Workforce
	    Skills mix
	    Unions
	    Turnover
		Human resources
		  Key people and skills
		  Turnover
			Human resources
			  Key people and skills
			  Turnover
				Staffing
				  Longevity and turnover
				  Experience
				  Replacement policies

Funding
  Total
  Percentage of sales
  Consistency over time
  Internally generated
  Government-supplied
		Findings
		  Total
		  Consistency over time
		  Percentage of sales
		  Reward systems
			Systems
			  Budgeting
			  Forecasting
			  Controlling
				Organisation
				  Centralisation
				  Functions
				  Use of staff

Source: as Table 11.2.

ing market evolution and devising unique competitive advantages. The analysis of social, political, economic and technological issues that may influence customer behaviour and competitive strategies is, therefore, of considerable importance. This aspect of the situation audit, and others, are discussed in some detail in Chapter 2 of Abell and Hammond's *Strategic Market Planning*.

Establishing objectives

After a suitable definition of the firm's business has been established and a comprehensive situation audit carried out, the firm may be in the position to establish objectives.

There is debate concerning the point in the strategic planning process at which objectives should be set. To some the setting of objectives should come before the process begins. However, others maintain that the argument depends on whether the objectives are to be vague and extremely long term, or whether they are to be very detailed and pragmatic. Clearly there is a role for both kinds of objectives in the overall strategic planning process. For example, American Telephone and Telegraph once stated that one of its major goals was the provision of a quality telephone service at a low cost for all the people. To satisfy this longer-term objecive, ATT may first have had to attain operational objectives, such as that of achieving a 10 per cent per annum compound growth rate in earnings per share over a three-year period.

Although the terms 'goal' and 'objective' are often apparently used interchangeably, it is possible to draw a clear distinction between them: goals being the long-term, open-ended attributes the firm seeks to acquire, for instance profit maximisation; objectives being short to medium term targets which must be achieved in order that it remains possible, ultimately, to attain the firm's goals.

Kotler[57] suggests that for objectives to be useful to an organisation, they should be not only realistic and consistent, but should also be hierarchical and quantitative. There are at least three reasons why firms should seek to perform the difficult task of formulating such objectives:[58]

1. Objectives define the organisation in its environment.
2. Objectives help co-ordinate decisions and decision-makers.
3. Objectives provide performance standards.

Hofer and Schendel[59] have identified four components that should be common to all objectives: an indication of the goal or attribute sought; an index for measuring the firm's progress towards it; a

Table 11.4   Simplified competitive analysis

Competitive dimensions			Competitors				Comments on data
			Us	A	B	C	
1. Product Position	Market Size	Growth per year	Market Share				
Line 1	$15M	0%	65%	20%	10%	5%	1. Not subject to share gain, manage for cash.
2	$30M	10%	25%	40%	15%	20%	2. Subject to share gain, A most vulnerable B, C less so.
3	$20M	15%	10%	25%	30%	35%	3. Subject to share gain, A, B, C equally vulnerable. Substantial unfilled need for a new product.
2. Pricing Strategy							B and C will be easiest to take share away from on price and it will be least expensive to maintain share taken away. A is more competitive, will require larger price differential: to gain and maintain share, and it is therefore more costly to take share away.
H = Price for margin		Line 1	C	C	C	H	
C = Price with market		2	C	L	C	C	
L = Price leader or very aggressive		3	C	L	C	C	
3. New Product Policy							Expect new products first from A, monitor market carefully to identify what they're working on—expect A to imitate earliest any new products introduced.
L = Leader		Line 1	L	L	F	F	
F = Follower		2	F	L	F	F	
		3	L	L	L	F	
4. Overall Marketing Strength							A strongest and equal to us. B and C vulnerable to more intensive selling effort offered by us.
No. Representatives		Line 1	5	10	15	15	
No. Distributors		2	40	35	30	30	
No. Salesmen		3	25	20	10	7	
5. Geographic Strength							We may be weak in district W and should consider adding salesmen, otherwise are equal or superior to competition.
No. Salesmen and Reps							
Territory E			9	7	7	6	
F			7	7	6	6	
G			5	8	7	6	
H			9	8	6	4	
6. Distributor Strength							A approximately equal in strength. B and C weaker and definitely vulnerable.
No. Distributors							
Territory E			12	10	8	7	
F			10	9	7	8	
G			10	9	7	7	
H			8	7	6	6	

target to be achieved; and an appropriate time frame within which the target is to be achieved. For objectives to be useful and meaningful to the management of a firm, they consider it to be important that each component is specified as precisely as possible.

Ansoff[60] considers that objectives provide 'the decision rules which enable management to guide and measure the firm's performance towards its purpose'. In a similar vein, Glueck[61] considers them to be the 'ends which the organisation seeks to achieve by its existence and operations'. In Drucker's[62] opinion, objectives are necessary for every area of a business whose performance and results

Table 11.4 *cont.*

Competitive dimensions	Competitors Us	A	B	C	Comments on data
7. Delivery norm (weeks)					Delivery improvements necessary in 1, 2 to be competitive. Improvement beyond competitive levels will not gain share. Improvement in line 3 will gain advantage against A, B and C according to sales force survey.
Product 1	6	6	4	7	
2	6	3	4	4	
3	6	6	7	9	
8. Penetration by Account Size (%) $ Market–all products					We're weak in medium and small accounts, need program to improve penetration and coverage there.
40 Large	40%	30%	15%	15%	
15 Medium	15%	30%	25%	30%	
10 Small	10%	30%	20%	40%	
$65M					

9. Probable Reaction to:				
Lower price	A –Immediate retaliation, continued price reduction to gain share back.			Cost in taking share away from A on price will be high. B and C more vulnerable.
	B,C –Weaker response. Will try to hold large accounts.			
New product	A –Will immediately match new product offering			B and to some extent C vulnerable to new product offering.
	C –May match immediately.			
	B –Eventually match.			
Increased sales coverage	A –Will Match.			B and C vulnerable in some measure to sales coverge, particularly if a new product is launched.
	B,C –Some Increase.			

KEY STRATEGIC CONCLUSIONS

1. *Product policy*: Focus on lines 2 and 3 where gain is possible by increased penetration and growth with the market and product modification for product 3.

2. *Competitive strategy*: Focus on taking share away from B and C, who are vulnerable to lower pricing and a new product innovation requested by salesmen. Selectively Take business away from competitor A–only up to the point where expensive price retaliation is expected.

3. *Marketing strategy*: Add three salesmen to territory G and one to F to build strength against key targets–B and C. Shift call pattern and develop marketing programmes for medium to small accounts where penetration is poor. Develop distributor program to capitalise on advantage over B and C.

4. *Service*: lowest in capacity to lower delivery time in product 2 to level competitive with B and C. Maintain competitive standards in other lines.

Source: C. Davis Fogg, 'Planning Gains in Market Share', *Journal of Marketing*, vol. 38 (July 1974).

directly affect the survival and prosperity of the enterprise. He has suggested that objectives need to be formulated for these areas: market standing; innovation; productivity; physical and financial resources; profitability; manager performance and development; worker performance and attitudes; and public responsibility. The most commonly used objectives concern the maximisation of net profit over short and long periods; the rate of new-product development; productivity; workforce motivation; and market share. Table 11.5 cites some commonly used objectives.

Table 11.5 **Some commonly used objectives**

Goal	Possible Indices	Objectives and time frame		
		Year 1	Year 2	Year 5
Growth	£ Sales	£100m	£120m	£200m
	Market share	10%	12%	20%
	Unit sales	10,000	12,000	18,000
Performance	£ Profits	£10m	£12m	£25m
	Profits/ sales	0.10	0.10	0.125
Utilisation of scarce resources	Return on investment	0.15	0.15	0.20
	Return on equity	0.25	0.26	0.30
Shareholder benefits	Dividends	£1/share	£1.10/share	£1.80/share
	Earnings per share	£2/share	£2.40/share	£3.00/share
Employees	Wage rates	£3/hour	£3.25/hour	£4/hour

Selecting and implementing strategies

It is a widely held view that having formulated objectives, the firm should then proceed with an analysis of its 'strengths and weaknesses'–otherwise described by Staudt[63] as 'an audit of the tangible and intangible resources'. The purpose of such an audit is to locate deficiencies in the firm's current mix of product-market strategies, and to identify strengths from which it can derive what Ansoff[64] calls 'advantageous synergistic effects'. Deficiencies will occur where a significant gap is found to exist between the current and projected strategic position of each of the firm's SBUs, in terms of growth, profit potential and risk, and that implicit to the objectives which have been formulated for them.

Ansoff visualised this gap by means of a pictorial representation of the firm's (or SBUs') current and projected future strategic position, as Figure 11.7 indicates. Ansoff's chart enables one to envisage the evolving trends of one dimension (or attribute of an objective) of the firm's performance with respect to time. It can also be used to examine the evolving trends of other dimensions of the firm's performance.

The size of the sales gap indicates the nature of the issues to which the firm's strategy must be addressed. The base-line position, or no

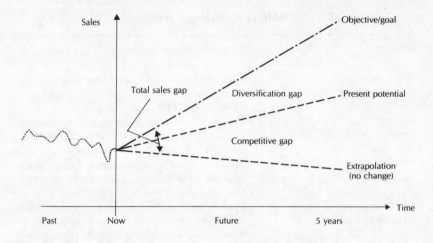

Figure 11.7 Ansoff's gap analysis chart

Source: As Table 11.6.

Table 11.6 Closing the 'competitive gap'

Strategic options	Actions
Market penetration	Increase productivity Increase marketing leverage
Market development	Identify new customers for existing products
New-product development	Widen customer base by developing new products

Source: H. I. Ansoff, *Corporate Strategy* (New York: McGraw-Hill, 1965).

change strategy, is viewed as being one of impending decline–the total sales gap widening as the firm fails to satisfy its growth objectives by redeploying resources to exploit emerging market opportunities, or counteract competitive threats. To close the 'competitive gap' the firm has three options (as conceived by Ansoff): these are displayed in Table 11.6. Where closing the 'competitive gap' will not achieve corporate growth objectives, given the firm's available mix of skills and resources, Ansoff's 'gap analysis' scheme proposes diversification as an answer (that is, closing the 'diversification gap').

Table 11.7   Strategic options

Strategy	General action required
Share-increasing (invest to grow)	High level of investment (greater than industry average) to gain a significant and permanent increase in market share.
Growth (invest to hold)	Moderate level of investment (less than industry average) to maintain the firm's competitive position in a rapidly expanding market.
Profit (harvest)	Minimum possible investment to maximise the application of the firm's current resources and skills and to generate large earnings.
Asset reduction (invest to rebuild)	Reorientation of the firm's mix of resources and skills to meet the needs of new market segments. Asset disposals and moderate investment is required.
Turnaround	Investment to achieve a rapid reversal of the decline in a business.
Liquidation/divestiture	Generate a large positive cash flow while withdrawing from business. No investment.

An alternative conceptualisation of the strategic options that are generally available to firms is discussed later; these options are summarised in Table 11.7.

The comparison of environmental threats and opportunities with the firm's current mix of resources and capabilities helps to identify alternative strategies. Furthermore, as Hofer and Schendel remark, 'it is the unique characteristics of the strategic opportunities and threats that a business faces, and not its basic strategic position, that determine the specific actions it should take to create effective competitive advantages'.[65] Analysing an industry to identify these unique threats and opportunities can, therefore, be seen to play an important role not only in determining what strategies are required, but also in implementing them. Ansoff's[66] outline of an industry analysis considers the industry's economic and competitive prospects; trends in growth, profitability and market shares; trends in demand, capacity utilisation, and the cost of entry and exit; and the likely direction and impact of anticipated technological innovations. Table 11.8 reproduces the factors that Hofer and Schendel consider to be important in identifying threats and opportunities within an industry. Table 11.8 is not exhaustive and other factors will, of course, be added to it in specific applications.

Glueck[67] has observed that many of the threats and opportunities firms confront arise as a result of changes that occur during the evolution of the market and industries in which they compete. It is

Table 11.8　Factors to consider in identifying unique opportunities and threats

Market factors	Industry factors	Supply factors
Size	Product differentiation	Raw material availability
Overall growth rate	Seller concentration	Supply/demand balance
Stage of product/market evolution	Barriers to entry	Supplier concentration
	Value added	Cost trends
Segmentation	Vertical integration	Import/export barriers
Segment growth rates	Capital intensity	
Buyer concentration	Economies of scale	
Price sensitivity and stability	Changes in product or process technology	
Distribution channels	Capacity utilisation	
Demand cyclicality	Industry profitability	
Demand seasonality	Inflation vulnerability	
Customer financial strength		
Export opportunities		

Source: adapted from C. W. Hofer and D. E. Schendel, *Strategy Formulation: Analytical Concepts* (St Paul, Minnesota: West Publishing Co., 1978).

important that the nature of such change is understood, for much the same reasons as an industry analysis is conducted, that is, to devise and implement strategic plans. Hofer[68] visualises in Figure 11.8 the general patterns of threats and opportunities which are known to arise at different stages in the evaluation of product-market segments. It indicates that major changes in a firm's strategic position occur when the nature of competition in an industry or market changes, that is, during the development, shake-out and decline stages of the evolution process. Major changes can also occur during the other stages of evolution, but, as Hofer[69] realises, 'it is much more difficult to do so since the bases for competition are usually already well established'. To further illustrate the possible associations between the stage of market evolution, a firm's competitive position and the strategy options available (see Tables 11.6 and 11.7), Hofer has constructed the matrix shown in Figure 11.9. The general strategy-making guidelines it offers are based on current research findings.

In order to implement the strategy it has to be translated into programmes for management action including: (i) medium-range operational/functional plans, e.g. marketing, new products, manufacturing, finance, etc., (ii) short-term tactical plans, and (iii) budgets. These plans express the firm's intentions in qualitative terms and help to co-ordinate the different functional operations of the enterprise. They also provide a means for measuring performance and permit the control of the operations.

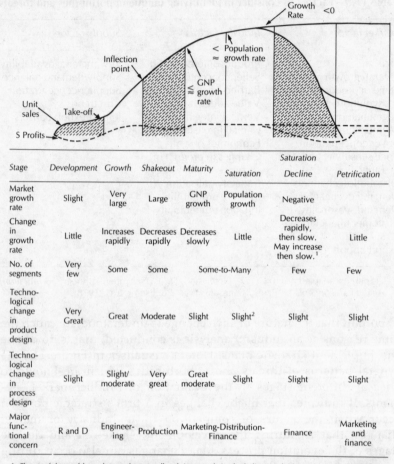

Stage	Development	Growth	Shakeout	Maturity	Saturation Saturation	Saturation Decline	Petrification
Market growth rate	Slight	Very large	Large	GNP growth	Population growth	Negative	
Change in growth rate	Little	Increases rapidly	Decreases rapidly	Decreases slowly	Little	Decreases rapidly, then slow. May increase then slow.[1]	Little
No. of segments	Very few	Some	Some	Some-to-Many		Few	Few
Technological change in product design	Very Great	Great	Moderate	Slight	Slight[2]	Slight	Slight
Technological change in process design	Slight	Slight/moderate	Very great	Great moderate	Slight	Slight	Slight
Major functional concern	R and D	Engineering	Production	Marketing-Distribution-Finance		Finance	Marketing and finance

1. The rate of change of the market growth rate usually only increases during the decline stage for these products that do not die, that is, that enter the petrification stage of evolution.
2. Although the rate of technological change in the basic design of the product is usually low during these stages of market evolution, the probability of a major breakthrough leading to a different kind of product that performs the same function increases substantially during these stages of evolution (substitution effects).
Source: C.W. Hofer, *Conceptual Constructs for Formulating Corporate and Business Strategy* (Boston, Intercollegiate Case Clearing House, no. 9–378–754, 1977).

Figure 11.8   Stages of product/market evolution

Koontz[70] points out that in order to make strategic planning work, equal pains should be taken in developing and implementing the strategies. He suggests that the following steps should be taken to implement the strategic plans.

1. Strategies should be communicated to all key decision-making managers.
2. Planning premises (assumptions) must be developed and communicated.
3. Action plan must contribute to and reflect major objectives and strategies.

Relative competitivie
position

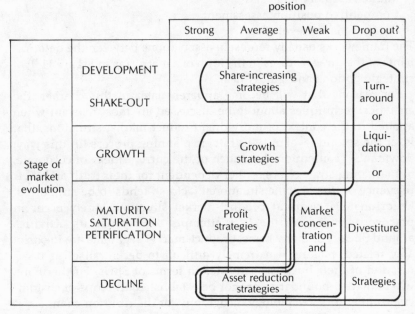

Figure 11.9   Recommended strategies

Source: C.W. Hofer, *Conceptual Constructs for Formulating Corporate and Business Strategy* (Boston: Intercollegiate Case Clearing House, no. 9–378–754, 1977).

4. Strategies should be reviewed regularly.
5. Consider developing contingency strategies and programs.
6. Making organisation structure fit planning needs.
7. Continue to teach planning and strategy implementation (in the form of day-to-day consideration and review of planning proposals and performance review).
8. Create a company climate that forces planning (e.g. using management by objectives).

Analytical techniques for strategic planning

The increased diversity of products or markets in which firms are engaged, combined with the constraints of limited resources, has encouraged firms to use strategic planning concepts to manage their products (SBUs) as they would manage a portfolio of investments. This, in turn, has led to the development of a number of analytical frameworks which assist in the process of analysis and decision-taking. The rationale on which these frameworks are based is largely composed of three aspects of strategy formulation:

Market/industry analysis
Competitive position assessment
Product-market evolution

The frameworks usually represent associations between the determinants of the three features in the form of a matrix (as in Figure 11.9) of strategic options and guidelines.

For reasons that will become apparent later in this chapter, the analytical techniques about to be discussed are most relevant when applied in the context of individual product-market situations, that is, at the second level of the strategic planning process. In this way, Bowman's[71] contention that much of the current ideas of corporate, or marketing strategy are 'rather dependent for their truth and their relevance on the specific situational factors', tends to be supported. Unfortunately, clear-cut product-market situations rarely occur in practice, even where the firm attempts to organise its activities around SBUs. For many firms, product-market segments are inextricably related, making it extremely difficult to decentralise the organisation of their business activities in terms of SBUs. Furthermore, where market boundaries cannot be established in terms of customers, competitors, technology, geography, or distribution channels, it becomes very difficult to divide a market into segments, and also to position specific products within them. A rule of thumb used in this respect by the Boston Consulting Group suggests that a stable market never has more than three or four significant competitors.[72]

Fundamental problems must be addressed concerning the delineation of product and market boundaries; the definition of meaningful units with which to measure performance; and the verification of tentative relationships assumed to exist between specific strategic variables and the performance of the firm. Related to these problems is the need to establish an analytical framework that can be applied reliably, not only in specific product-market situations, but also in broader strategic contexts, where uncontrollable environmental factors assume significant proportions. The major analytical techniques that are used to assess and develop product-market strategies will now be discussed with respect to the above mentioned problems.

The product life-cycle

Since the early 1960s, an increasing interest has been shown in the design of possible analytical frameworks with which to promote the process of strategic planning. In more recent years, four prominent conceptual frameworks have emerged as a result of the widely

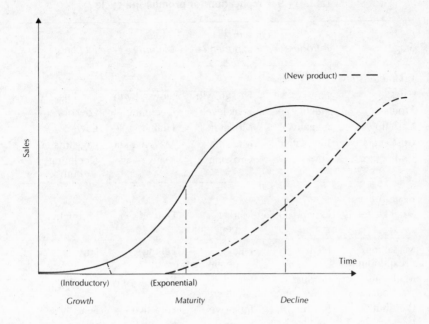

Figure 11.10   The idealised product life-cycle curve

Source: As Figure 11.9.

acknowledged empirical work of McKinsey and Co. at General Electric, the Boston Consulting Group, the Shell Group, and the Strategic Planning Institute, known respectively as: the Business Assessment Array; the Business Portfolio; the Directional Policy Matrix; and the Profit Impact of Marketing Strategy (PIMS) project.

The above frameworks have in common the intention to supplement management judgement, and to help to guide strategic thinking in order that product-market strategy decisions can be made on a rational basis. The traditional product life-cycle concept (see Figure 11.10; see also Figure 11.8) predates the development of these frameworks; being one of the first attempts to form an analytical framework for predetermining product-market strategy, it also shares their laudable intentions. It uses the stage in the product-life-cycle as the basis for proposing strategic guidelines[73] (see Table 11.9); these include specific recommendations on variables of the 'marketing mix', such as the type and level of promotion, product differentiation, pricing, distribution, etc.

Several authors have written extensively on the reasons why the response of the market to any given competitive manoeuvre differs

Table 11.9   Implications of product life-cycle

Stage	Introductory	Growth Exponential	Maturity	Decline
Characteristics				
Sales	Low	Fast growth	Slow growth	Decline
Profits	Negligible	Peak levels	Declining	Low or zero
Cash flow	Negative	Moderate	High	Low
Customers	Innovative	Mass market	Mass market	Laggards
Competitors	Few	Growing	Many rivals	Declining number
Responses				
Strategic focus	Expand market	Market penetration	Defend share	Productivity
Marketing expenditures	High	High (declining %)	Falling	Low
Marketing emphasis	Product awareness	Brand preference	Brand loyalty	Selective
Distribution	Patchy	Intensive	Selective	Selective
Price	High	Lower	Lowest	Rising
Product	Basic	Improved	Differentiated	Rationalised

Source: P. Doyle 'The Realities of the Product Life Cycle', *Quarterly Review of Marketing* (Summer 1976) pp. 1–6.

drastically at different stages of the life-cycle. Levitt,[74] Wasson[75] and Doyle[76] have prescribed in some detail the different patterns of management action that each stage of the product-life-cycle calls for: each author giving specific attention to how strategic objectives and the mix of marketing variables should be modified as the nature of competition changes. The patterns of Doyle's analysis are illustrated in Table 11.9. It is shown that competitive marketing strategy at any given stage must be shaped, not only according to the underlying trends of the product's life-cycle; similar trends in the market's life-cycle, implied at a higher level of aggregation, and the advanced recognition of the character of the next stage, are also shown to influence strategic response.

The idealised product life-cycle concept reveals an underlying pattern of sales development, but it largely ignores the complex variations that occur in practice. The basic characteristics of each stage are known to be determined independently of the absolute length of the product's life.[77] However, product life-cycles are also known to assume multifarious forms, not necessarily conforming to the stages of development outlined in the ideal life-cycle curve. Even for those cycles that follow the classical pattern of slow introductory and then exponential growth, the initial rates of sales development will vary greatly, especially where the product is a basic technological innovation. For example, the electric typewriter took twenty years to achieve an exponential growth rate; but sales of black and white television sets rose to a peak very rapidly, with no perceptible period of market development.

That sales development has characteristic stages underlines the commercial prudence of having a variety of products and markets with different present and anticipated growth rates. In the long term, the firm's survival depends on having a balanced mix of products that generate cash, and, as Figure 11.10 indicates, other promising new products that need cash to support growth during market development.

In practice, 'market share' and 'market growth rate' are two of the most fundamental factors to determine product-market strategy, measures of each being commonly used to establish strategic objectives. The influence of both these factors has been shown by several authors[78] to vary according to the different stages of the product life-cycle. Indeed, stage in the life-cycle is generally understood to be a proxy for management decisions as well as for 'market growth'. This quality has been exploited by some authors[79] who have developed analytical frameworks that offer strategic guidelines based on what they consider to be two broad components of strategic performance: stage in the product life-cycle, or rate of market growth; and competitive market position, expressed in terms of market share. The Product Evaluation Matrix of Wind and Claycamp and the Product/Market Matching Matrix of Enis typify the methods of analysis that have emerged in the foregoing fashion: Table 11.10 summarises the broad strategic guidelines they offer.

The cost of gaining market share varies at different stages in the product life-cycle.[80] Market share can be increased at relatively low cost during the growth stage, when capacity utilisation is high and customer purchasing habits relatively fluid. However, during the maturity stage, dominant competitors seek to defend their strategic position and, consequently, as Fruhan[81] observes, where competition is strong, market share is increased only at great cost. In the case of high added-value products, where the firm has a patent protecting some aspect of its product or process technology, or otherwise has a significant technical advantage, there are significant barriers to entry that will assist in the pursuit of market leadership. Nevertheless, as EMI recently found to its cost with the Body Scanner, competitors can enter the market and erode the dominant market share of the innovating firm where they attend, in great detail, to the particular needs to evolving market segments.

Table 11.10   Strategic guidelines for various product life-cycle stages and competitive positions

Competitive position	Product life-cycle		
	Growth	Maturity	Decline
Market leader (dominant market share)	Build market share; Reduce prices to discourage competition; Develop primary demand and channel strength.	Maintain market share; Advertise for brand loyalty; product differentiation; price with competitors	Harvest market share; Maximise cash flow; reduce product expenditures such as advertising and selling.
Market follower (low share)	Invest in R and D; advertising and distribution to increase market share; concentrate on a particular market segment; advertise for positioning.	Maintain or reduce market share; price to penetrate; reduce costs below the market leaders.	No product expenditures; withdraw from the market.

Source: D. Abell and S. Hammond, *Strategic Market Planning* (Englewood Cliffs, N.J.: Prentice-Hall, 1979) p. 185 (adapted by author).

It has been contested that the strategic guidelines based on the product life-cycle concept, and endorsed by authors such as Levitt,[82] can often lead to bad strategic marketing decisions.[83] Other work has produced similarly conflicting viewpoints on the value and efficacy of the product life-cycle as a strategic planning tool.[84] The main points of contention concern, first, the definition of 'products' and 'markets' for which the product life-cycle concept could be valid; and secondly, the extent to which the characteristic stages of the concept occur as a result of strategic decisions taken in response to changing market conditions.

As a strategic planning tool, the product life-cycle concept is considered to be deficient,[85] in that it cannot take explicit account of the influence of uncontrollable environmental elements on the evolution of products and markets. Additional inadequacies relate to the concept's failure to accommodate the economic and competitive prospects for an industry as a whole; the match of capacity utilisation to demand within the industry; technological innovation and the potential impact of new products; the cost of entering or leaving the industry; and the rate of growth of the industry. Indeed, it has been proposed by Kotler[86] that the traditional view of the product life-cycle be replaced by a theory that describes 'stages of market evolution'.

A further criticism of the product life-cycle as a basis for taking strategy decisions concerns the aggregation of product-market segments which must occur for the concept to be meaningful.[87] This 'aggregation' will be misleading where market boundaries cannot be delineated accurately; leading in turn to the inappropriate positioning of a product with respect to the life-cycle curve and inappropriate strategic guidelines.

The definition of the 'market' is important to the validity of the product life-cycle concept:[88] it not only prescribes the competitive arena in which a product is marketed, it also has a direct effect on how 'market share' and, hence, 'market growth' will be assessed. Ideally, markets should be defined on the basis of all products catering for the same consumer need.[89] Alternatively, they should group together customers who have in common situational or behavioural characteristics that are significant in a strategic sense.[90] However, in practice it is more common for markets to be defined in terms of several competing brands within a specific product category, perhaps perceived as substitutes by the consumer.

A relative, rather than absolute, measure of market share is used in the Boston Consulting Group's Business Portfolio. By measuring market share (competitive position) relative to the leading competitor, a pragmatic, if not conceptually defensible approach, is taken to the problems of 'market' delineation. It remains the responsibility of management to decide what market definition is most appropriate to what product-market situation. For this task considerable managerial expertise is required if the benefits of the technique are not to be lost. As Goold notes 'traditional product-market segments are frequently not the right basis for strategic business definition and should only be used where they can be justified in the light of the economics of competition in the business'. He prefers to define a business segment as being 'separate for the purpose of strategy if it is possible to establish and defend a competitive advantage in the segment alone, without needing to participate in other related segments'.[91]

Several attempts have been made to develop 'recycled' versions of the product life-cycle which are sufficiently comprehensive to provide a unifying concept for developing product market strategy. However, the analytical frameworks that will now be discussed have been shown to be more appropriate to the practical problems of taking product-market strategy decisions.[92] That is not to say that these techniques make the product life-cycle concept redundant. It is perhaps true to say that relevant aspects of the concept have been utilised in developing the underlying logic on which the frameworks are built.

Growth vectors

Alternative frameworks have been devised by several authors[93] offering broad strategic guidelines based on a two-dimensional analysis of product-market circumstances: in so doing, such frameworks are known to be more appropriate to the management of a strategic business unit than the product-life-cycle concept. The strategic components that are generally compared and assessed in this instance are: the degree of 'market newness'; and the degree of technological (product and process) newness.

The pre-eminent framework of this genre is, without doubt, Ansoff's[94] classic growth vector matrix. It dichotomises product-market strategy decisions as shown in Table 11.11, giving combinations through which growth can be achieved. The strategy options that are available to the firm are known to depend on the size of the gap* that exists between the current and projected strategic position of each of its SBUs, and that implicit to the objectives which have been formulated for them. Where the gap can only be closed as a result of some form of diversification, the various routes available to the firm are summarised in the diversification matrix of Table 11.12. Other writers such as Johnson and Jones, Karger and Murdik, and Craven have developed more sophisticated matrices which adopt further sub-divided categories of the firm's product-market scope. The detailed situations that these matrices describe not only provide general strategic insights, they also accommodate, in a limited fashion, the influence of external environmental forces on strategic decisions. However, they are only capable of offering very broad strategic guidelines in highly generalised product-market circumstances. For the practical purposes of strategic planning, a more detailed consideration is required of factors that influence strategic success in specific situations.

The business portfolio

The Boston Consulting Group's (BCG's) Business Portfolio (BP),[95] or Growth-Share Matrix,[96] is used to diagnose a business's strategic position. It assigns product-market strategies on the basis of a product's market growth rate and its market share relative to competitors. By relating cash flow to market share and market growth, it determines those products that represent opportunities for invest-

---

* See section 'Selecting and Implementing Strategies'; Table 11.6 and Figure 11.7.

Table 11.11   Ansoff's growth vector matrix

Product Market	Present	New
Present	Market penetration	Product development
New	Market development	Diversification

Source: H. I. Ansoff, *Corporate Strategy* (New York: McGraw-Hill, 1965); 'Strategies for Diversification', *Harvard Business Review* (Sept. Oct. 1957).

Table 11.12   Ansoff's diversification matrix

Products Customers	Related technology	Unrelated technology
Firm its own customer	vertical integration	
Same type	horizontal integration	
Similar type	Marketing and technology related concentric diversification	Marketing related concentric diversification
New type	Technology related concentric diversification	Conglomerate diversification

Source: as Table 11.11.

ment, those that should generate investment funds, and those that drain funds which should be liquidated or divested.

The basic concept on which BP is founded is what has become known as the experience curve effect. Study of this phenomenon has been advanced in recent years by the BCG[97] as a result of its work with firms in industries such as electronics.[98] Essentially the experience curve generalises the 'learning-effects'[99] that had earlier been found to occur in aircraft manufacture,[100] where assembly-line techniques were utilised for small-scale production runs, thereby achieving an experience curve with a slope of about 0.8.

The experience curve postulates that the length of time required to complete a task is inversely related to the number of times the task is performed; or, more specifically, that the total unit costs of producing, distributing and marketing a particular item decline by a fixed percentage (usually 10 per cent to 30 per cent) each time the cumulative number of units produced is doubled. The general form of the experience curve can be expressed in this way:[101] $y_n = an^{-b}$;

where y_n is the cost of producing, selling, etc., the nth item; n is the cumulative production; a is the cost of the first unit (i.e. where $n = 0$); and b is a parameter representing the learning rate. On linear axes the rate of cost decline is seen to be logarithmic (see Figure 11.11); on a logarithmic scale the decline is linear (see Figure 11.12).

Experience curve effects do not occur automatically. A precondition of the validity of the experience curve is that an explicit aim of management in functional areas of the firm, such as manufacturing, sales, distribution, purchasing and marketing, is the attainment of economies of scale. Other forces contributing to the experience curve effect are: investment in cost-saving equipment as volume increases; the development of specialised knowledge and skills; the substitution of cheaper or more efficient raw materials and technology; improved managerial decision-taking and labour efficiency.

As Figure 11.12 indicates, the experience curve for an industry (or market) has implications for the pricing policy of firms operating within it. Ideally, if the firm could predict the pattern of growth in a product market and the sensitivity of demand to changes in prices, the experience curve could then be used to predict the cash-flow positions arising from different pricing strategies. Under a *skimming* policy the firm with a new and unique product would earn monopoly profits by charging a high initial price and limiting the costs of launching the product. In this way it is possible to avoid the initial losses normally associated with the introduction of new products. But if imitative innovators are attracted by the margins available, growth in market share could be stifled, with a subsequent loss of competitive leverage unless price reductions are made to widen the products appeal. Under a *penetration* policy the firm with a new and unique product would sacrifice short-term profitability expedients. Instead it would pursue the longer-term growth in market share and cash flow which could occur if the firm consolidated its cost advantage by descending the experience curve ahead of the imitative innovators. For any firm, the question of which policy to pursue depends on its growth and profit objectives, and its assessment of the impact of environmental trends on competition within the industry.

An important conclusion drawn by the BCG from the experience curve, is that market share is a surrogate measure of a firm's position on this curve:[102] a firm (or SBU) with the largest share of a market, it suggests, will be the most profitable at the prevailing price level because it will have the lowest unit costs and highest margins (indicated by the point A in Figure 11.12); less 'experienced' competitors (indicated by the point B in Figure 11.12) will have lower market shares and, therefore, higher unit costs and lower margins. Consequently, the maxim in this instance is that margins, and generated cash flow, increase with relative market share.[103]

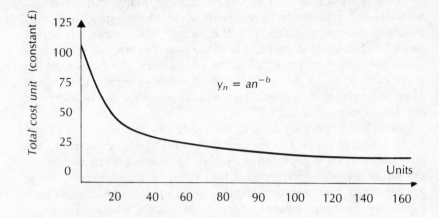

Figure 11.11   Industry experience curve using linear axes

Source: The Boston Consulting Group, *Perspectives on Experience*, no. 135 (1973) p. 149.

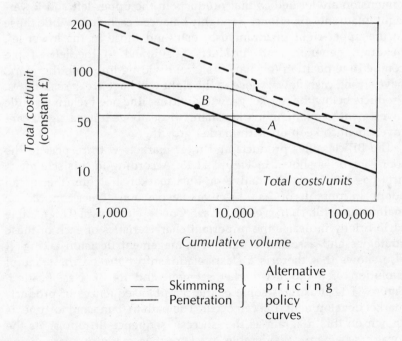

Figure 11.12   Industry experience curve using log/log scales

There is opposition to the view that in many industries (or markets), as experience curve analysis would suggest, the most profitable long-term strategy is the pursuit of a dominant market share.[104] The issues at the heart of the debate concern matters such as these: the cost of entering or leaving an industry; the creation of too much capacity in an industry; the profitability of firms on the fringe of an industry, or in a specialised market segment; the influence of anti-monopoly regulations.

One other important assumption underlies the approach of the BP.[105] The cash needed to support firms (SBUs) operating in rapidly growing markets is expected to exceed that needed for those operating in slower-growth markets; this being a consequence of the greater fixed and working capital requirements associated with expanding productive capacity and developing marketing leverage.

The Business Portfolio generally classifies products according to the criteria of competitive position (measured by market share relative to that of the firm's largest competitor) and market growth rate, adjusted for inflation (see Figure 11.13). This model can be further developed by dilating the point representing a product's position in terms of the given dimensions, to form a circle, the area (or diameter) of which is proportional to sales[106] (see Figure 11.14).

The lines that determine the HIGH and LOW divisions of each dimension are located so that products in the upper-left and lower-right quadrants experience a roughly balanced cash flow; while those in the upper-right quadrant use cash; and those in the lower-left quadrant generate cash. Products positioned to the left of the competitive position (or market share) dividing line will, therefore, have strong cash flows; those to the right will have weak cash flows. Products below the market growth dividing line need relatively little investment to maintain market share; those above it need significant investment to keep up with market growth.

The BP classifies products and their markets with respect to the four categories shown in Figure 11.13. According to this scheme, a firm has four basic alternative product-market strategies that it can adopt in pursuit of its objectives: expansion (Question Mark); maintenance (Star); harvesting (Cash Cow); withdrawal (Dog). Table 11.13 briefly indicates the important characteristics of each of these strategies and associated areas of management decision-taking. It also shows that there is a clear relationship between the stage of evolution of a product-market segment and its BP classification. Figure 11.14 illustrates some of the possible sequences of product-market development that can occur. The path to 'fame and fortune' is shown on this diagram as the 'success' sequence. It represents the ideal case where considerable investment is made in a promising new product (Question Mark) to support it during phases of market

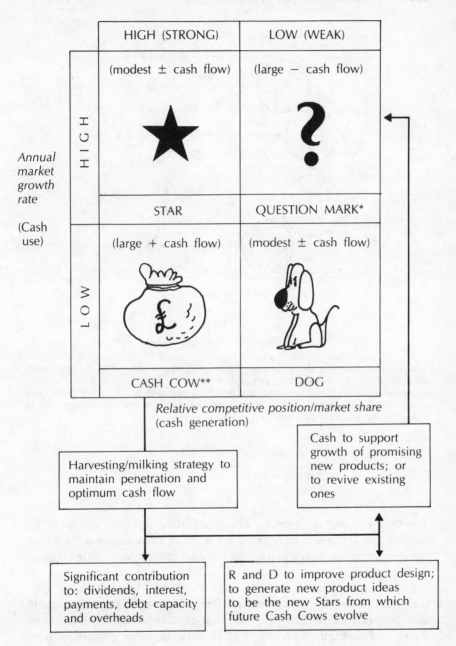

	HIGH (STRONG)	LOW (WEAK)
HIGH	(modest ± cash flow) ★ STAR	(large − cash flow) ? QUESTION MARK*
LOW	(large + cash flow) CASH COW**	(modest ± cash flow) DOG

Annual market growth rate

(Cash use)

Relative competitive position/market share
(cash generation)

Harvesting/milking strategy to maintain penetration and optimum cash flow

Cash to support growth of promising new products; or to revive existing ones

Significant contribution to: dividends, interest, payments, debt capacity and overheads

R and D to improve product design; to generate new product ideas to be the new Stars from which future Cash Cows evolve

Figure 11.13   The business portfolio and associated cash flow

*Also known as Wildcat or Problem Child.
** Examples of Cash Cows include Fry's Turkish Delight, Cadbury's Dairy Milk, Dreft, Carnation Evaporated Milk and the VW Golf.
Source: G. Day, 'Diagnosing the Product Portfolio', *Journal of Marketing*, vol. 42 (Apr. 1977) pp. 27–38 (adapted by the author).

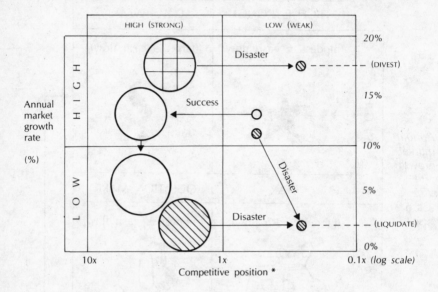

Figure 11.14   Sequences of product-market strategies

*Competitive position is largely measured by relative market share. This is plotted on a logarithmic scale to be consistent with experience curve effects. Relative market share is defined as the ratio of the firm's size to that of its largest competitors. Prior to 1976 this axis of the matrix was labelled 'relative market share'. The definition of 'the market' clearly influences the validity of this measure of competitive position.

development and growth, in order to obtain a strong competitive position; it is then managed as a source of cash (harvested) when market growth decelerates and the product enters the mature stage of its life-cycle.

In discussing the product-life-cycle it was stated that the long-term survival of a firm depends on there being a balanced mix of products that generate cash (Cash Cows/Stars)–the 'bread and butter' products–and, as Figures 11.10 and 11.15 indicate, other promising new products (Stars/Question Marks) that need cash to support growth during periods of market development. Determining the nature of this balance, and achieving it, is, therefore, of principal concern to management.

In the present era of low economic growth, pursuing the 'success sequence' is, for many firms, becoming an increasingly forlorn

Table 11.13   Brief guidelines associated with the BP analysis

Strategic management guidelines

STAR	Market growth is rapid. Shake-outs will occur as firms jostle for competitive position. Large cash balances are generated but heavy investment is required to maintain market share growth and consolidate competitive position. Low margins may be essential to defer competition; but longer-term prospects improve as growth slows, when large cash returns should be obtained. If investment is cut back during growth to gain cash returns in the short/medium term, the DISASTER sequence occurs, a STAR becoming a DOG.
CASH COW	A STAR becomes a CASH COW as market growth slows during maturity. Investment requirements are low and limited to those needed to reduce costs and maintain marketing leverage. Large cash surpluses are generated. Market positions become entrenched as the '3 or 4' dominant competitors consolidate their positions of strength. CASH COWS are managed for cash.
QUESTION MARK	QUESTION MARKS are managed to gain market share and strengthen their competitive position. To do so considerable investment is needed since rapid market growth occurs and cash generation is low as a result of low market share. The initial step of the SUCCESS sequence occurs when a QUESTION MARK becomes a STAR because of market share gains. However, if growth slows and competitive position is still weak, a QUESTION MARK becomes a DOG. Where STAR potential is not evident divestment is recommended. As a market contracts during decline because of, e.g. product substitution, a CASH COW becomes a DOG.
DOG	DOGS have relatively weak competitive positions in low-growth and mature markets. In most cases they have little potential for gaining market share and are not very profitable. However where it is possible to obtain a relatively strong competitive position in a market segment, a modest cash return may be generated (CASH DOG). Liquidation of DOG products (SBUs) is usually recommended.

mission. Not only are potential 'Cash Cows' and 'Stars' difficult to find, but the lifeblood of many firms is being supplied by products that the BP rationale classifies as Dogs. Considerable criticism has for some time been made of the BCG's belief that 'Dogs are essentially worthless' and that they should be liquidated or divested if possible.

Recent research[107] indicates that there are considerable managerial problems associated with eliminating the 'Dogs'. It has also been shown that in a wide range of stagnant industries firms can compete successfully with 'Dog' products.[108]

The apparent response of the BCG to criticism of its guidelines concerning 'Dogs' has been the emergence of the 'Cash Dog'. On the subject, Michael Goold[109] of the BCG states that, 'In a business where competition is mature and direct, that is where there is a little opportunity for product differentiation, or for competition based on serving the specific needs of particular customer groups through distinctive marketing approaches, it will be necessary to consider liquidation'. However, where firms operate with 'moderate' success in segments less exposed to the competitive dominance of the market leader, 'maintenance of position and competitive stability' are recommended for what must then be Cash Dogs. As Goold notes, 'The common factor in successful strategies of segment focus is that they permit the Dog to build some sort of competitive advantage in the segment that he lacks more generally.... Consequently, it is essential to analyse precisely how the economics of competition in the segment differ from those in the more broadly defined business, and whether they can offer any real protection from the strengths of the industry leader.'

Additional criticisms of the BP approach tend to focus on its over-simplified, and somewhat misleading, representation of possible strategy positions; and its use of the dimensions growth rate and market share, which are themselves considered to be inadequate descriptions of, respectively, industry attractiveness, and competitive position. As Wensley[110] concludes, this approach to strategy development 'encourages the use of general rather than specific criteria as well as implying assumptions about mechanisms of corporate financing and market behaviour which are either unnecessary or false'. Indeed, it has been observed that market leadership does not always offer the benefits of lower costs, more positive cash flow and higher profits. On the contrary: 'the number of highly viable companies occupying market "niches" is legion, and growing by the day'.[111] Recent trends that have favoured the development of greater specialisation in some markets include: the growth of private label consumer products; and the emergence of differential preferences in some industrial markets, for example computers, as customers become familiar with products, or develop relevant in-house expertise.

The BP also tends to overlook other important strategic factors which are more a function of the external competitive environment,[112] for example: technological change; barriers to entry; social, legal, political and environmental pressures; union and re-

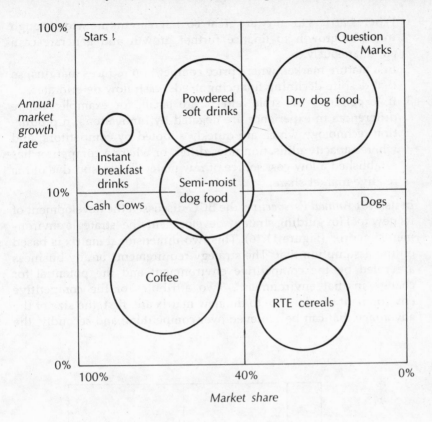

Figure 11.15   A portfolio of general foods' product line

Source: W.E. Cox Jr, 'Product Portfolio Strategy, Market Structure, and Performance', in *Strategy and Structure = Performance*, ed. H. Thorelli (Bloomington: Indiana University Press, 1977) p. 94 (adapted by author).

lated human factors; elasticity of demand; and cyclicality of sales. The application of the BP to strategic decision-taking is in the manner of a diagnostic rather than a prescriptive aid in instances where observed cash flow patterns do not conform with those on which the four product-market categories are based. This commonly occurs where changes in product-market strategies have short-term transient effects on cash flow. Further limitations occur in three specific situations:

1. Where barriers to entry are great, so that margins are wide enough in rapid growth to finance further growth and generate cash simultaneously.
2. In a mature market, where price competition reduces margins, so that despite declining financing needs, cash flow deteriorates.
3. If 'experience' or 'scale' effects are small, for example: where differences in experience are negated by innovations in production technology which are quickly adopted by competitors; and where capacity utilisation rates differ, or where a competitor has established a low-cost source of raw materials, irrespective of his relative market share.

In its 1981 *Annual Perspective*, the BCG discussed the development of its new tool for guiding strategy development–the 'strategic environments' matrix' (Figure 11.16). This two-dimensional matrix is based on the assumption that 'The strategy requirements of any business are ruled by the competitive environment and the potential for change in that environment'. Two attributes of the competitive environment of relevance to the new matrix are: first, the size of the advantage that can be achieved over competitors; and secondly, the

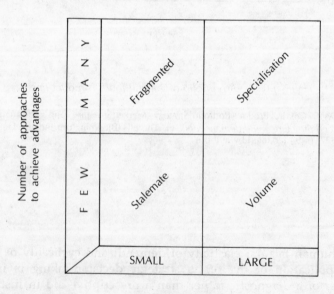

Figure 11.16   Strategic environments' matrix

Source: The Boston Consulting Group, *Annual Perspective* (Boston, 1981).

number of unique ways in which it can be achieved. The strategic environments' matrix combines these attributes to give four possible positions of strategy development. As BCG notes, 'There is a fundamental difference between businesses in which the size of the potential advantage that can be created by a competitor over all other competitors is large, and those in which it is small. There is also a basic difference between businesses that offer only one of a few ways to achieve advantages, and those that present several ways.' Further to what has been written in the 1981 *Annual Perspective*, very little is currently known about the application of this matrix.

Business assessment array

Although the Business Portfolio is widely discussed in the literature, there is very little published empirical evidence, outwith the PIMS work, to demonstrate that the assumptions it makes are indeed valid. For instance, the subject of some debate is the contention that preferential investment should be made in businesses operating in high-growth markets, as opposed to those in low-growth markets. Underlying the debate is concern for the validity of the assumption that it is 'easier' to gain market share in high-growth markets, and further, that there exists any quantifiable relationship between the ease with which market share can be gained and the rate of market growth. Wensley[113] argues that 'To justify a general bias towards high growth markets there must (therefore) be significant evidence that the long-run incremental benefits of market share gains in such markets are greater.'

In practice, the BP is known to have widespread appeal, despite its considerable limitations. It was reported in 1972[114] that more than 100 companies worldwide incorporated the ideas of the BP into their analyses of strategic issues: the compelling logic, apparent simplicity and intuitive appeal of the technique are in no small way responsible for this. Less interest has apparently been shown in the Business Assessment Array (BAA), or in its derivative, the Directional Policy Matrix (DPM).

Current thinking recognises that despite the insights provided by the BP, it frequently offers an inadequate analysis of strategic problems, especially in situations where experience curve effects are not known to occur. As Day[115] comments, 'when there are complex usage patterns and many alternative products/technologies which can satisfy customer needs, then the balance should shift toward a demand perspective'; that is, away from the costs-reduction strategies associated with periods of growth, to strategies based on

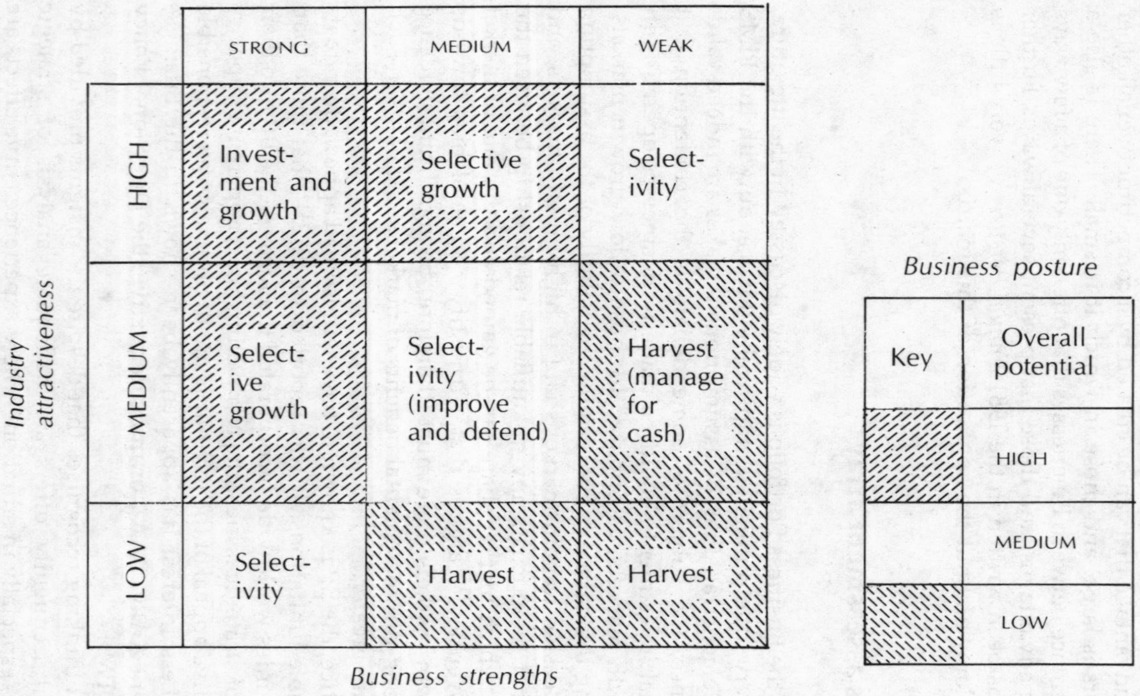

Figure 11.17 The Business Assessment Array and 'business postures'

Sources: B. Enis, 'Strategic Planning and the Product Life Cycle', Business (May–June 1980); D. Abell and S. Hammond, Strategic Market Planning (Englewood Cliffs, N.J.: Prentice-Hall, 1979).

segmenting customer needs. The inadequacy of the BP approach, therefore, is seen to become apparent where factors other than relative market share, or market growth, need to be used to assess the relative attractiveness of one investment opportunity compared with another.

Concern for the inadequacies of the BP is partly responsible for the development of a more elaborate, but similarly two-dimensional, framework by General Electric in consultation with McKinsey & Co. The simple, univariate measures of the BP have been replaced, in what has become known as the Business Assessment Array (see Figure 11.17) by these composite measures: 'business strengths', in terms of market share, but more importantly, in terms of characteristics such as capacity utilisation, level of integration, vulnerability to new technology, margins, company bargaining power, etc.; and 'industry attractiveness', in terms of market size, volatility of market share, growth rates, technological and sociopolitical trends, degree of concentration, unionisation, sources of leverage, etc.[116]

The BAA used by General Electric (GE) as a strategic planning tool combines six factors in measuring 'industry attractiveness', and nine in measuring 'business strengths'. These factors are thought to be generally representative of the more significant elements of a firm's internal and external environment, from which strengths and weaknesses and strategic threats and opportunities arise[117] (see Table 11.14).

Table 11.14   Measures used by GE

Industry attractiveness	Business strengths
Market size	Domestic market share
Market growth	World (export) market share
Profitability	Market share growth
Cyclicality/seasonality	Relative market share
Ability to recover from inflation	Product quality (substitution threats)
World scope	Technological skills (product, process, R and D)
	Costs (scale and experience)
	Marketing capability
	Relative profitability

The relative importance of such factors will vary from one firm (SBU) or industry to another, depending primarily on product-market characteristics and customer behaviour. For example, where technical sophistication is a source of competitive advantage, trends

Table 11.15   Some characteristics of the three main business postures of the BAA

Strategy	Invest/grow
Objective	Growth
Strategy characteristics	—Intensive pursuit of market share —Earnings generation subordinate to building dominant position —Focus predominantly on long-term results and payout —Emphasis on technical innovation and market development
Organisation characteristics	—Must enable future growth —Product or venture operations —Separate 'futures' from operations —Build technical competence —Strong international focus —Highly competent staff functions
Management characteristics	—Emphasis on entrepreneurs —Young, ambitious, aggressive —Strong development and growth potential —High-risk tolerance —Highly competitive by nature

Source: D. F. Channon, 'Commentary on Strategy Formulation', in *Strategic Management*, ed. D. E. Schendel and C. W. Hofer (Boston: Little, Brown & Co., 1979) (adapted by author).

in technological development will influence 'business strengths'; patent protection will influence 'industry attractiveness'.

The multivariate dimensions of the BAA encourage a more detailed analysis of a range of factors which influence the strategic position of a firm (or SBU) than that proposed by the BP approach. Two principal reasons for this are, first, that growth rate and market share alone are inadequate measures of a firm's potential long-term profitability; and, secondly, that the key success factors in each

Table 11.15 *cont.*

Selectivity/Earnings	Harvest/Divest
Earnings	Cash flow
—Intensive pursuit of maximum earnings —Focus balanced between long and short term —Emphasis on complex analysis and clear plans —Emphasis on increased productivity, cost improvement, strategic pricing	—Intensive pursuit of maximum positive cash flow —Sell market share to maximise profitability —Intensive pruning of less profitable products/segments —Emphasis only on short term
—Must provide flexibility at moderate cost —Matrix organisation (balance cost and people development) —Centralised product planning —Overseas sourcing operations —Pooled sales and distribution utilisation —Centralised finance	—Must be low cost/no frills —Functional structure (lowest cost) —Collapse product departments into functionally organised division —Reduce/eliminate R and D labs and forward engineering —Maximum pooling where cost effective —Combine manufacturing/engineering operations
—Emphasis on 'solid businessman' —Tolerates risks, but doesn't seek it —Comfortable with variety and flexibility —Careful, but not conservative —Trades off short-term, long-term risk/reward	—Emphasis on 'hard nosed' operators —Seasoned and experienced —Seeks high efficiency —Low change tolerance —Wants instant results, doesn't look ahead

situation will vary, as will the firm's objectives and the synergies it achieves. By placing emphasis as it does on a number of strategic variables, the BAA is capable of being a more comprehensive diagnostic tool in specific product-market situations. But, it is inevitable that a trade-off will occur between the comprehensiveness of the dimensions and the time wasted on considering irrelevant items.

The BAA diagnoses strategic position and possible strategy options (i.e. 'business posture') according to the firm's (or SBU's) location with respect to the two composite dimensions. Figure 11.17 displays the nine possible classifications and the three main 'busi-

Table 11.16   **Strategic guidelines associated with Figure 11.18**

Key	Strategic guidelines
1.	Market penetration to improve business position and build market share for long-term growth. Common during periods of market development and growth.
2.	Restore market position that has been lost. This is expensive in mature markets. Aim for growth in selected segments by differentiating products.
3.	Selective investment to strengthen (or weaken) positions in areas where market penetration (restoration) is not likely to be cost-effective.
4.	Maintain position as the market evolves; stabilise prices; reduce variable costs; maintain media coverage.
5.	Harvest the business, i.e. sacrifice market position so that cash is generated; avoid investment and rationalise.

Source: as Figure 11.18.

ness postures' which circumscribe them. Each business posture is associated with a different set of product-market objectives, management styles, important strategic factors and organisational structures (see Table 11.15).

As with the BP, the imaginary point that represents a firm's (or SBU's) location can be expanded to form a circle, the area (or diameter) of which is proportional to sales. Using sales as a third dimension of the BAA, Figure 11.18 graphically depicts a selection of possible business postures and strategic options: Table 11.16 briefly describes the strategic guidelines associated with each of them.

A large British electrical engineering multinational is also known to have made use of the BAA in strategic planning, at a parent-group level, and at the level of the Strategic Business Unit. This degree of utilisation is not uncommon in multi-product, multi-market firms, where analytical tools such as the BP and BAA find applications in contexts ranging from the management of investment funds to individual product management.

Like General Electric, this firm operates at an international level in a variety of markets, with a range of manufactured products and related services. In a similar way it uses measures of 'industry attractiveness' and 'business strengths' which represent complex combinations of strategically important variables: the measures generally replicate those of Table 11.14, but are specifically concerned with the strategic environment as it affects the firm.

The composite measures of the BAA are much less quantifiable than those of the BP, or the PIMS analysis. However, schemes have

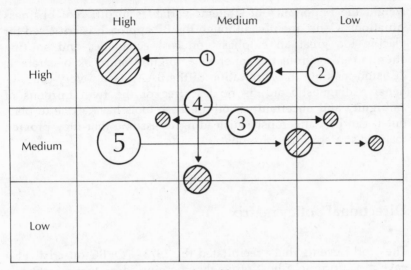

Figure 11.18   Selected business postures
Source: D. Abell and S. Hammond, *Strategic Market Planning* (Englewood Cliffs, N.J.:
    Prentice-Hall, 1979) p. 185 (adapted by the author).

Table 11.17   Possible weighting of composite measures used in the BAA

Industry attractiveness	Weight	Business strengths	Weight
Size	0.2	Market share	0.15
Growth	0.15	Distribution coverage	0.25
Price competiveness	0.15	Breadth of product line	0.05
Industry profitability	0.3	Raw materials costs	0.1
Cyclicality	0.05	Relative product quality	0.2
Competitive structure	0.1	Company image	0.15
Inflation	0.05	Advertising effectiveness	0.05
		R and D position	0.15
Total	1.00	Total	1.00

been devised in order that the various factors contributing to each
dimension can be scored and weighted according to their relative
importance (see Table 11.17). The available empirical work is insufficiently detailed to render the need for such arbitrary and subjective
weighting schemes redundant. The effective operation of these
schemes, as with the choice of level of aggregation mentioned above,
demands a high degree of management judgement, knowledge,
experience and foresight. Furthermore, their arbitrary nature is
underlined by the fact that there is no universal definition of how to

weight the importance of strategic variables in different business situations. Consequently, although the BP approach is criticised for placing too great an emphasis on cost economics and shifting attention away from the inherent ambiguity and risk of strategic decision-making, the application of the BAA, itself a very comprehensive diagnostic aid, is no less free of the twin burdens of ambiguity and uncertainty. Both of these tools have a role to play, but it can be dangerously misleading to assume that they provide realistic strategic prescriptions.

Directional policy matrix

The world events that precipitated the 1973–4 OPEC oil crisis also gave a platform to a host of newly emerging ideas that questioned the validity of strategic decision-making based on extrapolative corporate forecasts of quantitative factors. The Shell Chemical Company[118] found that traditional financial measures for guiding the allocation of resources within a diversified business, such as forecasted rate of return on capital employed, were, in some respects, becoming inadequate aids to strategic decision-making. To take consideration of some of the important qualitative factors that were seen to influence strategic planning in the petroleum-based sector of the chemical industry, a two-dimension matrix was derived.

The Directional Policy Matrix (DPM), as it is known, uses the two multivariate dimensions 'prospect for business (or market) sector profitability' and 'the company's competitive capabilities' (see Figure 11.19). The application of this matrix involves identifying, first, the main criteria with which to judge the prospects for a business sector (SBU); and, secondly, those criteria by which a company's position in a sector may be judged to be strong, average or weak.[119] These criteria are then used to establish separate ratings of the two principal dimensions, as shown in Figure 11.19. The main criteria that Shell applies in the context of the petroleum-based chemical business are shown in Table 11.18.

A business is assigned a rating of between one and five stars according to the degree to which it satisfies each of the criteria; the rating scales used by Shell for the criteria 'market growth rate' and 'market position' are shown in Tables 11.19 and 11.20 respectively.

There is clearly a considerable qualitative input to the DPM, as with the BAA. In Shell's case the assignment of ratings is reported[120] to be the responsibility of a group of functional specialists drawn from the business area under examination, general assistance being

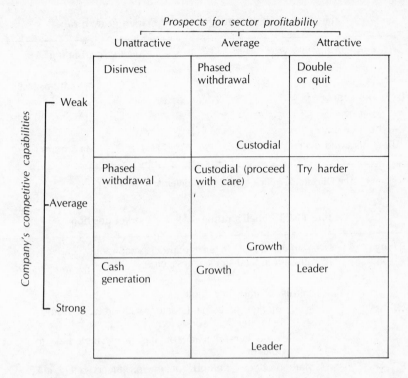

Figure 11.19   The directional policy matrix

Source: 'The Directional Policy Matrix — A New Aid to Corporate Planning' (Shell International Chemical Co., 1975).

Table 11.18   Shell's DPM criteria

Business sector prospects	Company's competitive capabilities
Market growth rate	Market position
Market quality	Production capability
Industry feedback situation	Product research and development
Environmental (regulatory) aspects	

provided by several non-specialists. The company's experience in applying the DPM has shown some criteria to be easier to express in quantitative terms than others: for instance, the impact of regulatory restrictions on the manufacture, transportation and marketing of petroleum products has been found to be largely quantifiable; but, it has been very difficult to quantify the importance of the factors

Table 11.19   Shell's rating scale for market growth rate

Sector growth rate per year	Market growth rating	
0–3 per cent	*	(Minimum)
3–5 per cent	**	
5–7 per cent	***	(Average)
7–10 per cent	****	
10 per cent and over	*****	(Maximum)

Source: 'The Directional Policy Matrix' (Shell International, 1975).

Table 11.20   Shell's rating scale for market position

Rating	Market position (in terms of process economics, capacity utilisation, feed-stock access, etc.)
*	Current position negligible
**	Minor market share–inadequate to support R and D and other services in the long term
***	Viable producer–not leader but has strong viable stake in the market
****	Major producer–a number of large producers, but no clear market leader
*****	Leader–pre-eminent market position–ability to lead, e.g. in terms of prices

Source: as Table 11.19.

'product range', 'product quality', and technical competence which, in combination, represent the criterion 'product R and D'. The inherent ambiguity of the DPM criteria can be addressed by posing a number of pertinent questions: some combination of the answers to these questions is judged and assigned a rating score. Some of the important questions posed by Shell to establish the rating of a business's market position are listed below:

1. Has the sector a record of high, stable profitability?
2. Can margins be maintained when manufacturing capacity exceeds demand?
3. Is the product resistant to commodity pricing behaviour?
4. Is the technology of production freely available or is it restricted to those who developed it?
5. Is the market supplied by relatively few producers?
6. Is the market free from domination by a small group of powerful customers?

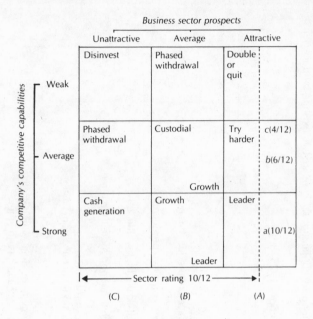

Figure 11.20   Comparison of competitive capabilities for product X

Source: S.J.Q. Robinson, R.E. Hichens and D.P. Wade, 'The Directional Policy Matrix –
Tool for Strategic Planning', *Long Range Planning*, vol. 11 (June 1978) pp. 8–15.

7. Has the product high added value when converted by the
   customer?
8. In the case of a new product, is the market destined to remain
   small enough not to attract too many producers?
9. Is the product one where the customer has to change his
   formulation or even his machinery if he changes suppliers?
10. Is the product free from the risk of substitution by an alternative
    synthetic or natural product?

   Converting an assessment of the two composite dimensions into a
matrix position is achieved by giving each star rating a numerical
value: thus, one, two, three, four and five stars are counted as zero,
one, two, three and four points respectively. In practice the criteria
are assigned ratings in half-star increments, thereby giving eight
half-star graduations between one and five stars. In some applications weightings are also assigned to each of the main criteria where
they are not of equal importance. To arrive at an overall rating in
such cases for 'business sector prospects' and for 'company's competitive capabilities' the scores and weightings are combined.
However, in many contexts this process is simplified where it is

Table 11.21 Hypothetical DPM application

Product sector: Product X is a semi-mature thermoplastic suitable for engineering industry applications. There are two existing producers in Western Europe and a third producer is currently building plant.

Sector prospects analysis (Western Europe, 1975–80)

	Stars	Points
Market growth	15–20% per year forecast	....	4
Market quality		
Sector profitability record?	Above average.	
Margins maintained in over-capacity?	Some price-cutting has taken place but product has not reached commodity status.	
Customer to producer ratio?	Favourable. Numerous customers; only two producers so far.	
High added value to customer?	Yes. The product is used in small-scale, high-value, engineering applications.	
Ultimate market limited in size?	Yes. Unlikely to be large enough to support more than three or four producers.	
Substitutability by other products?	Very limited. Product has unique properties.	
Technology of production restricted?	Moderately. Process is available under licence from Eastern Europe.	
Overall market quality rating:	Above average.	...	3
Industry feedstock	Product is manufactured from an intermediate which itself requires sophisticated technology and has no other outlets.	...	3
Environmental aspects	Not rated separately.	—	—
Overall sector prospects rating	Maximum points possible = 12		10

Companies competitive capabilities analysis (Competitors A, B and C)

	A	B	C
Market position			
Market share	65%	25%	10%
Production capability			
Feedstock	Manufactures feedstock by slightly outdated process from bought-in precursors	Has own precursors. Feedstock manufactured by third party under process deal	Basic position in precursors. Has own second process for feedstock
Process economics	Both A and B have own 'first generation' process supported by moderate process R and D capacity		C is licensing 'second generation' process from Eastern Europe
Hardware	A and B each have one plant sufficient to sustain their respective market shares		None as yet. Market product imported from Eastern Europe.
Overall production capability ratings	····(4)	···(2)	···(3)
	···(3)	···(2)	··(-)(1)
Product R and D (in relation to market position)	Marginally weaker ···(3)	Comparable ···(2)	Stronger ··(-)(1)
Overall competitors' ratings	10/12	6/12	4/12

Source: S. J. Q Robinson, R. E. Hichens and D. P. Wade, 'The Directional Policy Matrix—Tool for Strategic Planning', *Long Range Planning*, vol. 11 (June 1978) pp. 8–15.

Table 11.22   Interpreting the DPM positions (part A)

Keyword	Right-hand column (part A)
LEADER	*i.e. Strong competitive position in a sector with attractive prospects.* This firm will be the largest producer, and will have lowest unit cost (experience curve effects) and a commanding technical position (e.g. competitor A in Table 11.21). All resources necessary to hold this position should be made available. Growth is rapid, therefore investment in additional capacity will be required. Current cash flow may be insufficient to finance expansion. As growth slows, cash generated should be used to support expansion in other areas.
TRY HARDER	*i.e. Average competitive position in a sector with above-average prospects.* This firm is a market follower (e.g. competitor B in Table 11.21). Judicious application of resources is needed to strengthen position to become a leader. This position is acceptable in the short term but likely to become increasingly vulnerable to actions of leader, e.g. in terms of price.
DOUBLE OR QUIT	*i.e. Weak competitive position in a sector with above-average prospects.* Firms with products (SBUs) in this zone should select those that are likely to become future leaders (tomorrow's breadwinners) and fully support them, but abandon others. A diversification that places a firm in this position should only be made where prospects of achieving a stronger competitive position in the sector are good (e.g. competitor C in Table 11.21).

Source: 'The Directional Policy Matrix' (Shell International, 1975).

realistic to suppose that each of the main criteria can be given an equal weighting. Table 11.21 illustrates the application of the simplified DPM approach to assessing the strategic position of competitors in a particular business sector. The results of Table 11.21 can be plotted on the DPM, as shown in Figure 11.20.

The dimensions of the DPM are conveniently divided to give a 3 × 3 matrix with nine zones, each of which represents a unique combination of sector prospects and company strengths or weaknesses. The type of strategy associated with each zone is indicated by a key word, for example, TRY HARDER. In practice the zones are frequently found to assume an irregular shape, and often shade into each other or overlap. As Robinson[121] remarks, 'the most appropriate boundaries can only be determined after (further) practical experience of comparing business characteristics with positions plotted in the matrix'. A brief introduction to the interpretation of the matrix positions and the associated strategy guidelines is provided in Tables 11.22–11.24.

Table 11.23   Interpreting the DPM positions (part B)

Keyword	Middle column (part B)
GROWTH	*i.e. Strong competitive position in a sector with average prospects.* In this position there is no market leader, but two to four major competitors supported by commensurate production capability and product R and D (usually a four-star market position). Resources should be allocated to support growth as the market develops in anticipation of a reasonable rate of return (i.e. maintain market share). Sufficient cash should be generated to finance growth.
CUSTODIAL/ PHASED WITH- DRAWAL	*i.e. Average-weak competitive position in a sector with average prospects.* Products in these zones have distinct weaknesses in terms of their market position (below three star), process economics, hardware or feedstock. Custodial situations occur to weak firms operating in sectors where there are too many competitors. Cash generation should be maximised without committing further resources.

Source: as Table 11.22.

Table 11.24   Interpreting the DPM positions (part C)

Keyword	Left-hand column (part C)
CASH GENERATION	*i.e. Strong competitive position in a sector with below average prospects.* This occurs as a product approaches senility and is being substituted by other products. Profits should be maximised and cash used to support other ventures. No finance provided for expansion.
PHASED WITH- DRAWAL	*i.e. Average-weak competitive position in a sector with poor prospects.* Value of assets should be realised on a controlled basis to release resources for redeployment to other ventures. Earnings not likely to be significant. No finance provided.
DISINVEST	*i.e. Weak competitive position in a sector with poor prospects.* Money is lost periodically. Assets should be disposed of and resources redeployed. This usually occurs because of rapid technological advance or environmental change. Firms usually see such impending decline at the phased withdrawal stage.

Source: as Table 11.22.

The DPM approach is similar in many respects to that of the BAA: its multivariate dimensions incorporate a wide variety of the determinants of strategy; no explicit account is taken of the risk associated with various strategic options; definitions of 'businesses' and 'markets' are fundamental to its rationale; the application of subjective weighting schemes and the need for a considerable qualitative input from management makes it a very time-consuming and complicated technique to apply; and as a reliable prescriptive model it has considerable limitations. The DPM was originally conceived for applications in the petrochemical industry. Consequently, when applying this technique in other contexts the criteria used by Shell to define the composite dimensions will often need to be adapted. The extent to which this occurs will be the subject of management judgement.

PIMS

Despite their apparent differences, the BP, the BAA and the DPM all lean heavily on the belief that there is a direct relationship between market share and competitive strengths, profitability and the response of the market to variations in the marketing mix. This is not surprising, considering that the techniques are derived, to some extent, from important strategic issues originally revealed by the product-life-cycle concept. Marketing practitioners make similar assumptions when they adhere to the rule of thumb that suggests that high market share leads to high profit. To date the empirical work conducted by the PIMS group provides evidence which largely validates these assumptions. However, the reasons for this being so are not completely understood. Further work is needed to clarify the relationship between investment in market share and the associated change in profitability. Of this sort is Kijewski's work which uses the PIMS data to establish the nature of the relationship between the cost of gaining market share and different market conditions. That it is easier to gain market share in high-growth markets is disputed by Kijewski[122] who found that 'the cash costs of gaining share vary substantially between moderate and rapid growth markets. When the cash costs are appropriately adjusted for average point change in market share in each environment, the cost of a point in share is only slightly lower in the more rapidly growing markets (and, indeed, lowest in low growth markets).'

The Profit Impact of Marketing Strategy (PIMS) programme, managed by the Strategic Planning Institute since 1975, was initiated in

1960 by General Electric (GE) as an internal project. It originally sought to identify and weight the strategic variables that influenced the performance (measured in terms of ROI* and cash flow) of the eighty diverse businesses, then operated by GE. This early work developed a computer model, based on multivariate regression equations that identified those significant factors that influenced performance, weighting them according to their importance. A consistent relationship was demonstrated between market share and ROI, even when factors such as product quality and stage in the product-life-cycle had been allowed for.

The scope of the PIMS work was greatly expanded when, in the early 1970s, GE collaborated with the Marketing Science Institute at Harvard University to test the model in a variety of businesses and market environments. To do this a data bank was established that recorded empirical evidence of the strategic experiences of fifty-seven firms, collectively participating in over 600 businesses. As of 1980,[123] more than 200 firms, representing about 2,000 business operations, were participating in the PIMS project. These firms submit for analysis over 100 pieces of specific marketing, financial and competitive information on the activities of selected businesses (SBUs). The information is incorporated into the computer model which can then diagnose strategic position and identify, for each business, important factors to be considered in strategic planning.

The PIMS model is based on the concept that specific characteristics of a business and its market determine its strategic position and profitability. The firms that contribute to the PIMS data base are described in terms of the thirty-seven characteristics, including growth rate, market share, product quality, capacity utilisation, R and D spending, etc., which are thought to explain more than 80 per cent of the variation in performance.[124]

The main drawbacks of the BP and BAA are related to the user having to identify and assess the relative importance of the factors that influence their dimensions: i.e. 'market share' and 'market growth'; and 'industry attractiveness' and 'business strengths'. The PIMS research goes some way to overcoming these drawbacks by identifying the important determinants of the firm's performance, and their implications for its strategic position and prospects.

An important development of the PIMS work has been to show the ROI is closely related to relative market share.† It is noted elsewhere[125] that the data on which this relationship is based suggest that to earn a marginally acceptably ROI some minimum level of

---

* ROI: Return on Investment, i.e. pre-tax income/average investment (working capital + fixed capital).
† That is, the ratio of the firm's market share to that of its three largest competitors.

market share must be attained. This is consistent with the concept of 'critical mass' proposed by Ansoff whereby a firm must attain a given level of market share to achieve a level of ROI which permits it to continue in operation. Figure 11.21 shows that a strong relationship also exists between absolute market share and ROI: on average a difference of 10 percentage points in market share is accompanied by an increase of approximately 5 percentage points in ROI.[126] Table 11.25 groups some of the other important PIMS findings into three broad categories: attractiveness of the industry–market environment; competitive position; and capital structure.

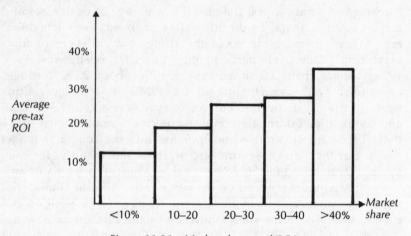

Figure 11.21   Market share and ROI

Source: R. Buzzell and B. Gale, 'Market Share – A Key to Profitability', *Harvard Business Review* (Jan.–Feb. 1974).

Conclusion

The work of the PIMS group focuses on the operations of the individual business (SBU). In so doing, it not only determines the specific variables that influence a firm's performance; it also quantifies this influence, so that the ambiguity commonly associated with assessing product-market strategy can be largely avoided. In this way the PIMS framework for analysis contrasts sharply with that of the BP, BAA and DPM where broad variables and general classifications are the order of the day. Consequently, PIMS deals explicitly with relationships that might otherwise be considered only on a superficial basis. However, PIMS gives no effective consideration of

Table 11.25 Selected PIMS findings

Attractiveness of industry–market environment

1. Market share is most profitable in vertically integrated industries.
1. R and D spending is most profitable in mature, slow-growth markets.
3. A narrow product range in the early or middle stages of the life-cycle is less profitable than at maturity.
4. Capacity utilisation is important when investment intensity (investment/value added) is high.
5. High relative market share (>75%) improves cash flow; high growth (>7%) decreases it.

Competitive position

1. High relative market share (>62%) and low investment intensity (<80%) generate cash; low share (<26%) and high investment intensity (>120%) results in a net use of cash.
2. High R and D spending (>37% sales) depresses ROI when market share is low (<26%).
3. High marketing spending (>11% sales) depresses ROI when market share is low.
4. High R and D and marketing spending depresses ROI.
5. A rapid rate of new product introductions in fast-growing markets depresses ROI.

Capital structure

1. Low or medium industry growth (<9%) coupled with low investment intensity (<80%) produces cash; high growth (>9%) and high investment intensity (>120%) is a cash drain.
2. A low level of new product introductions and low investment intensity (<80%) produces cash.
3. High investment intensity and high marketing intensity (>11% sales) drains cash.
4. Harvesting when investment intensity is low produces cash.
5. Building market share when investment intensity is high uses cash.

Sources: D. F. Abell and J. S. Hammond, *Strategic Market Planning* (Englewood Cliffs, N.J.: Prentice-Hall, 1979); S. Schoeffer, R. Buzzell and D. Heany, 'Impact of Strategic Planning on Profit Performance', *Harvard Business Review*, vol. 52 (March–April 1974) pp. 137–45; R. Buzzell and B. Gale, 'Market Share–A Key to Profitability', *Harvard Business Review* (Jan.–Feb. 1974) pp. 97–106; and R. Buzzell and F. Wiersema, 'Successful Share Building Strategies', *Harvard Business Review* (Jan.–Feb. 1981) pp. 135–44. (All adapted by the author.)

competitive advantage. It is also criticised on methodological grounds concerning the assignment of significance to individual variable coefficients and the interpretation of intra- and inter-group relationships in complex regression models.

Although the analytical frameworks of the BP, BAA and DPM are perhaps not as comprehensive as that of PIMS, they will require detailed product positioning and market segmentation information which is not readily available, or easy to collect.[127] However, without this information it is difficult to categorise a product-market situation accurately; this in turn undermining the validity of any strategic guidelines that may be offered.

A major cause for concern related to each of the frameworks discussed in this chapter is that they all ignore the needs and behaviour of the consumer, at a 'macro' and 'micro' level, concentrating instead on the functions a product fulfils. No explicit account is taken of the idea that the buyer perceives a product merely as a promise that he can fulfil a specific set of felt needs. The BAA and the DPM take the greatest cognisance of the customer by encouraging a comprehensive analysis of a business and its market. However, this very property is largely responsible for the considerable ambiguity of these techniques as strategic tools. BP emphasises the inherent balance between 'growth' and 'cash', forcing the firm to pursue a balanced portfolio with respect to cash generation/use and resource allocation. It takes no explicit account of customer motives, dealing instead with highly aggregated measures of customer behaviour such as 'market share'.

The strategic guidelines each framework offers are not a substitute for the application of sound managerial judgement, since it is possible that they will suggest misleading strategic options. Ideally, they should supplement and complement management expertise, also helping to stimulate creative management thought. Senior management will continue to play an important role in the process of deciding which framework is appropriate and in evaluating the product-market strategies they eventually suggest.

This chapter emphasises that the analytical frameworks it discusses are, in many ways, descriptive rather than prescriptive. It does not attempt to make any misleading or extravagant claims about their potential, preferring to remind the reader that ambiguity and risk are inherent to strategic decision-making.

Furthermore, it does not favour any one of the frameworks, preferring instead to highlight their pros and cons. In so doing, it hopes to stimulate thought, and provoke debate concerning the applications of these frameworks to the fundamental aspects of marketing strategy.

PART III

NEW DIRECTIONS
IN MARKETING

CHAPTER 12

Extending the marketing concept

Contents

Introduction

To this point we have been concerned with establishing a definition of marketing, with justifying the need for a sound theoretical foundation if the discipline is to grow, and with indicating how marketing has borrowed from other disciplines such as economics and the behavioural sciences in developing such a foundation. In this chapter we examine the extension of marketing thinking beyond the traditional areas with which it is usually associated–the sale of goods and services.

However, before undertaking a review of new areas for the application of the marketing concept, it must be recognised that there are divisions of opinion among practitioners concerned with selling industrial as opposed to consumer goods as to the applicability of a single theory of marketing. Accordingly, we consider the claimed differences between these two branches of marketing and dismiss them as being imaginary rather than real, and more a matter of degree than of principle.

Next, we devote some attention to the marketing of services. While virtually all definitions of marketing explicitly or implicitly subsume services as a category of product, there are differences between the two which merit somewhat fuller consideration than is usually accorded them and which we think are worth spelling out. Certainly there seem to be a number of service industries that have only recently recognised the possible relevance of the marketing concept, banking and insurance for example, while many other professions would still seem to lack any concept of consumer sovereignty and might well benefit from an understanding of marketing principles and practices.

Finally, we turn to consider an even wider spectrum of situations which may be broadly defined as 'non-business' where there would also seem to be scope for putting a marketing approach into use. Thus, while marketing is normally conceived of as a business function in which products or services are made available for purchase by consumers in consideration for a monetary payment, there are many other exchange relationships where the 'seller' is not seeking a monetary reward for his 'product'. The application of marketing ideas borrowed from the business function to non-commercial activities such as health-education programmes, the Church, voluntary organisations and so on, as well as to quasi-commercial situations, are increasingly regarded as a legitimate area for the extension of the marketing concept, and we conclude with a review of some recent contributions to an area which has been termed 'meta marketing'.

Industrial versus consumer marketing

In Chapter 1 we put forward the view that marketing might be defined as 'a process of exchange between individuals and/or organisations which is concluded to the mutual benefit and satisfaction of the parties' and that such a definition would imply that 'marketing' has existed since the very first exchange relationship was entered into. We also advanced the view that the rediscovery of marketing in the twentieth century is largely the result of the physical separation betwen producer and consumer, which is a direct consequence of mass production and mass consumption, and which has resulted in the evolution of complex and sophisticated institutions and methods to maintain contact between seller and buyer.

This separation is most marked in the case of mass consumption, packaged, convenience goods and it is with these that the 'new' marketing is most closely identified. Thus concepts such as 'market segmentation' and 'test marketing', and techniques such as sales promotion and media advertising, have developed to their present state largely due to the efforts of companies selling soap and detergents, tobacco and confectionery, and convenience foods, be they canned, frozen or freeze dried. It is also companies like Unilever, Proctor & Gamble, Heinz, Nestlé, British–American Tobacco, and the like, which manufacture these types of products, that have been most subject to criticism for the development and use of such marketing techniques–essentially on the grounds that such activities add costs, but not value, and effectively diminish competition in the market-place (that is, marketing costs are seen as a barrier to entry).

Without debating the rights and wrongs of such criticism, it seems to us that many producers of other categories of product wish to disassociate themselves from possible contamination and so claim that their branch or category of marketing is intrinsically different. Nowhere is this more marked than in the claimed differences between industrial and consumer-goods marketing. Implicitly we reject this contention, for, if it were true, there could be no justification for a book which seeks to prove the need for a sound theoretical basis to the discipline, for, as we indicated in Chapter 2, an essential feature of a theory is that it provides an acceptable general explanation of part of the real world. Explicitly we reject the supposed differences between the two areas on the grounds that premises on which they rest are merely differences in degree, and not in principle.

Thus a common difference between industrial and consumer marketing is claimed to rest in the differing buying motivations which characterise the purchase situation. But, as we endeavoured to show in Chapters 5, 7 and 8, it is our opinion that all buying decisions are the outcome of a process in which objective data are reviewed in the light of subjective judgement and perception. Because ultimate consumers spend less time evaluating performance criteria as expressed in a technical specification than do industrial buyers this is not to say that they are uncritical of the actual performance and satisfaction achieved. Certainly differences in emphasis upon different facets of the decision process are not sufficient to warrant the assertion that 'rational buying motives dominate the industrial market', which by implication infers that consumer buying is less rational, if not actually irrational. This is an arrogant presumption which destroys much of the force of the anti-marketing school's criticism for it contains the implication that one person is a better judge of another person's satisfaction than is that person himself. Perhaps Oscar Wilde best summarised this arrogance when he commented scathingly that 'An economist is a man that knows the price of everything but the value of nothing.'

A second basis for differentiating between industrial and consumer marketing–that 'industrial products are technically more complex'–has been dealt with in part in the preceding paragraph. Television sets, pocket calculators and quartz watches are all highly complex products purchased with apparent ease by ultimate consumers. Perhaps it is because the latter are using a satisfaction criterion–good reception, rapid computation, accurate time-keeping– that they do not bother unduly with 'how' this is achieved. In an industrial context we rather suspect that the same motives predominate–in fact technical specification is invariably a *sine qua non* for consideration as is an acceptable price range. Having normalised these two criteria it would seem that the industrial buying choice between competing alternatives must rest on other less tangible and more subjective factors such as expected or perceived reliability, quality of after-sales service, and so on.

Very similar arguments may be deployed against claims that there is a greater degree of concentration among industrial buyers (it depends upon the precise nature of the product, for example compare office supplies with the market for locally produced specialty products); that the scale of purchasing is greater (absolutely this is usually true but in relative terms, that is size of purchase *vis-à-vis* disposable assets, the reverse is often true); that industrial buying is a group process (so are many household purchasing decisions); that the role of service is greater (but compare consumer durables like cars, television sets, washing machines, etc.); and that credit plays a more important part (again compare consumer-durable purchases).

If we consider some of the concepts and ideas which we are seeking to integrate into a theory of marketing–some of which we have discussed in some detail in preceding chapters–then it would seem that they have equal relevance to both industrial and consumer marketing (and probably to any other branches of marketing as well). The concept of the marketing mix, propounded by Neil Borden,[1] incorporates those areas or elements which all decision-makers must needs consider in developing a strategy irrespective of the nature of their output, namely:

1. *Product planning.* Policies and procedures relating to
   (a) product lines to be offered–qualities, design, and so on;
   (b) the markets to sell–whom, where, when and in what quantity;
   (c) new-product policy–research and development programme.
2. *Pricing.* Policies and procedures relating to
   (a) the level of prices to adopt;
   (b) the specific prices to adopt (odd–even, etc.);
   (c) price policy–one price or varying price, price maintenance, use of list prices, and so on;
   (d) the margins to adopt–for company or for the trade.

3. *Branding*   Policies and procedures relating to
   (a) selection of trade marks;
   (b) brand policy–individualised or family brand;
   (c) sale under private brand or unbranded.
4. *Channels of distribution*. Policies and procedures relating to
   (a) the channels to use between plant and consumer;
   (b) the degree of selectivity among wholesalers and retailers;
   (c) efforts to gain co-operation of the trade.
5. *Personal selling*. Policies and procedures relating to
   (a) the burden to be placed on personal selling and the methods to be employed in (i) the manufacturer's organisation, (ii) the wholesale segment of the trade, and (iii) the retail segment of the trade.
6. *Advertising*. Policies and procedures relating to
   (a) the amount to spend, that is the burden to be placed on advertising;
   (b) the copy platform to adopt (i) product image desired, and (ii) corporate image desired;
   (c) the mix of advertising–to the trade, through the trade, to consumers.
7. *Promotions*. Policies and procedures relating to
   (a) the burden to place on special selling plans or devices directed at or through the trade;
   (b) the form of these devices for consumer promotions, for trade promotions.
8. *Packaging*. Policies and procedures relating to
   (a) formulation of package and label.
9. *Display*. Policies and procedures relating to
   (a) the burden to be put on display to help effect sales;
   (b) the methods to adopt to secure display.
10. *Servicing*. Policies and procedures relating to
    (a) providing service needed.
11. *Physical handling*. Policies and procedures relating to
    (a) warehousing;
    (b) transportation;
    (c) inventories.
12. *Fact finding and analysis*. Policies and procedures relating to
    (a) the securing, analysis and use of facts in marketing operations.

Similarly, the concept of market segmentation or the general model of buyer behaviour which we propose appears to offer equal benefit to different branches of marketing. In some, therefore, we feel that it is divisive to pursue differences between consumer and industrial marketing, not because there are no differences but because concentration on dissimilarity can only delay the development of a coherent and integrated theory. Once we have such a theory, then will be the time to increase its sophistication and explanatory power by distinguishing variations or departures from the accepted principles. However, we also feel that when such a time comes it will be found that a crude distinction between industrial and consumer markets will not suffice, for, as the above points suggest, there are likely to be as great if not greater differences within these two categories than there are between them.

The marketing of services

As indicated in the introduction to this chapter, most writers on 'marketing' claim that the term 'product' should be regarded as a collective noun which also includes services. In principle, as our dismissal of fundamental differences between industrial and consumer marketing indicates, we accept that any theory of marketing should be capable of application to both products and services. At the same time, it is important to recognise that the development of another splinter group of 'service marketers' has not yet emerged to join the industrial marketers, largely because the transfer of marketing techniques to service industries is of relatively recent origin.

In part this delay may be explained by the more personal nature of many services which has precluded the separation between the main parties to the exchange process–producer and consumer–that brought about the need for new institutions and techniques in the mass-consumption convenience-goods market. Similarly, interest in adopting techniques from the latter fields owes much to a desire to increase the productivity of the service industries.

Just as there are differences in degree in other areas of marketing, so we may anticipate similar dissimilarities developing in the service sector. Accordingly, it might be useful to outline some of the possible causes of disparity, for, in general, they are barely touched upon in many texts.[2]

While precise definition of a service presents some difficulties due to lack of agreement as to what should be included/excluded for statistical purposes, there can be no doubt that the service sector is the largest and most important of most advanced economies. Recent data for the United Kingdom illustrate this point (see Tables 12.1 and 12.2).

Not only is the service sector the largest in the economy, it is also the sector with the greatest growth potential and accounts for a

Table 12.1   Employees by industry group (1980)

Industry type	Category	Number ('000s)	%
Primary	Agriculture, forestry, fishing	370	3.17
	Mining and quarrying	344	
Secondary	Manufacturing	6,808	30.25
	Construction	1,265	5.62
Tertiary	Services*	13,726	60.96
Total		22,513	100.00

*Within the 'service' sector are included: gas, electricity and water supply, transportation, communication, the distributive trades, insurance, banking and finance, professional and scientific services, catering, national and local government services.

Source: Census of Employment.

Table 12.2   Gross domestic product by industry group (1980) (£m.)

Industry type	Category	Value	%
Primary	Agriculture, forestry, fishing	4,296	7.39
	Mining and quarrying	10,871	
Secondary	Manufacturing	48,060	23.41
	Construction	13,025	6.35
Tertiary	Services*	129,013	62.85
Total		205,265	100.00

*See the note to Table 12.1.

Source: CSO, *National Income and Expenditure* (HMSO, 1981).

disproportionately large share of any increase in consumers' discretionary purchasing power. Thus the service sector represents an attractive marketing opportunity, especially if it is amenable to the same scale economies as characterised the application of marketing technology to the sale of physical products.

However, as Stanton points out, 'Services possess distinctive characteristics which create marketing problems and result in marketing programs which are often substantially different from those found in the marketing of products.'[3] Among these characteristics Stanton singles out four for particular comment–intangibility, inseparability, heterogeneity, and perishability and fluctuating demand.

In essence it is a service's intangibility which distinguishes it from a physical product. Thus, while one can use objective criteria to describe the nature and performance of products, the same is only true to a limited extent of a service, for example, the value of an insurance policy on maturity, conditions or events under which it will mature, and so on. Clearly, the contention that customers are buying satisfactions or benefits becomes irrefutable in the case of services, and it may well transpire that the sellers of physical goods have as much to learn from the sellers of services when it comes to communicating a selling proposition as the latter have to learn from the former concerning other marketing techniques.

However, as indicated earlier, the transfer of marketing techniques has been delayed due to the *inseparability* of many services from the seller of the service, for example a haircut, beauty treatment, a taxi ride, car repairs, and so on and so forth. As a result of this personal involvement, the sale of many services has to be on a direct basis, which limits severely the scale of operation which is possible. On the other hand, many creators of services can employ agents to help improve their marketing coverage, an insurance agent, for example, while the package-tour brochure provides an excellent example of the application of advertising to create demand pull akin to that practised by many convenience-goods manufacturers.

A third factor that distinguishes many services is their heterogeneity, a natural outcome of the high level of personal involvement in the provision of such services. It is rather ironic that, while many manufacturers seek to differentiate their output to escape charges of homogeneity, it is the very lack of homogeneity which concerns many service organisations. For example, Stanton cites the uncertainty attached to many spectator sports concerning the standard or quality of the performance, while lack of consistency in repair services and transportation is a notable cause of customer complaint.

Finally, as Stanton points out, 'Services are highly perishable and they cannot be stored. Unused electrical power, empty seats in a stadium, and idle repairmen in a garage all represent business which is lost for ever. Furthermore, the market for services fluctuates considerably by seasons, by days of the week, and hours of the day.' It is this perishability and fluctuating demand that presents one of the greatest challenges to management in the creative combination of product planning, pricing and promotion functions to manipulate demand so that it corresponds more closely to the available supply. At first sight this may seem the very antithesis of the marketing-management concept, as it smacks of selling what one can make rather than making what one can sell. However, it is not difficult to see that by stimulating demand for under-utilised and perishable outputs, one is making a significant step towards maximising satisfaction from the use of scarce resources.

Although we suggested earlier that the delay in applying marketing ideas and techniques to the provision of services might be due, at least in part, to the more personal relationship between supplier and consumer, this is not to say that suppliers were truly customer-oriented. In fact, in many instances the reverse seems to have been (and still is) the case. Perhaps it is not without significance that several of the major examples cited by Theodore Levitt in his now classic 'Marketing Myopia'[4] were service industries. Thus the railroads failed because they conceived of themselves as being in the railroad business rather than in transportation; the movie business almost died because it ignored, then resisted, television, failing to see that films and television are both part of the entertainment business. Similarly, dry-cleaning, electric utilities and corner grocery stores have all suffered through a lack of sensitivity to customer needs.

Nowadays a similar problem seems to face many of the professions. Banking and insurance have gone some way towards catering to customer needs but still tend to adopt an approach which implies that they are doing you a favour by doing business with you, while their acolytes–accountants and solicitors–leave you in no doubt that this is the case. However, given present trends in consumer protection, there can be no doubt that unless these professions adopt a more sympathetic, dare one say marketing, approach to their clients, they are likely to find their monopolies exposed to close scrutiny and modification.

To sum up, the differences which distinguish services from products appear to be no greater nor more significant than those purported to differentiate between consumer and industrial goods. It follows, therefore, that the same principles and concepts should be of equal relevance to the marketing of services as to products notwithstanding the differences in degree and emphasis which will be called for. Thus the same sequence of market research, product/service planning and development, pricing, promotion, distribution, sale and after-sales service would seem to be equally appropriate to all marketing situations.

Broadening the marketing concept

If it is accepted that the same marketing approach is relevant to the sale of all goods and services, it does not seem a very big step to enquire whether the same philosophy and theory are not capable of still further extension to embrace all exchange relationships regardless of a cash or profit motivation. This very question provided the basis for a now famous article, 'Broadening the Concept of Marketing' by Kotler and Levy,[5] and has provided the foundation on which most subsequent discussion of the topic has been raised. Accordingly we consider it important to summarise and comment upon the main points made by Kotler and Levy.

The first point to be made is that most people regard marketing as a purely business activity involving functions such as product development, pricing, distribution and communication. However, in Kotler and Levy's view, 'marketing is a pervasive societal activity that goes considerably beyond the selling of toothpaste, soap, and steel', an assertion which they support by citing the marketing of politicians and film stars, student recruitment by American universities, and the raising of money for 'causes'. But if one examines these latter activities one finds that little attention has been given them by marketers, save perhaps in the context of public relations, and that only as a relatively minor aspect of advertising. In Kotler and Levy's opinion such neglect is unforgivable for it threatens to relegate marketing permanently to a narrowly defined business activity and ignores the challenge and potential for extending marketing ideas into a much wider social framework.

In the preceding section we drew attention to the fact that the tertiary, or services, sector of our economy, like that of most, if not all, advanced industrialised economies, is now larger than both the primary and secondary sectors combined. However, in making this point we did not distinguish between business and non-business organisations, although the subsequent discussion focused upon services provided mainly by the former. Kotler and Levy suggest that, while business enterprises will remain a dominant form of organisation, other types of non-business organisation will become increasingly important. Major unions, religious organisations, government and local-government departments, universities, philanthropic foundations, hospitals, and the like, would all seem to fall into this category. Further, upon analysis it appears that all must perform the classic business functions—finance, procurement, production, personnel management and marketing. But, while the other business functions may be clearly identifiable, the marketing function is often not recognised explicitly as such.

As examples Kotler cites the 'community relations' programmes run by many police forces in the United States, as part of an effort to improve understanding between the police and the public, the Metropolitan Museum of Art's development of a series of 'happenings' designed to persuade citizens that museums are not dull, uninteresting mausoleums, the efforts of health educationists to promote the harmful effects of cigarette smoking and persuade people to give up the habit, and so on. Clearly all these activities have parallels in this and many other countries and lend substance to the claim that 'All of these organisations are concerned about their "product" in the eyes of certain "consumers" and are seeking to find "tools" for furthering their acceptance.'

Just as services may be viewed as intangible products, and so may be amenable to marketing techniques, as argued in the preceding pages, so too are ideas, organisations and persons. However, if we are to extend successfully the marketing concept to these areas it seems desirable that we should give some attention to defining profit (an aspect neglected by Kotler and Levy), for it appears that a source of considerable resistance in many non-business organisations to the transfer of ideas and techniques from the business sector are the undesirable connotations associated with money profits. Thus it seems that much ill-formed criticism is often directed towards the business sector because it measures performance in terms of monetary gains (and losses) which socially are ranked as inferior to more spiritual and possibly less tangible benefits. But, in the long run, it is clear that the only justification for any form of organisation is that it improves human welfare. Faced with limited resources, it seems reasonable to ask that we measure the performance of all types of activity so that we may concentrate our efforts upon those which add most to this overall goal of maximising satisfaction. Accordingly, a concept of 'profit' or net surplus would seem to be just as appropriate in deciding priorities for education, social welfare, health services, and the like, and organisations providing such services should be encouraged to grapple with the problems of defining and measuring their contribution to society. Clearly, a first step in such an effort must be definition of the consumer need which is to be served and of the 'product' which will meet this need.

It should be stressed that the emphasis in the preceding sentence is rather different from that implied by the sequence–product, customer, tools–cited by Kotler and Levy, for this is a classical production orientation. If one is concerned with declining attendances in churches, with lack of enthusiasm for cultural opportunities provided by museums and art galleries, or lack of participation in the recreational activities offered by leisure centres, then the classical marketing approach of first identifying consumer needs and then relating them to the capabilities of the supplying organisation would seem to be the most important concept to communicate. Only if this is achieved is it likely that there will develop interest in marketing techniques, such as, for example, product-line pricing, or tools for dealing with problems of distribution and promotion.

In their analysis Kotler and Levy state that 'Nine concepts stand out as crucial in guiding the marketing effort of a business organisation.' They identify these as:
1. Generic-product definition.
2. Target-groups definition.

3. Differentiated marketing.
4. Customer-behaviour analysis.
5. Differential advantages.
6. Multiple marketing tools.
7. Integrated marketing planning.
8. Continuous marketing feedback.
9. Marketing audit.

Most of these terms are well known and understood by marketing practitioners, and do not merit elaboration here, although one example will help stimulate thought as to their relevance and transferability to a wider social context. Thus 'Churches at one time tended to define their product narrowly as that of producing religious services for members. Recently, most churchmen have decided that their basic product is human fellowship.'[6]

In our view, the major difficulty that faces any attempt to broaden the concept of marketing from the business to the non-business sector (sometimes referred to as 'meta marketing') lies not so much in demonstrating the utility of tools and techniques but in overcoming initial resistance to the materialistic connotation of 'marketing'. Perhaps one of our greatest weaknesses as practitioners is that we fail to practise what we preach and so tend to dismiss criticisms of marketing as ill-founded without considering that such expressed misgivings may be symptomatic of a much more radical concern and disillusionment, and, worse still, without doing very much to rectify what we regard as a misunderstanding of our true mission. In this belief we turn our attention in the next chapter to some of the main sources of criticism of marketing, for until we understand our critics we would seem to have little chance of persuading them that the marketing concept can be extended to embrace other, non-business areas of human activity.

CHAPTER 13

Marketing under attack[1]

Contents

Introduction

As indicated in the 'Preface to the First Edition', the thrust of this book has been concerned with establishing the need for a sound theoretical foundation on which to develop a discipline of marketing while recognising that the function and practice are of considerable antiquity. Based upon this argument we examined in Part II specific sub-areas within marketing to show how these had grown by borrowing concepts and ideas from other disciplines and then synthesising and developing these in a marketing context. And, in the preceding chapter, we reviewed the arguments in favour of extending the marketing concept into areas not traditionally associated with it–services and the outputs or 'products' of non-profit associations.

However, the title of this book is *Marketing: Theory and Practice*, and it would convey a false impression of the real-world situation if we were to close on a high point extolling the universality of marketing when it is quite clear that a number of serious reservations have been expressed concerning it. Accordingly, in this chapter we examine some of the major sources of marketing criticism.

Limitations of space preclude a full treatment of the multiplicity of sources of criticism, which Kotler[2] has classified into three main categories, namely:

1. *Marketing's impact on society*:
   (a) excessive materialism;
   (b) manipulation of demand;
   (c) neglect of social goods and costs;
   (d) cultural pollution;
   (e) excessive political power.
2. *Marketing's impact on business competition*:
   (a) anti-competitive acquisition;
   (b) barriers to entry;
   (c) predatory competition.
3. *Marketing's impact on consumer welfare*:
   (a) high prices;
   (b) deceptive practices;
   (c) high-pressure selling;
   (d) shoddy or unsafe products;
   (e) planned obsolescence;
   (f) minority discrimination.

Kotler's treatment extends to a full chapter (22) of thirty-eight pages and is strongly recommended for study. For our part we must be content with a more condensed analysis of two issues (which are subsumed within Kotler's major categories) that are frequently raised as an argument against a marketing philosophy–conservation and consumerism.

Conservation may be regarded as a general argument against a materialistic and consumption-dominated society which many consider to be synonymous with 'marketing', and will be discussed in the context of proposals for a zero-growth economy. Consumerism, for our purposes, will be reviewed as a particular example of focused and directed 'anti-marketing' thinking rather than in the all-embracing interpretation which includes conservation within it.

Conservation and marketing

At several points in this book we have adopted the economist's definition of the central problem facing world society as being 'maximising satisfaction from the utilisation of scarce resources'. Further, we have tended to emphasise maximising satisfaction, and have been critical of the economists' reluctance to incorporate subjective value judgements into concepts of choice and utility to any significant degree. In return, critics of marketing would argue that as a result of our emphasis upon satisfaction we tend to have lost sight of, or ignore, the constraint imposed upon consumption by the finite and scarce nature of many resources. In the early 1970s this scarcity was brought home to the affluent economies of the world with great force as a result of the Arab oil embargo and the energy 'crisis' which it precipitated. Certainly this single event provided a focus for a growing body of opinion directed against conspicuous consumption, which it previously had lacked, for it had a direct effect upon the man in the street whereas concern about long-term exhaustion of physical resources lacked this impact.

To some degree the lack of impact of the conservationist argument may be attributed to the failure of Thomas Malthus's gloomy prognostications to come to pass during the early nineteenth century. In his *Essay on the Principle of Population* first published in 1798 Malthus advanced the proposition that population has a universal tendency to grow at a geometric progression. However, Malthus also pointed out that this tendency is subject to certain checks and, in the first edition, emphasised natural and positive limitations–disease, famine and war. (It is less well known that in the revised edition of his *Essay* Malthus took a less pessimistic view and acknowledged the possibility of preventive checks through what may be described broadly as 'family planning'.) While Malthus's ideas had enormous influence upon his contemporaries and are cited as 'the basis for a stern revision of the English poor laws',[3] and while he will always enjoy an honoured place in the annals of economic thought for his statement of the principle of diminishing returns, the essential concept he propounded lost influence due to its failure to materialise.

As Samuelson notes,

> it is today recognised that his views were oversimplifications. In his discussion of diminishing returns, he never fully anticipated the miracles of the Industrial Revolution. In the next century technological innovation *shifted* production possibility curves *outward* and made possible better standards of living for more people. At the same time medical advances were prolonging human life and further lessening the positive checks to population. Nor did he realise that after 1870 in most Western nations, including the United States, family *fertility* as measured by actual number of children would begin to fall far short of family *fecundity*, or biological reproductive capacity.[4]

None of this is to suggest that the fundamental validity of Malthus's argument has ever been lost sight of, namely that there is a physical limit to the population which the world can support. However, the advances due to technological innovation have tended to diminish sensitivity to this constraint until the last two decades. In this latter period there has been a growing consciousness of our finite resource base which, in turn, has led to growing dissatisfaction with the way in which we have been using these resources; this has found expression in a number of ways.

Perhaps the most influential statement of this view is that contained in *The Limits to Growth*[5] which is an account of the first phase of the Project on the Predicament of Mankind which was sponsored by the Club of Rome 'in order to determine the limits of the world system and the constraints which this imposes upon population and consumption'.

Based upon its analysis of 'five major trends of global concern– accelerating industrialisation, rapid population growth, widespread malnutrition, depletion of non-renewable resources, and a deteriorating environment', the study team under Professor Denis Meadows concluded that:

> If the present growth trends in world population, industrialisation, pollution, food production, and resource depletion continue unchanged, the limits to growth on this planet will be reached sometime within the next one hundred years. The most probable result will be a rather sudden and uncontrollable decline in both population and industrial capacity.

The team further concluded that it was possible to alter the present trends and achieve a new equilibrium state, but that the sooner work started, the better the chances of success. In grossly simplified terms the remedy proposed is essentially a combination of population control and reduced consumption. While there is not universal support for the Meadows model, nor for the recommendations derived from it, there is a sufficient agreement to have given rise to what we term the 'zero-growth syndrome'.

The zero-growth syndrome

A major feature of the zero-growth syndrome is that it is anti-new-product development. Such opposition is patently misguided for it is clear that a very large proportion of all economic growth during this century is the result of technological innovation rather than increases in factor inputs. It is also clear that a major stimulus to technological innovation is the reward of above-normal profit which can be earned through developing successful new products. The importance of innovation is implicit in many of Meadows's recommendations and more than explicit in the following quotation:

Technological advance would be both necessary and welcome in the equilibrium state. A few obvious examples of the kinds of practical discovery that would enhance the workings of a steady state society include:

New methods of waste collection, to decrease pollution and make discarded material available for recycling;

More efficient techniques of recycling, to reduce rates of resource depletion;

Better product design to increase product lifetime and promote easy repair, so that the capital depreciation rate would be minimised;

Harnessing of incident solar energy, based on more complete understanding of ecological interrelationships;

Medical advances that would decrease the death rate;

Contraceptive advances that would facilitate the equalisation of the birth rate with the decreasing death rate.

It is clear that there is ample scope for innovation and new-product development in achieving and maintaining the desired steady state. Thus the criticism would seem to be directed not so much at the actual processes of new-product development but rather at some of its manifestations. Of these perhaps the most frequently criticised aspects are those embraced by the phrases 'product proliferation', 'planned obsolescence' and 'conspicuous consumption'.

Marketing and materialism

While it would be naïve to deny that marketing must bear some responsibility for all of these undesirable facets of modern society, it would be equally naïve to accept all the blame. We have already expressed the view that a central feature of marketing is that it seeks to measure consumer preferences and then satisfy them. If much of modern society is materialistic it should be remembered that materialism is not a new state—the only salient difference between twentieth-century materialism and that of previous centuries is that the condition is much more widespread now than hitherto. No longer is non-essential consumption the prerogative of the upper and middle classes—in the advanced economies it is the privilege of virtually all, and few would claim that increased consumption and the enhanced standard of living it confers is bad.

It would seem, therefore, that the criticism is directed at excessive consumption, not at improved consumption. However, as we have already suggested, marketing reflects society's wishes as much as it conditions and moulds them. Ever since the depression of the late 1920s and early 1930s the economic policy of most Western economies has been based upon the thinking of John Maynard Keynes. It was Keynes who postulated that a major cause of the depression and the unemployment that accompanied it was underconsumption. The Protestant Ethic extols the virtue of labour, so clearly the aim of government policy must be to stimulate consumption, for this will increase the demand for labour and alleviate the indignity of unemployment. This is admittedly a rather trite synopsis of economic thinking over the past thirty years or so, but there can be no denying that the maintenance of full employment has been a central plank in the platform of all political parties at all general elections ever since the Beveridge Report of 1944. (Some may question whether in fact this is true of the Thatcher government of the early 1980s. Our own view is that it is, but that an emphasis upon international competitiveness and greater individual productivity has been given even higher priority.)

The deficiency of this economic policy is very similar to the deficiency of the production- and sales-management orientations which preceded marketing as a managerial philosophy–all tend to stress quantity rather than quality. It would be more than invidious to blame business for implementing government, and therefore presumably society's, wishes in pursuing an expansionist policy, but this is just what we are in danger of doing. If, as now seems to be the case, we are more concerned with the conservation of resources than with their accelerated consumption, it would be more constructive if we were to allow management time in which to develop new policies and redeploy resources accordingly. Certainly it will take a long time to re-educate consumers to prefer durability to novelty and quality to quantity.

However, if it is necessary to re-educate consumers to prefer more durable products, to accept protein substitutes for fresh meat, to run smaller cars, to practise birth control, in fact to adopt willingly any significant change in their behaviour and/or consumption patterns, then surely marketing techniques will have a major role to play.

The impact of consumerism

Although it is often erroneously assumed that the consumerist movement owes its existence to the growth of conspicuous consumption in the 1950s and 1960s, and the reaction to it implicit in the writings of Vance Packard,[6] Rachel Carson[7] and Ralph Nader,[8] there appears to be a fundamental paradox in the apparent conflict between two activities–consumerism and marketing–both of which claim that their central interest is maximising consumer satisfaction.

However, a moment's reflection suggests that perhaps this seeming inconsistency is less contradictory than might appear at first sight.

As we have implied in the preceding paragraph, consumerism is no more an invention of the twentieth century than is marketing. Marketing has existed ever since man perceived the advantages to be gained from job specialisation, for, while such specialisation results in marked increases in productivity, it also creates the need for exchange so that individual producers may acquire products other than those which they make themselves. But as soon as men begin to enter into exchange relationships it becomes clear that there is a need for some system of rules to govern the nature of transactions, for, otherwise, the less scrupulous will take advantage of the customers with weak bargaining power. The protection of consumer interest is central to the consumerist movement so perhaps we should consider it unsurprising that increases in the level of marketing activity should be paralleled by an increase in activities designed to protect consumers.

For example, the growth of the medieval craft guilds resulted in a considerable increase in the supply of goods, and also resulted in the promulgation of devices to protect the consumer, for example the hallmarking of precious metals, as well as the evolution of voluntary codes of practice to govern standards of manufacture and trading. At the same time, certain common-law principles were evolved for the protection of both seller and buyer, such as the ruling that stolen goods purchased in market overt could not be recovered by their original owner. At a time when virtually all transactions took place in the open, and products lacked the homogeneity associated with mass production, such that individual goods might be readily identified, it seemed reasonable that one should acquire good title if buying stolen goods in the open market and in good faith. Under today's trading conditions the owners of stolen goods cannot be expected to have the same opportunity to recover their own property, and it has been necessary to change the law to reflect the changed situation. Similarly, the inherent complexity of many products, and of the distribution channels through which they pass between producer and consumer, demand modifications of earlier legislation designed to protect the consumer, such as the Sale of Goods Act of 1893.

At the present time, the consumerist lobby represents only a small proportion of all consumers, both in the United Kingdom, in the United States and in Europe. However, it is a very vocal and influential minority that has secured considerable success in persuading governments to enact legislation to improve the users' bargaining power and to protect them against misleading marketing practices. In the United Kingdom it is widely accepted that the consumerist movement is predominantly middle class (as the nature of the products reviewed in *Which?* clearly indicates), and that while its concern is with value for money its definition of value is essentially objective, and neglects, ignores and sometimes actively disapproves of any suggestion of subjective values created by promotional activity. None the less, active consumerists represent a sufficiently large market segment to warrant very close attention as a market opportunity. Moreover, unlike most market segments, consumerists are unusually articulate in spelling out exactly what it is they are looking for in terms of acceptable product specifications. Thus we would argue that consumerists represent a worthwhile marketing opportunity in their own right. If the consumerists' concern with brand proliferation, planned obsolescence, after-sales service, truth in advertising and lending, bio-degradable packaging and so on and so forth, represents the thinking of all consumers ten years from now, then there would seem to be very significant advantages in evaluating the precise nature of the consumerist demands and the development of goods and services to meet these demands today, for it will give the alert manufacturer ample opportunity to test-market a new strategy for prospering under these changed conditions.

In short, we return to our argument that the function of marketing is to maximise consumer satisfaction at a profit. If consumer demand changes then marketing should be the first to sense the nature and direction of this change and modify its own policies and practices accordingly. There is no fundamental conflict between consumerism and marketing–their basic objective is the same.

Marketing and inflation

Earlier in this chapter we suggested that the 'energy crisis' provided a focus for a rather diffuse body of opinion with the common feature that it was concerned with the irresponsible manner in which society was consuming scarce resources. We also suggested that this focus arose very largely from the fact that the consequences of the energy crisis had a direct and immediate effect upon the man in the street and so sensitised him to the validity of the conservationist's argument. As the citizens of most of the world's economies are aware the consequence of the energy crisis has been inflation–a condition which many argue is the direct result of excessive consumption. Marketing is frequently viewed as a consumption-oriented activity; therefore one solution to our problems is 'stop marketing'.

More specifically, inflation is seen as the direct consequence of an excess demand for goods and services, with the result that too much money is chasing too few goods. Given such a situation, we do not need to have taken a course in advanced economics to appreciate that the most likely outcome, at least in the short term, is an increase in price. After all, the function of the market is to equate demand and supply at an equilibrium price.

In fact the 'demand-pull' school of thought represents only one interpretation of the causes of inflation–the other most frequently cited causes being 'cost-push' and 'monetary' inflation. In simple terms, cost-push inflation is set in train when some groups of workers secure a substantial pay increase which leads in turn to an increase in the costs and price of their output. Consumers of the firm's output, faced with an increase in the cost of living and wishing to maintain parity of earnings with those who have just won a rise, put in their own claim. Further, in an inflationary situation, the second group of workers fear that by the time their claim is settled it will have been eroded by other price increases and taxation, and so will press for significantly more than they would be prepared to accept under more stable conditions. This escalation of wage claims gives rise to wage–price spiral in which the increase in the volume of money outstrips increases in the volume of goods and services available for consumption, and, once again, leads to too much money chasing too few goods.

An increase in the money supply is also viewed as the third main cause of inflation–'monetary' inflation. However, in the case of monetary inflation, the catalyst that initiates the inflationary spiral is an increase in the quantity of money rather than an increase in wages and costs. Such increases in the money supply usually take place when government exceeds its ability to raise revenue through increased taxes or borrowing and so must resort to printing more bank-notes in order to cover its commitments. Unfortunately, such increases in the money supply usually outstrip any increases in productivity, resulting once again in too much money chasing too few goods.

While these are grossly oversimplified representations of three main schools of thought concerning the causes of inflation, none the less they suffice to convey the basic point that a significant increase in the supply of money (or a significant decline in the supply of goods) will result in a rise in price, or, put another way, a decline in purchasing power. On a limited scale and in the short term, such fluctuations are to be expected and are no cause for concern. But, if they lead to a loss of confidence in the value of money, they set in train a vicious spiral of present consumption, rather than deferred consumption in the form of investment and saving, which acceler-ates price increases and wage demands designed to offset such price increases.

As noted earlier, critics of marketing are really supporters of the demand-pull school and so would seem to argue for the remedies appropriate to such inflation–a reduction in private purchasing power through higher taxes and credit restrictions, as well as a cut-back in public expenditure upon socially desirable projects such as schools, hospitals and other forms of social and welfare benefit. (In passing, one might observe that present stocks of cars and under-utilised capacity in many industries reflect excess supply rather than excess demand.) Of course, such policies are equally appropriate to cost-push inflation, although in this instance they are likely to be termed 'wage and price control'. Given this degree of similarity between the different forms of inflation and their cures, it seems reasonable to ask why marketing should be singled out for blame rather than, for example, restrictive-labour practices, insufficient investment in innovation, or simple bone-idleness. Without wishing to claim that marketing is wholly without fault, it would seem more constructive to recognise that our poor economic performance is the result of a combination of interdependent factors which need to be treated together.

Summary

In this chapter we have looked briefly at three sources of economic and social concern which have prompted observers to question the relevance of marketing. We have argued that these three sources of criticism–consumerism, inflation and the zero-growth syndrome–all spring from the same origin, a realisation that a continuation of present consumption patterns and trends is likely to result in exhaustion of the world's finite resources in the not too distant future.

We have suggested that marketing has been singled out for particular criticism on the grounds that it is frequently viewed as synonymous with demand stimulation, and excess demand is seen as the root cause of the projected disequilibrium. It is unnecessary to deny that demand stimulation is marketing's prime objective (although most marketers would, in fact, do so) in order to reject this criticism, for it would only be tenable if marketing's efforts to stimulate demand were concerned solely with *volume*. As all true marketing men know, marketing's prime preoccupation is maximising consumer satisfaction at a profit acceptable to the supplier–a point made forcibly by the British Printing Industries Federation in its magazine *Printing Industries*. For example, it was reported that

Printers cannot hope for better returns on capital when they are forced to lower prices merely to retain their present customers. In future they will have to rely on better marketing. ...The federation said printers should realise that better marketing was not necessarily concerned with selling the maximum volume at the lowest price to the greatest number of customers. *It might equally be selling the best at the highest price to a minority* [our emphasis].[9]

The report continued: 'In the present difficult times, member firms need to be quite a lot more profitable merely in order to survive.' Improved marketing is suggested as the appropriate remedy.

It is our view that there is no fundamental inconsistency between marketing and economic and social objectives–an improvement in the standard of living and the quality of life in general–even though the means of achieving these are subject to reconsideration at the present time. Rather, we view marketing as the business discipline best equipped to cope with such change, starting as it does with planning in order to determine the nature of consumer needs and then co-operating with all the other business functions to ensure that customers receive the right product at the right place, price and time. Further, if there is a need to educate people as to the need for conservation rather than conspicuous consumption, marketing and advertising men are probably better equipped to communicate this message than most other people. (Clearly a significant contributory factor to the present inflationary situation is a loss of consumer confidence–building consumer confidence is a major marketing activity.)

However, it also seems to us that marketing men must be prepared to stand up and be counted, and to use the skills they deploy so effectively in selling goods and services to communicate the relevance and value of marketing to the general public. If we fail to do this then perhaps marketing does not deserve a future.

Notes and references

Chapter 1

1. Philip Kotler, *Marketing Management*, 2nd edn (Englewood Cliffs, N.J.: Prentice-Hall, 1972) p. 6.
2. This follows a trichotomy suggested by Robert L. King in 'The Marketing Concept', in *Science in Marketing*, ed. George Schwartz (New York: Wiley, 1965). The discussion on these different orientations draws extensively on this source.
3. See *World Dynamics* (Cambridge, Mass.: Wright-Allen Press, 1971).
4. D. Meadows *et al.*, *The Limits to Growth* (London: Earth Island, 1972).
5. King, 'The Marketing Concept'.
6. *Marketing*, 2nd edn (London: Macmillan, 1974) pp. 26 ff.
7. Quoted from an unpublished paper, 'The Marketing Concept in General Electric', by Edward S. McKay.
8. General Electric Company, *Annual Report, 1952*.
9. 'An Interpretation of the Marketing Concept', *Advancing Marketing Efficiency*, Proceedings of the 41st National Conference, American Marketing Association (Chicago, 1959), cited in King, 'The Marketing Concept'.
10. See, for example, Vance Packard's books, *The Hidden Persuaders* (London: Longmans, Green, 1957) and *The Waste Makers* (London: Longmans, Green, 1961). Also Ralph Nader's *Unsafe at any Speed* (New York: Grossman, 1963).
11. Lawrence Abbott, *Quality and Competition* (Columbia University Press, 1955).

Chapter 2

1. Michael Halbert, *The Meaning and Sources of Marketing Theory* (New York: McGraw-Hill, 1975).
2. Robert D. Buzzell, 'Is Marketing a Science?', *Harvard Business Review* (Jan.–Feb. 1963).

3. P. D. Converse, 'The Development of the Science of Marketing–An Exploratory Survey', *Journal of Marketing* (July 1945) pp. 14–23.
4. W. Alderson and R. Cox, 'Towards a Theory of Marketing', *Journal of Marketing* (Oct. 1948) pp. 137 ff.
5. R. Vaile, 'Towards a Theory of Marketing', *Journal of Marketing* (April 1949) pp. 520–2.
6. R. Bartels, 'Can Marketing Be a Science?', *Journal of Marketing* (Jan. 1951) pp. 319–28.
7. K. D. Hutchinson, 'Marketing as a Science: An Appraisal', *Journal of Marketing* (Jan. 1952) pp. 286–93.
8. J. E. Jueck, 'Marketing Research, Milestone or Millstone?', *Journal of Marketing* (Jan. 1953) pp. 16 ff.
9. W. J. Baumol, 'On the Role of Marketing Theory', *Journal of Marketing* (Apr. 1957) pp. 413–18.
10. Buzzell, 'Is Marketing a Science?'.
11. Halbert, *The Meaning and Sources of Marketing Theory*.
12. W. J. Taylor, 'Is Marketing a Science Revisited?', *Journal of Marketing*, vol. 29 (July 1965) pp. 49–53.
13. Vaile, 'Towards a Theory of Marketing'.
14. Alderson and Cox, Towards a Theory of Marketing'.
15. Vaile, 'Towards a Theory of Marketing', p. 522.
16. Hutchinson, 'Marketing as a Science: An Appraisal'.
17. Ibid, p. 290.
18. Theodore Levitt, *Innovation in Marketing* (New York: McGraw-Hill, 1962).
19. Taylor, 'Is Marketing a Science Revisited?'
20. E. B. Weiss, 'Will Marketing Ever become a Science?', *Advertising Age*, vol. 33 (Aug. 1962) pp. 64–5.
21. Bartels, 'Can Marketing Be a Science?'.
22. Bartels in *Science in Marketing*, ed. George Schwartz (New York: Wiley, 1965) p. 47.
23. Hutchinson, 'Marketing as a Science: An Appraisal'.
24. C. Ramond, *The Art of Using Science in Marketing* (New York: Harper & Row, 1974).
25. G. C. Homans, *The Nature of Social Science* (New York: Brace & World, 1967).
26. *Webster's 7th Collegiate Dictionary* (London: G. Bell & Sons, 1971).
27. C. E. Lee, 'Measurement and the Development of Science and Marketing', *Journal of Marketing Research*, vol. 2 (Feb. 1965) pp. 20–5.
28. Bartels, 'Can Marketing Be a Science?'; A. S. C. Ehrenberg, *Data Reduction* (London: Wiley, 1978).
29. 'The Hunting of Advertising Effectiveness', *Admap* (Feb. 1975).
30. 'Towards an Alternative Advertising Theory', *Admap* (Jan. 1974).
31. *Marketing in a Competitive Economy* (London: Hutchinson, 1965).
32. Alderson and Cox, 'Towards a Theory of Marketing'.
33. Bartels, 'Can Marketing Be a Science?'.
34. A. W. Shaw, 'Some Problems in Marketing Distribution', *Quarterly Journal of Economics* (1912).
35. E. McGary, 'Some Viewpoints in Marketing', *Journal of Marketing*, vol. 17 (July 1953).
36. R. Bartels, 'The General Theory of Marketing', *Journal of Marketing*, vol. 32 (Jan. 1968) p. 32.
37. S. D. Hunt, 'The Nature and Scope of Marketing', *Journal of Marketing* (July 1976) pp. 17–28.

38. *Marketing Definitions: A Glossary of Marketing Terms*, compiled by the Committee on Definitions of the American Marketing Association (Chicago, 1960).
39. J. W. Newman, 'Marketing Science: Significance to the Profession of Marketing', in *Science in Marketing*.

Chapter 3

1. *The Meaning and Sources of Marketing Theory* (New York: McGraw-Hill, 1965).
2. *Journal of Marketing*, vol. 32 (Jan. 1968) pp. 29–33.
3. See particularly *The Development of Marketing Thought* (Homewood, Ill.: Irwin, 1962) and his contribution to *Science in Marketing*, ed. George Schwartz (New York: Wiley, 1965).
4. Arch. W. Shaw, 'Some Problems in Marketing Distribution', *Quarterly Journal of Economcs* (Aug. 1912): L. D. H. Weld, 'Marketing Functions and Mercantile Organisation', *American Economic Review* (June 1917); and Paul T. Cherington, *The Elements of Marketing* (London: Macmillan, 1920).
5. *Retail Selling and Store Management* (New York: Appleton-Century, 1913) and *The Economics of Retailing* (New York: Ronald Press, 1915).
6. Halbert, *The Meaning and Sources of Marketing Theory*, pp. 63–4.
7. Ibid.
8. Ibid., p. 24.
9. Ibid., p. 127.
10. Ibid., p. 23.
11. Alderson in R. J. Lawrence and M. J. Thomas, *Modern Marketing Management* (Harmondsworth: Penguin, 1971) p. 64.
12. W. Wentz, *Marketing* (St Paul, Minnesota: West Publishing Co., 1979) p. 5.
13. P. Kotler and G. Zaltman, 'Social Marketing: An Approach to Planned Social Change', *Journal of Marketing* (July 1971) pp. 3–12.
14. L. M. Dawson, 'The Human Concept: New Philosophy for Business', in *Marketing Concepts, Issues and Viewpoints*, ed. D. L. Kurtz (Morristown: D. H. Mark, 1972) p. 16.
15. J. T. Rothe and L. Benson, 'Intelligent Consumption: An Alternative to the Marketing Concept', *MSU Business Topics* (Winter 1974) pp. 29–34.
16. G. Fisk, 'Criteria for a Theory of Responsible Consumption', *Journal of Marketing* (Apil 1973) p. 24.
17. D. Harvey, *Explanation in Geography* (London: Edward Arnold, 1969).
18. M. Bunge, *Scientific Research: The Search for System* (Berlin: Springer-Verlag, 1967).

Chapter 4

1. George Katona, *The Powerful Consumer* (New York: McGraw-Hill, 1960).
2. Andrew Shonfield, 'Neglect of Psychology in Managing the Economy', *The Times* (24 Feb. 1971).
3. George Katona, *The Mass Consumption Society* (New York: McGraw-Hill, 1964).
4. Jennifer L. Drayton, 'Information Needs in the Furniture Market', unpublished report prepared for the Scottish Consumer Council (June 1977); Jennifer L. Drayton, *Consumer Interest in Product Labelling, Upholstered Furniture*, Reports on an Experiment in Informative Labelling (Office of Fair Trading, February 1981, and December 1982).
5. J. Jacoby, D. E. Speller and Carol A. Kohn, 'Brand Choice Behaviour as a Function of Information Load', *Journal of Marketing Research* (Feb. 1974).
6. Flemming Hansen, 'Psychological Theories of Consumer Choice', *Journal of Consumer Research*, vol. 3 (Dec. 1976).
7. Theodore Suranyi-Unger Jr, 'Consumer Behaviour and Consumer Well-Being: An Economist's Digest', *Journal of Consumer Research*, vol. 8 (Sept. 1981).
8. G. W. Allport, *The Nature of Prejudice* (Reading, Mass: Addison-Wesley, 1954).
9. See Philip Kotler, *Marketing Management: Analysis, Planning and Control* (Englewood Cliffs, N.J.: Prentice-Hall, 1967).
10. Ibid.
11. Ibid.
12. See C. Glenn Walters, *Consumer Behavior: Theory and Practice* (Glencoe, Ill.: Irwin, 1974).
13. Kotler, *Marketing Management*.
14. Alfred Marshall, *Principles of Economics* (London: MacMillan, 1927).
15. Francesco M. Nicosia, *Consumer Decision Processes: Marketing and Advertising Implications* (Englewood Cliffs, N.J.: Prentice-Hall, 1966).
16. See Walters, *Consumer Behavior*.
17. James F. Engel, David T. Kollat and Roger D. Blackwell, *Consumer Behavior* (New York: Holt, Rinehart & Winston, 1968).
18. Joseph Clawson, 'Lewin's Psychology and Motives in Marketing', in *Theory in Marketing*, ed. R. Cox and W. Alderson (Glencoe, Ill.: Irwin, 1950).
19. John A. Howard and Jagdish N. Sheth, *The Theory of Buyer Behavior* (New York: Wiley, 1969).
20. Michel J. Baker, *Marketing: An Introductory Text* (London: Macmillan, 1979).
21. Michael Laroche and John A. Howard, 'Nonlinear Relations in a Complex Model of Buyer Behaviour', *Journal of Consumer Research*, vol. 6 (Mar. 1980).
22. Gordon R. Foxall, *Marketing Behaviour: Issues in Managerial and Buyer Decision-Making* (London: Gower, 1981).
23. Bernard Berelson and Gary A. Steiner, *Human Behavior: An Inventory of Scientific Findings* (New York: Harcourt, Brace & World, 1963).
24. Peter J. McClure and John K. Ryans, 'Differences Between Retailers' and Consumers' Perceptions', *Journal of Marketing Research* (Feb. 1968).
25. Milton Blum and Valentine Appel, 'Consumer versus Management Reaction in New Package Development', *Journal of Applied Psychology* (Aug. 1961).

26. James C. Makens, 'Effect of Brand Preference upon Consumers' Perceived Taste of Turkey Meat', *Journal of Applied Psychology* (Aug. 1965).

27. Robert L. Brown, 'Wrapper Influence on the Perception of Freshness in Bread', *Journal of Applied Psychology* (Aug. 1958).

28. N. H. Pronko and J. W. Bowles, 'Identification of Cola Beverages I: A First Study', *Journal of Applied Psychology*, vol. 32 (1948). See also the following: Bowles and Pronko, 'Identification of Cola Beverages II: A Further Study', *Journal of Applied Psychology*, vol. 32 (1948); Pronko and Bowles, 'Identification of Cola Beverages III: A Final Study, *Journal of Applied Psychology*, vol. 33 (1949).

29. Ralph I. Allison and Kenneth P. Uhl, 'Influence of Beer Brand Identification on Taste Perception', *Journal of Marketing Research*, vol. 1 (Aug. 1964).

30. Mason Haire, 'Projective Techniques in Marketing Research', *Journal of Marketing* (1950).

31. Raymond A. Bauer and Stephen Greyser, *Advertising in America: The Consumer View*, Division of Research, Graduate School of Business Administration, Harvard University (1968).

32. J. A. Howard and J. N. Sheth, *The Theory of Buyer Behavior* (New York: Wiley, 1969).

33. C. L. Narayana and R. J. Markin, 'Consumer Behaviour and Product Performance: An Alternative Conceptualization', *Journal of Marketing*, vol. 39 (1975).

34. Jack Trout and Al Reis, 'The Positioning Era Cometh', *Advertising Age* (Apr. 1972).

35. Jack Springer, 'Put People in Positioning, New Products Expert Says', *Advertising Age* (Sept. 1972).

36. Berelson and Steiner, *Human Behavior.*

37. James H. Myers and William Reynolds, *Consumer Behavior and Marketing Management* (Boston: Houghton Mifflin, 1967).

38. Herbert E. Krugman, 'The Learning of Consumer Preference', *Journal of Marketing* (Apr. 1962).

39. Donald F. Cox, 'Clues for Advertising Strategists', *Harvard Business Review*, pt 1 (Sept.–Oct. 1961) pt II (Nov.–Dec. 1961).

40. Leo Bogart, *Strategy in Advertising* (New York: Harcourt, Brace & World, 1967).

41. T. S. Robertson, *Consumer Behavior* (Glenview, Ill.: Scott, Foresman & Co., 1970).

42. Ibid.

43. Carl I. Hovland, Irving L. Janis and Harold H. Kelley, *Communication and Persuasion* (Yale University Press, 1953).

44. Bogart, *Strategy in Advertising.*

45. Benton J. Underwood, 'Interference and Forgetting', *Psychological Review*, vol. 64 (1957).

46. Hermann Ebbinghaus, *Memory: A Contribution to Experimental Psychology*, trans. H. A. Ruger and C. E. Bussenius (New York: Teachers College, Columbia University, 1913).

47. Horace S. Schwerin and Henry H. Newell, *Persuasion in Marketing* (New York: Wiley, 1981).

48. Alfred A. Kuehn, 'Consumer Brand Choice as a Learning Process', *Journal of Advertising Research* (Dec. 1962).

49. Calvin S. Hall and Gardner Lindzey, *Theories of Personality* (New York: Wiley, 1957).

50. Berelson and Steiner, *Human Behavior.*

51. W. T. Tucker, 'Consumer Research: Status and Prospects', in *Consumer Behavior: Contemporary Research in Action*, ed. Robert J. Hillsway, Robert A. Mittelstaedt and M. Venkatesan (Boston: Houghton Mifflin, 1971).
52. Robert P. Brody and Scott M. Cunningham, 'Personality Variables and the Consumer Decision Process', *Journal of Marketing Research* (Feb. 1968).
53. Kathryn E. A. Villani and Yoram Wind, 'On the Usage of "Modified" Personality Trait Measures in Consumer Research', *Journal of Consumer Research*, vol. 2 (Dec. 1975).
54. Nicosia, *Consumer Decision Processes*.
55. Gardner Lindzey, *Assessment of Human Motives* (New York: Holt, Rinehart & Winston, 1960).
56. Ernest Dichter, *Handbook of Consumer Motivations* (New York: McGraw-Hill, 1964).
57. Harry Henry, *Motivation Research* (London: Crosby, Lockwood & Son Ltd, 1963).
58. Martin Fishbein, *Attitude Theory and Measurement* (New York: Wiley, 1967).
59. M. Bird and A. S. C. Ehrenberg, 'Consumer Attitudes and Brand Usage', *Journal of Marketing Research Society* (1970).
60. Timothy Joyce, 'Advertising, in *Consumer Behavior*, ed. A. S. Ehrenberg and F. G. Pyatt (Harmondsworth: Penguin, 1971).
61. H. C. Kelman, 'Attitudes are Alive and Well and Gainfully Employed in the Sphere of Action', *American Psychologist*, vol. 29, no. 5 (May 1974).
62. Foxall, *Marketing Behaviour*.
63. William D. Barclay, 'The Semantic Differential as an Index of Brand Attitude', *Journal of Advertising Research* (Mar. 1964).
64. Jon G. Udell, 'Can Attitude Measurement Predict Consumer Behavior?', *Journal of Marketing* (Oct. 1965).
65. Irving S. White, 'The Functions of Advertising in Our Culture', *Journal of Marketing* (July 1959).
66. Joseph A. Kahl, *The American Class Structure* (New York: Holt, Rinehart & Winson, 1957).
67. Stuart U. Rich and Subhash C. Jain, 'Social Class and Life Cycle as Predictors of Shopping Behavior', *Journal of Marketing Research* (Feb. 1968).
68. Pierre D. Martineau, 'The Pattern of Social Classes', in *Proceedings of the American Marketing Association*, ed. Robert L. Clewett (1957).
69. Sidney J. Levy, 'Social Class and Consumer Behavior' in *On Knowing the Consumer*, ed. Joseph W. Newman (New York: Wiley, 1966).
70. H. Gerth and C. W. Mills, *From Max Weber: Essays in Sociology* (London: Routledge & Kegan Paul, 1948).
71. L. Warner *et al.*, *Social Classes in America* (Chicago: Science Research Associates, 1949).
72. Solomon E. Asch, 'Effects of Group Pressure upon the Modification and Distortion of Judgments', in *Readings in Social Psychology*, ed. Eleanor E. Maccoby (New York: Holt, Rinehart & Winston, 1958).
73. M. Venkatesan, 'Experimental Study of Consumer Behavior, Conformity and Independence', *Journal of Marketing Research* (Nov. 1966).
74. James E. Stafford, 'Effects of Group Influences on Consumer Brand Preferences', *Journal of Marketing Research* (Feb. 1966).
75. Paul E. Green and Yoram Wind, *Multiattribute Decisions in Marketing*, (Hinsdale, Ill.: Dryden Press, 1973).

76. James Bettman and Michael A. Zins, 'Constructive Process in Consumer Choice', *Journal of Consumer Research*, vol. 4, no. 2 (Sept. 1977) pp. 75–85.
77. Jacob Jacoby, George J. Szybillo and Jacqueline Busato-Schach, 'Information Acquisition Behaviour in Brand Choice Situations', *Journal of Consumer Research*, vol. 3, no. 4 (Mar. 1977) pp. 209–16.
78. Jerome E. Scott and Peter Wright, 'Modelling an Organizational Buyer's Product Evaluation Strategy: Validity and Procedural Considerations', *Journal of Marketing Research*, vol. 13 (Aug. 1976) pp. 211–24.
79. James R. Bettman, Noel Capon and Richard Lutz, 'Cognitive Algebra in Multiattribute Attitude Models', *Journal of Marketing Research*, vol. 12, (May 1975) pp. 151–64.

Chapter 5

1. J. N. Sheth, *Is Industrial Marketing Really Different from Consumer Marketing?*' Working Paper 408 (University of Illinois, Champaign-Urbana, 1977); H. Henry, 'Goods or Services, Consumer or Industrial. The Rule is no Exception', *Admap* (Oct. 1979) pp. 520–6; J. A. Howard, *Consumer Behavior: Application of Theory* (New York: McGraw-Hill, 1977).
2. G. Balakrishna, 'Better Use of the Industrial Marketing Concept', *Industrial Marketing Management*, vol. 7 (1978) pp. 71–6; J. R. Pingry, 'Industrial Marketing: Myth or Reality', AMA Proceedings, *New Marketing for Social and Economic Progress* (1977) pp 483–6.
3. R. G. Cooper, 'Why New Industrial Products Fail', *Industrial Marketing Management* (Dec. 1975) pp. 315–26; National Industrial Conference Board, 'Why New Products Fail, October', *The Conference Board*, vol. 17 (Oct. 1964).
4. R. G. Cooper, 'The Dimensions of Industrial New Product Success and Failure', *Journal of Marketing*, vol. 43, no. 3 (Summer 1979) pp. 93–103; R. G. Cooper, 'Identifying Industrial New Product Success: Project New Prod', *Industrial Marketing Management*, vol. 8 (May 1979).
5. John Howard and Jagdish N. Sheth, *The Theory of Buyer Behavior* (New York: Wiley, 1969); F. M. Nicosia, *Consumer Decision Process: Marketing and Management Implications* (Englewood Cliffs, N.J.: Prentice-Hall, 1966).
6. J. N. Sheth, 'A Model of Industrial Buyer Behaviour', *Journal of Marketing*, vol. 37, (Oct. 1973) pp. 50–6.
7. J. Shingleton, 'The Customer as a Source of New Product Ideas', *Industrial Marketing Digest*, no. 1 (1981) pp. 107–13; E. A. Von Hippel, 'Has a Customer Already Developed Your Next Product', *Sloan Management Review*, vol. 8, no. 2, pp. 63–76; E. A. Von Hippel, 'The Dominant Role of the User in Semi-Conductor and Electronic Subassembly Process Innovation', *IEEE Transactions on Engineering Management*, vol. 18 (May 1977); E. A. Von Hippel, 'Transferring Process Equipment Innovations from Users–Innovators to Equipment Manufacturing Firms', *R & D Management*, vol. 8, no. 1 (1977); E. A. Von Hippel, 'Successful Industrial Products from Customer Ideas', *Journal of Marketing*, vol. 35, no. 1 (1978) pp. 39–49.

8. Sunil Mehrotra and William D. Wells, 'Psychographics and Buyer Behavior: Theory and Recent Empirical Findings', in *Consumer and Industrial Buying Behavior*, ed. A. G. Woodside, J. N. Sheth and P. D. Bennett (New York: North-Holland, 1977) pp. 49–65.
9. A. Koponen, 'Personality Characteristics of Purchases', *Journal of Advertising Research*, vol. 1 (1960) pp. 6–12.
10. E. Dichter, 'The Human Being in the Job of Buying', *The American Salesman*, vol. 4 (1959) pp. 42–53.
11. J. Pernica, 'The Second Generation of Market Segmentation Studies: An Audit of Buying Motivation', in *Life Style and Psychographics*, ed. W. D. Wells (Chicago: American Marketing Association, 1974) pp. 277–313.
12. W. D. Wells, 'Psychographics: A Critical Review', *Journal of Marketing Research*, vol. 12 (1975) pp. 196–213.
13. R. D. Hisrich and M. P. Peters, 'Selecting the Superior Segmentation Correlate', *Journal of Marketing*, vol. 38 (1974) pp. 60–3; J. H. Myers and J. Gutman, 'Life Style: The Essence of Social Class', in *Life Style and Psychographics*.
14. M. Fishbein, 'Attitude and the Prediction of Behavior', in *Readings in Attitude Theory and Measurement*, ed. M. Fishbein (New York: Wiley, 1967).
15. M. J. Rosenberg, 'Cognitive Structure and Attitudinal Effect', *Journal of Abnormal and Social Psychology*, vol. 53 (1956) pp. 367–72.
16. K. Lewin, *The Conceptual Representation and Measurement of Psychological Forces* (Durham, N.C.: Duke University Press, 1938).
17. J. R. Bettman, N. Capon and R. J. Lutz, 'Multiattribute Measurement Models and Multiattribute Attitude Theory: A Test of Construct Validity', *Journal of Consumer Research*, vol. 1 (1975) pp. 1–15.
18. J. E. Russo and B. A. Dosher, 'Dimensional Evaluation: A Heuristic for Binary Choice', unpublished working paper, Department of Psychology, University of California, San Diego (1975); J. R. Bettman and J. Jacoby, 'Patterns of Processing in Consumer Information Acquisition', in *Advances in Consumer Research Vol. III*, ed. B. B. Anderson (Chicago: The Association of Consumer Research, 1976) pp. 315–20; P. L. Wright and F. Barbour, 'The Relevance of Decision Process Models in Structuring Persuasive Messages', *Communication Research*, vol. 2 (1975) pp. 246–59; J. E. Russo and L. D. Rosen, 'An Eye Fixation Analysis of Multi-alternative Choice', *Memory and Cognition*, vol. 3 (1975) pp. 267–376.
19. M. J. Ryan and E. H. Bonfield, 'Fishbein's Inventions Model: A Test of External and Programmatic Validity', *Journal of Marketing*, vol. 44 (Spring 1980) pp. 82–95.
20. M. Fishbein and I. Ajzen, *Belief, Attitude Intention and Behavior* (Reading, Mass.: Addison-Wesley, 1975).
21. M. J. Ryan and E. H. Bonfield, 'Fishbein's Intentions Model: A Test of External and Programmatic Validity'; M. J. Ryan and E. H. Bonfield, 'The Fishbein Extended Model and Consumer Behavior', *Journal of Consumer Research*, vol. 2 (1975) pp. 118–36.
22. M. J. Ryan and E. H. Bonfield, 'Fishbein's Intentions Model: A Test of External and Programmatic Validity'.
23. J. R. Hauser and G. L. Urban, 'A Normative Methodology for Modelling Consumer Response to Innovation', *Operations Research*, vol. 25, no. 4 (July–Aug. 1977) pp. 579–619.
24. F. E. Webster Jr. and Y. Wind, 'A Generic Model for Understanding

Organisational Buying Behavior', *Journal of Marketing*, vol. 37, no. 2 (April 1972) pp. 12–19.

25. Sheth, 'A Model of Industrial Buyer Behavior'.

26. J. M. Choffray and G. L. Lilien, 'Assessing Response to Industrial Marketing Strategy', *Journal of Marketing*, vol. 42 (April 1978) pp. 20–31.

27. P. E. Green and V. Srinivasan, 'Conjoint Analysis Consumer Research: Issues and Outlook', *Journal of Consumer Research*, vol. 5 (Sept. 1978) pp. 102–23.

28. A. Madansky, 'On Conjoint Analysis and Quantal Choice Models', *Journal of Business*, vol. 53, no. 3, part 2 (1980).

29. M. Fishbein and I. Ajzen, 'Attitudes and Opinions', *Annual Review of Psychology* (1972) pp. 487–544.

30. A. Wicker, 'Attitudes Versus Actions: The Relationship of Verbal and Overt Behavioural Response to Attitude Objects', *Journal of Social Issues*, vol. 25 (1969) pp. 41–77.

31. B. Sternthal, A. Tybout and C. S. Craig, *Issues Underlying the Prediction of Behavior*, Working Paper (Graduate School of Management, North Western University, 1975).

32. P. J. Bem, 'Self-perception Theory', in *Advances in Experimental Social Psychology*, ed. L. Berkowitz (New York: Academic Press, 1972).

33. A. W. Wicker, 'An Examination of the "Other Variables" Explanation of Attitude–Behaviour Inconsistency', *Journal of Personality and Social Psychology*, vol. 19 (1977) pp. 18–30.

34. R. R. Dholakia, 'Influencing Buyer Behaviour: Process and Strategies', *European Journal of Marketing*, vol. 13, no. 5 (1979) pp. 282–93.

35. H. H. Kelley, 'The Process of Causal Attribution', *American Psychologist*, vol. 28 (1973) pp. 107–28.

36. G. I. Schulman and C. Worrall, 'Salience Patterns, Source Credibility and the Sleeper Effect', *Public Opinion Quarterly*, vol. 34 (1970) pp. 371–82.

37. K. Gronhaug and G. Zaltman, *Exploring Consumer Information Problems: Findings and Consumer Policy Implications*, ESSEC Seminar on Consumerism and Public Policy in the Field of Consumer Protection, Cergy, France (13 and 14 Dec. 1979).

38. R. W. Chestnut and J. Jacoby, 'Consumer Information Processing: Emerging Theories and Findings', in *Consumer Behavior and Industrial Buying behavior*.

39. J. R. Bettman, H. H. Kassarjian and R. J. Lutz, 'Consumer Behavior', in *Review of Marketing 1978*, ed. G. Zaltman and T. V. Bonoma (Chicago: American Marketing Association, 1978) pp. 194–229.

40. S. H. Chaffee and J. M. McLeod, 'Consumer Decisions and Information Use', in *Consumer Behavior: Theoretical Sources*, ed. S. Ward and T. S. Robertson :Englewood Cliffs, N.J. Prentice-Hall, 1973).

41. J. Jacoby, 'Consumer Reaction to Information Displays: Packaging and Advertising', in *Advertising and Public Interest*, ed. S. F. Divita (Chicago: American Marketing Association, 1974); J. Jacoby, D. E. Speller and C. A. Kohn, 'Brand Choice Behavior as a Function of Information Load', *Journal of Marketing Research*, vol. 11 (1974) pp. 63–9; J. Jacoby, D. E. Speller and C. A. Kohn-Berning, 'Brand Choice Behavior as a Function of Information Load: Replication and Extension', *Journal of Consumer Research*, vol. 1 (1974).

42. Wright and Barbour, 'The Relevance of Decision Process Models in Structuring Persuasive Messages'; Russo and Rosen, 'An Eye Fixation

Analysis of Multi-alternate Choice'; J. Jacoby, 'Consumer Psychology as a Social Psychological Sphere of Action', *American Psychologist*, vol. 30 (1975) pp. 977–87; J W. Payne, 'Heuristic Search Processes in Decision Making', in *Advances in Consumer Research Vol. III.*

43. A. Newal and H. Simon, *Human Problem Solving* (Englewood Cliffs, N.J.: Prentice-Hall, 1972).

44. W. K. Hall, 'Strategic Planning Product Innovation and the Theory of the Firm', *Journal of Business Policy*, vol. 3, no. 3 (1973).

45. R. W. Shoemaker and R. Shoaf, 'Behavioral Changes in the Trial of New Products', *Journal of Consumer Research*, vol. 2, no. 2 (1975), pp. 104–9.

46. J. A. Newall, 'A Perceived Risk Model of Industrial Buyer Behaviour: The Implication of Risk Handling Behaviour for Communication Policies in Industrial Marketing', PhD thesis, Cranfield Institute of Technology, School of Management (1975).

47. S. M. Cunningham, 'The Major Dimensions of Perceived Risk', in *Risk Taking and Information Handling in Consumer Behavior*, ed. D. F. Cox (Boston: Graduate School of Business Administration, Harvard University, 1967).

48. D. F. Cox, 'Risk Handling in Consumer Behavior', in *Risk Taking and Information Handling in Consumer Behavior.*

49. D. D. McFarlane and I. Horowitz, 'Risk and the Business Decision', *Business Horizons*, vol. X, no. 2 (Summer 1967) pp. 81–90.

50. L. B. Kaplan, G. J. Szybillo and J. Jacoby, 'Components of Perceived Risk in Product Purchase: A Cross-Validation', *Journal of Applied Psychology*, vol. 59, no. 3 (1959) pp. 287–91.

51. J. Jacoby and L. B. Kaplan, 'The Components of Perceived Risk', in *Proceedings of the Third Annual Conference of the Association for Consumer Research*, ed. M. Venkatesan (University of Chicago, 1972) pp. 382–93.

52. James Donnelly Jr. and Michael J. Etzel, 'Degrees of Product Newness and Early Trial', *Journal of Marketing Research*, vol. X (Aug. 1973) pp. 295–300.

53. Lyman E. Ostlund, 'Perceived Innovation Attributes as Predictors of Innovativeness', *Journal of Consumer Research*, vol. 1 (Sept. 1974) pp. 23–9.

54. Michael P. Peters and M. Venkatesan, 'Exploration of Variables Inherent in Adopting an Industrial Innovation', *Journal of Marketing Research*, vol. X (Aug. 1973).

55. S. T. Parkinson, 'The Role of Information in the Adoption of Industrial Innovation', MSc thesis, Department of Marketing, University of Strathclyde, Glasgow (1976).

56. P. J. Bern, M. A. Wallach and N. Kogan, 'Group Decision Making under Risk of Aversive Consequences', *Journal of Personnel and Social Psychology*, vol. 1 (1965) pp. 453–60.

57. N. Kogan and M. Zaleska, 'Levels of Risk Selected by Individuals and Groups when Deciding for Self and Others', *Proceedings of the 77th Annual Convention of the American Psychological Association*, vol. 4 (1969) pp. 423–4.

58. D. G. Marquis and H. J. Rietz, 'Effect of Uncertainty on Risk Taking in Individual and Group Decisions', *Behavioural Science*, vol. 14 (1969) pp. 281–8.

59. D. G. Pruitt and A. I. Teger, 'The Risky Shift in Group Betting', *Journal of Experimental Social Psychology*, vol. 5 (1969) pp. 115–26.

60. R. B. Zajonc, R. J. Wolosin, M. A. Wolosin and S. J. Shermann', 'Industrial and Group Risk-Taking in a Two-Choice Situation', *Journal*

of *Experimental Social Psychology*, vol. 4 (1968) pp. 89–106; R. B. Zajonc, R. J. Wolosin, M. A. Wolosin and S. J. Sherman, 'Group Risk-Taking in a Two-Choice Situation: Replication Extension and a Model', *Journal of Experimental Social Psychology*, vol. 5 (1969) pp. 127–40.

61. J. A. F. Stoner, 'Risky and Cautious Shifts in Group Decisions: The Influence of Widely Held Values', *Journal of Experimental Social Psychology*, vol. 4 (1968) pp. 442–59.

62. M. J. Baker and S. T. Parkinson, *Predicting the Diffusion of Industrial Product Innovation*, Final Report to the SSRC, Department of Marketing, University of Strathclyde, Glasgow (1976).

63. A. M. Kennedy, *The Adoption and Diffusion of New Industrial Products–A Literature Review*, Departmental Working Paper, IMS no. 1, Department of Marketing, University of Strathclyde, Glasgow (1979).

64. H. H. Kassarjian, 'Personality and Consumer Behaviour: A Review', *Journal of Marketing Research*, vol. 8 (1971) pp. 409–18.

65. D. P. Robin, L. M. Capella, S. R. Jones and B. S. Harmon, 'Attacking the Knowledge Gap Phenomenon'; W. Kamakura and R. J. Srivastava, 'Latent Trait Theory and Attitude Scaling: The Use of Information Functions for Item Selection and Handling of "Don't Know" Responses; J. C. Olson, 'Conceptualising and Measuring General Domains of Knowledge in Semantic memory'; G. Biehal and D. Chakravarti, 'Information Presentation Format and Task Goals as Determinants of Consumers' Memory Retrieval and Choice Processes'; R. R. Burke and T. K. Srull, 'The Acquisition and Transfer of Product Knowledge'; Eric J. Johnson, 'The "One-Sidedness" Effect and Learning to Make Better Decisions'; Ann Beattie, 'Effects of Product Knowledge on Comparison, Memory, Evaluation and Choice: A Model of Expertise in Consumer Decision-making'; Barbara Loken, 'Memory for Logically-Deduced Conclusions'; A. A. Mitchell and T. R. Smith, 'The Applicability of Computational Process Models for Representing Consumer Behavior'; E. J. Johnson and John Payne, 'Production Systems as Theories of Choice: Two Examples'; Barbara Hayes-Roth, 'A Cognitive Model of Planning'; T. R. Smith, R. Meyer and A. A, Mitchell, 'A Computational Process Model of Evaluation Based on the Cognitive Structuring of Episodic Knowledge'; E. F. Fern, 'Why Do Focus Groups Work: A Review and Integration of Small Group Process Theories'; M. C. Diamond, 'Right-Left: Male-Female: Premature Sexism in Consumer Research'; M. J. Ryan, 'Caveats Concerning Psychophysiological Measures in Consumer Research'; M. B. Gardner, 'Attribute Determinance–A Function of Past Memory'; J. Kisielius, 'The Role of Memory in Understanding Advertising Media Effects'. All these papers were presented at the Asociation for Consumer Research Meeting, St Louis (22–25 October 1981).

66. D. Brinberg, 'Validity Concepts in Research: An Integrative Approach'; A. A. Mitchell, 'Models of Memory: Implications for Measuring Knowledge Structures'; A. Taschian, R. O. Taschian and M. E. Slama, 'The Impact of Individual Differences on the Validity of Conjoint Analysis'; P. J. Cattin, 'Some Empirical Findings on the Estimation of Continuous Utility Functions in Conjoint Analysis'; L. Bozinoff, 'A Script Theoretic Approach to Information Processing'; J. E. Russo, 'When Can Process Tracing Data be Trusted?'; T. S. Robertson and J. Zielinski, 'Sociological Perspectives on Consumer Behavior'; J. Sheth, 'Consumer Research: Surpluses and Shortages'; F. Nicosia, 'Consumer Decision Processes: A Futuristic View'; H. Kassarjian, 'The Development of Consumer Be-

havior Theory'; J. P. Peter, 'Some Philosophical and Methodological Issues in Consumer Behavior Research'; A. G. Sawyer, 'Statistical Power and Effect Size in Consumer Research'. All these papers were presented at the Association for Consumer Research Meeting, St Louis (22–25 October 1981).

67. P. T. Robinson, C. W. Faris and Y. Wind, *Industrial Buying and Creative Marketing* (Boston: Allyn & Bacon, 1967).

68. Yoram Wind, 'Industrial Buying Behavior: Source Loyalty in the Purchase of Industrial Components', unpublished PhD dissertation, Graduate School of Business, Stanford University (1966).

69. Theodore Levitt, *Industrial Purchasing Behavior: A Study of Communication Effects* (Boston: Division of Research, Graduate School of Business Administration, Harvard University, 1965).

70. F. E. Webster Jr., 'On the Applicability of Communication Theory to Industrial Markets', *Journal of Marketing Research*, vol. V (Nov. 1968) pp. 426–8; F. E. Webster Jr., 'Word of Mouth Communication and Opinion Leadership in Industrial Markets', in *Marketing and the New Science of Planning*, ed. R. L. King, (Chicago: American Marketing Association, 1968) pp. 455–9.

71. Raymond E. Corey, *Industrial Marketing: Cases and Concepts* (Englewood Cliffs, N.J.: Prentice-Hall, 1968); D. H. Thain, C. B. Johnston and S. R. Leighton, *How Industry Buys: With Conclusions and Recommendations on Marketing to Industry*, a study sponsored by the Business Newspapers Association of Canada and the Toronto, Hamilton and Montreal Chapters of the National Industrial Advertisers Association (1959).

72. *How British Industry Buys*, a joint Industrial Market Research Ltd and Institute of Marketing Survey (1965).

73. H Buckner, *How British Industry Buys* (London: Hutchinson, 1967).

74. *Financial Times*, 'How British Industry Buys', Joint *Financial Times/* Industrial Market Research Ltd Survey (1974, 1978).

75. J. H. Platten, 'How Industry Buys', *Scientific American* (1955).

76. 'How Industry Buys–1970: A Study of the Systematic Procedure for Purchasing Materials, Component Parts and Equipment', *Scientific American* (1970).

77. Thain, Johnston and Leighton, *How Industry Buys: With Conclusions and Recommendations on Marketing to Industry*.

78. 'Readership Habits of Top and Middle Management', *Der Spiegel* (Oct. 1971).

79. Choffray and Lilien, 'Assessing Response to Industrial Marketing Strategy; W. J. Johnston, 'Communication Networks and Influence Patterns in Industrial Buying Behavior', PhD thesis, University of Pittsburgh, Pittsburgh, PA (1979); K. Gronhaug, 'Exploring a Complex Organisational Buying Decision', *Industrial Marketing Management* (6 Dec. 1977) pp. 439–44; R. E. Weigand, 'Identifying Industrial Buying Responsibility', *Journal of Marketing Research*, vol. 3 (Feb. 1966) pp. 81–4; J. R. McMillan, 'Role Differentiation in Industrial Buying Decisions', *Proceedings*, 1973 Educators Conference, Series no. 35, American Marketing Association, Chicago (1973) pp. 207–11; J. P. Kelly, 'Functions Performed in Industrial Purchasing Decisions with Implications for Marketing Strategy', *Journal of Business Research*, vol. 2 (Oct. 1974) pp. 420–34; J. M. Choffray, 'A Methodology for Investigating the Nature of the Industrial Adoption Process and the Differences in Perceptions and Evaluation Criteria Among Decision Participants', PhD thesis,

Massachusetts Institute of Technology, Cambridge, Mass. (1977); G. Zaltman, and T. V. Bonoma, 'Organisational Buying Behavior: Hypotheses and Directions', *Industrial Marketing Management*, vol. 6 (1977) pp. 53–60; A. G. Woodside and D. S. Sherrell, 'New Replacement Part Buying', *Industrial Marketing Management*, vol. 9 (1980) pp. 123–32.

80. Y. Wind, 'Organizational Buying Centre: A Research Agenda', in *Organizational Buying Behavior*, ed. G. Zaltman and T. V. Bonoma, (American Marketing Association, 1978) pp. 67–76.

81. R. E. Spekman and L. W. Stern, 'Environmental Uncertainty and Buying Group Structure: An Empirical Investigation', *Journal of Marketing*, vol. 43 (Spring 1978) pp. 54–64; R. E. Spekman, 'A Contingency Approach to Power Relationships within the Industrial Buying Task Group', unpublished PhD dissertation, Evanston, Northwestern University (1977); F. Nicosia and Y. Wind, *Behavioral Models for Market Analysis* (Hinsdale, Ill.: Dryden Press, 1977).

82. Ibid.

83. *Financial Times*, 'How British Industry Buys'.

84. P. Doyle, A. G. Woodside and P. Nichell, 'Oganisational Buying in New Task and Rebuy Situations', *Industrial Marketing Management*, vol. 8 (1979) pp. 7–11.

85. Robinson, Faris and Wind, *Industrial Buying and Creative Marketing.*

86. F. E. Webster and Y. Wind, *Organisational Buying Behavior* (Englewood Cliffs, N.J.: Prentice-Hall, 1972).

87. B. Klass, 'What Factors Affect Industrial Buying Decisions', *Industrial Marketing* (May 1961) pp. 33–8.

88. Sales Management, 'Profiles in Purchasing', *Sales Management* (1963).

89. F. E. Kast and J. E. Rosenzweig, 'General Systems Theory: Applications for Organisational Management', *Journal of the Academy of Management*, vol. 15 (1972) pp. 447–68.

90. K. Gronhaug, 'Exploring Environmental Influences in Organisational Buying', *Journal of Marketing Research* (Aug. 1976).

91. F. E. Webster Jr., 'Modelling the Industrial Buying Process', *Journal of Marketing Research* (Nov. 1965) pp. 370–76.

92. R. E. Weigand, 'Why Studying the Purchasing Agent is Not Enough', *Journal of Marketing*, vol. 32 (Jan. 1968) pp. 41–5.

93. P. Allen, 'Psychology of the Buying Decision', *Purchasing and Supply Management* (Dec. 1977) pp. 9–12.

94. E. H. Bonfield and T. W. Speh, 'Dimensions of Purchasing's Role in Industry', *Journal of Purchasing and Materials Management* (Summer 1977) pp. 10–17.

95. W. Feldman and R. Cardozo, 'The "Industrial" Revolution and Models of Buying Behaviour', *Journal of Purchasing* (Nov. 1969) pp. 77–88.

96. P. Lister, 'Identifying and Evaluating the Purchasing Influence', *IMRA Journal* (Aug. 1967) pp. 190–9.

97. J. M. Browning and N. B. Zabriskie, 'Professionalism in Purchasing: A Status Report', *Journal of Purchasing and Materials Management* (Fall 1980) pp. 2–10.

98. G. Strauss, 'Tactics of Lateral Relationships: The Purchasing Agent', *Administrative Science Quarterly* (Sept. 1962); G. Strauss, 'Work-Flow Frictions, Interfunctional Rivalry and Professionalism: A Case Study of Purchasing Agents', *Human Organisations*, vol. 23 (1964) pp. 137–49.

99. B. G. S. James, 'Emotional Buying in Industrial Markets', *Scientific Business* (Spring 1966).

100. J. Marrian, 'Marketing Characteristics of Industrial Goods and Buyers', in *The Marketing of Industrial Products*, ed. A. Wilson (London: Hutchinson, 1965) pp. 10–33.
101. Lister, 'Identifying and Evaluating the Purchasing Influence'.
102. Robinson, Faris and Wind, *Industrial Buying and Creative Marketing*.
103. G. A. Luffman, 'The Marketing of Industrial Raw Materials; the Role of Information in the Purchasing Process', MSc thesis, University of Manchester (May 1973).
104. J. G. White, 'Some Aspects of the Marketing of Machine Tools in Great Britain', PhD thesis, University of Manchester (1969).
105. Woodside and Sherrell, 'New Replacement Part Buying'.
106. 'The Purchasing Agent Gains More Clout', *Business Week* (13 Jan. 1975) pp. 62–3.
107. M. M. Bird and E. M. Mazze, 'Measuring the Efficiency of the Industrial Purchasing Department', *Industrial Marketing Management*, vol. 5, no. 1 (March 1976) pp. 17–23.
108. D. R. Rink, 'The Product Life Cycle in Formulating Purchasing Strategy', *Industrial Marketing Management*, vol. 5, no. 4 (Aug. 1976) pp. 231–42.
109. R. E. Spekman, 'Information and Influence: An Exploratory Investigation of the Boundary Role Person's Basis of Power', *Academy of Management Journal*, vol. 22 (March 1979).
110. P. Guillet de Monthoux, 'A Study of Organisational Buying for Industrial Marketing Purpose', paper presented at the Marketing Workshop of the European Marketing Education Association (May 1973).
111. K. J. Blois, 'The Growing Influence of Large Buyers', *IMRA Journal* (Feb. 1972) pp. 2–8.
112. Luffman, 'The Marketing of Industrial Raw Materials; the Role of Information in the Purchasing Process'.
113. White, 'Some Aspects of the Marketing of Machine Tools in Great Britain'.
114. M. A. Abdelrehim, 'Organisational Buying Behaviour: An Investigation into the Composition and Functions of the Buying Centre in Industrial Buying and its Marketing Implications', PhD thesis, University of Manchester (Dec. 1975).
115. A. Wallace, 'A Study of the Buying Process for New Products by Intermediate Marketing Organisations in the Channels of Distribution for Grocery Products', PhD thesis, University of Manchester (1976).
116. G. Brand, *The Industrial Buying Decision: Implications for the Sales Approach in Industrial Marketing* (London: Cassell, Associated Business Programmes, 1972).
117. L. Fisher, *Industrial Marketing, An Analytical Approach to Planning and Execution* (New York: Business Books, 1976); R. W. Hill, 'The Nature of Industrial Buying Decision', *Industrial Marketing Management* (Oct. 1972) pp. 45–55; T. J. Hillier, 'Decision-Making in the Corporate Industrial Buying Process', *Industrial Marketing Management*, vol. 4 (1975) pp. 99–106.
118. A. G. Woodside and J. L. Taylor, 'Observations of Buyer and Seller Transactions', *Advances in Consumer Research VI, Proceedings of the Association for Consumer Research*, 1977 Meetings, ed. Keith Hunt (forthcoming).
119. Robinson, Faris and Wind, *Industrial Buying and Creative Marketing*.
120. Ibid.

121. T. J. Hillier, 'Decision Making in the Industrial Purchasing Process', PhD thesis, Management Centre, University of Bradford (1973).
122. Brand, *The Industrial Buying Decision: Implications for the Sales Approach in Industrial Marketing.*
123. Webster, 'Modelling the Industrial Buying Process'.
124. James R. McMillan, 'Role Differentiation in Industrial Buying Decisions', in *Combined Proceedings Series 35*, ed. T. V. Greer, American Marketing Asociation, Chicago (1973) pp. 207–11; John F. Grashof and G. P. Thomas, 'Industrial Buying Centre Responsibilities: Self Versus Other Member Evaluations of Importance', in *Educators' Proceedings, Marketing 1776–1976 and Beyond*, ed. Kenneth F. Bernhardt, Series 39, American Marketing Association, Chicago (1976) pp. 344–7; J. R. Cooley, D. W. Jackson and L. L. Ostrom, 'Analysing the Relative Power of Participants in Industrial Buying Decisions', in *Educators' Proceedings, Contemporary Marketing Thoughts*, ed. B. A. Greenberg and Danny N. Bellenger, Series 41, American Marketing Association, Chicago (1977) pp. 243–6; J. A. Bellizzi, 'Product Type and the Relative Influence of Buyers in Commercial Construction', *Industrial Marketing Management*, vol. 8 (June 1979) pp. 213–20.
125. *Financial Times*, 'How British Industry Buys'.
126. Wind, 'Organisational Buying Centre: A Research Agenda'.
127. Webster and Wind, *Organisational Buying Behaviour.*
128. Sheth, 'A Model of Industrial Buyer Behaviour'.
129. K. K. Mackenzie, *A Theory of Group Structures: Vol. 1, Basic Theory: Vol. II, Empirical Tests* (New York: Gordon & Breach, 1976).
130. H. Hakansson, B. Wootz, O. Anderson and Paul Hangard, 'Industrial Marketing as an Organisational Problem', *European Journal of Marketing*, vol. 13, no. 3 (1979) pp. 81–93.
131. Paul Busch and D. T. Wilson, 'An Experimental Analysis of a Salesman's Expert and Referent Bases of Social Power in the Buyer-Seller Dyad', *Journal of Marketing Research*, vol. 13 (Feb. 1976) pp. 3–12.
132. P. B. L. Guillet de Monthoux, 'Organisational Mating and Industrial Marketing Conservatism–Some Reasons why Industrial Market Managers resist Marketing Theory', *Industrial Marketing Management*, vol. 4 (1975) pp. 25–36.
133. H. Hakansson and C. Ostberg, 'Industrial Marketing: An Organisational Problem', *Industrial Marketing Management*, vol. 4 (1975) pp. 113–23.
134. H. G. Gemunden, *Managing Inter-Organisational Conflict: Efficient Interaction Strategies for Buyer and Seller Organisation*, paper presented at 10th Annual Workshop on Marketing Research at EAARM Copenhagen (March 1981).
135. S. T. Parkinson, 'User-Supplier Interaction in New Product Development', PhD thesis, Department of Marketing, University of Strathclyde, Glasgow (1980).
136. J. N. Sheth, 'Recent Developments in Organisational Buying Behavior', in *Industrial Buying Behavior.*
137. Zaltman, in *Review of marketing 1978.*
138. See C. Glenn Walters, *Consumer Behavior: Theory and Practice* (Glencoe, Ill.: Irwin, 1974).
139. Lewin, *The Conceptual Representation and Measurement of Psychological Forces.*
140. Nicosia, *Consumer Decision Process: Marketing and Management Implications.*
141. A. R. Andreasen, 'Attitudes and Customer Behavior: A Decision

Model', in *New Research in Marketing*, ed. Lee E. Preston (Berkeley, California: Institute of Business and Economic Research, 1965) pp. 1–16.

142. J. F. Engel, D. T. Kollat and R. D. Blackwell, *Consumer Behavior*, 3rd edn, (Hinsdale, Ill.: Dryden Press, 1978).

143. J. Clawson, 'Lewin's Psychology and Motives in Marketing', in *Theory in Marketing*, ed. R. Cox and W. Alderson (Glencoe, Ill.: Irwin, 1950).

144. Howard and Sheth, *The Theory of Buyer Behavior*.

145. J. U. Farley and L. Winston Ring, 'Empirical Specification of a Buyer Behavior Model', *Journal of Marketing Research* (11 Feb. 1974) pp. 89–96.

146. Frank M. Bass, Edgar A. Pessemier and Donald R. Lehmann, 'An Experimental Study of Relationships between Attitudes, Brand Preference and Choice', *Behavioural Science*, vol. 17 (Nov. 1972) pp. 532–41; Paul E. Green and F. J. Carmone, *Multidimensional Scaling and Related Techniques in Marketing Analysis* (Boston: Allyn & Bacon, 1970); Paul E. Green and Vithala R. Rao, *Applied Multidimensional Scaling: A Comparison of Approaches and Algorithms* (New York: Holt, Rinehart & Winston, 1972); William L. Wilkie and Edgar A. Pessemier, 'Issues in Marketing's Use of Multi-Attribute Attitude Models', *Journal of Marketing Research*, vol. 10 (Nov. 1973) pp. 428–41.

147. David Aaker, 'Using Buyer Behaviour Models to Improve Marketing Decisions', *Journal of Marketing*, vol. 34 (July 1970) pp. 52–7; A. S. C. Ehrenberg, 'Toward an Integrated Theory of Consumer Behaviour', *Journal of the Market Research Society*, vol. 11 (Oct. 1969) pp. 305–37.

148. Donald R. Lehmann, T. V. O'Brien, J. U. Farley and J. A. Howard, 'Some Empirical Contributions to Buyer Behavior Theory', *Journal of Consumer Research*, vol. 1 (Dec. 1974) pp. 43–55.

149. Thomas F. Juster, *Consumer Buying Intentions and Purchase Probability* (Princeton, N.J.: National Bureau of Economic Research, 1964).

150. Green and Rao, *Applied Multidimensional Scaling: A Comparison of Approaches and Algorithms*.

151. Johan Arndt, 'Role of Product-Related Conservations in the Diffusion of a New Product', *Journal of Marketing Research*, vol. 4 (Aug. 1967) pp. 291–5.

152. G. R. Foxall, 'Marketing Models of Buyer Behaviour: A Critical View', *European Research*, vol. 8 (Sept. 1980) pp. 195–206.

153. M. J. Baker, 'Industrial Buying Behaviour and the Adoption of Innovation', in *Industrial Innovation*, ed. M. J. Baker (London: Macmillan, 1979).

154. A. M. Kennedy, 'Marketing Models of Buyer Behaviour: A Comment', *European Research*, vol. 7, no. 7 (April 1981).

155. Webster, 'Modelling the Industrial Buying Process'.

156. R. M. Cyert and T. G. March, *A Behavioral Theory of the Firm* (Englewood Cliffs, N.J.: Prentice-Hall, 1973).

157. Robinson, Faris and Wind, *Industrial Buying and Creative Marketing*.

158. Webster and Wind, 'A Generic Model for Understanding Organisational Buying Behavior'.

159. Robinson, Faris and Wind, *Industrial Buying and Creative Marketing*.

160. Webster and Wind, 'A Generic Model for Understanding Organisational Buying Behavior'.

161. Sheth, 'A Model of Industrial Buyer Behavior'.

162. Choffray and Lilien, 'Assessing Response to Industrial Marketing Strategy'.

163. Ibid.

164. 'A Methodology for Investigating the Nature of the Industrial Adoption

Process and the Differences in Perceptions and Evaluation Criteria Among Decision Participants'.

165. R. N. Cardozo and J. W. Cagley, 'Experimental Study of Industrial Buying Behaviour', *Journal of Marketing Research*, vol. 8 (Aug. 1971) pp. 329–34.

166. M. Cunningham and J. White, 'The Determinants of Choice of Supplier', *European Journal of Marketing*, vol. 7, no. 3 (Winter 1973).

167. D. R. Lehmann and J. O'Shaughnessy, 'Difference in Attribute Importance for Different Industrial Products', *Journal of Marketing*, vol. 38 (April 1974) pp. 36–42.

168. Hakansson *et al.*, 'Industrial Marketing as an Organisational Problem'.

169. Choffray and Lilien, 'Assessing Response to Industrial Marketing Strategy'.

170. Bellizzi, 'Product Type and Relative Influence of Buyers in Commercial Construction'.

171. F. Schuster, 'Bartering Processes in Industrial Buying and Selling', *Industrial Marketing Management*, vol. 7 (1978) pp. 119–27; Jack G. Kaikati, 'The Reincarnation of Barter Trade as a Marketing Tool', *Journal of Marketing*, vol. 40 (April 1976) pp. 17–24.

172. Wind, 'Organisational Buying Centre: A Research Agenda'.

173. Lowel E. Crow, Richard W. Olshavsky and John O. Summers, 'Industrial Buyers' Choice Strategies: A Protocol Analysis', *Journal of Marketing Research*, vol. 17 (Feb. 1981) pp. 34–44.

174. H. H. Kassarjian, 'Content Analysis in Consumer Research', *Journal of Consumer Research*, vol. 4 (June 1977) pp. 8–18.

175. J. R. Bettman, 'Data Collection and Analysis Approaches for Studying Consumer Information Processing', in *Advances in Consumer Research*, ed. W. D. Perreault Jr (Chicago: Association for Consumer Research) vol. 4 (1976) pp. 342–8.

176. J. W. Payne, M. L. Braunstein and J. S. Carroll, 'Exploring Predecisional Behaviour: An Alternative Approach to Decision Research', *Organisational Behaviour and Human Performance*, vol. 22 (1978) pp. 17–44.

177. Russo and Rosen, 'An Eye Fixation Analysis of Multi-alternate Choice'.

178. A. M. Kennedy, *Analysing Industrial Buyer Behaviour: a Descriptive Model of the Purchase Decision for a Specific Raw Material–Steel Plate*, Departmental Working Paper, University of Strathclyde, Glasgow (Oct. 1981).

179. R. M. Cyert, H. A. Simon and D. B. Trow, 'Observations of a Business Decision', *Journal of Business*, vol. 29 (1959) pp. 237–48.

180. Andrew M. Pettigrew, 'The Industrial Purchasing Decision as a Political Process', *European Journal of Marketing*, vol. 5 (Feb. 1975) pp. 4–19; J. D. Jick, 'Mixing Qualitative and Quantitative Methods: Triangulation in Action', *Administrative Science Quarterly*, vol. 24 (1979) pp. 602–11; John U. Farley, J. M. Hulbert and D. Weinstein, 'Price Setting and Volume Planning by Two European Industrial Companies: A Study and Comparison of Decision Processes', *Journal of Marketing*, vol. 44 (Winter 1980) pp. 46–54.

181. E. Braun, 'Constellations for Manufacturing Innovation', *OMEGA*, vol. 9, no. 3 (1981) pp. 247–53.

182. M. D. Cohen, J. G. March and Johan P. Olsen, 'A Garbage Can Model of Organisational Choice', *Administrative Science Quarterly*, vol. 17 (1972) pp. 1–25.

Chapter 6

1. S. H. Britt, 'The Right Marketing Mix for the Corporate Imagery Mix', *Business Horizons*, vol. XIV (Feb. 1971) pp. 87–8.
2. E. J. McCarthy, *Basic Marketing: A Managerial Approach*, 7th edn (Homewood, Ill.: Irwin, 1981) pp. 431–3.
3. Colin Gilligan and Geoffrey Crowther, *Advertising Management* (Oxford: Philip Allan, 1976) pp. 7–8.
4. S. W. Dunn and A. M. Barban, *Advertising: Its Role in Modern Marketing*, 5th edn (Hinsdale, Ill.: Dryden Press, 1982) p. 7–11.
5. Wilbur Schramm, *The Process and Effects of Mass Communications* (Urbana, Ill.: University of Illinois Press, 1955) p. 3.
6. John A. Howard, *Consumer Behavior: Application of Theory* (New York: McGraw-Hill, 1977) p. 9.
7. John A. Howard and J. N. Sheth, *The Theory of Buyer Behavior* (New York: Wiley, 1969); John A. Howard and l. Ostlund, *Buyer Behavior: Theoretical and Empirical Foundations* (New York: Alfred A. Knopf, 1973).
8. B. Ryan and N. Gross, 'The Diffusion of Hybrid Seed Corn in Two Iowa Communities', *Rural Sociology*, vol. VIII (March 1943) pp. 15–24.
9. George S. Day, 'Attitude Change, Media and Word of Mouth', *Journal of Advertising Research*, vol. II (Dec. 1971) pp. 31–40.
10. Labour Party, *Opposition Green Paper: Advertising* (London: The Labour Party, 1972) p. 55.
11. Donald F. Cox, 'Clues for Advertising Strategists', *Harvard Business Review*, vol. 39 (Nov.–Dec. 1961) p. 160.
12. Scott Ward, 'Consumer Socialization', *Journal of Consumer Behavior*, vol. 1 (Sept. 1974) p. 2.
13. Scott Ward, 'Children's Reactions to Commercials', *Journal of Advertising Research*, vol. 12 (April 1972) pp. 37–45.
14. Glen Smith, 'Children as the Target for Advertising', *Advertising*, no. 67 (Spring 1981) pp. 40–2; 'Research into the Effects of Advertising on Children', in Oyez Intelligence Report, *Advertising and Marketing to Children* (London: Oyez Publishing, 1980) pp. 54–62.
15. R. P. Adler *et al.*, *The Effects of Television Advertising on Children: Review and Recommendations* (Lexington, Mass.: Lexington Books, 1980).
16. The surveys in question are: Institute of Practitioners in Advertising, *Attitudes to Television Advertising* (London: Institute of Practitioners in Advertising, 1967); R. A. Bauer and S. A. Greyser, *Advertising in America: The Consumer View* (Cambridge, Mass.: Harvard Business School, 1968); Advertising Association, *Public Attitudes to Advertising– 1976* (London: The Advertising Association, 1976); Advertising Association, *Public Attitudes to Advertising–1980/81* (London: The Advertising Association, 1981).
17. D. H. Robertson, *Lectures on Economic Principles* (London: Staples, 1958) p. 169.
18. The original sources are: Daniel Starch, *Principles of Advertising* (Chicago: A. W. Shaw, 1923); E. K. Strong, *The Psychology of Selling* (New York: McGraw-Hill, 1925); C. H. Sandage and Vernon Fryburger, *Advertising Theory and Practice* (Homewood, Ill.: Irwin, 1935; 9th edn 1975) esp. pp. 79–86; Robert C. Lavidge and Gary A. Steiner, 'A Model for Predictive Measurements of Advertising Effectiveness', *Journal of Marketing*, vol. 25 (Oct. 1961) pp. 59–62; Russell H. Colley, *Defining*

Advertising Goals for Measured Advertising Results (New York: Association of National Advertisers, 1961) reprinted in *Modern Marketing Management*, ed. R. J. Lawrence and M. J. Thomas (Harmondsworth: Penguin, 1971) pp. 282–92; William J. McGuire, 'An Information Processing Model of Advertising Effectiveness', *Symposium on Behavioral and Management Science in Marketing* (Chicago: University of Chicago, 1969); M. Wayne DeLozier, *The Marketing Communications Process* (New York: McGraw-Hill, 1976) esp. pp. 219–20.

19. Thomas S. Robertson, *Consumer Behavior* (Chicago: Scott, Foresman, 1970) p. 46.
20. K. S. Palda, 'The Hypothesis of a Hierarchy of Effects: A Partial Evaluation', *Journal of Marketing Research*, vol. III (Feb. 1966) pp. 13–24.
21. B. Copland, 'An Evaluation of Conceptual Frameworks for Measuring Advertising Results', *Proc. Ninth Annual Conference* (New York: Advertising Research Foundation, 1963).
22. Hugh Murray, 'So You Know How Advertising Works?', *Mangement Decision*, vol. 17, no. 5 (1979) pp. 369–90.
23. Michael L. Ray, 'Marketing Communication and the Hierarchy of Effects', in *New Models For Mass Communication Research: Sage Annual Review of Communication Research, Volume II*, ed. Peter Clarke (Beverly Hills, California: Sage Publications, 1973) pp. 147–76.
24. H. E. Krugman, 'The Impact of Television Advertising: Learning without Involvement', *Public Opinion Quarterly*, vol. 29 (Fall 1965) pp. 349–56.
25. Brian Sternthal and C. Samuel Craig, *Consumer Behavior: An Information Processing Perspective* (Englewood Cliffs, N.J.: Prentice-Hall, 1982) p. 313.
26. Ibid, p. 67.
27. Ibid, p. 61.
28. George A. Miller, *The Psychology of Communication* (Harmondsworth: Penguin, 1970) pp. 21–49.
29. Peter L. Wright, 'The Harassed Decision Maker', *Journal of Applied Psychology*, vol. 59, no. 5 (1974) pp. 555–61.
30. Al Ries and Jack Trout, *Positioning: The Battle for Your Mind* (New York: McGraw-Hill, 1980) esp. pp. 33–42.
31. Keith Crosier, 'A New Strategy for Advertising to Over-Communicated Target Audiences', *Quarterly Review of Marketing*, vol. 7 (July 1982) pp. 13–21.
32. Ibid, p. 18.
33. Harold D. Lasswell, 'The Structure and Function of Communication in Society', in *Mass Communications*, ed. Wilbur Schramm, (Urbana, Ill.: University of Illinois Press, 1960) p. 117.
34. The three recent texts are: M. Wayne DeLozier, *The Marketing Communications Process* (New York: McGraw-Hill, 1976) esp. pp. 1–4, ,16–21, 170–3; Larry Percy and John R. Rossiter, *Advertising Strategy: A Communication Theory Approach* (New York: Praeger, 1980) esp. pp. 13–17; David A. Aaker and John G. Myers, *Advertising Management*, 2nd edn, (Englewood Cliffs, N.J.: Prentice-Hall, 1982) esp. pp. 233–5.
35. Wilbur Schramm and Donald F. Roberts (eds), *The Process and Effects of Mass Communications* (Urbana, Ill.: University of Illinois Press, 1971) p. 32.
36. David Aitchison, 'What Really Happens in TV Breaks', *Marketing* (Oct. 1977) pp. 41–5; Stephen Curtis, 'The Strange Case of the ITV Morons', *Campaign* (14 July 1978) p. 19.

37. For instance, see D. S. Leather, 'Fear-inducing Advertising', *Journal of the Institute of Health Education*, vol. 19, no. 2 (1981) pp. 45–6.

38. Aaker and Myers, *Advertising Management*, p. 35.

39. Ray, 'Marketing Communication and the Hierarchy of Effects', pp. 167–8.

40. Vivienne G. T. Price, 'Constraints and Opportunities in Children's Television Advertising', in *Researching Children*, Seminar Proceedings (Aarhus, Denmark: ESOMAR, Oct. 1978) p. 155.

41. Percy and Rossiter, *Advertising Strategy: A Communication Theory Approach*, p. 106.

42. Irving L. Janis and Seymour Feshbach, 'Effects of Fear Arousing Communications', *Journal of Abnormal Social Psychology*, vol. 48, no. 1 (1953) pp. 78–92.

43. Michael L. Ray and William L. Wilkie, 'Fear: The Potential of an Appeal Neglected by Marketing', *Journal of Marketing*, vol. 34 (Jan. 1970) pp. 54–62.

44. Leathar, 'Fear-Inducing Advertising', pp. 42–4.

45. Brian Sternthal and C. Samuel Craig, 'Humor in Advertising', *Journal of Marketing*, vol. 37 (Oct. 1973) pp. 12–18.

46. Leathar, 'Fear-Inducing Advertising', pp. 50–5.

47. For instance, see Major Steadman, 'How Sexy Illustrations Affect Brand Recall', *Journal of Advertising Research*, vol. 9 (Feb. 1969) pp. 15–20; Bruce J. Morrison and Richard C. Sherman, 'Who Responds to Sex in Advertising?', *Journal of Advertising Research*, vol. 12 (April 1972) pp. 15–19; Robert Peterson and Rodger Kerin, 'The Female Role in Advertisements: Some Experimental Evidence', *Journal of Marketing*, vol. 41 (Oct. 1977) pp. 59–63; M. Wayne Alexander and Ben Judd (Jr.), 'Do Nudes Enhance Brand Recall?', *Journal of Advertising Research*, vol. 18 (Feb. 1978) pp. 47–50.

48. Carl I. Hovland, Arthur A. Lumsdaine and Fred D. Sheffield, *Experiments in Mass Communication*, vol. III (Princeton: Princeton University Press, 1949) pp. 201–27.

49. E. W. J. Faison, 'Effectiveness of One-Sided Versus Two-Sided Mass Communications in Advertising', *Public Opinion Quarterly*, vol. 25 (Fall 1961) pp. 468–9.

50. R. L. Rosnow and E. J. Robinson (eds), *Experiments in Persuasion* (New York: Academic Press, 1967) pp. 101–2.

51. Carl I. Hovland, Irving L. Janis and H. H. Kelley, *Communication and Persuasion* (New Haven: Yale University Press, 1953) pp. 103–5.

52. Roger Collis, 'To Sell: Accentuate the Familiar, Eliminate the Negative and Sprinkle in the Positive', *International Management*, vol. 35 (Oct. 1980) pp. 53–5.

53. William J. McGuire, 'Personality and Susceptibility to Social Influence', in *Handbook of Personality Theory and Research*, ed. Edgar F. Borgatta and William W. Lambert (New York: Academic Press, 1969) pp. 1130–87.

54. DeLozier, *The Marketing Communications Process*, pp. 76–7.

55. Philip G. Zimbardo, Matisyo Weisenberg, Ira Firestone and Burton Levy, 'Communicator Effectiveness in Producing Public Conformity and Private Attitude Change', *Journal of Personality*, vol. 33 (March 1965) pp. 233–55.

56. Albert Mehrabian and Morton Weiner, 'Decoding of Inconsistent Communications', *Journal of Personality and Social Psychology*, vol. 6, no. 1 (1967) pp. 109–14.

57. D. Lowe Watson, 'Advertising and the Buyer–Seller Relationship', *Journal of the Market Research Society*, vol. 11 (April 1969) pp. 125–46; reprinted in *Modern Marketing Management*, ed. R. J. Lawrence and M. J. Thomas (Harmondsworth: Penguin, 1971) pp. 332–47, esp. pp. 331–42.

58. Aaker and Myers, *Advertising Management*, p. 459; DeLozier, *The Marketing Communications Process*, pp. 22, 73, 85, 87.

59. Marshall McLuhan, *Understanding Media: The Extensions of Man* (New York: McGraw-Hill, 1964) ch. 1.

60. William S. Blair, 'Attitude Research and the Qualitative Value of Magazines', *Attitude Research at Sea*, ed. Lee Adler and Irving Crespi, (Chicago: American Marketing Association, 1966) pp. 153–62.

61. See, for example, Gordon Oliver, *Marketing Today* (London: Prentice-Hall, 1980) p. 222.

62. Timothy Joyce, 'Attitude Research as a Measure of Media Values', *Admap*, vol. 17 (Dec. 1981) pp. 609–14.

63. Percy and Rossiter, *Advertiing Strategy: A Communication Theory Approach*, p. 173.

64. Aaker and Myers, *Advertising Management*, pp. 459–61.

65. Percy and Rossiter, *Advertising Strategy: A Communication Theory Approach*, p. 180.

66. James Coleman, Elihu Katz and Herbert Menzel, 'Doctors and New Drugs', in *The Effects of Mass Communications*, ed. Joseph T. Klapper, (Glencoe, Ill.: The Free Press, 1960) pp. 103–4; Gert Assmuss, 'An Empirical Investigation into the Perception of Vehicle Source Effects', *Journal of Advertising*, vol. 7 (Winter 1978) pp. 4–10; Douglas A. Fuchs, 'Two Source Effects in Magazine Advertising', *Journal of Marketing Research*, vol. 1 (Aug. 1964) pp. 59–62; David A. Aaker and Philip K. Brown, 'Evaluating Vehicle Source Effects', *Journal of Advertising Research*, vol. 12 (Aug. 1972) pp. 11–16.

67. Sonia Yuspeh, *On-Air: Are We Testing the Message or the Medium?*, Conference Paper (New York: J. Walter Thomson Co., November 1977), reported in Aaker and Myers, *Advertising Management*, pp. 466–7.

68. Keith Crosier, 'Puzzle Advertising', *Proc. Fourteenth Annual Conference* (Dublin: Marketing Education Group, July 1981) pp. 311–29.

69. Hovland, Lumsdaine and Sheffield, *Experiments in Mass Communication*, pp. 188–9; Carl I. Hovland and Walter Weiss, 'The Influence of Source Credibility on Communication Effectiveness', *Public Opinion Quarterly*, vol. 15 (Winter 1951–2) pp. 635–50; Herbert Kelman and Carl I. Hovland, 'Reinstatement of the Communicator in Delayed Measurement of Opinion Change', *Journal of Abnormal and Social Psychology*, vol. 48, no. 3 (1953) pp. 327–35.

70. DeLozier, *The Marketing Communications Process*, p. 79.

71. E. K. Strong, 'The Effect of Length of Series upon Recognition', *Psychological Review*, vol. 19 (Jan. 1912) pp. 44–7.

72. Hubert A. Zielske, 'The Remembering and Forgetting of Advertising', *Journal of Marketing*, vol. 23 (March 1959) pp. 239–43.

73. David Corkindale and John Newall, 'Advertising Thresholds and Wear-out', *European Journal of Marketing*, vol. 12, no. 5 (1978) pp. 329–78.

74. E. C. Strong, 'The Use of Field Experimental Observations in Estimating Advertising Recall', *Journal of Marketing Research*, vol. 11 (Nov. 1974) pp. 369–78; 'Space and Timing of Advertising', *Journal of Advertising Research*, vol. 17 (Dec. 1977) pp. 25-31.

75. John D. C. Little and Leonard M. Lodish, 'A Media Selection Model and its Optimization by Dynamic Programming', *Industrial Management*

Review, vol. 8 (Fall 1966) pp. 15–23; 'A Media Planning Calculus', *Operations Research*, vol. 17 (Jan.–Feb. 1969) pp. 1–35.

76. Colley, *Defining Advertising Goals for Measured Advertising Results*.
77. See, for example, David Corkindale and Sherril H. Kennedy, *Measuring the Effect of Advertising* (Farnborough, Hampshire: Saxon House, 1975) pp. 6–25 and 143–54.
78. For instance, Mark Lovell and Jack Potter, *Assessing the Effectiveness of Advertising* (London: Business Books, 1975).
79. Ibid, pp. 182–3.

Chapter 7

1. T. Levitt, *Innovation in Marketing* (London: Pan Books, 1962) p. 39.
2. See, for example, NEDO Publications London, *International Price Competitiveness and Export Performance–The Non-price Factors* (London: HMSO, April 1977); and NEDC Report on UK Product Design, *Corfield Report* (London: HMSO, January 1979).
3. See the discussion in E. Mansfield and J. Rapoport, 'The Costs of Industrial Product Innovation', *Management Science* (Aug. 1975) pp. 1380–6.
4. Reported in *Nielsen Researcher*, no. 1 (1982), published by A. C. Nielsen Co. Ltd, 1982.
5. B. Davis, 'New Product Development, High Risks, Few Winners', *Marketing* (18 March 1982).
6. P. Kotler, *Marketing Management: Analysis Planning and Control* 4th edn. (London: Prentice-Hall, 1980) p. 311.
7. D. A. Schon, *Technology and Change* (London: Delacorte Press, 1967).
8. Booz, Allen & Hamilton, *Management of New Products*, 4th edn (New York: Booz, Allen & Hamilton, 1968).
9. C. M. Crawford, 'Marketing Research and the New Product Failure Rate', *Research Management* (March 1977) pp. 29–31.
10. Reported in *Nielsen Researcher*, no. 1 (1982).
11. R. G. Cooper, 'Project New Prod: Factors in New Product Success', *European Journal of Marketing*, vol. 14, nos. 5/6 (1980).
12. See, for example, the review in B. Twiss, *Managing Technology Innovation* (London: Longman, 1974); and M. J. Baker and R. McTavish, *Product Policy and Management* (London: Macmillan, 1976).
13. N. R. Baker and W. H. Pound, 'R and D Project Selection: Where We Start', *I.E.E.E Transactions in Engineering Management*, EM-11, no. 4 (Dec. 1964).
14. T. E. Clarke, 'Decision Making in Technology Based Organisations: A Literature Survey of Present Practice,' *IEEE Transactions in Engineering Management*, EM-21, no. 1 (Feb. 1974).
15. A. Robertson and M. Fox, 'A Study in 'Real Time' of the Innovation Process in Two Science Based Companies', in *Industrial Innovation: Technology, Policy, Diffusion*, ed. M. J. Baker (London: Macmillan, 1979).
16. R. Rothwell, C. Freeman, A. Horsley, V. T. P. Jervis, A. B. Robertson and

J. Townsend, 'Sappho Updated: Project Sappho Phase II', *Research Policy*, vol. 3 (1974).

17. Cooper, 'Project New Prod: Factors in New Product Success'.
18. S. Myers and D. A. Marquis, 'Successful Industrial Innovations: A Study of Factors Underlying Innovation in Selected Firms', *National Science Foundation* (NSF) (1969) pp. 69–71.
19. National Industrial Conference Board, 'Why New Products Fail', *The Conference Board Record* (New York: NICB, 1964).
20. National Industrial Conference Board, 'The Marketing Executive Looks Ahead', *Experience in Marketing Management*, no. 13 (New York: NICB, 1967).
21. Reviewed in Rothwell *et al.*, 'Sappho Updated: Project Sappho Phase II'.
22. R. Rothwell, 'Innovation in the U.K. Textile Machinery Industry: The Results of a Postal Questionnaire Survey', *R and D Management*, vol. 6 (1976); and R. Rothwell, 'Innovation in Textile Machinery: Some Significant Factors in Success and Failure', *SPRU Occasional Paper Series*, no. 2 (1976).
23. C. F. Carter and B. R. Williams, *Industry and Technical Progress* (London: Oxford University Press, 1957).
24. R. Rothwell, 'The Characteristics of Successful Innovators and Technically Progressive Forms (with some comments on Innovation Research)', *R and D Management*, vol. 7 (1977) pp. 191–206.
25. Rothwell, 'Innovation in the U.K. Textile Machinery Industry: The Results of a Postal Questionnaire Survey'.
26. Davis, 'New Product Development, High Risks, Few Winners'.
27. P. Kraushar, editorial comment, in *Marketing* (Mar. 1982).
28. Cooper, 'Project New Prod: Factors in New Product Success'.
29. M. J. Baker, *Marketing New Industrial Products* (London: Macmillan, 1975).
30. S. T. Parkinson, 'New Product Development–An International Comparative Study', *R and D Management* (April 1981).
31. See R. W. Peterson, 'New Venture Management in a Large Company', *Harvard Business Review* (May–June 1967); and J. B. Gardner, 'Innovation through New Ventures: New Venture Concept in BOC', *R and D Management*, vol. 3, no. 2 (Feb. 1973).
32. B. C. Ames, 'Dilemma of Product/Market Management', *Harvard Business Review* (March–April 1971).
33. J. W. Lorsch and P. R. Lawrence, 'Organising for Product Innovation', *Harvard Business Review* (Jan.–Feb. 1965).
34. T. Burns and G. Stalker, *The Management of Innovation* (London: Tavistock Publications, 1966).
35. G. Zaltman, *Marketing: Contributions from the Behavioral Sciences* (New York: Harcourt, Brace & World, 1965).
36. A. Johne, 'Innovation, Organisation and the Marketing of High Technology Products', Ph.D dissertation, University of Strathclyde, Department of Marketing (1982).
37. M. Shanks, *The Innovators*, (Harmondsworth: Penguin, 1967).
38. F. A. Abu-Ismail, 'Predicting the Adoption and Diffusion of Industrial Product Innovation', unpublished PhD dissertation, University of Strathclyde (1976) ch. 3, pp. 53–103.
39. Carter and Williams, *Industry and Technical Progress*.
40. Ibid, p. 66.
41. A. S. Robertson provides a useful review of thirty such studies in 'Technological Innovation and the Management of R and D', in *Manage-*

ment Bibliographies and Reviews, ed. D. Ashton (Bradford: MCB Publications, 1977).

42. E. Von Hippel, 'A Customer Active Paradigm for Industrial Product Idea Generation', in *Industrial Innovation–Technology, Policy, Diffusion*, ed. M. J. Baker (London: Macmillan, 1979).

43. S. T. Parkinson and G. Avlonitis, 'Management Attitudes to Flexible Manufacturing Systems–An International Study', in *Proceedings 1st International Conference on F.M.S. I.M.E.* (Brighton, 1982).

44. Von Hippel, 'A Customer Active Paradigm for Industrial Product Idea Generation'.

45. S. T. Parkinson, 'The Role of the User in Successful New Product Development', *R and D Management* (July 1982).

Chapter 8

1. This description follows closely that contained in Michael J. Baker, Jennifer L. Drayton and Stephen T. Parkinson, *The Adoption of New Products* (Paris: Marcel Dassault, Jours de France Foundation, 1975).

2. *Laws of Imitations* (New York: Henry Holt, 1903).

3. See, for example, Everett M. Rogers, *Diffusion of Innovations* (New York: Free Press, 1902).

4. J. K. Ryan and N. Gross, 'The Diffusion of Hybrid Seed Corn in Two Iowa Committees', *Rural Sociology*, vol. 8 (1943).

5. J. S. Coleman, E. Katz and H. Menzel, 'The Diffusion of an Innovation among Physicians', *Sociometry*, vol. 20 (1967).

6. Rogers, *Diffusion of Innovations*.

7. R. Lavidge and G. A. Steiner, 'A Model for Predictive Measurements of Advertising Effectiveness', *Journal of Marketing*, vol. 25 (1961).

8. See, for example, R. Mason, 'An Ordinal Scale for Measuring the Adoption Process', in *Studies of Innovation and of Communication to the Public*, ed. Wilbur Schramm (Stanford University Institute for Communication Research, 1962) also K. S. Palda, 'The Hypothesis of a Hierarchy of Effects: A Partial Evaluation', *Journal of Marketing Research*, vol. 3 (1966).

9. T. S. Robertson, *Innovative Behavior and Communication* (New York: Holt, Rinehart & Winston, 1971); A. R. Andreasen, 'Attitudes and Consumer Behavior: A Decision Model', in *New Research in Marketing*, ed. Lee F. Preston (Institute of Business and Economic Research, University of California, 1965); and F. M. Nicosia, *Consumer Decision Processes* (Englewood Cliffs, N.J.: Prentice-Hall, 1966).

10. Or, alternatively, see Baker, Drayton and Parkinson, *The Adoption of New Products*.

11. Michael J. Baker, *Marketing New Industrial Products* (London: Macmillan, 1975).

12. This description follows closely that of 'A Model of the New Product Adoption Process', ch. 4 in *Marketing New Industrial Products*.

Chapter 9

1. A. Smith, *The Wealth of Nations*, Book 1, (London: J. M. Dent & Sons (Everyman Edition 1910), 1776–8) ch. III.
2. R. Simmat, *Scientific Distribution*, 2nd edn (London: Pitman, 1947) p. 85.
3. J. B. Jeffreys, *The Distribution of Consumer Goods* (Cambridge: Cambridge University Press, 1950).
4. L. P. Bucklin, *A Theory of Distribution Channel Structure* (University of California, Institute of Business and Economic Research, 1966) p. 6.
5. A. Rushton, 'Vertical Integration and Performance in Marketing Channels', *Proceedings of MEG Conference*, ed. M. J. Thomas (Lancaster, July 1982).
6. M. Guirdham, *Marketing: The Management of Distribution Channels* (Oxford: Pergamon Press, 1972).
7. R. F. Breyer, *The Marketing Institution* (New York: McGraw-Hill, 1934).
8. N. A. H. Stacy and A. Wilson, *The Changing Pattern of Distribution* (Oxford: Pergamon Press, 1958).
9. L. P. Bucklin, 'The Classification of Channel Structures', in *Vertical Market Systems*, ed. L. P. Bucklin (Glenview, Ill.: Scott, Foresman, 1970).
10. W. P. Dommermuth and R. C. Anderson, 'Distribution Systems: Firms, Functions, and Efficiencies', *MSU Business Topics*, vol. 17 (Spring 1969) pp. 51–6.
11. J. Gattorna, 'Channels of Distribution–State of the Art Review', *European Journal of Marketing*, vol. 12, no. 7 (1978).
12. James G. Miller, *Living Systems* (New York: McGraw-Hill, 1978).
13. R. E. Reidenbach and T. A. Oliva, 'General Living Systems Theory and Marketing: A Framework for Analysis', *Journal of Marketing*, vol. 45 (Fall 1981) pp. 30–7.
14. W. Alderson and M. W. Martin, 'Towards a Formal Theory of Transactions and Transvections', in *The Marketing Channel*, ed. B. E. Mallen (New York: Wiley, 1967).
15. G. Stigler, 'The Division of Labour Is Limited by the Extent of the Market', *Journal of Political Economy* (June 1951) pp. 185–93.
16. J. C. Palamountain, *The Politics of Distribution* (Cambridge, Mass.: Harvard University Press, 1955).
17. M. J. Baker, *Marketing: Theory and Practice*, 1st edn (London: Macmillan, 1976) ch. 6.
18. For lists, see W. J. Philpott, *Retailing Made Simple* (London: W. H. Allen, 1977).
19. D. Walters, 'Manufacturer/Retailer Relationships', *European Journal of Marketing*, vol. 13, no. 7 (1979) pp. 179–222.
20. Ibid.
21. J. A. Dawson and D. A. Kirby, *Small Scale Retailing in the UK* (London: Saxon House, 1979).
22. D. A. Kirby and D. C. Law, 'The Birth and Death of Small Retail Units in Britain', *Retail and Distribution Management* (Jan.–Feb. 1981).
23. F. Bechofer and B. Elliott, 'An Approach to a Study of Small Shopkeepers and the Class Structure', *European Journal of Sociology*, vol. 9 (1968) pp. 180–202.
24. Co-operative Union Ltd. *Co-operative Independent Commission Report* (Manchester, 1958).
25. D. K. Seaman, C. Blamires and R. Morgan, 'Micro Behaviour Modelling

as an aid to Retailer Strategy Planning', in *Market Research Society Conference* (London, 1981).

26. Monopolies and Mergers Commission, *Discriminatory Discounts to Retailers*, HC 311 of 13 May 1981.

27. W. N. Barnes, 'Socio Economic Influences on Distribution Levels in Western Europe', *Social Science Research Council Report* (London, 1979).

28. URPI, *The Mansfield Area Shopping Study* (Mansfield District Council, 1981).

29. URPI, *Superstores: The Impact on Shopping Patterns within the Scunthorpe Area* (Borough of Scunthope, 1981).

30. A. Gibbs, *An Analysis of Retail Warehouse Planning Enquiries* (Reading: URPI, 1981).

31. J. A. Dawson, 'The Impact of Marketing in the Urban Environment', *Retail and Distribution Management* (Sep.–Oct. 1977).

32. J. H. Kirk, P. G. Ellis and J. R. Medland, *Retail Stall Markets in Great Britain* (Ashford, Kent: Wye College, 1972).

33. Monopolies and Mergers Commission, *Trading Check Franchise and Financial Services*, Command Paper 62 (Dec. 1981).

34. S. F. Buck, 'The Changing Business Environment–in the 80s', *Market Research Society Conference* (London, 1980).

35. Ibid.

36. Walters, 'Manufacturer Retailer Relationships'.

37. D. Cook and D. Doyle, 'Marketing Strategies, Financial Structure and Innovation in UK Retailers', in Marketing Education Group, *Conference Proceedings* (Hull, 1978).

38. N. H. Borden, 'The Concept of the Marketing Mix', in *Science in Marketing*, ed. G. Schwartz, (New York: Wiley, 1965).

39. L. W. Stern and A. I. El-Ansary, *Marketing Channels* (Englewood Cliffs, N.J.: Prentice-Hall, 1979).

40. T. Twyman, 'Re-Classifying People', *Admap* (Nov. 1981).

41. B. Allt, 'The Future of Social and Economic Classification', *Admap* (May 1979).

42. P. Sampson, 'The M.R. Working Party on Socio Economic Grading', *Admap* (Feb. 1980).

43. J. Bermingham, J. Baker and C. MacDonald, 'ACORN–A Classification of Residential Neighbourhoods', *Admap* (May 1979).

44. R. J. Webber, *The National Classification of Residential Neighbourhoods*, Planning Research Applications Group (PRAG), Centre for Environmental Studies (London, Nov. 1977).

45. D. H. Granbois, 'Shopping Behaviour and Preferences', in *Selected Aspects of Consumer Behaviour*, ed. R. Ferber (Washington: National Sciences Foundation, 1977).

46. S. Douglas and C. D. Urban, 'Life Style Analysis', *Journal of Marketing* (July 1977).

47. Y. Wind and S. Douglas, 'Some Issues in International Consumer Research', *European Journal of Marketing*, vol. 8, no. 3 (1974).

48. R. Anderson and J. Engledow, 'A Factor Analytic Comparison of US and German Information Seekers', *Journal of Consumer Research*, vol. 3 (March 1977) pp. 185–96.

49. G. R. Foxall, 'Social Factors in Consumer Choice: Replication and Extension', *Journal of Consumer Research* (June 1975).

50. C. McLelland and J. Turner, 'Consumer Pre-purchase Information Seeking: A Comparison of Methodologies', unpublished working paper (Paisley College of Technology, 1980).

51. J. A. Howard, *Consumer Behavior: Application of Theory* (New York: McGraw-Hill, 1977) p. 9.
52. R. L. Davies, 'Effects of Consumer Income Differences on Shopping Movement Behaviour', *Tidschrift voor Economische en Sociale Geografie*, vol. 60, pp. 111–21, reprinted in *The Marketing Environment*, ed. J. A. Dawson (London: Croom Helm, 1979); R. L. Davies, *Patterns and Profiles of Consumer Behaviour* (University of Newcastle, Department of Geography, Research Series 10, 1973); R. L. Davies, *Marketing Geography* (Corbridge: Retail and Planning Associates, 1976).
53. S. P. Evans, 'A Relationship Between the Gravity Model for Trip Distribution and the Transportation Problem in Linear Programming', *Transportation Research*, no. 7 (1973) (pp. 38–61).
54. R. J. Garner, 'Towards a Better Understanding of Shopping Patterns', in *Geographical Essays in Honour of K. C. Edwards*, ed. R. H. Osborne, F. A. Barnes and J. C. Doornkamp, (Department of Geography, University of Nottingham, 1970) pp. 179–86.
55. A. Bruce, 'Why We Shop Where We Do', *Built Environment*, vol. 3, no. 6 (1974) pp. 280–4.
56. B. P. Holly and J. O. Wheeler, 'Patterns of Retail Location and the Shopping Trips of Low Income Households', *Urban Studies*, vol. 9 (1972) pp. 215–20.
57. S. Openshaw, 'Some Theoretical and Applied Aspects of Spatial Interaction Shopping Models', *Concepts and Techniques in Modern Geography*, vol. 4 (1975) pp. 1–38.
58. J. A. Dawson, *The Marketing Environment* (London: Croom Helm, 1979).
59. C. J. Thomas, 'The Effects of Social Class and Car Ownership on Intra-Urban Shopping Behaviour in Greater Swansea', *Cambria*, vol. 2, no. 1 (1974) pp. 98–126.
60. J. A. Dawson and D. A. Kirby, 'Outshopping from a British New Town', *Geo-Journal*, vol. 1, no. 4 (1978) pp. 57–70.
61. K. F. Stein, 'Explaining Ghetto Consumer Behaviour Hypotheses from Urban Sociology', *Journal of Consumer Affairs*, vol. 14, no. 1 (Summer, 1980).
62. N. G. Papadopoulos, 'Consumer Outshopping Research: Review and Extension', *Journal of Retailing* (Winter, 1980) pp. 41–58.
63. P. Doyle and I. Fenwick, 'How Store Image Affects Shopping Habits in Grocery Chains', *Journal of Retailing*, vol. 50 (Winter, 1974) pp. 39–52.
64. Seaman, Blamires and Morgan, 'Micro Behaviour Modelling as an Aid to Retailer Strategy Planning'.
65. B. L. Stern, R. F. Bush and J. F. Hair, 'The Self-Image/Store-Image Matching Process. An Empirical Test', *Journal of Business*, vol. 50, no. 1 (1977) pp. 63–9.
66. J. L. Ring, 'Retail Positioning. A Multiple Discriminant Approach', *Journal of Retailing*, vol. 55, no. 1 (1979).
67. Granbois, 'Shopping Behaviour and Preferences'.
68. P. Charlton, 'A Review of Shop Loyalty', *Journal of the Market Research Society*, vol. 15, no. 1 (Jan. 1973) pp. 35–51.
69. L. L. Berry, 'The Time Buying Consumer', *Journal of Retailing*, no. 4 (Winter 1979).
70. J. Guiltinan and M. Joyce, 'The Professional Woman–A Potential Market Segment for Retailers', *Journal of Retailing*, vol. 54, no. 2 (Summer 1978).
71. D. N. Bellenger and P. K. Korgaonkar, 'Profiling the Recreational Shopper', *Journal of Retailing*, vol. 56, no. 3 (Fall 1980).

72. S. H. McCall, 'Meet the Work Life', *Journal of Marketing*, vol. 41 (July 1977).
73. Stern and El-Ansary, *Marketing Channels*.
74. T. R. Lakshmanan and W. G. Hansen, 'A Retail Market Potential Model', *Journal of the American Institute of Planners*, vol. 31 (1965) pp. 134–44.
75. M. Pacione, 'Measures of the Attraction Factor–A Possible Alternative', *Area*, vol. 6 (1974) pp. 279–82.
76. J. Moseley, *Shopping in Berkshire: The Shopping Model* (Reading: Unit for Retail Planning Information, 1977).
77. I. D. Shepherd and C. J. Thomas, 'Urban Consumer Behaviour', in *Retail Geography*, ed. J. A. Dawson (London: Croom Helm, 1980).
78. URPI, *Hypermarkets and Superstores: Report of a House of Commons Seminar* (Reading: Unit for Retail Planning Information, 1976).
79. M. Lee and E. Kent, *Caerphilly Hypermarket Study Year Five* (London: Donaldsons, 1979); Department of the Environment (DOE), *The Eastleigh Carrefour Hypermarket after Three Years* (London: HMSO, 1978).
80. R. L. Davies and D. J. Bennison, 'Preliminary Effects of the Eldon Square Shopping Centre (Newcastle)', *Estates Gazette* (Nov. 1977 and April 1978).
81. D. L. Huff and R. R. Batsell, 'Delimiting the Areal Extent of a Market Area', *Journal of Marketing Research*, vol. 14 (Nov. 1977) pp. 581–5.
82. G. Heald, 'The Application of AID Programme and Multiple Regression Techniques to the Assessment of Store Performance and Site Selection', *Operational Research Quarterly*, vol. 20 (1972).
83. M. Simmons, 'Planning and Optimising Investment in Stores', *Journal of Market Research Society*, vol. 15, no. 4 (1973) pp. 207–24.
84. C. J. Clawson, 'Fitting Branch Locations, Performance Standards and Marketing Strategies to Local Conditions', *US Journal of Marketing* (Jan. 1974) pp. 8–14.
85. I. Fenwick, 'Forecasting Performance for Financial Outlets', *European Journal of Marketing*, vol. 13, no. 5 (1979).
86. Ibid.
87. Stern and El-Ansary, *Marketing Channels*.
88. A. E. Hall, 'Own Label Development in the UK Retail Sector', *Marketing Educators Group Annual Conference* (London: City University Grad. Business Centre, June 1976).
89. R. C. Curhan, 'Shelf Space Allocation and Profit Maximisation in Mass Retailing', *Journal of Marketing*, vol. 37 (July 1973) pp. 54–60.
90. R. A. Westwood, J. Palmer and J. Pymont, 'Manufacturer–Retailer Interface', *ESOMAR Proceedings–Product Range Policy in Retailing* (Breukelen, Netherlands, 1975).
91. J. Whitaker and J. Lay, 'The Evolution of Retail Research', *Market Research Society Conference* (1982).
92. P. S. H. Leeflang, 'Allocation of Shelf Space Over Article Groups–A Portfolio Problem', *ESOMAR Proceedings* (Lucerne, 1976).
93. E. E. Anderson, 'An Analysis of Retail Display Space: Theory and Methods', *Journal of Business*, vol. 52, no. 1 (1979) pp. 103–18.
94. P. McGoldrick and K. Sheath, 'Generic Products: Their Impact in the UK', *Journal of Retail and Distribution Management* (Sept.–Oct. 1981).
95. V. J. Cooke and T. F. Schutte, *Brand Policy Determination* (Boston: Allyn & Bacon, 1967).
96. J. Irvine and E. Fallaw, 'Own Brands or My Brands', *Admap* (Dec. 1979); T. O'Reilly, 'Re-inforcing the Brand', *Advertising*, no. 64 (May 1980) pp. 4–7.

97. H. Lind, 'Brands Caught Up in the Soap Box Paradox', *Campaign* (May 1979).
98. S. Broadbent, 'What Makes a Top Brand', *The Nielsen Researcher*, no. 3 (Oxford, 1979).
99. R.E. Frank and H. W. Boyd, 'Are Private Brand Prone Grocery Customers Really Different', *Journal of Advertising Research*, vol. 5, no. 4 (Dec. 1965).
100. T. R. Bryan, 'Retailers Private Label (Brands)', unpublished MA thesis, University of Bradford (1972).
101. Stern and El-Ansary, *Marketing Channels*.
102. P. Doyle and C. B. Weinberg, 'Effective New Product Decisions for Supermarkets', *Operation Research Quarterly*, vol. 24 (March 1973) pp. 45–54.
103. Monopolies and Mergers Commission, *Discriminatory Discounts to Retailers*.
104. J. E. Russo, 'The Value of Unit Price Information', *Journal of Marketing Research*, vol. XIV (May 1977).
105. J. B. Wilkinson, J. B. Mason and C. H. Paksoy, 'Assessing the Impact of Short-term Supermarket Strategy Variables', *Journal of Marketing Research*, vol. XIX (Feb. 1982) pp. 72–86.
106. M. Chevalier, 'Substitution Patterns as a Result of Display in the Product Category', *Journal of Retailing*, vol. 15, no. 4 (Winter 1975).
107. P. Doyle and I. Fenwick, 'An Experimental Design for Measuring Advertising Pay-Off', *Operational Research Quarterly*, vol. 26, no. 4 (1975) pp. 693–702.
108. L. W. Dyer, 'Scanner Bred Data Build a Launch Pad for Selling Flair', *Progressive Grocer* (Oct. 1979).
109. A. J. Della Bitta, K. B. Monroe and J. M. McGinnis, 'Consumer Perceptions of Comparative Price Advertisements', *Journal of Marketing Research*, vol. XVIII (Nov. 1981) pp. 416–26.
110. R. B. Haynes, 'Turning National Advertising into Regional Newspaper Advertising,' *Admap* (May 1979).
111. E. J. Ornstein, *The Retailers* (London: Associated Business Programmes, 1976).
112. Ibid.
113. Baker, *Marketing: Theory and Practice*, 1st edn.
114. Monopolies and Mergers Commission, *Discriminatory Discounts to Retailers*.

Chapter 10

1. M. J. Baker, *Marketing: Theory and Practice* (London: Macmillan, 1976).
2. G. Wadinambiaratchi, 'Channels of Distribution in Developing Economies', in *The Marketing Channel*, ed. B. Mallen (New York: Wiley, 1967).
3. L. P. Bucklin, 'A Normative Approach to the Economics of Channel Structure', in *Vertical Market Systems*, ed. L. P. Bucklin (Glenview, Ill.: Scott, Foresman, 1970).
4. J. P. Guiltinan, 'Planned and Evolutionary Changes in Distribution Channels', *Journal of Retailing*, vol. 50, no. 2 (Summer 1974).

5. Monopolies and Merger Commission, *Domestic Gas Appliances*, HC 703 Session 79/80, summarised in *Discounts to Retailers*, HC 311 Session 80/81, p. 111.
6. U. Weiss, 'China's Rural Marketing Structure', *World Development*, vol. 6 (1978) pp. 647–62.
7. R. E. Weigand, 'Fit Products and Channels to Your Market', *Harvard Business Review* (Jan.–Feb. 1977).
8. R. D. Michman, 'Foundation for a Theory of Marketing Channels', *Southern Journal of Business* (Nov. 1977) pp. 17–26.
9. R. Cox and T. F. Schutte, 'A Look at Channel Management', in *Marketing Involvement and Society*, ed. P. McDonald (Chicago: American Marketing Association, 1970).
10. J. Scitovsky, *The Joyless Economy* (New York: Oxford University Press, 1976).
11. P. McVey, 'Are Channels of Distribution What the Text Books Say?', *Journal of Marketing* (Jan. 1960) pp. 61–5.
12. J. Boddewyn, *Comparative Marketing and Management* (Glenview, Ill.: Scott, Foresman, 1969) pp. 108–18.
13. E. W. Lambert, 'Financial Considerations in Choosing a Marketing Channel', *MSU Business Topics* (Winter 1966) pp. 17–26.
14. James G. Miller, *Living Systems* (New York: McGraw-Hill, 1978).
15. R. E. Reidenbach and T. A. Oliva, 'General Living Systems Theory and Marketing. A Framework for Analysis', *Journal of Marketing*, vol. 45 (Fall 1981) pp. 30–7.
16. D. M. Lambert, *The Distribution Channel Decision* (National Association of Accountants and Society of Management, Accountants of Canada, 1978).
17. J. L. Gattorna, 'Effects of Innovation in Channels of Distribution', PhD thesis, Cranfield Institute of Technology (1977).
18. D. Walters, 'Manufacturer/Retailer Relationships', *European Journal of Marketing*, vol. 13, no. 7 (1979) pp. 179–222.
19. J. D. Thompson, 'Domains of Organised Action', in *Distribution Channels: Behavioral Dimensions*, ed. L. W. Stern (Boston: Houghton Mifflin, 1969).
20. R. K. Carter, 'The Effect of Domain Acceptance on Transfer of Resources and Goal Attainment: A Study of Inter-Organisational Relationship', PhD thesis, Michigan State University (1975).
21. M. Etgar, 'Sources and Types of Intra Channel Conflict', *Journal of Retailing*, vol. 55 (1979) pp. 61–8.
22. J. R. Brown and R. L. Day, 'Measures of Manifest Conflict in Distribution Channels', *Journal of Market Research*, vol. XVIII (Aug. 1981) pp. 263–74.
23. R. F. Lusch, 'Sources of Power: Their Impact on Intra Channel Conflict', *Journal of Marketing Research*, vol. XIII (Nov. 1976).
24. E. R. Cadotte and L. W. Stern, 'A Process Model of Dyadic Inter-organisational Relations in Marketing Channels', in *Research in Marketing*, vol. 2, ed. J. N. Sheth (Jai Press, 1979).
25. L. W. Stern and A. I. El-Ansary, *Marketing Channels*, 2nd edn (Englewood Cliffs, N.J.: Prentice-Hall, 1982).
26. Ibid.
27. T. Reve and L. W. Stern, 'Inter-organisational Relations in Marketing Channels', *Academy of Management Review* (July 1979).
28. R. F. Lusch, 'Intra Channel Conflict and Use of Power', *Journal of Marketing Research*, vol. XV (1978).

29. A. A. Ahmed, 'Channel Control in International Markets', *European Journal of Marketing*, vol. 11, no. 4 (1977) pp. 327–34.
30. I. Wilkinson, 'Power Conflict and Satisfaction in Distribution Channels', *International Journal of Physical Distribution and Materials Management*, vol. 11, no. 7 (March–April 1982).
31. M. Etgar, 'Channel Domination and Countervailing Power in Distributive Channels', *Journal of Marketing Research*, vol. XIII (Aug. 1976); M. Etgar, 'Channel Environment and Channel Leadership', *Journal of Marketing Research*, vol. XIV (Feb. 1977); M. Etgar, 'Selection of an Effective Channel Control Mix', *Journal of Marketing* (July 1978).
32. R. F. Lusch, 'Channel Conflict, its Impact on Retailer Operating Performances', *Journal of Retailing* (Summer 1976) pp. 3–12.
33. G. Zeitz, 'Inter-organisational Dialectics', *Administrative Science Quarterly*, vol. 25 (March 1980) pp. 72–88.
34. W. Alderson and M. W. Martin, 'Towards a Formal Theory of Transactions and Transvections', in *The Marketing Channel*, ed. B. Mallen (London: Wiley, 1967).
35. Lambert, *The Distribution Channel Decision*.
36. Miller, *Living Systems*.
37. J. W. Forrester, *Industrial Dynamics* (Cambridge, Mass.: MIT Press, 1961).
38. Zeitz, 'Inter-organisational Dialectics'.
39. M. Simmons, 'Measuring Trade Reaction: The Role of Market Research', *Market Research Society Conference* (1977).
40. D. Bloom, 'The Renaissance of Retail Auditing', in *Market Research Society Conference* (1980).
41. As reported by Whitaker and Lay, 'The Evaluation of Retail Research'.
42. M. T. Cunningham, 'Innovation in Sales and Distribution Systems', in *MEG Conference Proceedings* (Glasgow, 1973).
43. E. J. McCarthy, *Basic Marketing* (Homewood, Ill.: Irwin, 1971) pp. 7–20.
44. W. Alderson, 'Factors Governing the Development of Marketing Channels', in *The Marketing Channel*, ed. B. Mallen (New York: Wiley, 1967).
45. Alderson and Martin, 'Towards a Formal Theory of Transactions and Transvections'.
46. M. J. Baker, *Marketing: Theory and Practice*, 1st edn (London: Macmillan, 1976).
47. B. E. Mallen, *Principles of Marketing Channel Management* (Lexington, Mass.: D. C. Heath, 1977).
48. R. Cox, *Distribution in a High Level Economy* (Englewood Cliffs, N.J.: Prentice-Hall, 1965).
49. Wadimbiaratchi, 'Channels of Distribution in Developing Economies'.
50. B. Mallen, 'Functional Spin-off: A Key to Anticipating Change in Distribution Structure', *US Journal of Marketing* (July 1973) pp. 18–25.
51. Bucklin, 'A Normative Approach to the Economies of Channel Structure'.
52. J. Gattorna, 'Channels of Distribution–State of the Art Review', *European Journal of Marketing*, vol. 12, no. 7 (1978).
53. L. W. Stern and A. I. El-Ansary, *Marketing Channels* (Englewood Cliffs, N.J.: Prentice-Hall, 1979).
54. R. J. Ellis, 'Innovation in Retailing', *International Journal of Physical Distribution*, vol. 6, no. 3 (1976).
55. C. W. Lamb, 'Using the Principle of Postponement–Speculation to Analyse Channel Theory', *International Journal of Physical Distribution*, vol. 7, no. 5 (1978).

56. C. Le Boeuf, 'Consumerons-nous toujours plus de valeur ajoutee', an unpublished paper, Montpellier University (1981).
57. Mallen, *Principles of Marketing Channel Management*.
58. W. N. Barnes, 'Socio Economic Influences on Distribution Levels in Western Europe', *Social Science Research Council Report* (1979).
59. Lambert, *The Distribution Channel Decision*.
60. M. Christopher and G. Wills, 'Market Research as Action Research', in *Market Research Society Conference* (London, 1982).
61. T. Burns and G. M. Stalker, *The Management of Innovation*, (London: Tavistock Publications, 1961).
62. G. Johnson, 'The Dilemma of Channel Management', *International Journal of Physical Distribution and Materials Management*, vol. 11, no. 7 (April 1982).
63. S. L. Fink, J. Beak and K. Taddeo, 'Organisational Crisis and Change', *Journal of Applied Behavioral Science* (Jan.–Feb. 1981).
64. M. Guirdham, *Marketing: The Management of Distribution Channels* (Oxford: Pergamon Press, 1972).
65. Lambert, *The Distribution Channel Decision*.
66. B. Rosenbloom, *Marketing Channels–A Management View* (Hindsdale, Ill.: Dryden Press, 1978).
67. Monopolies and Mergers Commission, *Discriminatory Discounts to Retailers*, HC 311 of 13 May 1981.
68. T. L. Berg, 'Designing the Distribution Systems' in *The Social Responsibilities of Marketing*, ed. W. D. Stevens (Chicago: American Marketing Association, 1962).
69. D. W. Cravens, G. E. Hills and R. B. Woodruff, *Marketing Decision Making: Concepts and Strategy* (Homewood, Ill.: Irwin, 1976).
70. Rosenbloom, *Marketing Channels–A Management View*.
71. Lambert, *The Distribution Channel Decision*.
72. R. D. Michman and S. D. Sibley, *Marketing Channels and Strategy* 2nd edn (Columbia, Ohio.: Grid, 1980).
73. J. A. Narus, 'Development of a Marketing Channel Model Selection Process Model and its Demonstration in an Industrial Chemicals Business and in an Electronic Components Business', PhD thesis, Syracuse University (1981).
74. Rosenbloom, *Marketing Channels–A Management View*.
75. Lambert, *The Distribution Channel Decision*.
76. R. Simmat, *Scientific Distribution*, 2nd edn (London: Pitman, 1947).
77. P. Kotler, *Marketing Decision Making* (New York: Holt, Rinehart & Winston, 1971) pp. 291–5.
78. M. Corstjens and J. Doyle, 'Channel Optimisation in Complex Marketing Systems', *Management Science*, vol. 25 (Oct. 1979) pp. 1014–25.
79. Monopolies and Mergers Commission, *Discriminatory Discounts to Retailers*.
80. L. McAlister, 'An Optimisation Model of Distribution Channels Incorporating Behavioural Constraints' (University of Washington, Grad. School of Business Administration, Feb. 1980).
81. P. Zusman and M. Etgar, 'The Marketing Channel as an Equilibrium Set of Contracts', *Management Science*, vol. 27, no. 23 (March 1981) pp. 284–302.
82. D. J. Bowersox, M. B. Cooper, D. M. Lambert and D. A. Taylor, *Management in Marketing Channels* (New York: McGraw-Hill, 1980).
83. J. Esser and S. S. Komorita, 'Reciprocity and Concession Making in

Bargaining', *Journal of Personal and Social Psychology*, vol. 31 (1975) pp. 864–72.

84. J. R. Moore, 'A Comparative Analysis of Decision Criteria in Channel Formation', in *Combined Proceedings of AMA Conference* (Chicago 1974).

85. A. Wallace, 'A Study of the Buying Process for New Products by Intermediate Marketing Organisations in the Channels of Distribution for Grocery Products', PhD thesis, University of Manchester (1976).

86. A. M. Kennedy, *Industrial Purchasing Behaviour: A Review of Literature* (Department of Marketing, University of Strathclyde, Working Paper MWP 81/3).

87. J. Whitaker and J. Lay, 'The Evolution of Retail Research', in *Market Research Society Conference* (1982)

88. Stern and El-Ansary, *Marketing Channels*.

89. Lusch, 'Intra Channel Conflict and Use of Power'.

90. C. G. Walters, *Marketing Channels* (Goodyear Publishing, 1977).

91. N. Piercy, 'Marketing Information: The Corporate Battleground', *Proceedings of MEG Conference*, ed. M. J. Thomas (Lancaster, July 1982) pp. 376–99.

92. Stern and El-Ansary, *Marketing Channels*.

93. A. Rushton, 'Vertical Integration and Performance in Marketing Channels', *Proceedings of MEG Conference*, ed. M. J. Thomas (July 1982).

94. P. M. Dunne and H. I. Wolk, 'Marketing Cost Analysis: A Modularised Contribution Approach', *Journal of Marketing* (July 1977) pp. 83–94.

95. W. G. Brown and E. D. Rexton, 'Auditing Distribution Channels', *Journal of Marketing* (July 1978).

96. Lambert, *The Distribution Channel Decision*.

97. Rosenbloom, *Marketing Channels–A Management View*.

98. B. McCammon, 'Perspectives for Distribution Programming', in *Marketing Systems*, ed. L. P. Bucklin. (Glenview, Ill.: Scott, Foresman, 1970).

99. N. A. Highton and D. L. Chilcott, *Retailing: Management Controls and Performance Improvement* (London: Institute of Chartered Accountants, 1980).

100. M. T. Cunningham and D. A. Roberts, 'The Role of Customer Service in Industrial Marketing', *European Journal of Marketing*, vol. 8, no. 1 (1974).

101. M. Christopher, 'Logistics and the National Economy', *International Journal of Physical Distribution and Materials Management*, vol. 11, no. 4 (1981).

102. A. T. Kearney and C. J. Clarke, *Improving Productivity in Distribution* (London: A. T. Kearney Inc., 1980).

103. A. Rushton and J. Williams, 'Logistics–Neglected in the National Productivity Debate', *Logistics Today*, vol. 1, no. 1 (Jan. 1982) pp. 36–40.

104. D. Ray, J. Gattorna and M. Allen, 'Handbook of Distribution Costing and Control', *International Journal of Physical Distribution and Materials Management*, vol. 10, no. 5/6 (1980).

105. D. Firth *et al.*, *Distribution Management Handbook* (Toronto: McGraw-Hill Ryerson, 1980) pp. 60–3.

106. P. Gilmour, 'Customer Service: Differentiating by Market Segment', *International Journal of Physical Distribution and Materials Management*, vol. 12, no. 3 (1982).

107. M. A. Higby, 'An Evaluation of Alternative Channels of Distribution, An Efficiency Model', PhD thesis, Michigan State (1976).

108. D. J. Bowersox, *Logistical Management* (New York: Collier-Macmillan, 1978).

109. H. O'Brien, 'Limitation of the Computer in Load Planning', *IMH News* (Spring 1980) (IMH = Institute of Materials Handling).
110. T. Skjoett-Larson, 'Integrated Information Systems for Materials Management', *International Journal for Physical Distribution and Materials Management*, vol. 12, no. 3 (1982) pp. 45–55.
111. Lambert, *The Distribution Channel Decision*.

Chapter 11

1. T. Levitt, 'Marketing Myopia', *Harvard Business Review*, vol. 38, no. 4 (July–Aug. 1960) pp. 45–56.
2. P. Kotler, *Marketing Management–Analysis, Planning and Control*, 4th edn (Englewood Cliffs, N.J.: Prentice-Hall, 1979).
3. *European Societal Strategy Project Report*, European Foundation for Management Development and European Institute for Advanced Studies in Management (Dec. 1981).
4. Ibid, and see, for example, H. Igor Ansoff, *Managing the Process of Discontinuous Change*, parts I–IV, European Institute for Advanced Studies in Management, Working Papers 80–26, 80–36, 80–37 and 80–38.
5. P. F. Drucker, *The Practice of Management* (New York: Harper & Row, 1954).
6. H. Igor Ansoff, *Corporate Strategy* (New York: McGraw-Hill, 1965).
7. Levitt, 'Marketing Myopia'.
8. J. Bronowski, *The Ascent of Man* (London: Sir Joseph Causton & Sons Ltd, 1973).
9. C. W. Hofer and D. E. Schendel, *Strategy Formulation: Analytical Concepts* (St Paul, Minnesota; West Publishing Co., 1978).
10. *Managing the Process of Discontinuous Change; Corporate Strategy;* and 'Corporate Capability for Managing Change', SRI International Business Intelligence Program research report, no. 610 (1978).
11. M. J. Baker, 'Innovation–Key to Success', *Quarterly Review of Marketing* (Winter 1982) pp. 1–11.
12. A. D. Chandler Jr, *Strategy and Structure: Chapters in the History of American Industrial Enterprise* (Cambridge, Mass.: MIT Press, 1962).
13. H. Igor Ansoff, *Planned Management of Turbulent Change*, European Institute for Advanced Studies in Management, Working Paper 78–3.
14. Ibid.
15. Kotler, *Marketing Management–Analysis, Planning and Control*.
16. G. A. Steiner, *Strategic Planning–What Every Manager Must Know* (New York: The Free Press, 1979).
17. Drucker, *The Practice of Management*.
18. Chandler, *Strategy and Structure: Chapters in the History of American Industrial Enterprise*.
19. K. Andrews *et al.*, *Business Policy: Text and Cases* (Homewood, Illinois: Irwin 1965).
20. Hofer and Schendel, *Strategy Formulation: Analytical Concepts*.
21. D. F. Abell and J. S. Hammond, *Strategic Market Planning* (Englewood Cliffs, N.J.: Prentice-Hall, 1979).

22. 'Planning in an Uncertain World', series of reprints of articles appearing in the Management Page of the *Financial Times* (June 1981) Financial Times Ltd.
23. S. Thune and R. House, 'Where Long Range Planning Pays Off', *Business Horizons*, vol. 13 (1970) pp. 81–7.
24. Ansoff, *Corporate Strategy*.
25. Hofer and Schendel, *Strategy Formulation: Analytical Concepts*.
26. Andrews, *Business Policy: Text and Cases*.
27. Thune and House, 'Where Long Range Planning Pays Off'.
28. S. Schoeffler, R. Buzzell and D. Heany, 'Impact of Strategic Planning on Profit Performance', *Harvard Business Review*, vol. 52 (March–April 1974) pp. 137–45.
29. J. Eastlack and P. McDonald, 'CEO's Role in Corporate Growth', *Harvard Business Review*, vol. 48 (May–June 1970) pp. 150–63.
30. D. Herold, 'Long Range Planning and Organisational Performance: A Cross Validation Study', *Academy of Management Review*, (March 1972).
31. W. Guth, 'The Growth and Profitability of the Firm: A Managerial Explanation', *Journal of Business Policy*, vol. 2 (1972).
32. H. Igor Ansoff *et al.*, *Acquisition Behavior of US Manufacturing Firms* (Nashville, Tennessee: Vanderbilt University Press, 1971).
33. D. W. Karger and F. A. Malik, 'Long Range Planning and Organisational Performance', *Long Range Planning* (Dec. 1975).
34. V. Unni, 'The Role of Strategic Planning in Small Businesses', *Long Range Planning*, vol. 14 (April 1981).
35. Steiner, *Strategic Planning–What Every Manager Must Know*.
36. L. W. Rue and R. M. Fulmer, 'Is Long-Range Planning Profitable?' *Academy of Management Proceeding*, Boston (Aug. 1973).
37. G. Sheehan, 'Long-Range Strategic Planning and Its Relationship to Firm Size, Firm Growth, and Firm Variability: An Explorative, Empirical Investigation', unpublished PhD dissertation, University of Western Ontario (1975).
38. J. Quincy Hunsicker, 'The Malaise of Strategic Planning', *The McKinsey Quarterly* (Spring 1980) pp. 2–12.
39. R. Wensley, 'PIMS and BCG: New Horizons or False Dawn in Strategic Marketing', *Strategic Management Journal* (1981). See also 'Strategic Marketing: Betas, Boxes or Basics', *Journal of Marketing* (1981).
40. G. Day, 'Analytical Approaches to Strategic Market Planning', in *Review of Marketing 1981*, ed. B. Enis and K. Roering (Chicago: American Marketing Association).
41. H. Igor Ansoff, 'Managerial Problem Solving', *Journal of Business Policy*, vol. 2, no. 1 (Autumn 1971).
42. J. L. Bower, *Strategy as a Problem Solving Theory of Business Planning* (Boston: Harvard Business School, PB894, 1967).
43. See Kotler, *Marketing Management–Analysis, Planning and Control*; Steiner, *Strategic Planning–What Every Manager Must Know*; Abell and Hammond, *Strategic Market Planning*; and K. J. Cohen and R. N. Cyert, 'Strategy: Formulation, Implementation and Monitoring', *Journal of Business*, vol. 46, no. 3 (July 1973).
44. P. Lorange and R. Vancil' *Strategic Planning Systems* (Englewood Cliffs, N.J.: Prentice-Hall, 1977); and 'How to Design a Strategic Planning System', *Harvard Business Review* (Sept.–Oct. 1979) pp. 75–81.
45. T. Levitt, 'Planning in an Uncertain World'; P. Drucker, *Managing for Results* (London: Heinemann, 1964).
46. Hofer and Schendel, *Strategy Formulation: Analytical Concepts*.

47. G. Day, A. Shocker and R. Srivantava, 'Customer-Orientated Approaches to Identifying Product Markets', *Journal of Marketing* (Autumn 1979) pp. 8–19; Lorange and Vancil, *Strategic Planning Systems*.

48. H. Igor Ansoff and J. Leontiades, 'Strategic Portfolio Management', *Journal of General Management* (Autumn 1976) pp. 113–21.

49. P. Drucker, *Managing for Results* (London: Heinemann, 1964).

50. Ansoff, *Corporate Strategy*.

51. Levitt, 'Marketing Myopia'.

52. D. F. Abell, *Defining the Business: The Starting Point of Strategic Planning* (Englewood Cliffs, N.J.: Prentice-Hall, 1980).

53. P. F. Drucker, *Management: Tasks, Responsibilities and Practice* (New York: Harper & Row, 1973).

54. Abell and Hammond, *Strategic Market Planning*, pp. 48–50.

55. The Boston Consulting Group, *Annual Perspective* (1981).

56. Abell and Hammond, *Strategic Market Planning*, pp. 51–4.

57. Kotler, *Marketing Management–Analysis, Planning and Control*.

58. W. F. Glueck, *Business Policy: Strategy Formation and Management Action* 2nd end (Tokyo: McGraw-Hill, 1976).

59. Hofer and Schendel, *Strategy Formulation: Analytical Concepts*.

60. Ansoff, *Corporate Strategy*.

61. Glueck, *Business Policy: Strategy Formation and Management Action*.

62. Drucker, *The Practice of Management*.

63. T. Staudt, 'Program for Product Diversification', *Harvard Business Review*, vol. 32, no. 6 (1954) pp. 121–31.

64. Ansoff, *Corporate Strategy*.

65. Hofer and Schendel, *Strategy Formulation: Analytical Concepts*.

66. Ansoff, *Corporate Strategy*.

67. Glueck, *Business Policy: Strategy Formation and Management Action*.

68. C. W. Hofer, *Conceptual Constructs for Formulating Corporate and Business Strategy* (Boston: Intercollegiate Case Clearing House, no. 9-378-754, 1977) pp. 7–32.

69. Ibid.

70. H. Koontz, 'Making Strategic Planning Work', *Business Horizons*, vol. 19 (April 1976) pp. 37–47.

71. E. Bowman, 'Epistemology, Corporate Strategy and Academe', *Sloan Management Review* (Winter 1974) pp. 35–50.

72. The Boston Consulting Group, 'The Rule of 3 or 4', *Perspectives*, no. 187 (1976).

73. T. Levitt, 'Exploit the Product Life Cycle', *Harvard Business Review* (Nov.–Dec. 1965) pp. 81–94.

74. Ibid.

75. C. Wasson, *Dynamic Competitive Strategy and Product Life Cycles* (St Charles, Ill.: Challenge Books, 1974).

76. P. Doyle, 'The Realities of the Product Life Cycle', *Quarterly Review of Marketing* (Summer 1976) pp. 1–6.

77. Wasson, *Dynamic Competitive Strategy and Product Life Cycles*; Doyle, 'The Realities of the Product Life Cycle'.

78. Y. Wind and H. Claycamp, 'Planning Product Line Strategy: A Matrix Approach', *Journal of Marketing*, vol. 40 (Jan. 1976) pp. 2–9; D. Cravens, 'Marketing Strategy Positioning', *Business Horizons* (Dec. 1975) pp. 53–68; B. Catry and M. Chevalier, 'Market Share Strategy and the Product Life Cycle', *Journal of Marketing*, vol. 38, no. 4 (1974) pp. 29–34; B. Enis, 'Strategic Planning and the Product Life Cycle', *Business* (May–June 1980) pp. 10–18.

79. Ibid.
80. W. Fruhan, 'Pyrrhic Victories in Fights for Market Share', *Harvard Business Review*, vol. 50 (Sept.–Oct. 1972) pp. 100–7.
81. Ibid.
82. Levitt, 'Exploit the Product Life Cycle'.
83. N. Dhalla and S. Yuspeth, 'Forget the Product Life Cycle Concept', *Harvard Business Review*, (Jan.–Feb. 1976) pp. 102–12.
84. R. Polli and V. Cook, 'Validity of the Product Life Cycle', *Journal of Business* (Oct. 1969) pp. 385–400; B. Enis, R. La Garce and A. Prell, 'Extending the Product Life Cycle', *Business Horizons* (June 1977) pp. 46–56.
85. Enis, La Garce and Prell, 'Extending the Product Life Cycle'.
86. Kotler, *Marketing Management–Analysis, Planning and Control*.
87. Dhalla and Yuspeth, 'Forget the Product Life Cycle Concept'.
88. Enis, La Garce and Prell, 'Extending the Product Life Cycle'.
89. J. Sissors, 'What is a Market', *Journal of Marketing*, vol. 30 (July 1966) pp. 17–21.
90. Wasson, *Dynamic Competitive Strategy and Product Life Cycles*.
91. Michael Goold, 'Why Dicey Definitions Are So Dangerous', *Financial Times* Management Page (16 Nov. 1981); also, 'How "Dogs" Can be Given More Bite', *Financial Times* Management Page (13 Nov. 1981).
92. Enis, La Garce and Prell, 'Extending the Product Life Cycle'.
93. A. Johnson and C. Jones, 'How to Organise for New Products', *Harvard Business Review* (May–June 1957); F. Karger and K. Murdick, 'Product Design, Marketing and Manufacturing Innovation', *California Management Review* (Winter 1966); see also Ansoff *et al.*, *Acquisition Behaviour of US Manufacturing Firms*.
94. Ansoff, *Corporate Strategy*; Ansoff, 'Strategies for Diversification', *Harvard Business Review* (Sept.–Oct. 1957) pp. 113–24.
95. B. Henderson, 'The Product Portfolio', *Perspectives*, no. 66 (Boston: Boston Consulting Group, 1970).
96. Polli and Cook, 'Validity of the Product Life Cycle'.
97. B. Henderson, 'The Experience Curve', Reviews I to V, *Perspectives Series* (Boston: Boston Consulting Group, 1968).
98. B. Hedley, 'Strategy and the Business Portfolio', *Long Range Planning* (Feb. 1977).
99. W. Hirschmann, 'Profit from the Learning Curve', *Harvard Business Review*, vol. 42 (Jan.–Feb. 1964) pp. 125–39.
100. T. P. Wright, 'Factors Affecting the Cost of Airplanes', *Journal of Aeronautical Sciences*, vol. 3 (1936).
101. Henderson, 'The Experience Curve'.
102. Ibid.
103. Sissors, 'What is a Market?'
104. C. Baden Fuller, *The Implications of the 'Learning Curve' For Firm Strategy and Public Policy*, London Business School, Working Paper (1981).
105. B. Henderson, 'The Growth Share Matrix of the Product Portfolio', *Perspectives*, no. 135 (Boston: Boston Consulting Group, 1973).
106. G. Day, 'Diagnosing the Product Portfolio', *Journal of Marketing*, vol. 42 (April 1977) pp. 29–38.
107. G. J. Avlonitis, 'Product Elimination: A Neglected Phase of Innovation', *Marketing Education Group Conference Proceedings* (July 1981) pp. 3–50.
108. R. Hamermesh and S. Silk, 'How to Compete in Stagnant Industries', *Harvard Business Review* (Sept. 1979) pp. 161–8.
109. Goold, 'Why Dicey Definitions Are So Dangerous'.

110. R. Wensley, 'Strategic Marketing: Betas, Boxes or Basics', *Journal of Marketing* (1981).
111. C. Lorenz, 'Why the Boston Theory is on Trial', *Financial Times* Management Page (11 Nov. 1981) p. 14.
112. Day, 'Diagnosing the Product Portfolio'.
113. Wensley, 'Strategic Marketing: Betas, Boxes or Basics'.
114. 'Meads Technique to Sort Out the Losers', *Business Week* (11 March 1972) pp. 124–30.
115. G. Day, 'Strategic Market Analysis: Top-Down and Bottom-Up Approaches', *MSI working paper*, 80/105 (Aug. 1980).
116. P. Lorange, 'Divisional Planning: Setting Effective Direction', *Sloan Management Review* (Autumn 1975) pp. 77–91.
117. Ansoff, *Corporate Strategy*, p. 126, Table 8.1.
118. 'The Directional Policy Matrix–A New Aid to Corporate Planning' (Shell International Chemical Co., 1975).
119. S. J. Q. Robinson, R. E. Hichens and D. P. Wade, 'The Directional Policy Matrix–Tool for Strategic Planning', *Long Range Planning*, vol. 11 (June 1978) pp. 8–15.
120. Ibid.
121. Ibid.
122. V. Kijewski, 'Marketing Share Strategy: Beliefs vs. Actions', PIMS Letter 9/2 (Cambridge, Mass.: Strategic Planning Institute, 1978).
123. R. Buzzell and B. Gale, 'Market Share–A Key to Profitability', *Harvard Business Review* (Jan.–Feb. 1974) pp. 97–106; and R. Buzzell and F. Wiersema, 'Successful Share Building Strategies', *Harvard Business Review* (Jan.–Feb. 1981) pp. 135–44.
124. Abell and Hammond, *Strategic Market Planning*.
125. Buzzell and Gale, 'Market Share–A Key to Profitability'; and Buzzell and Wiersema, 'Successful Share Building Strategies'.
126. Ibid.
127. Y. Wind and V. Mahajan, 'Designing Product and Business Portfolios', *Harvard Business Review* (Jan.–Feb. 1981) pp. 155–65.

Chapter 12

1. See George Schwartz (ed.), *Science in Marketing* (New York: Wiley, 1965).
2. An exception to this is William J. Stanton, *Fundamentals of Marketing*, 4th edn (New York: McGraw-Hill, 1975), and we draw heavily on this source in this section. Another source to be consulted is John M. Rathmell, *Marketing in the Service Sector* (Cambridge, Mass.: Winthrop, 1974) which contains many useful references.
3. Stanton, *Fundamentals of Marketing*.
4. Levitt, 'Marketing Myopia', *Harvard Business Review* (July–Aug. 1960).
5. Philip Kotler and Sidney J. Levy, 'Broadening the Concept of Marketing', *Journal of Marketing*, vol. 33 (Jan. 1969) pp. 10–15.
6. Ibid.

Chapter 13

1. This chapter draws heavily upon an article first published in *Industrial Advertising and Marketing* (Spring 1975) and thanks are extended to the editor for permission to reproduce this material.
2. Philip Kotler, *Marketing Management*, 2nd edn (Englewood Cliffs, N.J.: Prentice-Hall, 1972).
3. P. A. Samuleson, *Economics*, 4th edn (New York: McGraw-Hill, 1958).
4. Ibid, p. 21.
5. D. Meadows *et al.*, *The Limits to Growth* (London: Earth Island, 1972).
6. See his *The Waste Markers* and *The Hidden Persuaders*.
7. See her *Silent Spring* (Harmondsworth: Penguin, 1970).
8. See his *Unsafe at Any Speed.*
9. From the *Financidl Times* (24 Dec. 1974).

Index